THE CROOKED RIB

THE CROOKED RIB

AN ANALYTICAL INDEX

*to the Argument about Women
in English and Scots Literature
to the End of the Year 1568*

By

FRANCIS LEE UTLEY

1970

OCTAGON BOOKS

New York

Copyright, 1944
by The Ohio State University

Reprinted 1970
by special arrangement with Ohio State University Press

OCTAGON BOOKS
A DIVISION OF FARRAR, STRAUS & GIROUX, INC.
19 Union Square West
New York, N. Y. 10003

LIBRARY OF CONGRESS CATALOG CARD NUMBER: 74-120672

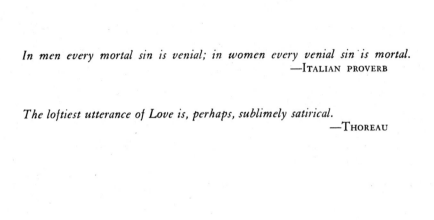

In men every mortal sin is venial; in women every venial sin is mortal.
                                        —ITALIAN PROVERB

The loftiest utterance of Love is, perhaps, sublimely satirical.
                                        —THOREAU

PREFACE

There is a special diplomatics appropriate to the study of satire and defense of women. The background must be sketched, but the formulae discounted. Sociology, psychology, and economics may seem the major clues to interpretation; but to extract anything like accuracy from the records we must also consider the large part played by literary convention. This book is no short history of women. Its primary task is to record the crucial documents and to contribute toward their understanding by some attention to their genesis, their kinds, and the details of their literary history. A field so extensive demands sharp qualification in literary definition, in the use of allied disciplines, and in the period to be covered.

Our most essential terms, *satire* and *defense,* require at once the pruning shears. We cannot include every antagonistic or every laudatory word about women uttered in a certain epoch. The task of establishing a criterion is much more difficult than that experienced by students who have concentrated on other medieval and renaissance types. Greene had a simple test of form for the carol; Child one of origin and transmission for the popular ballad; Rollins one of contemporary title and typographical format for the broadside ballad; Lewis one of conventional setting for the love allegory. But the forms, the origins, and even the aims of the authors whom we shall consider are all too mixed, and we are forced to rely on two simple tests for a satire or a defense: that the subject matter be women primarily, and that the intent and attitude be exaggerated or controversial. Since the human mind has not yet succeeded in making literature or those who create it thoroughly logical, there will be many borderline cases where a subjective element has crept into the hopeful compiler's choice. I have tried to use the tests as consistently and as simply as possible without undue rigidity of classification.

Some may cavil at a lack of constant reference to allied disciplines—to the social sciences in particular. Few literary forms hold more fruitful implications for the study of mankind or man than those before us. Even in these self-conscious days the literary student will recognize that satire on women is neither insignificant nor uninteresting. On its lowest level it can amuse or satisfy sheer curiosity. On a higher level it will serve in part to explain why social reformers of the present still encounter the old masculine conservatism. On the highest level it may lead us at least a short distance into the realm of truth. A literary approach need not deny the impact of external forces on the question of woman's status. Without some psychological corrective one might, for instance, accept innocently the perennial charge of woman's lasciviousness, instead of observing that an accusation which so contradicts the axioms of Ellis and his successors may be, among other things, the half-humorous projection of the never too celibate or even monogamous male. Without some sociological corrective one is apt to land squarely in the midst of the institutional fallacy, which charges celibacy and the medieval Church with all the sins which went on in the medieval world, and forgets the longevity of some of the sins adduced. Without some economic corrective one is apt to emerge with the oversimplification of the class fallacy, which dramatizes the aristocracy as consciously grinding women under heel along with the proletariat, and ignores the position of great power and privilege held by certain women of every medieval class, or the amelioration of woman's status which is a direct and intentional product of feudalism at its best. Without some attention to anthropology one is apt to toy with the race fallacy, which claims that all worship of women is Aryan and all satire Oriental. My first chapter will attempt a modest warning against some of these pitfalls. It will also be concerned with the challenging uses of the literary discipline, without which many have been misled by the notion of a "typical medieval attitude towards women," a "shocking well-known view," a faulty abstraction which takes no account of the total imaginative content of these early periods—of the strong elements of drama, symbolism, and jest which must be weighed if we wish to arrive at any satisfactory equation with the attitudes of our own times.

Finally, we must choose an arbitrary limit in time itself, a task which grows more difficult the more we dwell on the continuity of the themes we are discussing. To define the backward limit of our study is simple enough. It is a mere matter of language; however old the genres of satire and defense may be, they are

not an extant part of the literature written in English before the
thirteenth century. But the forward limit must be arbitrary.
Medieval themes or forms do not die with 1400 or even with 1500.
To ignore at least some part of the English Renaissance is to
obscure a crucial stage in the development of our genres. Yet any
date set up within the Renaissance as a limit will find its objectors,
and the end of that period has never been defined. Despairing,
therefore, of finding perfect agreement among critics, I have risked
an unconventional end point, 1568, to which I have held as
closely as our knowledge of the dates of anonymous pieces will
permit. I have chosen this date simply because it has permitted
me to include without argument the remarkable collection completed in 1568 by George Bannatyne, a manuscript which contributes about one-fifth of the poems in the Index. We are not certain
how early some of Bannatyne's poems are; though the bulk of
them are of the sixteenth century, no small number were composed in the two preceding centuries. We are sure of the forward
limit to their composition, and thus the work of the compiler is
immeasurably aided by the choice of the year 1568. I may venture
one critical support for this date: after the second third of the
century of Elizabeth it is unusual for any artist of the stature of
Chaucer or Dunbar to devote himself to the *querelle des femmes*
in anything more than an epigram or a digression. Spenser and
Shakespeare, at any rate, relegate it to a subordinate position and
mingle it with other literary themes until its formal character is
diminished or wholly lost. Katherine and Petruchio, Beatrice
and Benedict, the Bower of Bliss and the Garden of Adonis recall
the old controversy, but in a fashion rich and strange.

F. L. U.

ACKNOWLEDGMENTS

It is a happy task to name those generous masters and colleagues who have made this book possible. I would have lacked the courage to undertake and the method of prosecuting this study if it had not been for George Lyman Kittredge, whose death has kept it from being a better book. So many others have helped me that I can make no satisfactory list of them. In the earlier stages of work there were six who gave especially valuable counsel: Professors Hyder E. Rollins, Bartlett J. Whiting, C. Grant Loomis, Hamilton M. Smyser, Eileen Power, and Franklin B. Williams, Jr. Without the generosity of the authorities of Harvard University in appointing me Charles Dexter Scholar in the summer of 1934, or the many subsequent grants in aid from the Graduate School of The Ohio State University, I should never have been able to consult the many authorities at firsthand. My debt to libraries is especially great in the case of the Bodleian, the British Museum, Cambridge University, Trinity College (Cambridge), Lambeth Palace, Pierpont Morgan, Huntington, Harvard College, and Ohio State. One's gratitude to libraries is also a matter of persons: I must thank especially the unflagging efforts and expert advice of Miss Maud D. Jeffrey and Miss Alice D. McKee of Ohio State, Mr. Robert H. Haynes of Harvard, Miss Irene J. Churchill of Lambeth Palace, Dr. E. L. Pafort of Pierpont Morgan, and Mr. Herman R. Mead of Huntington. In the latter stages of compilation the help of Professor Archer Taylor, Mrs. Helen Estrich, and Mr. Rossell Hope Robbins has been generously offered. Fortunately Brown and Robbins' *Index of Middle English Verse* appeared in time to permit the hasty insertion of a number of corrections and to make several extranumeral additions in Index I (besides **22a, 41a, 67a,** and **271a** from other sources): **37a, 93a, 106a, 113a, 123a, 149a, 233a,** and **298a.** The margin of error in my Introduction has been greatly diminished by the advice of Professors Robert M. Estrich, John Harold Wilson, Harold R. Walley, and Viva Boothe. Professor William R. Parker has supplemented his reading of the Introduction with an attentive check of Index I; his counsel has been always kind, sometimes disturbing, and never intolerant. He has prevented me from many slips by allowing me complete access to his manuscript index of printers and booksellers to 1640. Another manuscript index, compiled under his direction by Mr. W. Edson Richmond and subsidized by the Graduate School of The Ohio State University, has aided me with its co-ordination of entries in *Stationers' Register* and *Short Title Catalogue*. For help in proofreading I am indebted to Mr. Bernard I. Duffey and Dr. Frederick J. Hoffmann. Mrs. Nancy M. Dasher has kindly helped prepare the manuscript for the printer—no easy task. The greatest debt of all cannot be paid by words, that which I owe to three women who at various stages in this work have constituted themselves my critics and, wittingly and unwittingly, saved me from a thousand masculine blunders: Virginia Loomis, Professor Ruth Hughey, and another Ruth—my wife.

F. L. U.

CONTENTS

INTRODUCTION

INTRODUCTION

I. THE MOTIVE FORCES BEHIND MEDIEVAL SATIRE AND DEFENSE OF WOMEN

The forces which combined to produce satire and defense of women are part of a complex process. In defining these forces we can only try to clear our lenses of their obscuring fogs: our religious environment, our sex, our personal experience, or our membership in a middle-class world. Perhaps we can select without too great distortion a number of intermingled forces, some of which have been overstressed and some neglected. Excessive emphasis has perhaps been placed on five of them: an arbitrary division in time, the Middle Ages; a place and a culture, the Orient; an ideal, asceticism (and its visible expression, the medieval Church); a class, the *bourgeoisie;* and an individual experience, that of the poet. Each of these is significant, but none should be treated as though it existed in a vacuum. Moreover we should not ignore four others too seldom considered: another culture, that of Greece and Rome; a psychological factor, sex antagonism; a common human characteristic, the desire for entertainment; and another ideal, courtly love, which is the product of another class, the aristocracy.

Of the commonly accepted factors the most general and probably the most baseless is that of *Zeitgeist*—the assumption that satire on women is a peculiar product of the Middle Ages. The error is as old as the forward limits of this study. Early medieval defenses of women repeatedly assert the falseness of the men who write satire, and with the Renaissance this charge becomes historical in nature. When humanism and reformation merge to make Elizabethan England at least outwardly a new thing, the *ad hominem* argument becomes a matter of chronology, and the "false men" are identified with an unenlightened or "monkish" past. The myth is full-grown in Puttenham's *Arte of English Poesie,* where the author, discussing the lamentable state of poetry in the "time of Charlemaine and many yeares after him," attributes the distich

> Fallere flere nere mentiri nilque tacere
> Haec quinque vere statuit Deus in muliere

to "some forlorne louer, or els some old malicious Monke."[1]
He was probably unaware that Chaucer had used it,[2] perhaps
even unaware how little of a monk or forlorn lover Chaucer himself might be. Thus, in a century when satires on women were
pouring off the presses in quantity unimagined in the times of
Chaucer or Charlemagne, a critic could characterize the Middle
Ages by one Latin scrap. The worst historical blunders about
"monkish satire" appear to stem from the eighteenth century
and after, when the idea of progress gets into full swing.

The error is in part fed by a somewhat literal reading of the
romanticism, the boasts, and the cynicism of medieval writers
themselves. When Huizinga makes Deschamps' satire against
marriage and squalling children a sign of the "pessimism" of the
later Middle Ages he is exalting the *laudator temporis acti* into a
sworn witness of his time.[3] When Mackay, discussing Dunbar's
Tua Mariit Wemen and the Wedo (**336**), says "it is vain to deny
that their conversation represents a corrupt condition of society
and a special depravity in the sex, which in better times maintains
the standard of purity,"[4] he appears to be unaware that the
chanson de mal mariée which forms the frame and substance of
this poem is as old as the twelfth century and as new as the
present day. When Routh correlates certain lines of John Barker
(1561),

> Neibourhed nor love is none,
> Treu dealyng now is fled and gone,

with the passing away of *noblesse oblige* and the rape of the abbey
lands by Henry VIII's bourgeois favorites,[5] he forgets that Barker
merely repeats the ancient and proverbial formula of the Abuses
of the Age: "Love is lechery, Wit is treachery." We must not
convert the eternal note of sadness into a document of the times.
An age cannot be judged by its sermons any more than by the
warden's book at the Old Bailey. What documentary evidence
exists in a saint's life, a *fabliau,* a defence of women, or a satire
on them is a very delicate matter to ascertain. The Middle Ages
is "neither a sordid tragedy of ecclesiasticism nor a splendid inter-

[1] Ed. Gladys D. Willcock and Alice Walker, Cambridge, 1936, p. 14.
[2] *Wife of Bath's Prologue*, III, 401–402. See also **166**.
[3] *The Waning of the Middle Ages*, London, 1927, pp. 25–27.
[4] Introduction to *The Poems of William Dunbar*, ed. John Small, Edinburgh (STS, XVI), 1883–93, I, lxxxvii.
[5] *CHEL*, III, 111.

lude, but the testing ground wherein many seeds were sown, some good, some bad.'"[6]

The Middle Ages did not give birth to the controversy over women any more than it did to love itself. Both are timeless and universal. Greece and Rome made their contributions as well as the Orient; and the most prolific age of English satire on women is the sixteenth century, when Renaissance and Reformation were in vigorous motion. Satire on women is as old as the Egyptian Book of the Dead and as new as the American comic strip. It will not co-operate when the apostles of progress attempt to correlate its rise and fall with the emancipation of women from man's yoke.

But the Middle Ages did in some measure transform the eternal theme. First, it provided its own rich and gaudy pageant of life, from which men abstracted anew in accordance with old conventions. Above all, it formalized satire, just as it formalized love; it devoted countless single poems to the subject of woman's vice and virtue. In the classics such formalization is rare; aside from epigrams and trifles we may name only a few extant pieces: the work of Semonides of Amorgos, a play or two of Aristophanes, some dialogues of Lucian, the Theophrastus used by Jerome, a few poems by Horace, and most famous of all, the Sixth Satire of Juvenal. With the Fathers, theological and didactic intent begins to make this artistic device more frequent. The best known example is Jerome's *Against Jovinian;* there are treatises on chastity and marriage by Ambrose, Augustine, Origen, Tertullian, and many others. Their satire on women derives equally from classical convention and from Scripture. Christianity was bound to affect sexual *mores* in many ways, but like many another reform, its exact results are difficult of estimate. If it has improved the status of women by making them an important factor in the social and spiritual pattern, it also appears to have diminished in some respects the independence of the Roman matron. Cultures began to merge—Germanic, Greek, Jewish, Roman; the result was conflict and outspoken concern over woman's position. Outside of the formal moralistic treatises there was little strict satire on the sex until the time of twelfth century rejuvenation. From this period on, Latin and the vernaculars are full of satire and defense, to which the Middle Ages contributed its gift for the creation of new genres. The medieval formulae are retained in

[6] C. G. Crump and E. F. Jacob, *The Legacy of the Middle Ages,* Oxford, 1932, p. 172.

the Renaissance when, quantitatively speaking, the controversy over women is at its height.

One common form of chronological limitation has been the undue weight placed upon the defense of women by witness of the Virgin Mother. Henry Adams has done much to help us understand her commanding place in the emotions of medieval man and her relationship to the chivalric ideal. Too much dwelling on his distinguished work can, however, lead to the false assumption that the worship of Mary is a product of the twelfth century. Its artistic flowering may be; but both art and ritual had nurtured the cult of the Virgin from the very beginning of Christianity. Again, when Adams proceeds to call the *Roman de la Rose* "the end of true mediæval poetry," we cannot help wondering how short a space of time he allots to an age which at times has been thought to comprise some fifteen centuries; he seems to bind it within two hundred years or less. Even the *Roman* as a whole is not allowed to stand, for he characterizes the divergences between Guillaume de Lorris and Jean de Meun as matters of time rather than of temper. The "monkey-like malice" of Jean is exiled from the ideal epoch.[7] Had Adams faced the consequences of his metaphor he might have come nearer the truth. For if Jean is to be thought of as the malicious ape of Lorris, as the *simia Dei,* correct dualism would demand that this Devil who parodies divine creation be coeval with the God he imitates. And so, essentially, he is. Guillaume dreamed his dream "Ou vintieme an de mon aage," and recorded it some five years later;[8] Jean continued it when he was middle-aged, the master of a lifetime's study. The contrast between youth and age should not be used to mark epochs.

The chronological error, so deeply seated in the thought of modern critics and historians, needs formal denial. The exponents of woman's worth have been confined to no single period in time: Plato, Euripides, Zeno the Stoic, St. Paul, Eleanor of Aquitaine, Christine de Pisan, Gerson, Vives, Mary Wollstonecraft, John Stuart Mill. These names form no steady progression; they are a series of brilliant flashes against the dark background of conser-

[7] *Mont-Saint-Michel and Chartres,* Boston, 1936, pp. 245-48. Contrast C. S. Lewis, *The Allegory of Love,* Oxford University Press, 1936, pp. 144-45. Adams' "short Middle Ages" is, of course, the result of his desire to illustrate his dynamic theory of history (see *The Education of Henry Adams,* Boston, Mass., 1927, p. vii). I am concerned with certain end products of his theory, not with the theory itself.

[8] *Le Roman de la Rose,* ed. Ernest Langlois, Paris (SATF), 1914-24, I, 2: II, 2.

vatism. Convention is the substance of literature; individuality the accident without which it would lack savor. Occasionally the conventions as a whole clot or intensify into new significance. We need not be puzzled by the twelfth century's rejuvenation of both sensual love and asceticism, or be led to the conclusion that satire originated with Hildebrand's reforms and defense with Eleanor of Aquitaine. The twelfth century, like the sixteenth or the twentieth, was a time when the human mind was awakened to the world within and the world without; when the old axioms were restated in a revolutionary way; when oppositions grew sharp because the eyes of men and women were opened to some of the fundamental paradoxes of existence. The Middle Ages is a time of creation in satire and defense in so far as it provides a formal frame for conventional abstractions from life. The literary fact ought not lead to too ready a sociological conclusion.

A second factor, the Orient, is commonly used to explain why the Middle Ages had a view of women differing somewhat from that of the classical era. Critics have gone to Asia Minor in their search for influences to account for the supposedly great contrast. We encounter, for instance, these jottings in an established authority: "Contempt for female character is primarily monastic. Influence of the East is also unmistakable (cf. the position of women in the Arabian Nights)."[9] Or, elsewhere, Christianity "has given a new prominence and dignity to the female sex."[10] Again, "the Rabbis over and over again teach the utter inferiority of women; they put a definite seal as it were on the degraded life of the female sex which for ages has been lived by women in the East as in the West. Jesus of Nazareth and His Disciples, on the other hand, first taught the equality of the sexes in the eye of God, and by so doing worked a complete revolution in the life of the women of the future."[11] Such statements as these involve flat contradictions. On the one hand, Christianity is supposed to have exalted the position of women above the inferiority to which the East had subjected them; on the other, it fostered an oriental asceticism which lowered the status of the Roman matron.

These paradoxes are the result of an a priori selection of documents. Suppressing for the moment all contradictory evidence,

[9] *CHEL*, III, 551.
[10] Sir John Seeley, *Ecce Homo*, London, 1890, p. 298.
[11] H. D. M. Spence's Introduction to Paul Isaac Hershon, *Genesis: with a Talmudic Commentary*, London, 1883, p. xi.

one might as easily define the classical ages as "Oriental," "medieval," and "paternalistic" in their view of women. Liberated in fact as the Roman matron was, she was guarded by the law against feminine frailty. The *Regulae* of Ulpian, a compiling jurist of the third century, contain the following dictum: "Mutus, surdus, furiosus, pupillus, femina neque familiae emptor esse neque testis libripensve fieri potest" (xx. 7). Both the theory and the practice must have affected Christianity, for some of the Apostles and many of the Fathers were Roman citizens. If we turn backwards to fifth century Athens we find great exponents of women's emancipation, among them Plato and Euripides. But at the same time Aristotle is insisting on the inferiority of women. Among the larger mammals (including man, and for some reason excluding the bear and the leopard) we are told that "the female is less spirited than the male . . . softer in disposition . . . more mischievous, less simple, more impulsive, and more attentive to the nurture of the young; the male, on the other hand, is more spirited than the female, more savage, more simple, and less cunning."[12] Woman is considered an impotent male, the substance or material which cannot generate without the essence or form of the higher sex.[13] Demosthenes makes a threefold division which appears to be not poetry but fact: "Mistresses [ἑταίρας] we keep for the sake of pleasure, concubines [παλλακὰς] for the daily care of our persons, but wives [γυναῖκας] to bear us legitimate children and to be faithful guardians of our households."[14]

Unless, therefore, we are willing to exclude Greece and Rome from the fundamental tradition behind Christianity, we cannot say that the Fathers derived their less idealistic attitudes toward women solely from the East. Nor need we detract from the contribution of Jesus himself when we say that feministic tendencies existed before him. Like all religious leaders, he exalted the individual human being; and women, like men, could only gain by his teaching. Martha and Mary are in some sense the counterparts of Jerome's Paula, Rolle's spiritual sisters, and John Knox's Mrs. Bowes. But to assume that the spiritual high point of the

[12] *Historia Animalium,* 608*ab*; see the translation of D'Arcy W. Thompson in *The Works of Aristotle,* ed. W. D. Ross, Oxford, 1908-1931, Vol. IV.

[13] *De Generatione Animalium,* 728*a*.

[14] *In Neaeram,* 122; tr. A. T. Murray, *Demosthenes: Private Orations III,* Cambridge, Mass., 1939, p. 445. For similar triads in Chaucer and in Daude de Pradas, which show the interpenetration or at least the parallelism of cultures, see R. M. Estrich, "A Possible Provençal Source for Chaucer's *Hous of Fame,* 300–310," *MLN,* LV (1940), 342–49.

founder of Christianity obliterated the valleys of conservatism or created something wholly novel is to deny the lessons of history.

Oriental conservatism has nothing peculiar about it; the Orient is as conservative and as liberal as the world at large. "Let us not here be beguiled by any of the old formulas, of which 'the changeless East' is one of the most familiar and one of the most untrue."[15] If the East were as changeless as the label implies, it could not have been the influence on the West which all, in varying degrees, will grant it to have been. A changeless view of women is usually attributed to two races, the Arabs and the Jews. When we speak of Judaism we remember Eve and forget Deborah; we recall that "it is better to dwell in a corner of the housetop, than with a brawling woman in a wide house" (Prov. 21:9) and we ignore the virtuous woman whose price is far above rubies, whose husband's heart "doth safely trust in her," who will "do him good and not evil all the days of her life" (Prov. 31). The portrait of the virtuous woman may, like that of Patient Griselda, have been later turned to satiric uses; but surely that was not the intention of the Hebrew idealist who climaxed his words with "Give her of the fruit of her hands; and let her own works praise her in the gates." Those who rejoice over the liberation of women under Christianity often forget that the attitudes of the Jews themselves were subject to extensive evolution in the medieval period; for the Rabbis contributed as much to reform as the Church. Whether Jesus rebelled against "the Talmud" (that ill-defined term) is a matter of dispute. One scholar at least has noted that the *Midrash Rabba* possesses not only a fine psychological sense of women's frailty, but also a full appreciation of the talents of the sex and the virtues of matrimony.[16] Apart from eccentric parties like the Essenes, a people which had the Messianic hope could have viewed celibacy only with repugnance. One of the most renowned humanistic defenders of women, Cornelius Agrippa (1486–1535), was an avowed student of the Cabbala.[17]

Aware of the complex testimony offered by Old Testament,

[15] Abrahams, Bevan, and Singer, *The Legacy of Israel*, Oxford, 1928, p. 176.

[16] J. Fürst's Introduction to August Wünsche, tr., *Bereschit Rabba*, Leipzig, 1881, p. viii. See also the liberalizing tendencies displayed in Solomon Zucrow, *Women, Slaves and the Ignorant in Rabbinical Literature*, Boston, Mass., 1932.

[17] Lulu M. Richardson, *The Forerunners of Feminism in French Literature of the Renaissance from Christine of Pisa to Marie de Gournay*, Baltimore and Paris, 1929, pp. 53–64.

Talmud, and Midrash, we may except the Hebrews from the orientalism supposed to have influenced the Fathers, and still be tempted to assign the responsibility to Mohammedanism, polygamy, and the spread of Arabic culture. Here our radically different view of marriage clouds our vision, and we forget that the harem had its roots in economic necessity. If Jerome had his Paula, Mohammed had his Kadija. Arabic culture in the Andalusia of the eleventh century granted considerable freedom to women; we find Wallada conducting a salon not unlike that of Eleanor of Aquitaine.[18] Just how greatly the Arabs influenced the rise of courtly love in eleventh-century Provence is still unclear, but the theory has able exponents,[19] and in any event our understanding of Arab views does not demand the acceptance of any particular theory of transmission. All one insists is that those who call upon oriental documents revealing that woman's place is in the harem give equal prominence to the exalted love poetry of Saracenic civilization, which ranged like that of the West from sensuality to spiritual sublimity. If we concede that the asceticism of the Monks of the Thebaid played some part in the writings of the Christian Fathers, we should not deny the possible inspiration which Moorish romanticism gave to courtly love. The alternative is to minimize all communion between East and West.

Nor should we dwell excessively upon a third factor governing the rise of satire on women, the ascetic ideal. There is no doubting that celibate thought repeated the old charges against the sex. Perhaps the nadir of asceticism is reached in the thirteenth century *Hali Meidenhad,* which attempts to deter a virgin from marriage by describing the horrors of pregnancy:

> Þi rudie neb schal leanen, & as gres grenen. Þin ehnen schulen doskin, & under þon wonnen; & of þi breines turnunge þin heaued ake sare. Inwið þi wombe, swelin þe bitte, þat beoreð forð as a water bulge; þine þarmes þralinge, & stiches i þi lonke, & i þi lendene sar eche riue, Heuinesse in euch lime. Þine brestes burðen o þine twa pappes, & te milc strunden þat te of strikeð. Al is, wið a welewunge, þi wlite ouer warpen. Þi muð is bitter, & walh al þat tu cheowest, & hwat mete se þi mahe hokerliche underfeð; þat is, wið unlust, warpeð hit eft ut.[20]

[18] John Jay Parry, tr., *The Art of Courtly Love by Andreas Capellanus,* New York, 1941, p. 12.

[19] Parry, pp. 7–13; see Power, "The Position of Women," in Crump and Jacob, *Legacy of the Middle Ages,* p. 407.

[20] Ed. Oswald Cockayne and rev. F. J. Furnivall, London (EETS, XVIII), 1922, p. 49.

Our natural indignation at this travesty of motherhood may lead
to false conclusions. So violent a form of asceticism should not
be attributed to the Church as a whole. *Hali Meidenhad* is a
cento of passages from St. Ambrose,[21] and thus a survival of the
propagandizing days of Christianity, which perforce resorted to
the cloister to avoid compromise with a world corrupt in more
things than sexual morals. It is intended for the ears of confirmed
virgins, and we may surmise that its intemperate language
involves not a little *fraus pia* to console the already cloistered
nun, with her half-suppressed longings for maternity. We need
not assume that it was broadcast to the majority of women; its
appearance in only one manuscript may possibly suggest its
limited appeal. And even this treatise provides its own antidote:
the nun is exhorted not to despise the widow or the wedded,
since a mild wife or a meek widow is better than a proud virgin.
God bestowed His favor on the Blessed Virgin more for her
humility than for her virginity.[22]

The ethos of the more rigid forms of monasticism is not the
total ethos of the medieval Church, which comprised all states,
all sexes, and all opinions. The monk of the twelfth century (or
of the ninth)[23] was no hermit like St. Anthony; nor was he of
necessity corrupt. Our Protestant division of Church and State,
of theory and practice, may lead us to misinterpret the medieval
attitudes toward both.[24] We are not justified in identifying one
fragment of the Church Universal with the Church itself.

The celibacy of the secular clergy, so often urged as the primal
cause of misogyny, was by no means a thing established in the
first thousand years of Christianity. With the libels of the Reformation in the way of clear vision we may feel that the many
jests about priests' wives are evidence of unparalleled corruption,
whereas these jests mean simply that the Middle Ages harbored
the usual conflicts among *mores*, law, and ideal. About 1074
Hildebrand attempted repressive measures; his work was continued by Anselm and by the Lateran council of 1215. But it is

[21] J. M. Campbell, "Patristic Studies and the Literature of Medieval England,"
Speculum, VIII (1933), 476.
[22] Cockayne and Furnivall, pp. 58–63.
[23] Philip S. Allen, *Medieval Latin Lyrics*, Chicago, 1931, p. 30.
[24] Ernest Barker, "The Conception of Empire," *The Legacy of Rome*, ed. Cyril Bailey,
Oxford, 1923, pp. 82–89. See also Blanche H. Dow, *The Varying Attitude toward
Women in French Literature of the Fifteenth Century: the Opening Years*, New York,
1936, p. 20; E. K. Chambers, *The Mediæval Stage*, Oxford, 1903, II, 97–113.

significant that the Lyons council of 1273, explicitly named by
Matheolus as the efficient cause of his notorious attack on women,
did not postulate universal celibacy for clerics but merely defined
bigamy as the second marriage of widows, and forbade it to the
clergy.[25] Conservative elements in the Church always had denied
that an unchaste life on the part of the celebrant voided the sacra-
ments. The more extreme forms of asceticism, of which this
sacramental doctrine is but one example, owe as much to the forerunners of Protestantism as to orthodox Catholic belief, a point
often obscured by Luther's break with the whole idea of celibacy.
If clerical celibacy is the major source of satire on women, we
must explain why England, notably unfriendly to the Hilde-
brandian reforms,[26] could yet produce its full share of satires.
Matheolus is evidence that a single poem might owe its genesis
to a local manifestation of celibate zeal; but to attribute the whole
twelfth-century rejuvenation of satire to Hildebrand is to make
too much of one particular. The same century is the beginning
of artistic expression for many attitudes toward women besides
the satirical: the sensual lyric of the Goliards and the troubadours,
the medieval romance, the study of the psychology of lover and
lady, the codification of courtly love. Like the sixteenth century
it is a time of happy contrasts; it has its parallels with both the
Bower of Bliss and the Garden of Adonis, with the Ovidian
humanist and the Puritan, with Rabelais and the moralists who
later assimilated the ideal of chastity to something very different—
monogamous marriage.

   If, as is often implied, asceticism meant otherworldliness and
hence the denunciation of that carnal creature who chains our
thoughts to earth, we must ask why Richard Rolle and other
ascetics surrounded themselves with women and with surprising
rigor kept themselves out of the popular controversy. Though
we may single out individuals whose ethical and religious con-
viction led them to make woman the symbol of that arch enemy,
the Flesh, we must concede that such individuals are confined to
no time or sect. Semonides of Amorgos, Juvenal, St. Jerome,
John Knox, and Schopenhauer agree on this point and on little
else. The picture should not be oversimplified by a Freudian

   [25] A.-G. van Hamel, ed., *Les Lamentations de Matheolus*, Paris, 1892–1905, pp.
cvii–cxiv.
   [26] Henry C. Lea, *History of Sacerdotal Celibacy in the Christian Church*, 3rd ed.,
New York, 1907, I, 333 and *passim*.

paradox; yet there is something to be said for regarding the few serious satirists as exhibiting more than the normal need for repression. The devil appeared to St. Anthony in very pleasing guise. Rolle, when he rebuked a woman for wearing that vain headdress satirized as "horns," was asked why he, a spiritual man, had looked at her so closely as to know what she was wearing.[27] The world was surely too much with the bitter poets who wrote *De Coniuge non Ducenda* (75) and "The beistlie lust, the furious appatite" (282). The worldly lawyers, the one literate class which we may with confidence separate from the clergy, were quite as interested as the clergy itself in antifeminine satire.[28]

Monasticism merely provided a congenial atmosphere for the eternal debate over women. The phenomenon is parallel to the "monkish" intensification of the poetic themes of contempt for the world and the imminence of death, but parallel only, and not identical. It recalls the romantic intensification of the themes of freedom and rebellion, the twentieth-century preoccupation in its *Waste Lands* with "O tempora, o mores," the Elizabethan revival of the theme of patriotism, the Wordsworthian return to a love for nature, the courtly emphasis on themes of love and honor. The twelfth century was a time of humanism, when men's minds awoke to Aristotle, and Abelard gave life to the old ethical and theological controversies in his *Sic et Non*. The age-old quarrel about woman's worth could not escape revival in a time when there was an equal passion for reason and for love, for violent indulgence and for violent renunciation. No greater abuse of a word exists than the common use of *goliardic* to mean ascetic satire on women. When the Archpoet wrote in his *Confessio*

> Si ponas Ypolitum
> hodie Papie,
> non erit Ypolitus
> in sequenti die:
> Veneris in thalamos
> ducunt omnes vie,
> non est in tot turribus
> turris Aricie,

---

[27] *The Fire of Love*, ed. Ralph Harvey, London (EETS, CVI), 1896, p. 28.
[28] See Gustav Gröber, *Geschichte der Mittelfranzösischen Literatur. I*, Berlin and Leipzig, 1933, p. 247; and, for an extensive treatment, Howard G. Harvey, *The Theatre of the Basoche*, Cambridge, Mass., 1941.

he was scarcely identifying himself with Hippolytus before the visit to Pavia. Although, as Allen says, the Goliards were lacking in reverence for women,[29] they were not lacking in approval.

Otherworldliness is as responsible for the praise of women as for their accusation. The Wife of Bath has perhaps more than any other person given currency to the fiction of "monkish" satire:

> For trusteth wel, it is an impossible
> That any clerk wol speke good of wyves,
> But if it be of hooly seintes lyves,
> Ne of noon oother womman never the mo (III, 688-91).

But she is a special pleader, and in any event Chaucer probably means by "clerks" not priests or monks but those who do the world's writing. The Wife's opponent, the Clerk of Oxford, is as much a defender of women as a satirist; in all his tales he says less harm of the sex than do those uncloistered souls the Wife and the Merchant. Certain active enemies of celibacy and of chaste marriage, like Andreas Capellanus and Guillaume de Lorris, were clerics. And one pious writer of "hooly seintes lyves," a direct product of asceticism and of the medieval Church, shows that the Wife was too scornful of valuable allies:

> Whanne men [sitteþ] in hare hayt: vp hare ale-benche,
> And habbeþ þe pycher & þe coppe: & þe botyler to schenche,
> Þanne is hare iangle & hare game: to deme som sely wenche,
> Þat god ȝeue þat some of ham myȝte: in þe ale-ffat a-drenche![30]

Thus we cannot agree with one critic who attributes Lydgate's satire on women to his "serious and melancholy turn of mind," and speaks of how that poet's celibacy soured his temper "as is observed of old bachelors in our days";[31] with another who refers to "asceticism with its gross view of married life";[32] or with a third who traces the genesis of *Griselda* and *The Taming of the Shrew* to the "ignorant abuse of women" which "prevailed in literature—abuse springing mainly out of the vile prejudices and superstitions of the medieval Church."[33] Such judgments have

[29] *Medieval Latin Lyrics*, p. 246.
[30] Beatrice D. Brown, ed., *The Southern Passion*, London (EETS, CLXIX), 1927, pp. 68-71.
[31] *The Works of Thomas Gray*, ed. Edmund Gosse, London, 1884, I, 400-408. Since Gray was himself an old bachelor, there may be more jest than earnest here.
[32] Thomas R. Lounsbury, *Studies in Chaucer*, London, 1892, I, 114.
[33] J. W. Hales, in *Originals and Analogues of Some of Chaucer's Canterbury Tales*, Oxford University Press (Chaucer Society), 1928-37 (Hales's essay originally appeared in 1875), p. 175.

damaged the reputation of "ascetic" twelfth-century satirists like
Marbod of Rennes and Hildebert of Le Mans, and have given a
false estimate of the forces which produced them.[34] The point is
seen more clearly if we turn to the most influential of all medieval
satirists, Jean de Meun. To charge this clerical student of women
with his cloth is to close one's eyes to his reputation as the Voltaire of the Middle Ages, the encyclopedist and scourge of his
times; it is to ignore his partiality for the senses, his attacks on
celibacy, his love for Ovid, and his naturalism. We are not obliged
to repeat the libels of Christine de Pisan, who was a polemicist
and not a historian. We should err as greatly in attributing
Rabelais's *esprit gaulois* to his somewhat tenuous connection with
the cloister. And what of Chaucer, who was no cleric, in the
religious sense, at all?

No doubt it is this residue of distinguished satirists which has
led many students to supplement asceticism with a fourth factor,
that of the *bourgeoisie*. Apropos of Jean de Meun Miss Waddell
has remarked that "there is nothing in Latin to touch the sheer
brutality of the vernacular";[35] and this statement seems to need
no great qualification. The economic version of history is too
strong a bulwark to be ignored. The long history of English
satire on women, with its renaissance flowering and its adaptation
by the Puritans, cannot be written without reference to the share
of the middle class as author and as audience. Chaucer surely
perceived something of the truth when he placed his broader
satirical ironies in the mouths of the Wife of Bath and the Merchant, those very bourgeois souls, when he ameliorated the position of the Clerk and made the gentle Franklin the exponent of
courtly marriage (as the Knight and the Squire were of romantic
love). When in *The Parliament of Fowls* he appears to identify
the heretics of courtly love solely with the non-noble classes he
is merely following the aristocratic habit of ascribing no good
to the *vilain,* an ill-defined creature of abuse who might be anything from the poorest serf who stole a partridge to the wealthiest
burgher who refused to open his purse strings to a noble lord.
We may recall the extremities of Bertran de Born's strictures on
the wealthy peasantry.

[34] Contrast the summary of these authors in August Wulff, *Die Frauenfeindlichen
Dichtungen in den Romanischen Literaturen des Mittelalters*, Halle, a. S., 1914, pp. 19–24,
with the more sensitive treatment in Helen Waddell, *The Wandering Scholars*, 7th ed.,
London, 1934, pp. 97–100.
[35] *The Wandering Scholars*, p. 211.

It is hard sometimes to disassociate the bourgeois from the
clerical factor. In an age when the education of the middle
classes was largely dependent upon clerical status, when the major
path from one class to another was that of the Church, it is not
surprising to find many satirists who derive their jests equally
from the monastic ideal and from the bourgeois spirit. In the
twelfth and thirteenth centuries the rebellious temper of the
awakening middle class appears, for instance, in the *fabliaux* and
in the *Roman de Renart*. "The authors of these works tested
ideals and conventions by the touchstone of everyday life, and
fearlessly questioned the authority of all who had power over
them, and especially the authority of the aristocracy, of the clergy,
and of women."[36] Rebelling against the clergy they might often
be a part of it—no paradox, since the most violent anticlericalism
is often the product not of indifferent laymen but of the less-
favored ranks of the clergy.

We must beware, however, of the oversimplification which
speaks of "the bourgeois contempt for women and the cavalier
deference for women,"[37] or the kindred division between severely
ascetic and cynical bourgeois misogyny.[38] Too much can be made
of the sterility and conservatism of the nobility.[39] Folk and *bourgeoisie* have their own conservatism;[40] submerged or emerging
groups cling hard to what they know, and fear that they may be
the victims of a change in the social frame. This may account for
woman's own hesitancy in approving "reforms" for her sex,
for that feline form of satire which deplores the individualist
among women to a degree undreamed of by most men. Too
much has been said of the bourgeois reaction to courtly love. We
shall see later how organically rebellion and acceptance, satire and
defense, can be joined to one another.

The nobility itself was not totally unversed in satire which
betrays a class prejudice. One constant form of accusation is that
against the bourgeois wife, who threatened the framework of
society by aping her betters. Andreas Capellanus asserts that the
most exalted forms of *cortoisie* are not meant for the middle-class

---

[36] F. P. Wilson, ed., *The Batchelars Banquet,* Oxford, 1929, p. ix.

[37] Eleanor P. Hammond, *English Verse between Chaucer and Surrey,* Durham, N. C.,
1927, p. viii.

[38] See Th. M. Chotzen, "La 'Querelle des Femmes' au Pays de Galles," *Revue Celtique,* XLVIII (1931), 43–44.

[39] Hammond, pp. 3–9.

[40] See Routh in *CHEL,* III, 93.

woman; the sophisticated *pastourelle* reveals the low regard of
the chevalier for the morality of the shepherdess. Reverence for
women, in other words, had its qualifications; the true recipients
of *Minnedienst* were noblewomen. Sumptuary laws were enacted
to curb the desire of the middle-class wife to dress like her
superiors. Chaucer jests at the guildsmen's wives who feel that

> It is ful fair to ben ycleped "madame,"
> And goon to vigilies al bifore,
> And have a mantel roialliche ybore[41]

and at the Miller's wife who is

> as digne as water in a dich,
> And ful of hoker and of bisemare.[42]

When he portrays the tradesmen's wives who fight to be the first
in line at a religious service he is speaking to his courtly friends;
for we are told that the truly noble sought to avoid the precedence
which was their due, that "the struggles of politeness, which some
forty years ago were still characteristic of lower-middle-class eti-
quette, were extraordinarily developed in the court life of the
fifteenth century."[43] Eternal theme the Easily Consoled Widow
may be, recurring as it does in China and Greece, in Petronius
and in Voltaire; but we may suspect that the Wife of Bath's
failure to mourn her husbands was in part her lack of courtly
sensibility. The bourgeois widow lacked the leisure to indulge
in the elaborate mourning which led Madame de Charolais to
confine herself ceremoniously to her bed for six weeks.[44]

We too often assess the middle classes of these early centuries
as if they were ourselves, and forget that our own bourgeois ideals
have been subject to several hundred years of change. When we
object to the hyperbolic praise of a sovereign or of a woman we
need not assume that a medieval townsman would do the same.
Modern distaste for hero worship owes something to Thomas
Paine and to the English novel. We cannot confine the irreverence of the *fabliau* to the town or the idealism of love poetry to
the chateau, any more than we can be sure how many workers
read the proletarian novel today. Defense of women by witness
of the Virgin Mother is not the product of the aristocracy alone;

[41] *General Prologue*, I, 376–78. See also entries **262** and **268** in Index I.
[42] *Reeve's Tale*, I, 3964-65.
[43] Huizinga, *Waning of the Middle Ages*, p. 34.
[44] Huizinga, p. 43.

a burgher or a peasant was just as capable of seeing the sorrowing Mother of the Crucifixion in stained glass or sculpture and of enacting her story in drama. History and our present-day attitudes may even suggest that the *bourgeoisie* is to a large degree responsible for the emphasis on mother-sentiment in such sixteenth-century defenders as Pyrrye (94) or Gosynhill (347). Though the tradesman often lacked the courtier's skill in expressing his more delicate emotions, we must recognize that family feeling had its roots in economic and social necessity. In the early days, at least, the bourgeois moved in a limited circle; his home was apt to be small and his wife and children too near to be ignored. Children were the hope of their ambitious fathers. The price of a virtuous and industrious wife was above rubies; one might wive and thrive (70). In contrast the nobleman's interest in family was less grounded in necessity and more in need of conventional supports. Valuable as a good wife might be, her place as a chatelaine could be taken by others. She might bring dowry and land and quarterings on the escutcheon, but she could bring dynastic quarrels too. One's son might be an avowed enemy, a threat to one's own supremacy. Bourgeois culture, therefore, was as potentially favorable to women as aristocratic. Economic factors demanded that the *bourgeoisie* develop "a greater sense of the normal personality of women than . . . either the Aristocracy or the Church," for the *femme sole* was a factor to be reckoned with in trade, and an ambitious housewife was the source of prosperity in the home.[45] If the wider reading public created by printing meant an increase in the number of satires, it was responsible as well for a host of defenses.[46]

There is one major difficulty in calling a tendency bourgeois or proletarian or courtly—the problem of the individual chosen to expound the tendency. The school of Arras in thirteenth-century France is evidence that bourgeois poets could write in the "courtly" tradition.[47] Those who were deprived of noble birth did not accept without protest the aristocratic stigma that they could not love. It is true that the more subtle manifestations of love might suffer in less sophisticated hands, but this is the fault

[45] Eileen Power, in *Legacy of the Middle Ages*, pp. 407, 410–12.

[46] Louis B. Wright, *Middle-Class Culture in Elizabethan England*, Chapel Hill, N. C., 1935, pp. 464, 506–507.

[47] Gaston Paris, *La Littérature Française au Moyen Age*, pp. 203–205. See also Crump and Jacob, *Legacy of the Middle Ages*, p. 190; E. K. Chambers and F. Sidgwick, *Early English Lyrics*, London, 1926, p. 276.

of education and not of class. Educate a bourgeois like Chaucer and you may have a hand more deft than that of Charles of Orleans.

Nowhere is the danger of too sharp a division between bourgeois and noble more apparent than in the use which has been made of the book which Geoffrey, Knight of la Tour-Landry, wrote for his daughters in the late fourteenth century (150). It is almost as precious a record of the ordinary life of women as the instructions of the Menagier of Paris to his wife. The Knight's tolerance toward the *bourgeoisie* has led some to identify his views with the Menagier, but he does not throw chivalry completely overboard: "thus pore men canne chaste her wyues with fere and strokes, but a gentille woman shulde chastise her selff with fairenesse."[48] Kilgour has rightly shown that a difference might exist between the ideals of a courtly sophisticate and a provincial nobleman like Geoffrey.[49] But the Knight's critique of courtly love is not necessarily due to bourgeois influence. A provincial knight was in fact less likely to encounter the ideas of the town than a greater noble. What Geoffrey shared with the Menagier was the heritage of the Church—a mutual piety which came from religious treatises with their counsels of harmony in marriage and their disapproval of courtly irreverence and adultery. To them, as to John Knox two centuries later, the court was Sodom. And there is an ironic element in Geoffrey's book; his wife is the one who rebels outspokenly against the code which was supposed to exalt womankind.

We are obliged, in short, to treat Geoffrey as the complex personality that any human being is, not as the representative of a type or class or state. Satire, defense, or a crude or delicate blend of the two, all rest in large part on another factor than time, place, ideal, or class—the personal experience of the individual. Of the commonly ascribed factors none is more perilous to interpret. Especially is this true of the Middle Ages, for which letters and contemporary biographies are almost non-existent, the canon of a poet's work is often unsettled, and even the baffling and one-sided evidence of the Public Records Office is rare. In this aura of doubt many have seized blindly upon the supposed

[48] *The Book of the Knight of La-Tour-Landry*, ed. Thomas Wright, London (EETS, XXXIII), 1868, p. 28.
[49] Raymond L. Kilgour, *The Decline of Chivalry*, Cambridge, Mass., 1937, pp. 109–122.

autobiography of a poet's own work, and argued, as Allen points
out, in a vicious circle: we reconstruct a life from a poem and
then proceed to criticize the same poem in the light of our conjectures.[50] Goliardic poetry, for instance, is lacking in the "reverence for women" which we find in Dante or Lord Tennyson.
Hence we conclude that the wandering scholars invariably lived
dissolute lives. Hence *Iam dulcis amica* becomes a coarse and
sensual poem, however much it may have borrowed from the
Song of Songs.

What one may call the autobiographical fallacy often depends
as well upon too close attention to the letter of early authorities.
When Christine de Pisan employs the *ad hominem* argument
against Jean de Meun,[51] and calls him rake and ribald, we may
forgive her. We have seen what seventeenth-century polemics did
to Milton, or modern enemies and false friends to Nietzsche. It
is easy to conclude that if your opponent argues what you feel to
be satanic notions he must be a devil in his personal life. If he
calls woman sensual and grasping he must have frequented "the
wrong kind of woman."

The essence of this sort of strained biography is the failure
to perceive that an artist's work, static and firm as it may appear
when neatly collected between covers, is the product of a lifetime,
of many moods, many experiences, and many social forces. Above
all we must remember that drama plays no small part in satire.
Pierre Col, replying to the arguments of Christine, had the wit
to understand that Jean de Meun's La Vieille and Le Jaloux were
"personnaiges"—dramatic creations— and that Jean "fait chascun
personnaige parler selonc qui luy appartient."[52] The dramatic setting of the Marriage Group has in some measure saved us from
assuming that Chaucer was the Merchant or the Wife of Bath,
although we have been more often tempted by the notion that he
was the Clerk or the Franklin. With *The House of Fame* in
mind, some have even concluded that he hated his wife for wak-
ing him up early in the morning.[53] Our eyes are still blurred by

[50] Allen, *Medieval Latin Lyrics*, pp. 16, 294. The *reductio ad absurdum* would seem
to be the reconstruction of a composer's biography from his music. See E. M. Dent, "The
Historical Approach to Music," *Authority and the Individual*, Cambridge, Mass., 1937,
p. 363.
[51] See Dow, *Varying Attitude toward Women*, pp. 164–67.
[52] Charles F. Ward, *The Epistles on the Romance of the Rose and Other Documents
in the Debate*, University of Chicago Press, 1911, p. 68.
[53] On this and on the general subject of Chaucer's "misogyny" (an absurd enough
term), see T. R. Lounsbury, *Studies in Chaucer*, London, 1892, I, 112–15.

romantic miasma, by the knowledge that Lord Byron tried to live his Byronism, by the fictional autobiographies which the Provençal *chansonniers* appended to the poems of a Jaufre Rudel, by the forgivable desire to know everything we can of a personality whose verse has spoken personally to us. "Even he who has sufficient intelligence to perceive the folly of speculative biography may not always have the strength to avoid it."[54] Each writer presents his special problem—a prose writer like Conrad who wrote much conscious autobiography in the guise of fiction,[55] a poet like Browning whose poetic statement about his own love is confirmed by external biography, the less certain case of a satirist like Matheolus whose "bigamy" is attested both by his own statement and by external history, the uncertain case of a poet like Chaucer whose poetic words are supported by no unequivocal documents at all, and the completely baffling case of the author of *De Coniuge non Ducenda,* about whom we know nothing except that he must have existed in the twelfth or thirteenth century.

When, in a surge of enthusiasm for modern feminism, we attribute satires on women to unhappy marriages, unrequited love, or clerical bitterness, we should beware the categorical imperative. To attribute all the satires in our index to marital catastrophe would be to create the greatest unconscious satire of all. Since personal experience can be taken as a name for all the causal stimuli which combine to make a poet put pen to paper— among them the act of composition itself—it can be reckoned a factor in the debate over women. Perhaps, if we define it largely and imaginatively enough, we may even call it the major factor. But to peep and botanize upon a satire for the purpose of recovering a bit of domestic gossip is to defeat the very end of poetry. *Weltschmerz* or universal satire may derive its immediate stimulus from a divorce, a rebuff, a new love, a dyspeptic attack, or an extra mug of ale; but to deny that a competent poet writes obliquely is to destroy poetic and scholarly truth at once. A stumbling writer who writes on a manuscript margin "I se where is but litill truste" (**105**) may directly reveal his inarticulate grief, or a rebellious lover may force real sorrow into the procrustean

[54] Lounsbury, I, xiv-xv.
[55] Even Conrad objected to too much literal reading of his "autobiography." See Edward Crankshaw, *Joseph Conrad,* London, 1936, pp. 15-18; G. Jean-Aubry, *Joseph Conrad: Life and Letters,* New York, 1927, II, 73.

bed of convention, but the satirist proper is usually conscious of his duty to a particular audience and to the world at large.

Thus we must qualify the commonly ascribed factors behind medieval satire on women. We must be as cautious in advancing others less frequently mentioned: the classics, sex antagonism, the jesting spirit, and the literary convention known as courtly love. Yet they surely deserve as much attention as those I have been discussing.

We have already had some evidence in the words of Ulpian, Aristotle, and Demosthenes that classical law and literature could be at times as harsh in their judgment of woman's status as the supposedly ascetic twelfth century. References to women are scattered, and only rarely crystallize into so obvious a form as the iambics of Semonides of Amorgos or the Sixth Satire of Juvenal; but most of the content and even the expression do not greatly differ from those of Christian centuries. Except in its conciseness Juvenal's

> certe sanus eras; uxorem, Postume, ducis?
> dic, qua Tisiphone, quibus exigitare colubris?

provides no contrast to the early sixteenth-century

> O man more than madde, what ys þi mynde? (**223**)

or to Lydgate's translation of *De Coniuge non Ducenda,*

> Glory vnto God, laude and benysoun
> To Iohn, to Petir, & also to Laurence,
> Which haue me take vnder proteccioun
> From the deluge of mortall pestilence,
> And from the tempest of deedly violence,
> And me preserved I fell not in the rage
> Vnder the yoke and bondis of mariage (**75**).

The wanton she-wolf, wife of Ysengrin and mistress of Renart, is rhetorical kin to Semonides' cunning Vixen, tetchy Bitch, stubborn and promiscuous She-Ass, lecherous Cat, fastidious Mare, and spiteful and ungainly Ape. Few medieval poets exceeded the intensity of passion manifest in Semonides' portrait of one woman made by Zeus

> of a bristly Sow; all that is in her house lies disorderly, defiled with dirt, and rolling upon the floor, and she groweth fat a-sitting among the middens in garments as unwashed as herself.[56]

---

[56] J. M. Edmonds, ed. and tr., *Elegy and Iambus,* London, 1931, II, 217.

It is unnecessary to search in the Orient or in the localized events of the twelfth century for the origins of clerical and lay satire on women; we should not attribute Jerome's *Against Jovinian* to his Eastern travels if by so doing we obscure the existence of his Roman predecessor and kindred spirit, Juvenal.

Gladstone, living in the time of triumphant middle-class liberalism, once drew a portrait of women in Homer's "Heroic Age."[57] One of his ideals was that of chivalry toward woman (much altered from its feudal form), another that of housewifely virtue. In Homer he sought and found just what he wanted: the loyalty of a party leader, the courage of imperialism, and the family affection beloved of the bourgeois public and the Queen. But what are we to say of the strife of Agamemnon and Achilles over Briseis? Or of the hateful Thersites, whom the Middle Ages would have called Malebouche or Wikked-Tunge, and who charges the Grecian leaders with uxoriousness and effeminacy?[58] The leader himself, Agamemnon, speaks from personal experience when he says in Hades "there is nothing so cruel and shameless as a woman," and warns Odysseus that even though Penelope is something of an improvement on Clytemnestra, he should still keep his masculine counsel.[59] These satirical nuggets are a corrective to the idealized portraits of Andromache and Helen; we must include them in the ledger when we estimate the views of Homer (one or many) or of the heroic age which long preceded the *Iliad* and *Odyssey,* an age which these poems themselves romanticize. When Ker observed that epic incorporated all the other literary modes—tragic, comic, pastoral, and heroic—we may infer he meant satiric also.[60]

Or let us turn to Rome, to a writer whose philosophical intentions might lead us to expect consistency. Cicero could attack love in terms not inappropriate to a medieval celibate.[61] He could oppose the growing legal freedom of women sponsored by the Voconian law,[62] and yet place a defense of the same law into the

---

[57] *Studies on Homer and the Homeric Age,* Oxford, 1858, III, 479–520. For more successful treatments of Roman and Greek attitudes toward women see August Wulff, *Die Frauenfeindlichen Dichtungen,* pp. 3–13; F. A. Wright, *Feminism in Greek Literature,* London, 1923; E. F. M. Benecke, *Antimachus of Colophon and the Position of Women,* London, 1896; Hans Licht, *Sexual Life in Ancient Greece,* London, 1933.

[58] *Iliad,* ii, 211–42.

[59] *Odyssey,* xi, 404–461.

[60] *Epic and Romance,* London, 1926, pp. 19–34.

[61] *Tusculanes,* iv, 32–36.

[62] *De Senectute,* v, 14.

mouth of another.[63] He bestowed education and regard on his daughter Tullia and approved the training of Spartan women, which by conservative Greeks had been held to be one of the greatest threats to masculine comfort. In short, there is something to be had on both sides in Homeric Greece and in Cicero's Rome. Athens and Rome retained the controversy despite the just view of some sociologists that the Spartan Wars and the Punic Wars were focal points for the emancipation of women as significant as the First World War itself.

Feminism of a sort existed in Greece and Rome—we need name only the Pythagoreans, Plato, and Plutarch. But we need not conclude, therefore, that the Middle Ages plunged women into unparalleled subjection from which they have only lately been released again. If Ovid was the inspiration of courtly love, he was also a fertile source of satire. Guillaume de Lorris and Jean de Meun are both Ovidians. We may trace two streams of medieval satire: Juvenalian indignation with its warning against marriage—Jerome, Theophrastus, Marbod of Rennes, *De Coniuge non Ducenda,* the *Epistle of Valerius to Rufinus;* and the Ovidian revelation of the way to a woman's heart, a revelation realistic and artful, manifest in the Goliards, Jean de Meun, Boccaccio, Chaucer, and the rebellious lover poems. Each tradition involves many variations, many nuances of mood; neither is part of a dynastic line, but each depends on renewed inspiration and at times blends with the other. Together they account for the major portion of medieval satire, and what is most important, they both have classical prototypes. There is nothing to surprise us in the fact that two times of great activity in satire, the twelfth and the sixteenth centuries, are also times of classical revival. Jean de Meun may owe his encyclopedism and many of his examples against women to his era and to monasticism, but he is also indebted to the humanists of Chartres.[64] And the scholars Pierre and Gontier Col, who defended him against Christine, are often called the forerunners of the French Renaissance.

Satire therefore runs through both the classical and the medieval periods, turned no doubt a fraction to left or right by various moral fashions such as Christian asceticism and Grecian masculinism, but retaining in general a remarkably straight channel.

---

[63] *De Republica,* iii, 10.
[64] See Lewis, *Allegory of Love,* p. 122.

Today the world may have slowed the current by indifference and a concern for other issues, but it has not stopped it up. For there are other factors than literary borrowing and sociological institutions which impel satire forward—the related themes of sex antagonism and jest.

Sex antagonism, the strut of the male and the clever coquetry of the female, surely played its part. It is a factor too ancient, too unconscious, to need much illustration; but it should not be overlooked. Perhaps it is revealed in the comb of Chauntecleer

> redder than the fyn coral,
> And batailled as it were a castel wal.

When Chaucer had his Cock show off his learning with

> *Mulier est hominis confusio,*—
> Madame, the sentence of this Latyn is,
> "Womman is mannes joye and al his blis,"

he recognized the conflict as clearly as does our own time. And Chaucer knew the response of the female, her capacity for consoling her lord and master even though her counsels were "ful ofte colde." Perhaps there is a bit of shrewish malice in those laxatives she recommends for idle dreams. Man's satire on women is one of his prerogatives, a sign of physical snobbery which has not yet failed. Without it, without the ambiguous and jesting battle of courtship, the affairs of love would be in a parlous state.

The recognition of the biological and psychological factor should not cause us to assume that Christine de Pisan is typical of her sex or Jean de Meun of his. Women can satirize women as well as men can. Christine and Hélisenne de Crenne, noted feminists both, were far from ignoring the failings of their sex.[65] Marie de France could repeat the conventional attacks on women; as Foster Damon puts it: "Marie, being woman, could not idealize her sex as the men did; and once the essential adoration was punctured, the heart was gone out of the whole system."[66]

In truth we may say that women would rather be talked about scandalously than ignored. It is a grave error which concludes that medieval satire was confined to the cloister or the soldier's campfire. Perhaps it was frequent enough in the alehouse, but some of our satires will tell us that medieval women

[65] Richardson, *Forerunners of Feminism*, p. 75.
[66] *PMLA*, XLIV (1929), 968. One French reviewer was somewhat hardheaded, I believe, in his denial of satire in Marie; see *Romania*, XXX (1901), 158–59.

were not absent from what was twenty years ago considered the
masculine castle. Women heard the wanton *fabliaux* as well as
men, and the satirical apologies and ambiguities of Chaucer and
Lydgate testify to a mixed audience. When Lydgate like many
another satirist qualifies his invective with a double-edged apology, we can hardly assume that there were no women to hear
him:

> For thouh it fall that oon, or two, or three
> Haue doon amysse, as therefore God forbeede
> That other women which stable & feithful be
> Should be atwited off ther ongoodliheede. . . .
> A gallid hors, the sooth yff ye list see,
> Who touchith hym, boweth his bak for dreede. . . .
> But goode women haue ful litil neede
> To gruchch or frowne whan the trouthe is lernyd.[67]

The same poet counted eight or more noble ladies among his
patronesses,[68] and he would have found it difficult to hide from
them his most ambitious work. His jest about the galled jade
wincing was as dependent upon a mixed audience as the "gaude"
of Chaucer's Pardoner, when he barred his absolution to

> any womman, be she yong or old,
> That hath ymaad hir housbonde cokewold.

Chaucer was Lydgate's master in "amphilogies" as in many
another artistic device. The disciple could not duplicate the complexity of tone in the passage where Chaucer is discussing Pertelote's counsel to take no heed of dreams:

> Wommennes conseils been ful ofte colde;
> Wommannes counseil broghte us first to wo,
> And made Adam fro Paradys to go,
> There as he was ful myrie and wel at ese.
> But for I noot to whom it myght displese,
> If I conseil of wommen wolde blame,
> Passe over, for I seyde it in my game.
> Rede auctours, where they trete of swich mateere,
> And what they seyn of wommen ye may heere.
> Thise been the cokkes wordes, and nat myne;
> I kan noon harm of no womman divyne (VII, 3256-66).

Chaucer may have learned the trick from Jean de Meun or his
successors, Deschamps or Machaut. Jean's apologies are on a

[67] *Lydgate's Fall of Princes*, ed. Henry Bergen, London (EETS, CXXI-CXXIV),
1924-27, I, 190.
[68] *DNB*, XII, 307; Karl J. Holzknecht, *Literary Patronage in the Middle Ages*, Philadelphia, 1923, pp. 100-101.

slightly more serious level. He prays that women will not blame
him if they find anything "mordanz e chenins" about his words,
for he does it but to teach, not out of spite. His purpose is that
of the omnivorous encyclopedist: "Car il fait bon de tout saveir."
Women should not call him liar; he has it all on the authority
of ancient books; if he lies "li preudome" lie, and like them he
intends but "profiz e delectacion."[69] Contrast Chaucer's confusion
of the issue in the remarks on Pertelote. First the flat proverbial
libel that women are fatal counselors, and the time-honored
example Eve. Then a hint of satire in the other direction; are
the smug words "ful myrie and wel at ese" exactly flattering to
Adam? Then Chaucer, or rather the speaker (for all these words
are strained through the consciousness of the confessor to a nun-
nery) says "Pass it over! I said it but in jest," and adduces serious
authority to support the joke. As if this were not enough, he must
in his patent digression cast the blame on Chauntecleer, who has
not been speaking for some little time. Finally the ambiguous
line "I kan noon harm of no womman divyne." Who can say
whether *divyne* is adjective or verb, whether the speaker denies
all harm in woman or only in "hooly seintes lyves?"

The irony defies analysis; but we can be sure that no lonely
group of men would enjoy this passage with the zest of a mixed
audience. When Ausonius in the third century writes the following complacent epigram his wife was certainly peering over his
shoulder:

> Laidas et Glyceras, lasciuae nomina famae,
> Coniunx in nostro carmine cum legeret,
> Ludere me dixit falsoque in amore iocari.
> Tanta illi nostra est de probitate fides.[70]

The tone is identical with that of Chaucer's Host, who fears that
"somme of this meynee" might tell his wife if he details her
vices there, for "of hir tonge a labbyng shrewe is she" (IV, 2419).

Jest, the civilized veneer for sex antagonism, is thus another of
the prime factors in the debate. At no time in history did the
tedious hours demand more spontaneous public entertainment
for parties of both sexes than the age of the baronial hall. The
efflorescence of both courtly love and satire may be more easily
attributed to this physical fact than to any other. Yet nowhere

[69] *Roman de la Rose*, ed. Langlois, IV, 94–96.
[70] *Carmina*, xix, 39.

do we find literal-mindedness among students making "ernest of game" more perversely than here, when the Court of Love is made into a political institution, and satire is deprived of the feminine audience which gave it piquancy. The alliance of satire with courtly festivity is made certain by its intrusion into the fortune-game (**201**), the riddle (**275**), and the holly-ivy carol (**86**). If formal satire were merely the product of serious asceticism, or even of the jesting cloister, more would have been preserved from before the twelfth century. Like its near relation, the love lyric, it has vanished because it seemed in those times too trivial and too profane for preservation. Whatever the personal taste of scribes, a monastic scriptorium could not waste precious hours and vellum on poems which lacked due piety and weight.

Sheer accident is no doubt one of the major reasons for the scarcity of extant satire in Old English. All the dwelling on those lines in Tacitus which assert the mystical reverence for women among Germanic tribes is not enough to convince us that the Anglo-Saxons knew no wanton jests or songs about the sex's frailty. What misogyny we find preserved is largely serious in tone, but it is evidence that the satirical theme was not absent from Hrothgar's hall. Thryth, who is contrasted in *Beowulf* (1931–62) to Hygelac's queen, is a case in point; and the war-inciting heroines of Norse saga further suggest that the words of Tacitus are one-sided. The commanding place of women in sympathetic magic existed elsewhere than in Germania, and it should not be taken as a uniquely Teutonic contribution to the courtly codes of Andreas Capellanus or Wolfram von Eschenbach.

Misogyny thus doubtless existed before the Middle English period, and it continued after it was over. The courtly ideal and its satirical counterpart lost some of their centrality in the Renaissance, but not their place in the realm of sport. When Iago's invention produces the old epigrams on women fair and wise, black and witty, fair and fond, foul and foolish, Desdemona says "These are old fond paradoxes to make fools laugh i' the alehouse." Yet she answers each quip, and by a teasing chiding encourages Iago to his most lame and impotent conclusion.[71] Tragic foreshadowing this banter may be, it is nevertheless part of ancient heritage (see **343**). The courtly Desdemona is less exercised about alehouse humor than a pious writer we have already quoted.

[71] *Othello*, II, 1. Compare *Hamlet*, III, 1.

She does not miss the point like our somewhat sober males. Satire on women, often frivolous in the Renaissance, has become today the province of newspaper humor, the detective story, and the comedy of manners, fictional and dramatic. Was jest therefore absent in medieval times?

Indeed Iago's special brand of antithetical humor could not have existed without the Middle Ages. Huizinga has remarked that the line of demarcation between seriousness and pretense was never less clear than in the medieval period,[72] when one's place in the framework and one's orthodoxy on major issues made extraordinary liberties possible on matters which counted less. Since there was no doubting His existence, even the name of God could be used with a flippancy which seems blasphemy to us. Our time is self-conscious about trifles, for an idle remark common in one social group may expel us from another, and when we speak of women we must choose our words with care. By contrast Dame Alisoun could jest with Scripture, Christ at Cana, Solomon's wives, and St. Paul, and yet fear no inquisition:

> Poul dorste nat comanden, atte leeste,
> A thyng of which his maister yaf noon heeste.
> The dart is set up for virginitee:
> Cacche whoso may, who renneth best lat see (III, 73-76).

Satire demands a norm, a vantage point. There is a difference between the Middle Ages, the whole structure of which was normative and anchored, and the eighteenth century, when the norm was something vainly struggled toward. This may account for the disapproval of satire on women in critics such as Gray and Pinkerton and somewhat later, Grosart,[73] and for our own difficulties in evaluating it. What may have bothered some eighteenth century readers was their sense of progress and reform; if they had satirized women with the words of the Middle Ages they would have meant them, and how could society exist if women were abolished? The Middle Ages could never have dreamed of the alternative of Euripides, whose Hippolytus suggests that procreation be accomplished by a miracle of Zeus in an entirely masculine world.[74] When medieval writers satirized physicians, lawyers, tailors, millers, and priests there was no implication that society might live without them, or even that

---

[72] *Waning of the Middle Ages*, p. 217.
[73] See the odd remarks of Grosart quoted by Wright, *Middle-Class Culture*, p. 486.
[74] *Hippolytus*, lines 616–24, tr. Arthur S. Way, *Euripides*, London, 1912, IV, 213.

reform was possible or desirable. How could we live without—
or reform—plumbers and mothers-in-law today? Medieval satire
accepted the thorn in the side and made a jest of it, and the logic
went no farther than the poem itself.

This accounts for the mingled tone of many satires. When
Chaucer makes fun of women or of courtly love he is attempting
neither to abolish a code nor to transform a sex. He is merely
participating in a very courtly game, which fits excellently into
medieval pomp and ceremony, themselves only half-serious.[75] His
trepidation before Alceste, his modest pose that he is only a servant of love's servants (the Pope, in short) and not himself a
lover—these are part of the ritual in that worldly church known
as the Temple of Venus. Satire was an integral part of "the olde
daunce." The opposition was fictional; the pretense that the
eagerly listening women who were a conditioning factor of satire
must be elaborately apologized to or deprived of a view of the
sinning poem was pretense and nothing more. Only a few virulent moralists could have pictured the opposition as more serious;
they no doubt felt the enemy was the Devil himself. But the
simpler fiction was on the whole the more successful. Even in
the fifteenth century, when the frame had hardened into such
brittle rigidity that it was about to crack, we find satire and parody
almost alone among the genres surviving on a level which will
interest untutored modernity.[76] As its presence in anthologies
shows, satire still attracts us. We can turn to it with a mock-
serious purpose, and combat the entrance of the Wife of Bath
into modern politics. Defenses of women interest us less, for we
feel that that point has been made too often. We lack the code
of formal politeness which made the exaggerations of courtly
panegyric themselves a pleasure for noble idle hands and ears.

I have long been anticipating our final factor, courtly love,
lest it now appear too much a paradox to say that this is one of
the most powerful reasons for the flourishing of medieval satire
on women. I do not mean that satire is a bourgeois or "monkish" reaction to courtly love. An individual poem may parody
the system (see, for instance, 226); a didactic treatise may be so
far removed from the world as to turn its face from earthly love
entirely (127). But in its highest form satire is itself as codified

[75] Huizinga, *Waning of the Middle Ages*, pp. 31–35.
[76] Huizinga, *Waning of the Middle Ages*, p. 279; for modifications of his point of
view see Crump and Jacob, *Legacy of the Middle Ages*, p. 156.

as courtly love and merges with it. It is a clear recognition of the torments of the flesh, and must be reckoned with when love is formalized. True Tristan or true Troilus are those rare lovers who sustain the tragic malady; but many an accepted lover writes his renunciation and many a forsaken lover his rebellion. A cleric may escape the torment by seeking another code, but he will feel the burning:

> I ne wot quat is love,
> Ne i ne love ne lovede nouth;
> But wel i wot wo so lovet
> He brennet harde in his youth.
> I ne wot quat is love,
> Ne love me never bond;
> But wel I wot wo so lovet
> Reste havet he non (**103**).

A bourgeois may seek escape through common sense and laughter. But the courtly lover must acknowledge the canker in the Rose.

Scattered and unassimilated satire on women is eternal, but formalized satire is coeval with formalized love, for both seek to put order into the irrational. The causes of the courtly code are deep in politics and society and religion, and we cannot pause to treat them here, or to clarify the subtle distinctions which exist among Chrétien de Troyes, the troubadours, trouvères, and minnesinger, Dante, Andreas, de Lorris, and Chaucer. The reaction between courtly love and satire is mutual and continuing; as in other medieval phenomena like profane and secular verse and music, the cult of chivalry and the cult of the Virgin, the arrow points both ways. *Odi et amo* is older and newer than Catullus. When the Middle Ages formalized love—a necessity, we are told, in times of violent passion,[77]—the ambivalent hate was included in the formula. At the beginning of the fifteenth century the Duke of Burgundy, Jean sans Peur, founded in Paris the "Cour Amoureuse" for the defense of woman's honor, and accepted as members Pierre and Gontier Col and Jean de Montreuil, the exponents of Jean de Meun, as well as their feminine antagonist Christine de Pisan.[78] The charter of the order forbade satires on women at its proceedings,[79] a provision which recognized that Malebouche could not be exiled from the ranks of the defenders.

[77] Huizinga, *Waning of the Middle Ages*, p. 96.
[78] Dow, *Varying Attitude toward Women*, p. 138.
[79] Dow, p. 137.

When Alain Chartier a few years later wrote *La Belle Dame sans Mercy* (**82**) he aroused a storm of protest on the grounds that he was reviling womankind. But though his Merciless Beauty was something of a novelty as a literary phrase,[80] there was nothing new about the concept. If it be argued that Chartier and the "Cour Amoureuse" come at a time of decline, we need only turn to Chrétien, in whose *Lancelot* the courtly paradox is outlined in the boldest terms. After Lancelot has sought Guinevere by humiliating himself so far as to ride in a cart reserved for criminals and by suffering the agony of a journey across the sword-bridge, she rewards him by refusing even a kind word, since he had paused for a moment before entering the cart while Reason debated with Love.[81] Lewis has rightly called this an allegory of love;[82] it is a prototype of Chartier and of the two parts of the *Roman de la Rose*.

In an idle moment we may wonder how the medieval *domina* could stand to have lovers grovel at her feet. However much she may have loved the fiction, the fact goes absolutely contrary to biological and psychological necessity. Pursuit in love which is not met by some form of response defeats its own purpose. If courtly love ever in reality left the realm of sport we must assume that the original fiction was a mere amelioration of the noble and passionate male's real wooing. However courtly love deplored the satirical germ it was forced to contain it; this was the recalcitrant fact which caused the code to take so many forms in different writers. And the more mature the writer the harder it was to suppress the irrepressible. Gawain, the gem of courtesy, does not rebuke the Green Knight when he bursts into an invective which may seem more appropriate to a homily than to a romance:

> Bot hit is no ferly þaʒ a fole madde
> & þurʒ wyles of wymmen be wonen to sorʒe;
> For so watʒ Adam in erde with one begyled,
> & Salomon with fele sere, & Samson eftsoneʒ,
> Dalyda dalt hym hys wyrde, & Dauyth þer-after
> Watʒ blended with Barsabe, þat much bale þoled.
> Now þese were wrathed with her wyles, hit were a wynne huge
> To luf hom wel & leue hem not, a leude þat couþe.[83]

[80] See B. J. Timmer, *English Studies*, XI (1929), 20–22.

[81] See the edition of Wendelin Foerster, Halle, 1899, pp. 140–42, 159–60.

[82] *Allegory of Love*, p. 30. It is difficult to acknowledge my debt to Lewis in this discussion of the final factor. I knew that satire and feminism have never existed apart; but Lewis's analysis has helped immeasurably in clarifying the medieval picture.

[83] *Sir Gawain and the Green Knight*, ed. Sir Israel Gollancz, London (EETS, CCX), 1940, p. 90.

The sentiment does not really differ from that of Chaucer's Goose: "But she wol love hym, lat hym love another!" It is somewhat less courteous than the Goose's heresy, that is all—and this in a courtly romance, hymning the master lover. Of course there is an underlying heresy in the whole poem, when the author praises chastity and rebukes adultery in the figure of Gawain, who trod the sword-bridge between reverence for women and reverence for marriage. But that is the essential point: the courtly ideal, being a civilized code superimposed on another, the moral code of Christianity, involved contradictions which in the more subtle authors could not be ignored. There were none but fictional resolutions for the conflict between the adulterous courtly system and celibacy or chaste marriage, and the setting up of the fiction demanded mention of the conflict. The simultaneous view that women are merciless and full of pity, that they bring a man to honor and bring him to his doom, that they should be reverenced and reviled—these paradoxes are the very essence of the courtly tradition. Codify it men might try, but the war went on within the frame. Otherwise why the interminable debates, the jeu-partis, the palinodes; why the repeated myth of the poet who has sinned against the law of Love—Chaucer in the *Legend,* Gavin Douglas in *The Palice of Honour;* why the continued pop-ularity of both parts of the *Roman de la Rose?* As one thirteenth-century poet says:

> Loue is softt, loue is swete, loue is goed sware.
> Loue is muche tene, loue is muchel kare.
> Loue is blissene mest, loue is bot ȝare.
> Loue is wondred and wo, wiþ for to fare (**171**).

He imprisons the conflict between the walls of antithesis, but his rhetoric accentuates rather than resolves the difficulty.

Chaucer's relationship to the system has been much obscured. Although his Theseus is amused at the two young gamecocks who fight to the death for an Emilye who has bestowed a nod on neither, the great Duke is still willing to admit that he would have done the same when he was young. When one critic opens our eyes to the way in which Chaucer may well have revised his prologue to the *Legend* by inserting a comic complexity of tone into what purports to be a defense of woman and the religion of love,[84] we need not assume that Chaucer's bourgeois blood is

---

[84] Robert M. Estrich, "Chaucer's Maturing Art in the Prologues to the *Legend of Good Women*," *JEGP*, XXXVI (1937), 326–37.

revealing itself in his old age. He is speaking neither from the
alehouse nor from the guildhall, but from the court which had
adopted him. When he gathers wit with age he is simply the
more mature courtier; he plumbs more successfully the depths of
the tradition. He arrives at his own expression of the conflict
between reverence and satire. But he is no stout Cortes; he has
predecessors who each seek resolution—Andreas, Dante, Petrarch,
Jean de Meun. The seeds of controversy are present in *The Parliament of Fowls;* whatever satire the more awkward birds are
led to utter, there is no doubt that the tercelets rule the hierarchy.
The noble birds can exile neither the Ten Commandments nor
vulgar common sense; yet the courtly code retains its ultimate
power however the decision is postponed in the end.

Courtly love is always an escape from these twin heresies,
and more than one courtly lover has suspected at times that reason
was on the other side. The Gawain-poet attempted reconciliation
with chastity and Chaucer's Franklin with marriage; these
attempts merely underline the paradox. "Some politicians hold
that the only way to make a revolutionary safe is to give him a
seat in Parliament. The Duck and Goose have their seats in
Chaucer's *Parlement* for the same reason; and for the same reason
we have satire on women in Andreas, we have the shameless
Vekke in the *Rose,* we have Pandarus in the Book of Troilus,
and Dinadan in Malory, and Godfrey Gobelive in Hawes, and
the Squire of Dames in the *Faerie Queene.*"[85]

Asceticism and courtly love, defense and satire are all alike
present, merging and conflicting, in the climactic Christian centuries. We find the same abyss in the twelfth century as in the
fifteenth; it yawns before us when Aucassin cries:

> In Paradise what have I to do? I care not to enter, but only to have
> Nicolette, my very sweet friend, whom I love so dearly well. For into
> Paradise go none but such people as I will tell you of. There go those
> agèd priests, and those old cripples, and the maimed, who all day long
> and all night cough before the altars, and in the crypts beneath the
> churches. . . . To Hell go the fair clerks and the fair knights who are
> slain in the tourney and the great wars, and the stout archer and the
> loyal man. With them will I go. And there go the fair and courteous
> ladies, who have friends, two or three, together with their wedded
> lords.[86]

[85] Lewis, *Allegory of Love,* pp. 172–73.
[86] *Aucassin and Nicolette,* tr. Eugene Mason, London, 1910, p. 6.

Nor is the defiance confined to youth alone; it bursts from the lips of the Wife of Bath:

> Allas! allas! that evere love was synne!

When Chaucer ends the tragic mockery of Troilus with a moral counsel to lovers the paradox vibrates through his lines:

> *O yonge, fresshe folkes, he or she,*
> In which that love up groweth with youre age,
> Repeyreth hom fro worldly vanyte,
> And of youre herte up casteth the visage
> To thilke God that after his ymage
> Yow made, and thynketh *al nys but a faire*
> *This world, that passeth soone as floures faire.*

There is a complexity of purpose here that would make Donne call the "naive" Chaucer brother. It was St. Paul himself who set down the irreconcilable conflict that blends in satire and in defense, in courtly love and rebellion within the frame: "For I delight in the law of God after the inward man: But I see another law in my members, warring against the law of my mind, and bringing me into captivity to the law of sin which is in my members" (Rom. 7:22-23). Courtly love, which strives to erect one law into a code half jesting and half serious, cannot write it down without absorbing the law which wars on it.

The quarrel about women was endless because its arguments, example and *ad hominem,* could be turned either way. If the satirists urged that man alone was created from earth in God's image, the defenders asserted that woman, being made of man, was of finer stuff than earth.[87] Debate and palinode demanded a suspension of disbelief, easier to attain in an age when there was nothing shameful about belief. The very Provençals who invented courtly love had satirists among them.[88] Andreas Capellanus, who codified their teachings, wrote a final book rejecting love; his eye was on Ovid's *Ars Amatoria* and its *Remedia Amoris.* Chrétien's *Lancelot* had its *Erec and Enid.* One critic believes that Guillaume de Lorris might well have written a palinode if he had lived to finish his poem.[89] Whatever the truth of this somewhat startling statement, the palinode was not long awaited, for Jean de Meun soon wrote a conclusion for the great vernacular *Art of Love.* In the thirteenth century Matheolus wrote his vicious

[87] Chotzen, *Revue Celtique,* XLVIII (1931), 66.
[88] Wulff, *Die Frauenfeindlichen Dichtungen,* pp. 166–76.
[89] Lewis, *Allegory of Love,* pp. 122, 136.

Lamentations, the most comprehensive satire produced by the Middle Ages; a century later Jehan Lefevre translated him and then apologized with *Le Livre de Leesce.* Dante diverged from the main stream with an amazing resolution of heavenly and earthly love, but high as his concept of the force which moves the sun and other stars might be, he still gave sinning lovers the easiest place in Hell. Petrarch wrote courtly poetry which began a fashion it took some centuries to end, and he wrote also the tale of Griselda. Boccaccio and Chaucer piled satire and defense on one another in inextricable confusion; the contrasts among *L'Amorosa Fiammetta, Il Corbaccio,* and *De Claris Mulieribus* are matched by those in *Troilus,* the *Merchant's Tale,* and the *Legend.* Even the author of the ironic *Quinze Joyes de Mariage* promised a palinode, which he probably never lived to write.[90] The mingling of praise and blame went on—in Alain Chartier, Hoccleve, Lydgate, Dunbar, Hawes, Nevizanni, Rabelais, Erasmus, and in a host of minor English writers. Nor was the blend confined to France, Italy, and England; it appeared in a Catalan Pere Toroella, in a Dutchman Dirk Potter van der Loe, and in a Welshman William Kynwal.[91]

The view which resolves opposites in this way is the *Sic et Non* of the woman question. Whatever the difference in the canons of poetry and philosophy, there is a parallel with Abelard and Aquinas and Bernard. In symbolism the Middle Ages had its method of reconciling the ideal world and the real world, death in life and life in death, heaven and earth. "The world, objectionable in itself, became acceptable by its symbolic purport."[92] Eve with all her vices became the prototype of Mary, with all her perfection of beauty, intelligence, and virtue—better than all earthly women and men too:

> þu ert briht & blisful ouer all wummen,
> and god ðu ert & gode leof ouer all wepmen.[93]

We are so far from this kind of thinking that we can scarcely comprehend its usefulness in the medieval synthesis. Puritanism has separated heaven and earth to the detriment of both. "For oh, the hobby-horse is forgot!" Perhaps this is why we are so embarrassed by the carnival spirit of Dunbar's ribald Shrove

[90] Huizinga, *Waning of the Middle Ages,* p. 114.
[91] Chotzen, *Revue Celtique,* XLVIII (1931), 67–71.
[92] Huizinga, *Waning of the Middle Ages,* p. 187.
[93] Carleton Brown, *English Lyrics of the XIIIth Century,* Oxford, 1932, p. 3.

Tuesday poem, presented to the Queen (**177**). No doubt it also helps explain why Pinkerton remarked with such acrimony of Dunbar's *Now of wemen this I say for me* (**219**): "A paltry piece in praise of women. *Non defensoribus istis* . . . The point of it is that Christ had a woman for mother, but no man for father." Yet symbolist thought, which "permits of an infinity of relations between things,"[94] was seeking an answer to the same questions as the Deism of Pinkerton's own century, with its Argument by Design.[95] Today, no doubt, we have rightfully renounced symbolism as a primary intellectual tool. But science will permit us the consolations of poetry, and perhaps *Der Zauberberg* and *The Waste Land* may help us in some measure to overcome the barriers to an understanding of the Middle Ages. Even scientists will recognize the value of symbolic myths, like Galileo's cannon ball, Archimedes' bath, or Newton's apple. There is more than one field of knowledge where we can within limits benefit emotionally and intellectually by *Credo, ut intelligam.*

A failure to take into account the symbolic approach to life and the universe will cause us unduly to exaggerate the gap between satire and defense, and to be disturbed when the same person tries his hand at both. The harm has not been confined to the medieval period. Exuberant over feministic progress, some have called Euripides and Milton, those keen-eyed students of women, misogynists.[96] This is the result of assuming that if an author presents evidence on both sides of the question he is of necessity honest or "sincere" about one side only. Even enthusiastic defenses have been twisted into irony, because they were written too long before Christine de Pisan (see **42, 340**). Yet, if defense was rare or non-existent in the thirteenth century, Jean de Meun need never have bothered to apologize to his feminine listeners. Writer and epoch alike reveal the impossibility of asserting one side of the controversy without taking account of the other. In some measure Milton and Euripides represent the "realistic" approach to women favored by modernity, and they may therefore be contrasted to the medieval symbolists who dealt

[94] Huizinga, *Waning of the Middle Ages,* p. 187.

[95] A closer and more modern parallel to symbolism, so useful in resolving the paradox of courtly love and satire, might be Whitehead's "patterned intensity of feeling arising from adjusted contrasts." See Stephen Lee Ely, *The Religious Availability of Whitehead's God,* University of Wisconsin Press, 1942, p. 25.

[96] William R. Parker, "A Word on 'Misogyny,'" *Milton's Debt to Greek Tragedy in Samson Agonistes,* Baltimore, 1937, pp. 129–35, analyzes this misconception.

with the problem in another fashion. But both Middle Ages and
modernity recognize that truth involves some statement of the
ambivalence unavoidable in a world which has two sexes in it.
The symbolism of Eve and Mary is the medieval solution.

The greatest satirists therefore knew that they were in the
midst of a controversy which had untold implications for morality
and pleasure. Jerome answered Jovinian, Meun Lorris, and Andreas, Chaucer, and Rabelais themselves. When, as in a satire
like *The Epistle of Valerius to Rufinus,* or a panegyric like "Bot
fals men make her fingres feld" (42), there was no undertone
of controversy, the result was flatness beyond compare. A bitter
poem once ascribed to Dunbar, "The beistlie lust, the furious
appatite" (282), is no exception; its undertone and its excellence
lie in the very sharpness of its one-sided and passionate rhetoric.
Our unsatisfactory experience with many a lesser satire or defense
has often led us to overlook the inseparable nature of courtly love
and mockery, of earnest morality and irrepressible mirth, and to
characterize a whole epoch as unfriendly toward one-half of
creation. The courtly code reconciles itself to hard fact and to
Christian ethics by incorporating them, and thus nourishes, re-
vives, and in combination with other forces gives depth and
meaning to satire on women.

When the accident is stripped away we see that satire and
defense are, in substance, both eternal and in a state of perpetual
flux. Each age puts its mark on the controversy: Juvenal colors
it with ancient piety, Jerome with ascetic fervor, Chrétien with
aristocratic paradox, Chaucer with worldly amusement, and Rabelais with fleshly gusto. The argument receives genetic impulses
from the monk, the preacher, the bourgeois, the Arab and Jew,
the individual poet, the male and female, the jester, and the
courtly lover; but none of them is alone responsible for the formal
praise or blame of women. If any of these elements had been
absent, the quarrel about woman's worth would not be the complex and fascinating subject which it was and is today.

II. THE GENRES OF SATIRE AND DEFENSE

Often called an era of formlessness in art and letters, the Middle Ages merits the charge in so far as it lacks certain of the subtleties and triumphs of classical symmetry. Yet, in spite of the diffuseness of medieval romance and didactic poetry, many of the forms we know and praise have their origin in this period: moral and domestic drama, allegory, romance, and exhortation; sonnet, roundel, and carol; ballad and debate; and in some measure even epic, pastoral, comedy, and tragedy. Much of this is formalism rather than form, but we need not always judge these medieval genres by their worst exemplars. Romance can be *Aucassin* and *Sir Gawain* as well as *Guy of Warwick;* satire on women the *Wife's Prologue* as well as Hoccleve's rambling *Dialogue* (28); defense *The Nut-Brown Maid* as well as the diffuse and mechanical *ABC* (42). The medieval poet's work is particularly susceptible to classification, for he was no more ashamed to borrow a conventional structure than a well-known tale. Chaucer, Boccaccio, and Petrarch all used the Tale of Griselda with independent success; and all three likewise gave their individual stamp to satire or allegory.

Defense and satire often possess technical settings which are not organic. They may be superficially dramatic, narrative, or lyric;[1] they may employ stanzaic patterns like rime royal, octave, or quatrain; they may adorn the expression with rhetorical alliteration or the ABC frame; or they may be accidentally carols, ballades, sonnets, or that too-inclusive type called ballad. Such variety tells us nothing about the art of satire or defense; it merely illustrates the perennial need for tricking out shopworn themes with poetic ingenuity. But there are several categories which are organically hospitable to our controversy: the *chanson d'aventure,* the confession, the debate, the catalogue, the proverb and epigram, the parody, the lying-song, and the fortune-game.

One of the most successful forms into which satire was cast was the *chanson d'aventure,*[2] which, if theories of origin are cor-

---

[1] I have usually suppressed narrative and drama from the Index, since these forms are usually complex in purpose. The inclusion of separate *exempla* would be burdensome. Although *The Seven Sages* (ed. Killis Campbell, Boston, 1907) has been excluded because at least half its stories are not about women, it should not be forgotten here. Shrew plays like *Tom Tyler* and some of the *Canterbury Tales* could not of course be ignored.

[2] See W. Powell Jones, *The Pastourelle,* Cambridge, Mass., 1931; Helen E. Sandison, *The "Chanson d'Aventure" in Middle English,* Bryn Mawr, Pa., 1913; Alfred Jeanroy, *Les Origines de la Poésie Lyrique en France au Moyen Age,* 3rd ed., Paris, 1925, pp. 84–101.

rect, comes rightfully by its interest in women, whose spinning wheels played some part perhaps in its rhythm, subject, and refrain. Popular as its beginnings might be, it has left its traces on the sophisticated love-vision, and hence on *The Book of the Duchess, Le Roman de la Rose,* and Spenser's *Prothalamion.* In essence it is a dramatic lyric, in which the pensive poet goes out for fresh air and overhears a confession or a dialogue. He may remain a mere auditor or, at times, as in the *pastourelle* (often considered a separate form), he may become a participant. The *chanson d'aventure* or *chanson dramatique* has several well-defined subdivisions; of special interest to us are the *pastourelle,* the forsaken maid's lament (*chanson de jeune fille*), the nun's complaint (*chanson de nonne*), the wife's lament (*chanson de mal mariée*), and the husband's lament (*chanson de mal marié*). The *pastourelle,* with its seducing courtier and clever-witted shepherd lass, offers no English specimens which participate in the quarrel, although we recall Henryson's *Robene and Makyne,* in which a maid pays off Robin's earlier indifference in the same coin. French *pastourelles* often stress a woman's inability to say no to a seducer, but in England there are few examples of such a denouement, and we may perhaps conclude with Miss Sandison that prudery prevented the wholesale borrowing of less delicate poems composed in France.[3] Although it differs in origin and form from Ovid's sophisticated *Heroides* (**280**), the forsaken maid's lament is similar in intention. Not all of these lovelorn ladies can be said to defend their sex by word or by example, and all are too sympathetic for satire, but a few draw an abstract moral of the wickedness of men which brings them within our range of vision (**43, 316, 319**). The *chanson de nonne* is rare in England, a sure sign that this kind of lyric, in which a nun in springtime bewails the cloister which has deprived her of love, owes nothing to the Protestant spirit. We can point to only one example, which is allegorized and ambiguous in message— the fifteenth century *Why I Can't Be a Nun* (**30**). But when we turn to the *chanson de mal mariée* and its masculine counterpart we find copious material which is both English and controversial. Of the wife's laments in our index only one is a true defense (**18**); the rest are ribald satires in which women discuss the failings of their husbands with all the ardor of the Wife of Bath

[3] Sandison, pp. 66–67.

herself (78, 135, 172, 251, 256). Occasionally the dialogists are a wife and husband (141), but usually, as in the classic *Tua Mariit Wemen and the Wedo* (336), the speakers are a pair or more of wanton gossips who wash down their complaints with a sufficiency of ale or wine. The *mal marié*, on the other hand, can spare neither time nor money for conviviality, for his shrewish wife will not permit him. His complaint is usually a monologue (20, 32, 45, 91, 245, 305, 333, 400, 401), but on one occasion he tells his sorrows to his sympathetic mother (200), and on another to a friend (327).

So closely related to the *chanson de mal mariée* that at times the two cannot be distinguished is the confession, the medieval origin of which is obvious enough. *The Wife of Bath's Prologue* and its prototype, the revelations of La Vieille in the *Roman de la Rose,* are true confessions—ironic exposures of vice even as the speaker attempts to defend herself. Since Chaucer through the framework of the *Tales* overhears the Wife's long harangue, the effect is similar to that of the dramatic *chanson,* and we may well ask how much of his lively wit was owing to the more popular form. Perhaps Chaucer used the confession even more successfully when he had his Pardoner give away his professional secrets; and his two essays in the genre are worthy ancestors to the later flowering of the type in the France of Rousseau and the Germany of Goethe and Thomas Mann. The most elaborate development known to English readers is Gower's *Confessio Amantis,* in which an aged but kindly lover presents the courtly code and his own renunciation of it. Many of the masculine renunciations of love, such as Kennedy's *Against Mouth-Thankless* (26) and Copland's *Complaynte of them that ben to late maryed* (17), involve something of a confession of past follies, but for our purposes the outstanding use of this kind of revelation is in the *chansons de mal mariée* and the gossip's songs (33, 107, 328; see also 206, 277).

The dramatic setting of the *chanson d'aventure* is also present in one of the most charming semi-lyric traditions with which we have to deal, the bird-debate. This is a special development of the Old French *débat* in which the dialogue is conducted by two birds, and which always posits as its subject the question of woman's worth. The exact relationship of our English examples to the Continent is difficult to discover in the present state of our knowledge; for although the earlier debates of this type usually possess a Latin or French title, no exact equation with these languages has ever been worked out. Parliaments of birds were frequent enough in French during the thirteenth and early fourteenth centuries; we may cite *Florance et Blancheflor (Le Jugement d'Amour)*, the *Geste de Blancheflour et Florence, Melior et Idoine, Li Fablel dou Dieu d'Amours, De Venus la Deesse d'Amor,* and Jean de Condé's *La Messe des Oisiaus.*[4] In a larger sense these contributed to the formation of the bird-debate, since both invoke the conventional associations of spring, birds, and love-divinities. But the confining of the debate to two specific birds is, so far as I know, peculiar to the English; and the French parliaments are usually occupied with a very different problem, the relative merits of knight and clerk as lover (see **167**). In the absence, therefore, of clear parallels or certain sources, one wonders whether the manuscript titles *Altercacio Inter Filomenam et Bubonem* and *Le Cuntent Parentre le Mauuis & la Russinole* (**112, 273**) really reflect foreign sources or consist of a mere appeal to authority similar to that of Chaucer's Lollius.[5]

The first bird-debate, *The Owl and the Nightingale* (1189?–1217?), is also the earliest piece in our index. Women are defended by the courtly Nightingale and opposed by the jangling Owl. This is not the sole theme of the poem; no agreement exists, in fact, as to the poem's exact theme or whether it has one. But it merits a place among our satires and defenses because of the impetus it gives both controversy and bird-debate genre. There is no question as to the meaning of *The Thrush and the Nightingale (ca.* 1275); it sets clearly the opposition between the Thrush with his examples of evil women and the Nightingale, who routs him with a stirring appeal to woman's perfection as manifest in the Virgin Mary. Both of these early poems have a juristic or legal quality, which suggests an attribution to the one literate non-clerical class, the lawyers. We must wait another century (1309?–1410?) for our third exemplar, Clanvowe's

[4] See Ernest Langlois, *Origines et Sources du Roman de la Rose,* 1891, pp. 19–20: W. A. Neilson, *The Origins and Sources of The Court of Love,* Boston ([Harvard] Studies and Notes, VI), 1899, pp. 36–38, 41–42, 67; W. E. Farnham, "The Fowls in Chaucer's Parlement," *University of Wisconsin Studies in Language and Literature,* No. 2, Madison, 1918, pp. 362–64.

[5] Th. M. Chotzen, *Revue Celtique,* XLVIII (1931), 79, names a few French debates concerning women (none of them involving birds as well). His suggestion that the Welsh bardic dispute may have had something to do with the tradition deserves study.

Cuckoo and the Nightingale (286), which among other things discusses at length the problem of faith in love. The Chaucerian echoes in this poem remind us that the master himself had written *The Parliament of Fowls,* a related poem which makes some remarks about the courtly code, but which is too much concerned with other matters and too divergent in form to fit our scheme. In the second half of the fifteenth century the tradition appears to be breaking down; in one interesting poem the feministically inclined Nightingale becomes a misogynist, and his old position is taken by a lovelorn Clerk (129). The same displacement is evident in a much finer poem written shortly after, Dunbar's *The Merle and the Nychtingaill* (139), where the Nightingale's exalted refrain, "All luve is lost bot vpone God allone," is victorious over the Merle's "A lusty lyfe in luves scheruice bene." Thomas Feylde's *Contrauersye bytwene a Louer and a Jaye* (313— 1509?–1535?) once more presents a courtly human speaker and a misogynistic bird, who is triumphant. Although its two contenders are both human, the spirit behind *The Dialogue between a Clerk and a Husbandman* (31—late fifteenth century) is essentially that of the bird-debates, and its alternating refrains "Quia amore langueo" and "Turn up hyr haltur and let hyr goe" remind us of Dunbar.

The *débat* and its congeners, dialogue, *jeu parti, tenson, conflictus,* and colloquy, had many variations in England in which birds were not the actors. Of those in which women win the victory we may mention *The Nut-Brown Maid* (36), Guillaume Alexis' *Le Debat de l'Omme et de la Femme* (355), Sir Thomas Elyot's *Defence of Good Women* (53), and Edmund Tilney's *Flower of Friendshippe* (40). Misogyny, heavenly love, or uncourtly rebellion carry off the honors in Lydgate's *Mumming at Hertford,* where wives and husbands submit their plea to the King (190); in William Walter's *Spectacle of Louers* (66); in the carol *In Villa* (180); in the *Dialogue bytwene the Commune Secretary and Jalowsye* (342); and in Wyatt's "A Robyn Joly Robyn" (202, see also 191), which with its legalistic and Gallic touches reminds us of the original bird-debates. The argument reaches a stalemate in the Holly and Ivy poems (86), Erasmus' *Coniugium* (184), and the dialogues of Pyrrye and Tusser (113, 70).

We may pass more briefly over the remaining forms. There

is the catalogue, or compilation of examples, which makes its
appeal not to logic but to symbolism. It may apply equally to
evil women and masculine martyrs (**205, 317, 350**; see also the
exemplum collections **52, 271a**), or to noble women whether
amazonic, chaste, or the martyrs of man's lust. The second group
is ultimately derived from Ovid's *Heroides* (**280**); it was extensively cultivated by distinguished authors like Boccaccio (**236**),
Chaucer (**12**), Christine de Pisan (**46**), Cornelius Agrippa (**214,
237**), and Bishop John Aylmer (**84**), as well as by minor poets
(**247, 367**). Such argument by example appears in many poems,
such as *The Thrush and the Nightingale,* where it is not the
primary formal element. *The Thrush* is a brilliant display of the
symbolic nature of the argument, not too well apprehended in
modern times; here feminism triumphs over misogyny's many
examples with true economy, for it only takes the precedent of
God's Mother to dismiss the case for the prosecution. Closely
allied to the catalogue are the tapestry-poem and the pageant-
poem, both of which testify to the marriage between art and literature in the later Middle Ages. Lydgate's *Bicorne and Chichevache* (**227**) is an example of the first; the pseudo-Chaucerian
Nine Ladies Worthy (**247**) perhaps of the second.

The medieval "proverb," a practical clothing of abstract morality, is, as Huizinga has shown,[6] related to the argument by example. The proverb (**275, 287, 293, 332, 348**; see also the collections **14, 25, 292, 213**) reveals that the Elizabethan epigram
had a native ancestor as well as a classical one (**10, 11, 27, 48,
56, 74, 122, 149, 155, 295**); the essence of both is brevity and
wit, useful and too seldom employed adornments to the controversy. Proverbial lore or sententious remark may easily be the
starting point for other satires, especially when they can be made
to fit a carol burden, such as

> Man, bewar of thin wowyng,
> For weddyng is the longe wo (**165**).

This and the Lydgatian *Warning to Beware* (**166**) are veritable
proverbial centos. The temptation to fall back upon traditional
wit explains why so much fifteenth-century poetry opens with a
good line and exhausts itself in catalogue and rhetoric of the
worst type:[7] the poet begins with lively but borrowed wisdom

[6] *Waning of the Middle Ages,* pp. 208–211.
[7] Huizinga, p. 276.

and through lack of dramatic sense or saving irony has really nothing more to say after he has begun. He did not always dwindle out, however, as *Merciles Beaute,* attributed to Chaucer, will demonstrate (**403**). The proverbial structure of many of our satires is strikingly shown by a late thirteenth-century poem in MS. Harley 2253, which contains among its lines the germ of three of our pieces: "wilde ase þe ro" (see **322**); "lord, þat hast me lyf to lene" (see **169**); and "vnwunne haueþ myn wonges wet" (see **340**).[8]

Another sub-genre is the parody of the courtly love poem (**93, 106, 168, 176, 192, 204, 341, 383, 403**), in which the disconsolate lover's malady heretically allows him to sleep and grow fat. Closely related are the parody defense (**192**) and the satirical panegyric of one's lady (**95, 161, 194, 195, 221, 226, 277, 294, 321, 325, 335**; see also **149, 155**). The last type, which ridicules the ever-present catalogue of charms, is assured its place in literature not only by the boisterous roguery of its conception, but by its culmination in Shakespeare's "My mistress' eyes are nothing like the sun." Perhaps none of our genres has been more displeasing to modern eyes than these attacks on ugly wenches (often the product of sour grapes) and of aged women who remain coquettish. One editor, too much the heir of romantic humanitarianism, was even unwilling to assign a poem to Lydgate because he disliked the type—even though manuscript tradition and other tests favored the ascription (**194**). Yet there are prototypes in Horace, in Martial, and in the Greek Anthology; and in spite of its often cruel and obscene results the idea has a philosophical basis of some distinction, the physiognomical doctrine that beauty of countenance mirrors that of the soul within (and vice versa). The very same argument was employed by defenders of women on the grounds of their beauty. In addition to these three varieties of irreverent parody, there are countless ironic defenses or ironic exhortations to women to fortify themselves in their power over men, the most famous of which is the Clerk's *Envoy* (**81**; see also **22, 79, 121, 136, 143, 220, 230, 261, 264, 265, 272, 274, 275, 304, 307, 322, 326, 334, 358, 359, 360, 386**). And there is a parodic or ironic element in the "lying-song," which often begins as a *chanson d'aven-*

---

[8] *An Old Man's Prayer,* in Carleton Brown, ed., *Religious Lyrics of the XIVth Century,* Oxford, 1924, pp. 3–7.

ture, and mushrooms into a fantastic collection of impossibilities which are the conditions of one's trust in womankind (4, 15, 16, 69, 116, 203, 351, 353, 354, 357, 360, 361). This kind of poem would have its singular charm even if it had not been the source of one of England's finest lyrics, Donne's "Go and catch a falling star," and had not survived in American tradition as "The barefoot boy with shoes on" of our childhood.

Such, then, are the major formal settings which medieval satirists and defenders, not infrequently with true artistic integrity and skill, used to vary and to give rhetorical form to their somewhat hackneyed jests and arguments. But there are many other sub-genres based on content rather than form: on satirical intent alone, on feministic intent alone, or on the desire to mingle praise and dispraise.

Of the satirical class by far the most common is a type of poem essentially formless except for its unity of content, though when it extends to encyclopedic length it may be graced with the title treatise or essay. Over fifty of the kind could be enumerated, among them Chaucer's *Merchant's Prologue and Tale* (339), the *Romaunt of the Rose* (181), and the *Scholehouse of Women* (292).

Another genre based on content is the Rebellious Lover poem, wherein a poet with greater or less seriousness describes the torments he has suffered and announces his determination to abandon his cruel fair.[9] Such apostasies from Love's service are conventional enough developments of the courtly code in spite of the pretense that they are not, and many of them can by no stretch of the imagination be called satirical. Of over sixty poems of the type which I have listed, many are somewhat doubtful entries. My criterion, necessarily subjective, has been to include them when there is no serious residue of expressed or implied worship for one's lady (when they are not what Salomon calls "pseudo-revolts"), and when there is enough universal sentiment to justify the inference that the poet considers his merciless or unfaithful lady symbolic of women in general. A good example of a marginal poem which I have not included is the thirteenth-century lyric which begins with passionate and all-inclusive melancholy

[9] The type has been excellently studied by Louis B. Salomon, *The Devil Take Her,* Philadelphia, Pa., 1931.

> Lutel wot hit anymon
> Hou derne loue may stonde,
> bote hit were a fre wymmon
> þat muche of loue had fonde.
> þe loue of hire ne lesteþ no wyht longe,
> Heo haueþ me plyht & wyteþ me wyþ wronge.
> Ever & oo, for my leof icham in grete þohte,
> y þenche on hire þat y ne seo nout ofte.

Since the opening is a perfect blend of individual and universal sentiment, we seem to be entering upon a satirical attack on woman's inconstancy. But instead of ending with revolt the poet comes back into the fold:

> ffayrest fode vpo loft,
> my gode luef, y þe greete.
> ase fele syþe & oft
> as dewes dropes beþ weete,
> ase sterres beþ in welkne, ant grases sour ant suete.
> whose loueþ vntrewe, his herte is selde seete.[10]

Such an orthodox rebellion is the very reverse of satire, for it implies that one must worship one's lady no matter how tyrannous she may be. Alain Chartier was soundly berated by his contemporaries for making his *belle dame sans merci* speak a bit too tartly to please the servants of Venus, and for universalizing the situation too successfully (82). But if true heresy is not one of the elements in the courtly code at the very beginning, as in Chrétien or Andreas, it was well developed by the end of the fourteenth century, when Chaucer or another wrote *Merciles Beaute* (403). And by the sixteenth century the rebellion is an almost too common form, much loved by Wyatt, Turbervile, and Alexander Scott, and by the anonymities which cluster in the anthologies of Tottel and Bannatyne. When, in other words, the courtly code has become nothing but a polite veneer, we may almost hazard a conjecture that the latter-day cavalier is expected by his lady to show some resentment over his mistreatment, and that rebellion is in effect one of the accepted methods of wooing. The form as a whole is strangely on the verge of satire and never quite there; but a disgruntled lover, whatever his motives, can speak as harshly as the fabled monk in a cloister. Perhaps the most amusing branch of this genre is that which urges the casting off of love in terms of hunting and hawking: "Then plukkyd y

[10] Carleton Brown, ed., *English Lyrics of the XIIIth Century*, Oxford, 1932, pp. 162–63 (from MS. Harley 2253).

of here bellys and let her fly." This well-cultivated theme (**7**, **31**,
62, **104**, **108**, **222**, **225**, **271**, **344**, **365**) is the true ancestor of
the "hunting-shooting-fishing Englishman" of the nineteenth
century, the country lumpkin who cannot love.

A closely related type is that of Renunciation: Farewell to
Earthly Love. So frequently do we encounter the pattern of
Worship—Rebellion—Renunciation that we must doubt the efficacy of attempts to reconstruct a poet's biography on the basis
of such a sequence. It is so normal for youth to love, for the
prime age to grow rebellious, and for old age to renounce that
we may assume that any poet who wished could hurry the process
for effect. In short, the Wife of Bath's words are not gospel:

> The clerk, when he is oold, and may noght do
> Of Venus werkes worth his olde sho,
> Thanne sit he doun, and writ in his dotage
> That wommen kan nat kepe hir mariage!

We cannot argue, for instance, that Dunbar's courtly lyrics were
all written when he was young, his rebellions when he reached
middle age, and his renunciations when he was old. For if the
extremes of passion could mellow with age, so could the sharpness of uncompromising asceticism. Dunbar and Rabelais appear
to have renounced not love, but their cloth; and of Luther what
are we to say? When they were older Chaucer and Jehan Lefevre wrote defending palinodes to atone for earlier satire; and
Gower wrote his courtliest poem, the *Confessio Amantis,* after
Vox Clamantis and the *Miroir de l'Omme* were behind him. The
sympathetic old lover or servant of Love's servants was a favorite
pose of Gower, of Chaucer, and of their predecessor Machaut in
Le Livre du Voir-Dit.[11] Our some forty renunciations are not
necessarily the product of impotent age, but of all stages of ma-
turity and all ranks of society.

Whatever its origin, the renunciation of love is essentially a
didactic branch of satire on women, and it is closely related to
the warning to beware in the choice of mistress or wife. This
type includes some of the husband's complaints already discussed,
as well as a form more entertaining than didactic, the bachelor's
rejoicing (**83**, **97**, **130**, **278**, **281**, **364**).[12] The usual form, however, is that of a general admonition against marriage (**65**, **124**,

[11] See Huizinga, *Waning of the Middle Ages,* p. 109.
[12] This class is allied to the wanton picaresque carol: see R. L. Greene, *The Early English Carols,* Oxford, 1935, nos. 415–18.

158, 165, 190, 218, 227, 274, 378, 400) or love (**166, 222, 289, 381**). Here also may be classed the influential *De Coniuge Non Ducenda* (**75**), Chaucer's *Bukton* (**208**), a poem which emphasizes the conversion of virtuous maidens to wicked wives (**54**), and three sets of paradoxes against marriage and life in general with their answers (**163, 162; 259, 260; 343**).

But certain late Puritanical poems agree with St. Paul that it is better to marry than to burn (**342, 363, 255**; compare **306**). From the very beginning St. Jerome had counseled that prospective husbands choose their wives with the care of a horse-trader, and Deschamps and Chaucer echoed his words. As the Wife of Bath says to one of her old husbands:

> Thow seyst we wyves wol oure vices hide
> Til we be fast, and thanne we wol hem shewe,—
> Wel may that be a proverbe of a shrewe!
> Thou seist that oxen, asses, hors, and houndes,
> They been assayed at diverse stoundes;
> Bacyns, lavours, er that men hem bye,
> Spoones and stooles, and al swich housbondrye,
> And so been pottes, clothes, and array;
> But folk of wyves maken noon assay,
> Til they be wedded; olde dotard shrewe!
> And thanne, seistow, we wol oure vices shewe.[13]

In order to help out the process there were instructions enough and to spare which discussed the perils of disparity in rank, virtue, wisdom, and the like (**25, 113, 122, 159, 123a, 151, 179, 271a, 285, 375, 393**), but above all the evil results when old January married May (**9, 17, 24, 27, 183, 224, 256, 266, 401**), a theme elaborated in both the *Wife of Bath's Prologue* (**58**) and the *Merchant's Tale* (**339**). Such counsels were not exclusively the product of satire; they were also a fundamental bulwark of the sober marriage treatise. But satirists played havoc when they took on the role of sober teachers.

Other satires were built around specific charges against women: pride and obstinacy and desire for the mastery, lasciviousness, jealousy, garrulity, vanity, greed and extravagance, caprice, infidelity, physical inferiority, and the manifold dangers which threaten men who trifle with them. Pride and obstinacy form the nucleus of the shrew literature, especially of that riotous

[13] III, 282–92. On the history of the convention see F. L. Utley, *MLN*. LIII (1938), 359-62.

form (set often in the *chanson d'aventure* frame) known as the fight for the breeches, a prototype of *The Taming of the Shrew* (5, 32, 45, 76, 157, 177, 190, 193, 305). Woman's lust is treated in the wanton song (172) and in many a Rebellious Lover poem, as well as in one of the most amusing pieces in our collection, a burlesque recipe for the reconstruction of chastity (117). Woman's garrulity is the basis of the confession and the gossips' song; vanity of the satire on fashion (39, 65, 169, 182, 211, 232, 233, 240, 262, 296, 309, 369); gluttony of the alewife and drinking poem (33, 107, 172, 195, 249, 251, 277, 336, 368, and many of the *chansons de mal mariée*);[14] infidelity and caprice of the rebellious lover poem; and the threat to man's domestic peace, life, and salvation, of most renunciations of carnal love and the antithetical poems on love's sweet peril (170, 171; see 3, 160).

Of the 403 pieces in our list, about 85 favor the other side of the argument and merit the name defense, a much larger proportion than we might expect. That satire still bulks larger in quantity is not entirely the fault of the times, but in part a tribute to its taste. For, honorable as they may be, defenses are on the whole more long-winded, less unified, and less witty and amusing; they represent sobriety which protests when it is being teased. The best defenders, like Chaucer in the *Legend,* are not above a bit of mockery themselves, but in the main defense demands more extraneous rhetorical aids and provides less real humor or point than satire does. The friends of women were forced to call on courtly allegory or the bird-debate, on the ABC form usually devoted to the Virgin Mary (42), on alliteration (115), or on the aureate diction common to fifteenth and sixteenth centuries (247, 313). Erasmus was one of the very few to succeed in putting wit into defense (189), and even his tone is mixed.

What it comes down to is that the defenders have little to say beyond stating sober truth. The exaggerated position of satire has the whole Seven Deadly Sins to draw upon; only when the satirist is serious does he fail miserably, and for the same reason as the defender, because woman is really neither good nor bad.

[14] Here, as in the closely related *fabliau,* the convivial author's sympathy is often mixed. On *The Twelve mery gestys of one called Edyth* (1525), a jestbook of picaresque intent which is too interested in its heroine (a real person) to be called a satire, see *CHEL.,* III, 553.

She is chaste and she is beautiful, what then? No doubt this accounts for the lists of Amazons (247, for instance), common in an age which was shocked to its marrow by the real Joan of Arc; feminists seem to have wished to bestow upon women some of the traits to which the more active sex is natural heir. Imaginative defense on a high level is in part outside the bounds of our index, since it appears in the realms of courtly love, where a number of impossibilities are established as first principles, and controversialists agree to disagree. Consequently Christine and other late defenders cling tenaciously to the courtly jargon even when the heart is going out of it, and the Virgin Mother, symbol of perfection, is interminably (and sometimes beautifully) called upon as a staple of medieval defense. "Womanhede" is played upon as an emotional term and rarely subjected to the light of day (142).[15] Defenders, forced to the wall by outrageous jest, take over the methods of satirists and, rather than contravert their lack of logic, use the empty arguments by example, by beauty, and *ad hominem* until they reach surfeit.

No argument is more popular than the last mentioned, which attributes satires to the sensuality and frustration of wicked men (see especially 379). Outside of Christine's attack on Jean de Meun, perhaps the best expression of this theme is in Gower's *Confessio Amantis,* where Misogyny, one of the worst sins against Love, is classified as a type of pride or surquidry and exemplified by Narcissus.[16] The usual practice is to compose a warning to women against false and vicious men who lie in wait to steal their honor (19, 49, 110, 115, 140, 142, 144, 147, 152, 160, 178, 288, 307, 316, 379, 397), a genre best represented by Hoccleve's translation of Christine's *L'Epistre au Dieu d'Amours* (49), which was known in the sixteenth century as *Le Contre Romant de la Rose.*[17] Most of these poems argue didactically that woman has only one real virtue, that of chastity.[18] Closely associated with this doctrine, and only occasionally suggesting a wider scope for woman's moral development, are the descriptions of a virtuous woman (38, 98, 126, 150, 234, 283, 337, 388, 389), a genre of which the tale of Griselda (261)

---

[15] Chaucer especially was given to a connotative expansion of this word (for some fifteen examples see J. S. P. Tatlock and A. G. Kennedy, *A Concordance to the Complete Works of Geoffrey Chaucer,* Washington, 1927, p. 1076).

[16] Book I, lines 2254–2366.

[17] Dow, *Varying Attitude toward Women,* p. 145.

[18] See Power, in Crump and Jacob, *Legacy of the Middle Ages,* p. 404.

is the classic example.[19] Such defenses are the product of didactic
clerics rather than courtly gentlemen, for although the courtly
code worshipped women, it rarely defended them on satisfactory
moral grounds. Chivalry did foster the defending palinode, which
tends to answer satire with examples of woman's beauty, nobility,
and kindness to men.[20] A final type, which counters the perennial
advice to beware in marriage, is the commendation of matrimony
(184, 189, 253, 303, 371). The independent existence of this
form is largely confined to the sixteenth century, before which
it is imbedded in longer moral treatises on a variety of subjects.[21]

But the most significant product of the Renaissance is the
mingling of praise and dispraise, a derivative perhaps of the
ambiguities and ironies of Chaucer, and perhaps of the triumph
of observation over authority. As Miss Hammond pointedly
says, "After a long period of attempt to modify life, men began
more correctly to report it."[22] Type-satire and its equivalent,
exaggerated defense, no longer held the appeal they once had;
the old genres of opposition dissolved into something more formless and more like life itself. Type-satire had been the result of
medieval ideation, of that special kind of philosophical realism
which dealt with abstract essences rather than with irreconcilable
facts. Chaucer early began to probe into character as well as to
repeat the stock types—his Wife of Bath owes her universality
to a mingling of the two objectives. From the outset the debates
had pretended to show both sides of the question, though most
of them at first had ended by championing women. A mixed
tone was found in the ironic defenses, since irony was then as
always the means of coating satire in order to win an audience,
or of fictionally resolving a poet's mental pattern "paralyzed by
conflicting drives."[23] In the last category is such a poem as Henry
Sponare's, which defends women by comparing them not too
favorably with their biblical sisters (234); or the piece frankly

[19] See also a host of treatises listed in Alice A. Hentsch, *De La Littérature Didactique
du Moyen Age*, Cahors, 1903.

[20] 12, 28, 49, 67a, 94, 101, 125 (answering 292), 145, 162 (answering 163),
186, 252, 260 (answering 259), 288, 291 (probably answering 85), 298 (answering
6), 323 (possibly answering 292 or 313), 340, 343, 347 (answering 292), 367, 373
(answering 318), 379. This list includes all poems which purport to be defending
palinodes, even when the original satire is not known. Identifiable satirical palinodes
are rare in English; only *Merchant's Tale* and the *Scholehouse of Women* (339, 292)
occur to me.

[21] See also the marriage treatises listed below, p. 72n.

[22] *English Verse between Chaucer and Surrey*, p. 30.

[23] David Worcester, *The Art of Satire*, Cambridge, Mass., 1940, p. 141.

called *In Praise and Dispraise of Women* (**286**); or Pyrrye's appeal to the public with a little tract containing one satire, one defense, and one warning to be cautious in the choice of a wife (**94, 113, 210**). Such products of the sixteenth century suggest that the controversy had descended to such a level that the participants scarcely knew what they were about, when form and content had both gone by the board as methods of unifying satire or defense, and when it is thus useless any longer to speak of genres.

III. THE HISTORY OF ENGLISH SATIRE AND DEFENSE
TO 1568

To trace the strict beginnings of English satire and defense one must first refer to its French and Latin forebears, insular and continental.[1] Among the numerous Latin writers whose satire in more comprehensive works preceded the writings of independent satires we may single out Marbod of Rennes (1035–1123), Hildebert of Tours (1057–1133), Bernard of Morlas (*ca.* 1140), Alexander Neckam (1157–1217), and Bongiovanni of Mantua (first half of thirteenth century). Independent satires began to flourish in the late twelfth or early thirteenth centuries; most notable among them is the anonymous *De Coniuge Non Ducenda,* which Wulff assigns to the beginning of the thirteenth century, and which kept its popularity to the sixteenth (**75**). Of some eighteen poems cited by Wulff from the thirteenth century we may give special mention to *Dolopathos,* an ancestor of the *Seven Sages,* and to Adam of Barking's *Arbore sub quadam.* Outstanding prose satire is incorporated in Petrus Alphonsus' *Disciplina Clericalis* (written between 1106 and 1112), Andreas Capellanus' *De Arte Honeste Amandi* (*ca.* 1184–86?), the *Polycraticus* of John of Salisbury (1120?–1180), Albert of Brescia's *Liber consolationis et consilii* (1246?), and the *Chronica* of Fra Salimbene (born 1221). Independent prose satires are the *Dissuasio Valerii ad Rufinam Philosophum Ne Uxorem Ducat,* by

---

[1] The most complete treatment will be found in August Wulff, *Die Frauenfeindlichen Dichtungen in den Romanischen Literaturen des Mittelalters bis zum Ende des XIII. Jahrhunderts,* Halle a. S., 1914. What is secondhand in my summary is based on Wulff, who studies Latin, French, Italian, Provençal, and Spanish satire. Further useful bibliography will be found in Theodore Lee Neff, *La Satire des Femmes dans la Poésie Lyrique Française du Moyen Age,* Paris, 1900, pp. vii–x. Neff's treatment is topical rather than historical.

Walter Map (*ca.* 1120?–1208?),[2] and the *De Dissuasione Uxoria-
tionis* of Andreas Fieschi (early thirteenth century).

In Provence satires were composed by Marcabrun of Gascony
(1140–1185), Peire de Bussignac (late twelfth or early thirteenth
centuries), the Monk of Montaudon (fl. 1180–1213), Peire Car-
dinal (1225?–1272), and in Catalonia by Serviri of Girona (*ca.*
1260–1280). Satire is incorporated within the longer French
works of Étienne de Fougères, chaplain of Henry II of England
(fl. 1170), and above all in *Le Roman de la Rose*. Meun's continuation of the *Roman* belongs to the later years of the thirteenth century, shortly before the appearance of the *Lamentations*
of Matheolus or Mahieu. About the same time appeared a considerable number of shorter pieces: *L'Évangile des Femmes, Le
Blasme des Femmes, Le Blastange des Fames,* Bozon's *De la
Femme et la Pye, De la Chinchefache* (see **227**), and *Le Dit
des Cornetes* (see **232**). In the fourteenth century Jehan Lefevre
translated Matheolus, and Deschamps wrote his encyclopedic
Miroir de Mariage.

Such a listing, which merely skims the surface of satirical
production on the continent and in other languages than English,[3] cannot be duplicated in these early years for English itself.
As Anglo-Norman and Anglo-Latin literature testifies, this lacuna
is merely the result of the scarcity of any vernacular writing, and
owes nothing to the national temper. *The Owl and the Nightingale* (1189?–1217?) takes up the *querelle,* but only incidentally.
When the thirteenth century is in full swing the English contribution begins to show itself with three poems opposing exaggerated fashions (**169, 211, 369**), another attacking woman's
garrulity (**254**), two poems on the perils of love (**170, 171**),
two defenses (**140, 340**), and a second bird-debate (**273**). In
the fourteenth century the number increases; there is record of
some eighteen satires and defenses, and of fourteen more hover-
ing around the turn of the century. The first fifty years produced
little more than had the thirteenth: a *chanson de mal mariée*
(**18**), two scraps about woman's frailty (**4, 178**), and two

---

[2] See Max Manitius, *Geschichte der Lateinischen Literatur des Mittelalters,* Munich.
1911-1931, III, 265. Wulff makes the conventional error of attributing this work to
Jerome or to Valerius Maximus.

[3] Welsh satire and defense, which we must omit from consideration, have been
treated by Theodor M. Chotzen, *Recherches sur la Poésie de Dafydd ab Gwilym,* Amster-
dam, 1927, pp. 201–258, 286–90: and "La 'Querelle' des Femmes' au pays de Galles,"
Revue Celtique, XLVIII (1931), 42-93.

defenses (212, 42), one from a French ABC poem. Apart from a disquisition on the perils of love (103) and a fine defense (145), the activity at the end of the century is almost wholly due to Chaucer's inspired borrowing and unquestioned individuality: his *Legend of Good Women* (12); his ambiguous poems which bestow gentle mockery on the courtly code without renouncing it (176, 208, 325, 326); and his Marriage Group (58, 81, 261, 303, 339), which views the controversy through the eyes of the feministic but slightly tarnished Wife of Bath, the mildly satirical Clerk, the cynical Merchant, and the mellow Franklin. Longer works by Gower, Usk, Rolle, Langland (?), and the "Pearl Poet" exhibit a small amount of satire and defense, but separable satire in this period is almost a monopoly of its greatest writer. Chaucer's dominance is clearly traceable to his unparalleled knowledge of Latin and French writers—of Jerome, Walter Map, Jean de Meun, Deschamps, and Machaut, and possibly of Lefevre's Matheolus.

With the exception of a satire on fashions (65) and the piquant story of Tutivillus, a little devil who sets down the names of women who chatter in church (329), all the poems written at the end of the century or the beginning of the next are connected in one way or another with Chaucer. Three rebellious lover poems (148, 175, 403) have been ascribed to him; another, the *Romaunt of the Rose* (181), is either in part due to him or duplicates a translation of his now lost. Hoccleve's burlesque on the courtly panegyric dedicated to Lady Money (235) is clearly an attempt to repeat the success of Chaucer's *Purse* (325). Lydgate's *Horns Away!* carries on the satire on fashions which is a favorite subject of sermons then and now, and which had received a side glance in the portrait of the Wife of Bath. Lydgate's two ironic defenses (307, 334) are a crude attempt to master Chaucer's ambiguous pose; his *Epistle to Sibille* (283), based upon the Bible, may also owe something to Chaucer's more serious feminism. Clanvowe's *Cuckoo and the Nightingale* (286) has been attached to the Chaucerian apocrypha; whatever its exact date or authorship there is no doubt that it was written by a disciple who caught Chaucer's spirit and used at times his very words. Like the early bird-debates, this late contribution to the genre ends in the victory of woman's champion.

If we include these pieces just mentioned, which cannot be exactly dated, we may estimate a hundred or so satires and defenses on record for the fifteenth century—a sure sign that Chaucer's pioneer work had been well done. His disciples, Lydgate, Hoccleve, Henryson, and Dunbar, each make valuable contributions to the debate. We must reckon also with the vigorous participation of certain French poets and polemicists who popularized the quarrel—Christine de Pisan, Jean Gerson, Pierre and Gontier Col, Jean de Montreuil, Martin le Franc, the anonymous author of *Les Quinze Joyes de Mariage,* and Alain Chartier.[4]

At the very outset of the century France brought new life to the old argument. It was in 1399 that Marshal Boucicault founded his "Ordre de l'Escu Vert à la Dame Blanche" for the defense of woman's interests and honor, and in 1400 that the Dukes of Bourbon and Burgundy organized the "Cour Amoureuse" for a similar purpose. Significant as these gestures were, they were of small import compared to the controversy linked with the name of Christine, herself a member of the latter order.[5] The first blows in "La Querelle de la Rose" were struck in 1399 by Christine in *L'Epistre au Dieu d'Amours* (**49**) and by Jean Gerson, "le grave, l'honnête Gerson,"[6] in his *Sermo contra Luxuria.* Instead of preferring vague charges against false lovers in the manner of the courtly panegyrics of prior centuries, these two defenders of women seized upon one outstanding culprit, Jean de Meun, and made his treasonable continuation of the *Roman de la Rose* their central argument. Gerson, chancellor of the University of Paris, was moved as much by his feeling about the naturalism and "libertinism" of Jean as by any consideration for women; but Christine is a veritable *champion des dames.* She penetrates to the very heart of the satirical para-

---

[4] For the many satires and defenses of the XV century see Abel Lefranc, "Le Tiers Livre du 'Pantagruel,' " *Grands Écrivains Français de la Renaissance,* Paris, 1914, II, 252-60; Blanche H. Dow, *The Varying Attitude toward Women in French Literature of the Fifteenth Century,* New York, 1936.

[5] The bibliography is large. For some of the most useful treatments see Dow, *Varying Attitude toward Women,* pp. 128–224; Richardson, *Forerunners of Feminism,* pp. 12-34; Rose Rigaud, *Les Idées Féministes de Christine de Pisan,* Neuchatel, 1911; Huizinga, *Waning of the Middle Ages,* pp. 100–106. Most of the documents of the *querelle* are collected by Charles F. Ward, *The Epistles on the Romance of the Rose and Other Documents in the Debate,* University of Chicago Press, 1911. For convenience I follow Dow's chronology of the debate (pp. 223-24) even when it is conjectural.

[6] A. Jeanroy, Introduction to *Les Quinze Joies de Mariage,* tr. M.-L. Simon, Paris, 1929, p. xi.

dox, to the men who claim that women are unchaste and frail, and who nevertheless exercise all their masculine wit and strength in seduction:

> Et comment donc quant fresles et legieres,
> Et tournables, nyces et pou entieres
> Sont les femmes, si com aucuns clers dient,
> Quel besoing donc est il a ceulz qui prient
> De tant pour ce pourchacier de cautelles?
> Et pour quoy tost ne s'i accordent elles
> Sanz qu'il faille art n'engin a elles prendre?
> Car pour chastel pris ne fault guerre emprendre. . . .
> A foible lieu faut il donc grant assault?[7]

These two defenses, interesting as they are to us, would not be a landmark in French literary history if they had not been answered by three short Latin epistles (1400–1401?) by Jean de Montreuil, who politely attempted to keep on Gerson's good side while vigorously defending Jean de Meun. On September 13, 1401, Gontier Col entered the lists with a letter to Christine, and championed Meun on humanistic grounds.[8] The *Querelle* proper comprises some twenty documents; each debater had his rebuttal, and Christine (the only woman in the controversy) had more to say than all the rest together. After the ending of the debate itself Christine produced her *Livre de la Cité des Dames* (46) and its sequel, *Le Livre des Trois Vertus*, both composed apparently in the years 1404–1405.

Like any literary figure who gains more than his share of modern study, Christine has been maligned for conservatism and praised for revolutionary ardor. The truth is somewhere between; she is neither a great reformer, a "militant suffragist," nor an apologist for things as they were. She had, like the modern newswoman, to live on good terms with the men whose prerogatives of authorship she was invading, and her frank admissions of the weaknesses of her sex reveal this necessary compromise. Even in the role of defender she calls upon the man-made codes of courtly love and of Christian didacticism. She is as much of a professional writer as Lydgate, and as conventional and prolix; both of them wrote for a living in a time when artists were useful and subordinate purveyors to the hierarchies of Church

---

[7] *Oeuvres Poétiques de Christine de Pisan*, ed. Maurice Roy, Paris, 1886-96, II, 13.
[8] For the part of the Cols in the debate see Alma LeDuc, "Gontier Col and the French Pre-Renaissance," *Romanic Review*, VIII (1917), 145-58.

and State. In some measure we must agree with the common
charge of poetic mediocrity in Christine.[9]

But if she is not a poetic innovator, her verses do contribute
something new in tone and subject matter. As a phenomenon she
is unusual enough—an occasional Hrotswitha or Marie de France
does not contravene the common assumption that most medieval
writers were men.[10] And neither of these two predecessors of
hers shows any remarkable sympathy for the sex. What are the
reasons for this sudden articulateness on the part of a woman?
No doubt they are personal in part; she was the product of a
remarkable education. Her father, Thomas of Pisa, was an
erudite bibliophile, physician, and astrologer, and gave her many
of the advantages usually confined to a great lady, and something more, his own inspiration.[11] But she was no *grande dame,*
and her future was by no means assured. After the deaths of
her father and her husband, Étienne de Castel, secretary and
notary to the King, she was thrown at the age of twenty-five
upon her own resources, with three children to support.[12] She
was a true *femme sole,* with writing as her only means of liveli-
hood, and her misfortune was the making of her. The usual
great lady would never have had to work; the usual hard-
working bourgeoise would never have had the education. This
rare combination of necessity and training went together with
no small measure of personal courage and talent to produce a
woman who understood the sufferings of her sex and had the
tongue to say so. She was aided by other less personal factors:
by the decadence of chivalry and the somewhat hysterical attempts to revive it (in which even a woman's efforts were acceptable), by the breaking down of the framework of society and
the consequent uncertainty about woman's exact position, and
by the awakening of some sense of the need for legal and social
reform in *mores.*[13] These are the reasons why she is woman's
representative, though not a representative woman of her time.

Her work has much of originality—not the heights of Pla-

[9] See, for instance, Richardson, *Forerunners of Feminism,* pp. 13-14; Rigaud, *Les Idées Féministes,* p. 116; Raymond L. Kilgour, *The Decline of Chivalry,* Cambridge, Mass., 1937, p. 129.
[10] The small number of studies in Alice Kemp-Welch's *Of Six Mediæval Women,* London, 1913, which includes a sensitive and illuminating estimate of these two and of Christine, will indicate the truth of my remark.
[11] Kemp-Welch, pp. 117-23.
[12] Kemp-Welch, p. 121.
[13] On the last see Dow, *Varying Attitude toward Women,* p. 132.

tonic inspiration, but a new note natural to an age of prose. She was competent to deal with her masculine rivals, whose distinguished names reveal that she had enough erudition and spirit to draw fire from the best. Even her conservative ally, Gerson, looks forward rather than backward; for if Meun, the Cols, and Montreuil anticipate the era of Montaigne and Rabelais, Gerson is a worthy prototype of the Council of Trent. Christine has irony and wit and sometimes subtlety, no mean weapons in such a controversy, and weapons all too rare among the earlier defenders of women. Her admission that women have their faults is a wise departure from the humorless defense by one-sided example; though she is a true enough child of her times to use this argument, she knows how to anticipate her opponents in its use. She does not underrate her present antagonists, or even the dead Jean de Meun;[14] her polemics do not minimize themselves by confining the argument to that of *ad hominem*. Above all, she is a woman, and writes not out of mere gallantry; like the Wife of Bath she speaks from experience as well as from authority. Against the usual lack of shadows in the estimates of women, who were "either deified or . . . evil incarnate," she attempts to remedy the evil "not by shouting in the market-place, but by studying men and women as God made them and as she found them."[15] Like Chaucer and Euripides, she writes about women not out of a false abstraction but out of observation and meditated wisdom; and unlike them she can look within herself for testimony. She is even keen enough to penetrate to economic and social fundamentals, to recognize that women's position of trust and power when their husbands were away at business or war manifests more toleration of the sex than the conventional charges against Eve implied.[16] Hence her *Querelle* towers not in literary merit but in social significance above the work of other fifteenth-century satirists and defenders, Alain Chartier's *La Belle Dame sans Mercy* and the controversy which it aroused (*ca.* 1424?—see **82**), Martin Le Franc's *Champion des Dames* (1440–42), and *Les Quinze Joyes de Mariage* (before 1450?—see **274**).

Some echoes of this French activity were bound to reach England, where Chaucer had already paved the way. *Le Quinze*

---

[14] See Dow, p. 167.
[15] Kemp-Welch, *Of Six Mediæval Women*, p. 129.
[16] Power, in Crump and Jacob, *Legacy of the Middle Ages*, pp. 418–19.

Joyes and Christine's *Cité des Dames* (**274, 46**) had to wait a century—until French was less common in England—to be translated; but Chartier's work was translated by Sir Richard Ros, perhaps shortly after Chartier had himself visited England. Christine reached English ears when, a year or two after *L'Épistre au Dieu d'Amours* was written, it was paraphrased by the young Chaucerian Hoccleve (**49**). So the major contributions of Chaucer and Christine merged to make the fifteenth century a time when every author who raised his head above the crowd must participate in the popular and ambiguous quarrel.

The first half of the century was dominated by Lydgate, whose determination to please everybody and to cultivate all of the traditional genres led him to compose both satire and defense. In addition to the early pieces we have mentioned, he paraphrased the French fable of *Bicorne and Chichevache,* of the fat monster who eats patient husbands and the lean one who suffers from a diet of patient wives (**227**); he translated the thirteenth-century *De Coniuge Non Ducenda* (**75**); he played his part in the rise of drama with his *Mumming at Hertford,* in which shrews and their husbands contend for the mastery (**190**). Burlesque panegyric and general satire (**249, 387, 57, 72**) are both attached to his name. His cultivation of Chaucerian ambiguity extended to his longer works; he was much addicted to translating a satirical passage with embellishments and rebuking his original in the bargain. *Reason and Sensuality* (from *Les Échecs Amoureux*), the *Troy-Book* (from Guido delle Colonne), and the *Fall of Princes* (from Laurent de Premierfait and Boccaccio) all contain long passages of this sort. The *Fall of Princes* is of special importance, since scribes and even Lydgate himself were in the habit of culling satirical and defending passages from it and presenting them as separate poems (**142, 185, 220, 317, 350**). Despite his disclaimers, his use of irony and "amphilogies," and at least two outright defenses (**142, 283**), his contemporary fame was as a satirist, and he merited a playful rebuke from scribes like Shirley and from the courtly author of *A Reproof to Lydgate* (**186**). While he lacked Chaucer's grace and wit and insight, he was perhaps as influential in giving wide currency to formalized satire and defense in the next two centuries. He was not alone; Hoccleve paraphrased Christine and attempted an imitation of the Canterbury Marriage Group (**49, 28**); John Audelay used the popular new carol form for didactic defense (**38, 144, 147**); Lydgate's example in the *Fall of Princes* was followed by an anonymous author who translated a portion of Boccaccio's *De Claris Mulieribus* but, like Chaucer in the *Legend,* tired of the task before he was done (**236**); the tradition of the Rebellious Lover got under way (**7, 104, 105, 188, 396**); an interesting fortune-game mingled praise and dispraise (**201, 366**); and an unusual adaptation of the *chanson de nonne* was written (**30**).

Production, or at least preservation, increased greatly in the last half of the century—certain evidence that Lydgate, Chaucer, and the French *querellistes* had as great an effect upon the controversy as the invention of printing did. It is during this period that we begin to witness the compilation of wholesale manuscript anthologies, and that we see scribes taking a part in the debate through their powers of selection. In the thirteenth and fourteenth centuries only two anthologies, MSS. Digby 86 and Harley 2253, showed much concern with the controversy; these two had scribes who copied satirical jest and courtly gesture from French, Latin, and English. But it is not really until Chaucer's works begin to be collected that the *querelle* becomes a passion of copyists. The Marriage Group needed no compiling; its important contribution to the debate appears in some sixty manuscripts (usually devoted to the *Tales* as a whole). Feminists may find consolation in the fact that, whenever the Group was broken up, the gentle irony of the *Clerk's Tale* was most popular and the bitterness of the *Merchant's Tale* least so. In only one of the sixty manuscripts, MS. Cambridge University Library Gg. 4. 27, do we find the Group accompanied by other pieces of interest to us in any number—two of them Chaucer's own and one Lydgate's (**12, 326; 387**). Real anthologizing begins with Shirley and his fellows about the middle of the century,[17] and this tendency is apparently inspired by the desire to include Chaucer and Lydgate within one compass. The celebrated MS. Fairfax 16, written before 1450 and containing twelve pieces which interest us, is apart from the Shirleian tradition, although it fell into the hands of one of Shirley's collectors,

---

[17] In this estimate and others I have considered as worthy of comment manuscripts containing five or more pieces relating to the controversy. Index III provides a full list of manuscripts and other authorities, in which the contents of less important collections may be studied.

John Stow.[18] It represents Chaucer and his disciples with distinction, with five poems by the master, two by Lydgate, and
one reproving him, Hoccleve's *Letter of Cupid,* Clanvowe's
Cuckoo and the Nightingale, the fortune-game called *Ragman
Roll,* and Chartier's *La Belle Dame sans Mercy.* Two manuscripts
from the hand of Shirley (who died in 1456) are of special value
because they contain his marginalia: Trinity Cambridge R. 3. 20
with four poems by Lydgate and one by Hoccleve; and Ashmole
59, with five by Lydgate, an anonymous satire on fashions, and
an epitome of Chaucer's *Legend* (**80**). Harley 2251, derived
from Shirley, has eight by Lydgate and one by Chaucer. At the
end of the century two manuscripts in the Rawlinson collection,
C. 86 and C. 813, contain six and eight pieces respectively; and
the Chaucerian MS. Cambridge University Library Ff. 1. 6 has
seven. Two others are of even greater interest: MS. Trinity
Cambridge R. 3. 19, with thirteen satires or defenses, six by or
ascribed to Lydgate, Chaucer's *Legend, Piers of Fulham, La Belle
Dame,* and four others which crept into the Chaucerian apocrypha
by virtue of the editor Stow's use of the codex; and Bodleian
Eng. poet. e. 1, which Thomas Wright believed was a portfolio
of the wares of a professed minstrel. External evidence does not
confirm this romantic interpretation, but there is no doubt that
the manuscript is of vastly more popular character than the
Shirleian codices and the other Lydgate-Chaucer collections. All
of the fourteen pieces which concern us are anonymous: twelve
are carols, three belong to the Holly and Ivy tradition, one is a
riddling poem, one a conventional satire without the carol burden,
ten oppose women by outright satire, warnings against marriage,
bachelor's rejoicing, lying-song techniques, and ironic defense, one
is a debate which ends in the misogynist's victory, two mingle
praise and dispraise, and one is a defense. None of the fifteenth-
century anthologies is a better clue to what the late medieval
audience liked; the collection must have appealed equally to
baronial hall, market place, and alehouse.

The last half of the century is characterized by this increase
in anthologizing, by the use of printing, and by the rise of a
Scottish school. The old anonymous genres contined to flourish:
an obscene but lively *chanson de mal mariée* (**172**); a host of

---

[18] Eleanor P. Hammond, *Chaucer, a Bibliographical Manual,* New York, 1908, pp.
333-34. This summary of manuscripts has been greatly aided by Miss Hammond's
pioneer work.

carols in addition to those found in MS. Bodleian Eng. poet. e. 1 (88, 137, 203, 243, 257, 270); a bird-debate with misogyny the victor (129); a conventional satire against vanity with a French source (182); and several sprightly parodies of the courtly lyric (95, 168, 221, 226, 335). Caxton contributes a translation of the *Book of the Knight of La Tour-Landry* (150), written a century before and already once put into English; at about the same time another narrative collection, *The Spektakle of Luf,* was translated by the Scottish "Master" G. Myll from a Latin source not yet identified (271a). Perhaps Caxton's most amusing attempt to exploit the traditional quarrel lies in his epilogue of 1478 to Lord Rivers' translation of Guillaume de Tignonville's *Les Dits Moraulx.* The printer suggests that some fair and noble lady has silenced Lord Rivers, who had once "thought that Socrates spared the sothe. And wrote of women more than trouthe." But, says Caxton, we must not malign a great philosopher so readily, for the women of Greece had different manners than our own, who are

> right good / wyse / playsant / humble / discrete / sobre / chast / obedient to their husbondis / trewe / secrete / stedfast / euer besy / & neuer ydle / Attemperat in speking and vertuous in alle their werkis. or atte leste sholde be soo.

Thus he emphasizes by remark the passage he pretends to deplore, and compounds the crime by separating the sayings of Socrates from their context and placing them at the end, so that the gallant may rend the leaf from the book—and nobody will miss it.[19] But despite this essay into courtly ambiguity, Caxton can scarcely be said to anticipate the part which the printers of the next century were to play in the *querelle.*

At the same time we find lively pens at work in Scotland; but the only writer besides Myll who with certainty can be dated before 1500 is the Dunfermline schoolmaster, Robert Henryson, whose *Garmont of Gude Ladeis* (388) recalls Oliver de la Marche's *Le Parement des Dames,* and whose *Testament of Cresseid* adds a narrative moral to Chaucer's *Troilus*—a semi-satirical moral on woman's wantonness which Chaucer despite his apologies to Alceste would never have dared to compose, but which for two succeeding centuries was the sixth book of

[19] W. J. B. Crotch, ed., *The Prologues and Epilogues of William Caxton,* London (EETS, CLXXVI), 1928, p. 22.

his romance and helped to convert Chaucer's complex heroine, "sliding of corage," into the wanton creature of Shakespeare.[20]

Henryson may serve as a bridge to the sixteenth century, during which the medieval tradition of satire and defense grew in scope and was transformed. The last 68 years we have to treat contribute some 250 of our 400 pieces. This startling quantitative climax to our controversy has several causes. Two of them, the history of manuscripts and the invention of printing, are commonly and justly adduced. The paleographer offers several reasons for the dearth of documents in the early Middle Ages: the small reading public (court and clergy, and not all of either), the cost of vellum, the fastidious care with which scribes worked, and above all the loss of early manuscripts through fire, battle, hard usage, and sixteenth-century reforming zeal. In part the great increase in fifteenth-century satire and defense is due to Chaucer and Christine, but it owes something as well to the spread of education, the substitution of paper for vellum, and the development of high-speed (and careless) non-monastic scribes. In addition to these factors were two others. One is the progressive attention to the English vernacular; by the fifteenth century we no longer need to turn to Anglo-Latin and Anglo-French to assess the extent of the controversy. Another, primarily ideological, is the serious turn the debate was beginning to take. With the widening horizon of the sixteenth century the problem of woman's position grew more acute. Although jest was not absent from Renaissance satire, we may agree with Lefranc that the *querelle*

> prend un caractère plus sérieux et une allure plus serrée. Elle profite du progrès général des esprits, de la conaissance plus solide des deux antiquités, de la rénovation des études juridiques, du développement de la médicine et de toutes les sciences d'observation.[21]

Some of the most violent attacks on women appear when the advanced ideas of moralists and reformers collide with the universal conservatism. We may perhaps note a parallel in the history of socialist and collectivist theory, which in the early nineteenth century was somewhat academic, but in times of transition like our own arouses bitter antagonism and fervent defense of the old order.

[20] See H. E. Rollins, "The Troilus-Criseyde Story," *PMLA*, XXXII (1917), 383–429.
[21] *Grand Écrivains de la Renaissance*, II, 260.

So long as we recognize the difficulty of accurate dating within narrow limits, we may for convenience' sake divide this last period into two parts, from 1500 to 1540, when the *Scholehouse* controversy began, and from 1540 to 1568.

Activity in Scotland, incipient before the turn of the century, burst into full expression with William Dunbar, who is more than any other person responsible for the enthusiasm north of the border. For sheer quantity and quality he towers above his contemporaries in both Scotland and England, and commands a position as distinctive as that of Chaucer a century earlier. He is as much a master of medieval genres as he is of meters; he runs the gamut from ribald and brilliantly conceived confessions of the *chanson de mal mariée* type, *The Twa Cummeris* and *The Tua Mariit Wemen and the Wedo* (**251, 336**), to a noble and aureate defense by witness of Mary (**219**). His *Merle and the Nychtingaill* (**139**) is no crude opposition of earthly and divine love; it sets up the eternal paradox so skillfully that it must have appealed alike to courtly churchmen and to Catholic courtiers. He can parody courtly love, as in the burlesque panegyric *Of Ane Blakmoir* (**161**) and the ironically reversed *To a Lady* (**199**); he can rebel entirely in three renunciations of love which reflect the preoccupation with death which came to all men when the old happy faiths were breaking up (**215, 60, 372**); he can descend into the depths of wanton abandon with *To the Quene* (**177**); he can write with equal fervor of worldly passion in *Bewty and the Prisoneir* and *The Thrissil and the Rois,* and of the Blessed Virgin in that pyrotechnic masterpiece *Haile, sterne superne.* His gentle satire on an ale-wife, *Kind Kittok* (**195**), is balanced with the whipping and stripping *Of the Ladyis Solistaris at Court* (**301**). He is thus an overwhelmingly favorable specimen of the wit and variety harbored by the controversy in its transitional period.

Other Scottish *querellistes* nearly contemporary with him are Gavin Douglas, in whose *Prologue to the Fourth Book of the Aeneid* the tale of Dido's sufferings is made to release its moral of the power, slights, and viciousness of wanton love (**381**); "Mersar" (if the poet of Bannatyne is really Dunbar's lamented "makar") with two warnings against wanton men (**19, 300**); Walter Kennedy, with one conventional farewell to love and another obscene renunciation full of *double entente* (**154, 26**);

and Sir David Lyndsay, whose *Satire of the Three Estates* incorporates a farcical treatment of marriage, and who also wrote a lively attack on the long trains then in fashion which cleansed the city streets at no improvement to themselves (**262**).

Anonymity was passing in England as well as Scotland. The most fertile producers of satire south of the Tweed were John Skelton and Robert Copland, both of whom lived and wrote in the old century and the new. Skelton composed wanton songs and burlesque treatments of the rebellious lover theme (**187, 279, 383**); he contributed in somewhat oblique fashion to the tradition of palinode by virtue of his charming tributes to ladies of the court in *The Garland of Laurel*. But his fame as a satirist is largely due to his essay into roughhouse grotesquerie, *The Tunnyng of Elynour Rummyng,* one of the most popular poems of the century and still a favorite (**277**).

The position of Robert Copland (fl. 1496–1547?) is not, like that of Dunbar, Skelton, or Chaucer, the result of genius; but rather, like that of Lydgate, the product of a capacity for hard work and a knowledge of foreign tongues. Like Lydgate again, he was a professional writer, but whereas Lydgate had been dependent on the patronage and favor of courtiers and wealthy burgesses, Copland's success was due to his connection with Wynkyn de Worde. Two of his pamphlets, the ill-starred *Seuen sorowes that women haue when theyr husbandes be deade* (**377**), and the robust *Gyl of Braintfords Testament* (**35**), are apparently original compositions. Two others are translations from the French: *A complaynt of them that be to soone maryed* (**67**) and its sequel, *The complaynte of them that ben to late maryed* (**17**). He may also have provided additional verses for Lydgate's *Pain and Sorrow of Evil Marriage* (**75**). From the beginning de Worde recognized the popularity of the controversy, and in the years 1507–1509 he swelled the total of English satires by printing two other translations, either of which may be by Copland, and both of which enliven English literature with deft Gallic wit: *The .xv. Joyes of maryage* (**274**) and *The gospelles of dystaues* (**79**). *The Boke of Mayd Emlyn* (**380**), a jestbook which issued from John Skot's press between 1507 and 1525, seems to allude to *The gospelles* and is certainly rebuked by Copland in his *Seuen Sorowes*. Other printers, Rastell and Berthelet, sponsored satires from the hand of John Heywood which likewise echo French literature (**25, 76**). De Worde himself continued to profit by the controversy with William Walter's *Spectacle of Louers* (**66**), Thomas Feylde's *Contrauersye bytwene a louer and a Jaye* (**313**), *An !nterlocucyon with an argument betwyxt man and woman* (**355**—from the French of Guillaume Alexis), and John Ryckes' *Ymage of Loue* (**127**).

We shall later discuss the specific contributions of humanism to the *querelle,* but here we may mention something of what was going on in the continental arena, which as usual sets the tone for English literature a quarter of a century in the future. A vigorous Neo-Latin debate, humanistic and international, centered about the names of the German Cornelius Agrippa, the Dutch Erasmus, the Spanish Vives, the Italian Nevizzani, and the French satirist André Tiraqueau with his opponent Amaury Bouchard. In Spain vernacular *querelles* had been conducted by many authors, among them Juan de Flores, Lucena, and the Arcipreste de Talavera;[22] in Italy by Jacopone da Todi, Fra Salimbene, Boccaccio, and Castiglione;[23] and in Germany by Hugo von Trimberg, Der Stricker, and Hans Sachs, to name only a few.[24] Of these continental writers Vives carried Spanish gallantry to England; Castiglione brought Italian courtesy (at the start largely through the medium of France); and Barclay's translation of Brant's *Narrenschiff,* along with the work of Erasmus, made some slight contact with Germanic Europe. The lack of strong Flemish and Dutch influence is noteworthy, considering how many English printers came from the Low Countries.

On the whole the English derive their inspiration as before from French and Latin. Signal contributions to the *querelle* in

[22] See Wulff, *Die Frauenfeindlichen Dichtungen,* pp. 178-83, 193-96; Barbara Matulka, *An Anti-Feminist Treatise of Fifteenth Century Spain,* New York, 1931, and "The Feminist Theme in the Drama of the Siglo de Oro," *Romanic Review,* XXVI (1935), 191-231; Jacob Ornstein, "Misogyny and Pro-Feminism in Early Castilian Literature," *MLQ,* III (1942), 221-34.

[23] Wulff, pp. 139–65, 189–92; Luigi Valmaggi, *Lo Spirito Antifemminile nel Medioevo,* Turin, 1890; Carlo Pascal, "Misoginia Medievale," *Studi Medievali,* II (1906-1907), 242-48; see also Pascal's *Poesia Latina Medievale,* Catania, 1907, pp. 151-84. Valmaggi's lecture, a charming though popular treatment which deserves to be better known, is not to be found either in Harvard, the British Museum, or the Library of Congress. Professor Eileen Power was kind enough to let me photostat her copy.

[24] Franz Breitzmann, *Die böse Frau in der deutschen Litteratur des Mittelalters,* Berlin (Palaestra, XLII), 1912; Archer Taylor, *Problems in German Literary History of the Fifteenth and Sixteenth Centuries,* New York, 1939, pp. 124-41, 165-72. Taylor, whose primary concern is with German marriage treatises, supplies extensive bibliography and commentary on the entire woman question.

France were Symphorien Champier's *La Nef des dames ver-
teueuses* (1504); the first printing of Martin le Franc's *Le Champion des Dames* (written about 1440 and printed in 1530), which
evoked a violent reply in Gratian du Pont's *Controverses dex
sexes masculin et feminin* (1534); Jean Bouchet's *Le Iugement
poetic de l'honneur feminin* (1538); and Hélisenne de Crenne's
Epistles familieres et invectives (1539). An important new element, neo-Platonism, enters the debate with Antoine Héroet's
La Parfaicte Amye (1542), which owes a good deal to Castiglione's *Il Cortegiano* (1528, translated into French in 1537).[25]
The emulation of a noted exponent of women's emancipation
like Plato was bound to lead to defense; and Héroet inaugurated
a series of elaborate debates which took place in Lyons under
the guidance of Maurice Scève.[26]

The humanists who wrote in Latin were less likely to be
defenders. Nevizanni's *Sylva Nuptialis* (1521) was the vortex
of the Neo-Latin *querelle* and had great influence in France;
full as it is of outright misogyny, it nevertheless borrows all the
apparatus of the New Learning.[27] Nevizanni and his fellow
humanist, Tiraqueau, would have faded from memory if it were
not for the undoubted part they played in the production of
"cette énorme parenthèse qu'est le tiers livre" of Tiraqueau's
friend Rabelais. The Third Book was published in 1546, twelve
years after the great *satura* had been set for the first time before
a race of gourmets. It is largely concerned with a specious debate
between Panurge, who *will* have a wife, and his many counselors,
including Pantagruel, who interprets the advice of others in a
highly misogynistic vein. The result is essentially pessimism
about marriage, although it is scarcely celibate. Bédier and
Hazard put it tartly: Rabelais's "opinion sur ces questions est
celle que l'on pouvait attendre d'un médicin et d'un moine: ce
n'est pas un madrigal."[28]

Humanism in England appears to have borrowed little from
Rabelais; we have only one piece which can even conjecturally
be ascribed to the influence of the Third Book, *The Image of
Idleness* (**158**, written in 1558?). But another of Rabelais's masters, Erasmus, and his fellow spirit Vives (1492–1540) both play

[25] Richardson, *Forerunners of Feminism*, p. 78.
[26] Richardson, p. 85.
[27] Lefranc, *Grande Écrivains de la Renaissance*, II, 263.
[28] *Historie de la Littérature Française Illustrée*, Paris, 1923, I, 156.

a large part in conditioning the English mind.[29] Vives's influence
is indirect; his *De Institutione Christianae Feminae* (1523, translated about 1529 by Richard Hyrde and often reprinted) is a
landmark in the history of woman's liberal education, but its
tone is too didactic to warrant inclusion here.[30] Vives's most
significant disciple was probably Sir Thomas Elyot, whose Platonic or Lucianic dialogue, *The Defence of Good Women* (**53**),
written during the thirties, is said to be "a slightly disguised
defence of Queen Catherine" of Aragon.[31] When we speak of
the feminism which begins in the Renaissance it is largely of
such educators as Vives that we are thinking. Yet we should
recall that Spanish gallantry had flourished since the days of
the Andalusian Moors, and that Vives occupies a position in
relationship to Catherine and to her daughter Mary Tudor[32]
very similar to that held toward Eleanor of Aquitaine by poets
and philosophers centuries before. It is not improbable that
some connection exists between the many satires on women published by de Worde during the last ten years of his life (1525–35)
and the fact that woman's emancipation has as its most notable
exponent a favorite of the unpopular queen, who lost his position
at court and suffered imprisonment when he opposed Henry's
divorce in 1528. If we are bound by the old shibboleths we find
sufficient contradiction here: a Catholic at once a humanist and
defender of women, who finds himself at odds with the scarcely
gallant founder of English Protestantism. The uncelibate Henry
had good reason to listen to satires on women, and it was even
charged at the time that satirists found an excellent road to both
royal and popular favor (see **323**). There is nothing really surprising in these historical paradoxes when we consider that among
the most violent antagonists of the sex in the late sixteenth
century was such a Puritan as John Knox.

Of even greater influence than Vives is Erasmus, whose medi-
ating role shows how complex the attitude of the humanist might
be. Like Vives he had written a didactic treatise, *De Matrimonio
Christiano* (1526), which sets the new tone for woman's educa-

[29] As their use as symbols in Edmund Tilney's *Flower of Friendshippe* (1568)
indicates (see **40**).
[30] It is well summarized by Hentsch, *De la Littérature Didactique*, pp. 214-23; extracts
from Hyrde are printed by Foster Watson, *Vives and the Renascence Education of
Women*, New York, 1912.
[31] Watson, p. 19.
[32] Watson, p. 1.

tion and for the ideal of partnership in marriage.[33] Although this was not translated into English during the Renaissance, its opinions found their way into other works by Erasmus: the shorter treatise *Encomium Matrimonii* (253—1518), translated about 1530 by Richard Tavernour; and three of the colloquies of the 1523 edition—*Pamphilus* (189) and *Adolescens et Scortum* (238), translated by Nicholas Leigh and printed in 1568, and *Coniugium* (184, see also 337), translated by an unknown hand and printed in 1557. These pieces are excellent witness to Erasmus' Catholic merging of the new humanism and the medieval spirit. The *Encomium*, for instance, owes something to Plato and to other classics; *Adolescens et Scortum* to Lucian and to medieval religious treatises; *Coniugium* to the Socratic myth and to contemporary observation; *Pamphilus* to personal experience and to the medieval *débat*. Erasmus' didactic side causes him to deplore prostitution and exalt marriage, but his irrepressible wit leads him to call upon the eternal themes of satire. He was not the innovator that Vives was, and apparently owes his conversion to woman's cause in part to Sir Thomas More.[34] But he has many gifts—sensitivity, understanding, a refined psychology, a talent for striking observation, and a sense of social necessity—which bring him "hors de pair entre tous les savants de son époque."[35] We need hardly term his opinions a bit unstable as Miss Richardson has done;[36] his realistic observation and universal erudition merely combined to tear down the old distinctions of black and white in a fashion which appealed to his contemporaries and should appeal to us today. As a reformer he steers the way between unworldly theory and the facts of life; as a satirist he strikes one of the first great blows against type satire, and reveals woman as a human being, full of flaw and of good intention—the very creature she was to become in Elizabethan drama. Nowhere does his special genius appear more clearly than with regard to our controversy.

Erasmus, despite his love of the dialogue form, can scarcely be labeled a neo-Platonist; his jests about the higher love in *Pamphilus* remind us of Voltaire. The airy realms of the Idea, such as are envisioned in Héroet's *La Parfaicte Amye* and in

[33] For a good summary of his work see Richardson, pp. 46–53.
[34] Watson, *Vives*, p. 18; see also Richardson, p. 53.
[35] Lefranc, *Grands Écrivains de la Renaissance*, II, 264.
[36] *Forerunners of Feminism*, p. 42.

Castiglione's *Il Cortegiano*, are more congenial to the courtier than to the humanist. Miss Foxwell's attempt, however, to link Wyatt with Héroet's school of Lyons falls down on the basis of simple chronology (see **160**), for Héroet's book appeared the very year of Wyatt's death. What may be garnered of the Platonic spirit in Wyatt is more likely due to his direct knowledge of Italian; as a defender of women (**160**) he is more of a medieval courtier than we are apt to realize. He engages in frequent rebellion against his lady (**92, 109, 196, 202, 276, 338, 346**), in philosophical renunciation (**61**), and even in a burlesque of the catalogue of charms (**395**). He does have a serious streak in him which sets him apart from his fellow courtiers, whose extant contribution to satire seems to be largely that of wanton songs (see **29, 120, 207, 271**; and **97, 83, 364**). But the deeper note is struck by Surrey's renunciation of love (**390**) and by Lord Vaux's rebellion (**228**). Perhaps we may also see something of courtly taste in *The Nut-Brown Maid* (**36**) in spite of its popular clothing; and certainly such taste is exhibited in Brian Anslay's translation of Christine's *City of Ladies* (**46**) and in David Clapham's englishing of Cornelius Agrippa (**237**, see also **214**).

During the next thirty years, the last we have to treat, satire increases in the same numerical progression. Year after year broadsides and pamphlets on women flood the presses. So extensive is the material that it may be only cursorily treated; we shall confine ourselves to the notable *querelle* evoked by *The Scholehouse of Women,* to the broadside activity, to the anthologizing tendency in manuscript and print, and to a brief examination of the special factors which the Renaissance introduced into the controversy.

Great names were not attracted to the debate during this period; only minor writers like George Turbervile, Alexander Scott, and Edward Gosynhill may be singled out. The last of these may not have written as much of the *Scholehouse* controversy as he is said to; but his name would mean little to us without it. This tempest in a teapot is a true *querelle des femmes,* involving charge and countercharge and polemical allusion to the other participants; and unless we except the mild skirmishes over Chaucer's Marriage Group and *The Reproof to Lydgate,* it is the only real *querelle* in English. Here for the first time, probably, do we find English defenders becoming conscious of their social import, and it is possible that their opponents also sense the spirit of the age.

There is perhaps no mere coincidence in the two milestones in this controversy, the publication in 1541 of *The Scholehouse of Women,* and the revival of the argument in 1560. The first date had been preceded by more than thirty years of de Worde's commercialization of satire and defense, by twenty years of humanistic interest in woman's education, and by fifteen years of Henry VIII's divorces and the consequent perusal of the whole structure of religious sanctions as they related to sex. And 1560 represents the beginning of the reign of England's greatest woman ruler.

The *querelle* opens with the printing of the anonymous *Scholehouse* (**292**), a conventional enough satire, though one of the most comprehensive yet written in this century. Its notoriety is hard to account for, unless it is due to the poem's encyclopedic scope (in earlier years the imposing length of their poems had done much to set up Jean de Meun and Matheolus as whited sepulchers), or to the existence of a growing band of defenders influenced by humanism and Reformation alike.[37] In high places

[37] Elyot's *Defence* (**53**), for instance, was printed by Berthelet in 1540 and reprinted in 1545; the same printer brought out Agrippa's *Commendation of Matrimony* in 1534, 1540, and 1545, and Agrippa's *Of the Nobilitie and Excellencie of VVomankynde* (**237**) in 1542. This is a convenient place to list a number of Renaissance treatises on marriage which are peripheral to our subject. A number of them, as will be seen, cluster around the years 1530-40 (the number in parentheses refers to the *STC*):

1. (24320). Bishop Cuthbert Tunstall, *In Laudem Matrimonio oratio,* R. Pynson, 1518.
2. (12799-801). William Harrington, *The comendacions of matrymony,* John Skot, 1528; reprinted by Redman in the same year and by Rastell (n.d.).
3. (24856-63). Vives, *A very frutefull and pleasant boke called the instruction of a christen woman, Turned into Englysshe by R. Hy[r]de.* T. Berthelet, [1529?]. Reprinted in [1540?], 1541, 1547, 1557 (twice), 1585, 1592.
4. (10493). "The Matrimony of Tyndale," proscribed in 1530-32, and perhaps either identical with Tyndale's Exposition on Corinthians 7, or by William Roy. See F. J. Furnivall, *Political, Religious and Love Poems,* London (EETS, XV), 1866, p. 34; Robert Steele, *Transactions of the Bibliographical Society,* XI (1909-1911), 203-215; J. F. Mozley, *William Tyndale,* London, 1937, p. 345.
5. (10508). Erasmus, *A Sermon* [on the Marriage at Cana], R. Wyer, [1532?].
6. (201-202). *The Commendation of Matrimony, made by Cornelius Agrippa, & translated into englishe by David Clapham.* The *STC* lists only the 1540 and 1545 editions of Berthelet; but I have seen a microfilm of British Museum pressmark 8416.a.31, which specifies no printer and is dated 1534.
7. (1723-24). T. Basille [Thomas Becon], *The golden boke of christen matrimonye,* J. Mayler for J. Gough, 1542. Reprinted in 1543. At a cursory glance this appears to be remarkably like the next item.
8. (4045-53). Heinrich Bullinger, *The Christen State of Matrimonye,* tr. Myles

many things were happening to sharpen the perennial taste for
satire: the long succession of Henry's queens, the dissolution of
monastic life, the quarrels over the legitimacy of Mary and Elizabeth, and the Statute of Six Articles (1539), which hampered the
reforming tendency by reaffirming the celibacy of the priesthood
(see **361**). In 1542 Robert Wyer printed *A Dyalogue defensyue
for women* (**323**), by Robert Vaughan or Robert Burdet, which
does not mention the *Scholehouse* by name but has been thought
an answer to it. Apparently in the same year appeared another
defense, Edward Gosynhill's *Mulierum Pean* (**347**), which explicitly names the *Scholehouse* and in turn is named by it. For a
few years, during which (1544) Parliament officially recognized
Mary and Elizabeth as heirs to the throne and (1547) Henry VIII
died, I find no mention of the *Scholehouse*. But about 1550 (?)
there was published *The vertuous scholehous of vngracious women*
(**337**), translated from a work by the German reformer Wolfgang Resch, who seems to have been aware of the model of
Erasmus' *Coniugium* (**189**). The translator's title is probably a
gratuitous allusion to the original *Scholehouse*. About the same
time Charles Bansley also made allusion to the primal tract in
*A Treatyse Shewing and Declaring the Pryde and Abuse of
Women Now A Dayes* (**39**). Some ten years later John Kynge
developed renewed interest in the *querelle;* in 1557–58 he obtained
a license to print both the *Scholehouse* and a new rebuttal, Edward
More's *Defence of Women* (**125**). If extant documents tell the
whole story, he put off until 1560 the publication of this laborious
essay in fourteeners and any other items he may have been col-
lecting. It is conceivable that the age-old controversy had suddenly become dangerous with the issuing of John Knox's *First
Blast of the Trumpet against the monstruous regiment of Women*

Coverdale, n.p., 1541. Reprinted [1543?], 1543, 1546, 1552 (four times), 1575.
9. (18787). Joannes Oecolampadius, *A sarmon to yong men and maidens*, tr. J.
Fox, H. Powell [1548?].
10. (18841). [Anon.], *The Order of Matrimony*, Anthony Skoloker, 1548.
11. (12104). *A fruteful Predication . . . of D. Mart. Luth. concernynge matrimonye*
and *A briefe Exhortacion vnto the maryed couple*, both appearing as appendices
to *The vertuous scholehous of vngracious women* [Walter Lynne? ca. 1550?]
(see **337**).
12. (24855). Vives, *The office and duetie of an husband*, tr. T. Paynell, J. Cawood,
[1553?].

For studies of this kind of reformation treatise see Archer Taylor, *Problems in
German Literary History*, pp. 124-41, 165-72; and William and Malleville Haller, "The
Puritan Art of Love," *Huntington Library Quarterly*, V (1942), 235–72.

(64) at Geneva in 1558, and the accession of Elizabeth to the throne in the same year.[38] If so, with the answer of John Aylmer (84) to Knox in 1559 the danger seems to have passed, and in 1560 Kynge published with identical title-page borders and format three tracts on the subject, *The Scholehouse,* More's *Defence,* and *The Proud Wyues Pater Noster* (240), the last reprinted at least once within the next eight years and relicensed in 1581–82. Undated but apparently belonging to a period very close to 1560 are two other tracts from Kynge's press, *A dialogue bytwene the commune secretary and Jalowsye, Touchynge the unstableness of Harlottes* (342) and a reprint of Gosynhill's *Mulierum Pean.* Kynge's gamble may have inspired the heir of Robert Copland, William Copland, to publish Robert's *Seuen Sorowes* (377) and to reprint *The Deceyte of Women* (52). John Allde testifies to the continued popularity of the original *Scholehouse* by reprinting it in 1572. Thus ended an unusually lengthy episode in the commercialization of the debate.

Meanwhile the controversy in general had attracted the interest of two minor poets who have not been wholly forgotten, George Turbervile and Alexander Scott. In 1567 Turbervile published his translation of Ovid's *Heroides* (280) and his one-man imitation of *Tottel's Miscellany,* called *Epitaphes, Epigrams, Songs and Sonets.* Among the twenty-two poems which he devoted to our subject, the largest number from the hand of any one author, there is nothing to equal the work of those earlier dominant figures, Chaucer and Dunbar. Most of his pieces are short, the reflection of a mood and no considered indictment of the sex. Perhaps only one of them, the *Dispraise of Women, that allure and love not* (356), is a thoroughly generalized satire. Five are epigrams derived ultimately from the Greek Anthology (10, 27, 74, 155, 295) and three are probably original poems in the same vein (149, 330, 331). Turbervile's rebellious lover poems are similar to those in *Tottel's Miscellany;* some have a specious classical apparatus which seems to sever them from the usual medieval exemplar (34, 68, 111, 314, 315), but one casts off his lady in the old metaphor of falconry (344) and others follow the tradition of describing love as Hell (315, 330-331). Turbervile also calls upon the Neo-Latin paradox with regard to the choice of a

[38]Kynge was fined for printing *The Nut-Brown Maid* (36) without license in 1558–59.

wife (162-163). Although he grounds his one really generalized attack on women on his own experience (356), we must on the whole consider him as a poet who seeks an audience rather than expression for an inner agony.

Alexander Scott is almost as indefatigable, with some sixteen poems touching upon the debate. He lacks Turbervile's taste for epigram, and his general tone reveals the conservative medievalism of genre and sentiment prevailing in Scotland. Against his many conventional courtly pieces we may place seven rebellious lover poems (63, 138, 153, 160, 164, 250, 312, 320). In three of them the rebellion develops into an outright renunciation of worldly passion. He offers us also a defense of women and a plea for temperate love (71), a didactic defense warning women against wicked men (152), and a palinodic pair, *Ane Ballet maid to the Derisioun and Scorne of Wantoun Wemen* with its counterpart directed toward sensual men (392, 394). This pair is interesting evidence of the prejudice of the times: women are scourged for a particular vice, lasciviousness, whereas men are merely encouraged abstractly to renounce the vice to which flesh is heir. Like his English contemporary, Scott is a mere patient cultivator of the old modes.

Most of the minor poets who took part in the debate deserve discussion only as entries in the anthologies which housed their work. Such manuscript collections as can be assigned to the first forty years of the century are on the whole courtly. Two harbor the poems of Wyatt: MS. Egerton 2711 with seven satires or defenses and MS. Additional 17492 with eight. MS. Additional 31922, with five contributions, is a compilation of the lighter lyrics which appealed to the court of Henry VIII. Only one of the anthologies of this period, MS. Balliol College 354, is truly popular; it owes its existence to the assiduity of Richard Hill, a merchant of London who during the thirties included among his accounts and personal history a host of poems, some no doubt the result of oral transmission, and many clearly belonging to the fifteenth century. Among the nine satires and defenses which Hill preserved for himself and for posterity are seven or eight carols: a fight for the breeches (5), a poem favoring Holly (87), a lively gossips' song which reminds us of Skelton's *Elynour Rummyng* (107), an ironic defense with destroying burden (136), a parody complaint (168), a debate travestying the Easter prose *Victimae Paschali* in which the misogynist is victor (**180**), a poem in praise and dispraise (**264**), and an amusing lying-song telling us of the Utopia in which women are to be trusted (**351**). In answer Hill has only one clear defense, *The Nut-Brown Maid* (**36**). Whatever its bias, Hill's Commonplace Book is good testimony that antiquarian zeal need not destroy a sense of humor.

This short list exhausts the significant anthologies of the first forty years of the century with one exception, the Chaucerian collection of William Thynne (1532). The easy standards early editors erected for Chaucer's canon are here well displayed, and they have been perhaps too often scourged. The apocryphal pieces which crept into Thynne and Stow and Speght may be in part the result of credulity, but in the days when manuscripts were beginning to be printed the editors may well have been moved merely by a desire to use Chaucer as a convenient peg on which to hang old works which pleased them. Of the sixteen items for us in Thynne nine correctly belong to Chaucer and three to his school: Henryson's *Testament of Cresseid* (**1**), *The Romaunt of the Rose* (**181**), and Clanvowe's *Cuckoo and Nightingale* (**286**). Two are translations: Chartier's *La Belle Dame sans Mercy* (**82**) and Hoccleve's Christine (**49**). One is an excellent *Praise of Women* (**21**), perhaps of Lydgate's time; another, *The Remedy of Love* (**255**), may be contemporary with Thynne himself. All, by virtue of tone, allusion, or influence, have reason to exist in a collection devoted in the main to Chaucer. But when Stow revised Thynne in 1561 he exercised no such care in selection; of his ten additions only one (**175**) has had any success in clinging to the canon. Four are by or ascribed to Lydgate (**142, 307, 387; 166**), and one is an epitome of the *Legend of Good Women* (**247**). They all appear to result from Stow's antiquarian search in Lydgate and Chaucer manuscripts; seven of the ten can be attributed to his use of the fifteenth-century MS. Trinity Cambridge R. 3. 19, which we have already remarked as an anthology valuable for us. Stow was scribe as well as editor; MS. Additional 29729 contains five pieces in his hand—four by Lydgate (**57, 190, 387** twice) and one by Burgh (**269**).

These Chaucerian collections show that a sixteenth-century poet who wrote satire might be a conscious imitator of a still-honored master as well as an unconscious repeater of the tradition.

They also may have stimulated the production of miscellanies by the line of printers which begins with Richard Tottel, in whose celebrated anthology, published in 1557, occur some twenty-one of our poems. No book better shows the intimate relationship between manuscript and early print; the transition, in other words, from John Shirley to Colard Mansion to William Caxton. Tottel has epigrams like that about the new-married student who might have had fame, but who

> In knitting of him selfe so fast,
> Him selfe he hath vndoon (11).

Or the epigrammatic form runs over into the miniature debate, as in the pair of poems in which William Gray's epitaph, attributing his death to his wife's "Spitefull tong," is answered by another urging the double happiness which came when death parted the ill-matched couple (159, 122). The same tendency is manifest elsewhere in *Tottel's*; in Thomas Norton's *Against women either good or badde* and its palinode (6, 298); in a lover's complaint and a lady's rebuke (318, 373); and in the paradoxes for and against wedding exchanged by N. Vincent and G. Blackwood (259, 260). There is a dramatic defense which hearkens back to the medieval forsaken maid's lament (319); a novel defense on the basis of Dame Nature (23); and a sober counsel on the choice of a wife which urges that virtue, not fame or beauty, should turn the scales (285). By far the overwhelming mass of poems to concern us are those of a Rebellious Lover or his close associate, the renouncer of earthly love (47, 61, 99, 196, 228, 294, 318, 338, 390, 396). All of the poems added in the second edition which merit a place in our index are of the same genre (62, 109, 114, 373, 391). *Tottel's Miscellany* is thus as much of a climax to the Middle Ages as it is a prelude to the Renaissance.

The only other printed collection coming within our scope is *A Handful of Pleasant Delights,* preserved complete only in its 1584 revision, but probably first printed in 1566. Its special value is as an *omnium gatherum* of broadsides. In the last years which we are treating our controversy is overwhelmed by the fugitive and grosser realm of Autolycus' pack. *A Handful* is unusual in containing four poems which favor women and only two which oppose them. There is the usual debating pair, a maid's lament and her lover's rebellious answer (316, 108). *A Warning to*

Wooers begins with the devastating "Ye loving wormes come
learne of me" (**393**); a didactic defense hymns the joys of virginity, perhaps ironically (**98**); and another warns women
against wicked men (**397**). Nothing better reveals the hands
into which chivalry has fallen than a fourth defense (**288**) by
one I.P., whose other conjectural claim to fame is a broadside on
"A meruaylous straunge deformed Swyne."

Few of the ephemeral pieces from these early days of broadside writing have survived in their original form; yet even at the
beginning we find the predecessors of Samuel Pepys and Bishop
Percy at work. Two manuscripts, Cotton Vespasian A. 25 (about
1578?) and Ashmole 48 (1557–65?) are invaluable. Except when
the *Stationers' Register* offers confirmation, most of their contents
are hard to date; but I have thought them representative enough
to merit inclusion in the Index. MS. Cotton contains a rhetorical
description of love as folly (**3**), a fight for the breeches which puts
an untimely end to the honeymoon (**45**), two poems asserting
that women will have their will (**218, 289**), an exhortation to
marry your equal (**375**), and a defense arguing that satirists are
crying sour grapes (**379**). MS. Ashmole contributes all of sixteen poems, many of them by John Wallys and Henry Sponare.
As usual there are rebellious lover poems (**15, 128, 241**); there
is Lord Vaux's well-known renunciation, which was also in
Tottel's Miscellany (**99**); there are two *chansons d'aventure,* one
ironically revealing a widow's sorrow (**78**) and the other describing the sufferings of a clownish husband (**200**). A run of the
mill satire derives its authority from Boccaccio and Guido (**134**);
a roundabout satire laments the sad life of a cuckold (**48**); some
figurative obscenity on what women most desire (**132**) and at
least five ironic defenses (**121, 349, 358, 359, 386**; see also **78**)
keep the pot a-boil. Protestantism reveals itself in a lying-song
opposed to the cleric's way with woman's affections (**15**) and in a
pathetic lament for the lapse of woman's virtue since Biblical
times (**234**). Of special interest is a poem which, disgorging a
flood of alliterating adjectives, demands that men try to be as good
as the women they dispraise (**115**).

These manuscripts give a panorama of the genres which
appealed to popular taste in the third quarter of the sixteenth
century. But we should deprive the reader of the pleasures of
Tantalus if we failed to mention a number of entries in the *Sta-*

tioners' Register which correspond to nothing extant. The *Register,* begun in 1557, manages to cover the last ten years of our period, and consoles us somewhat for the destruction of single-sheets and for the complete loss of some 796 ballads stored in a cupboard in Stationers' Hall and never registered.[39] Rollins lists an avalanche of titles[40] we should like to know more about:

(34) *a godly ballett agaynste fornication &c*
(241) *a breffe brygement of maryage and so what Jogges the Wyves geves on the elbowe*
(339) *a commyssion vnto all those whose wyves be thayre masters*
(345) *the Comonycation betwene the husbounde and the wyf and Dyscommodytes of maryage*
(358) *The complaynte of a Wedowe that now Weded ys / with a Warnynge to women to tyke hede of this*
(531) *the Defence agaynste them that commonlye Defame women*
(532) *a Defence of mylke maydes agaynste the terms of Mawken*
(544) *a Dyscription betwene man and Woman*
(934) *the frutes of love and falshod of Women*
(978) *god send me a wyffe that will Do as I saye*
(980) *Godes greate and marvelus thretenynges to Women for thayre offyndyng*
(1027) *a ballet of good wyves*
(1042) *of the greate myschances yat hapened vnto men throwe the Cruelnes of wycked Women*
(1165) *howe women the wytty and Worthy to trane*
(1203-04) *I will have a Wydow yf ever I marye*
(1206) *I will say as I do fynde my wyfe to me ys nothynge kynde*
(1208) *I wysshe all bachelars well to ffayre*
(1212) *yf a Weked Wyfe may have hyr Will*
(1216) *yf lovers lenger at the Worste*
(1222) *the Image of evell Women*
(1258) *intreatinge of the stadfastnes of Women*
(1465) *ye lamentinge of a yonge mayde who by grace ys fully stayde*
(1552) *Love*
(1656) *of a man that wold be vnmaryed agayne*
(1662) *mannors for matrons*
(1820) *Mother damnables ordinary*[41]
(1854) *my wyfe she wyll do all she can take mastrye as better hande*
(2096) *the plague Jolasy with examples to avoyde the same*
(2165) *the prayse of the vayne beauty of women*
(2228) *quene Sabbe and kynge Salomon*

[39] Hyder E. Rollins, *MLN,* XXXIV (1919), 350.
[40] The numbers preceding each title refer to entries in his *An Analytical Index to the Ballad-Entries in the Registers of the Company of Stationers,* printed as part of *Studies in Phililogy,* XXI (1924), 1-324.
[41] Licensed in 1656. The others are all dated before 1568, but it was felt that the modern reader would not wish to overlook such a prototype to *The Shanghai Gesture.*

(2275) *Reporte of the Wyttye answeres of a beloved mayden*
(2291) *the Rewardes of vngodly Lovers*
(2595) *a ballett of the talke betwene ij maydes*
(2624) *thoughe fondly men wryte thayre myndes Women be of gentle kynde*
(2645) *to all vnchaste maydes and Wyves*
(2874) *a Warnyng for Wydowes that aged be / how lusty yonge yough and age can agre*
(2883) *a Warnynge to all maydes that Brewes thayre owne bane*
(2884) *a Warnynge | to | all Wanton Wyves to fle from follye | the | lenghte of thayre lyves*
(2926) *Wherby women may beware*
(3055) *you [v]vyves to your husboundes be tru and leve Well*
(3074) *a yonge womans skyll / and how she became mistress and Ruled at hyr Wyll.*

This worthy successor to Pantagruel's Library of St. Victor is wholesale evidence of the survival of medieval genres. One scholar who felt the fascination of these textless titles too strongly was John Payne Collier, whose ballad manuscript, unfortunately seen by no eye but his own, contained six compositions which I have been unable to suppress from the Index (**59, 73, 89, 119, 311, 382**; compare Rollins 820, 936, 117, 1214–15, 1042, 3006–3007).[41a] It seems almost a shame that posterity has had better luck than Collier in finding authentic candidates to fit some of these *Register* entries (see **382, 119, 73, 59**). A few other unidentified titles in the *Register,* not named as ballads, should not be ignored:

> [A] *compendious abstracte contayninge a mooste Delectable conference betwene the wedded lyf and the syngle by master Henry Hake* (Arber, I, 330—see **156**); *An hundreth poyntes of evell huswyfrye* (I, 294—see **70**); *To ye prayse of good women ye [xxxj] chapeter of ye Proverbis* (I, 378—compare, **283, 388**); *The husbande to his wyfe* (I, 95); *The Dyscryption of the howse of an harlott* (I, 213); *The xx orders of Callettes or Drabbys* (I, 208).[42]

If broadside writing existed north of the Tweed we have little record of it. But the poetry of the time, high and low, popular and aristocratic, has been preserved to us largely through the efforts of two collectors, George Bannatyne and Sir Richard Maitland. The latter's great contribution to our index is the

---

[41a] The information that Collier's "ballad manuscript" is apparently in the Folger Shakespeare Library came too late to my attention to be of use. It is discussed, still with doubt and reservation, by Giles E. Dawson, in *English Institute Annual: 1942,* New York, 1943, pp. 90–96.
[42] Although the last item is listed as if it were extant by Routh in *CHEL,* III, 97, I have been unable to identify it.

so-called *Maitland Folio* (MS. Pepys 2553, preserved at Magdalene College, Cambridge), which was compiled in the main of earlier pieces during the years 1570–85,[43] and which records twenty-one of our entries. Of these, nine are by or ascribed to Dunbar, one by Alexander Scott, and two by Kennedy. The rest consist of a lively satire on old January's love, unquestionably modeled on Chaucer (24); two satires on fashions, one by Maitland himself (233, 268); the tale of the Man Who Married a Dumb Wife (352); a young wife's complaint about her old husband, by Clapperton (135); a husband's lament over his shrewish wife which aptly follows the last (333); an *Advice to Gallandis* against sensual lust, by Balnevis (222); a punctuation poem of English origin which ends as an ironic defense (22); and an attack on the corruption of the law courts through wanton high-born dames (297). Maitland's variety and comprehensiveness bring great credit to Scotland for permitting medieval letters to flower so late, a phenomenon which owes much to the constant stimulus from France, which during this period was at once more conservative and more humane than England.

But Maitland's many satires and defenses are few compared to what we find in that neglected anthology completed "in tyme of pest" by George Bannatyne (MS. Advocates' Library I. I. 6). It has been remarked that Caxton

> printed what suited his serious courtly clientèle, but not the lyric and dramatic masterpieces of his own time. He did not necessarily despise them; he left them where they belonged, in the taverns, at the crossroads, in ladies' bowers and in the church-yards. This habit of mind persists into the nineteenth century, and we have only hints of what it has lost us.[44]

It is precisely because Bannatyne was a true antiquary, the very reverse of Caxton, that he has helped us so much. He was one of the wiser antiquaries who preserves the work of his own time along with that of the past; Allan Ramsay, long recognized as a pioneer of eighteenth-century collectors, would not have been the editor he was if he had not had access to Bannatyne. I have gone so far as to consider this manuscript the culmination of my study, since its more than eighty medieval and early renaissance

[43] The *Maitland Quarto* (MS. Pepys 1408) has only three of our pieces. The Reidpeth MS. (Cambridge University Library Ll. 5.10) contains eight satires and defenses, but most of them are from the *Folio*.

[44] W. L. Renwick and Harold Orton, *The Beginnings of English Literature to Skelton*, London, 1939, p. 29.

contributions to the *querelle* sum up the debate and in a sense embalm it.

That Bannatyne was an editor as well as a scribe is evidenced by his organization of the manuscript into books. Our pieces are listed under ballads of wisdom and morality, under merry ballads, and under ballads of love—the last divided into orthodox songs of love, ballads of love's remedy and against evil women, ballads praising women and against evil men, and ballads renouncing blinded love. Besides the work of Dunbar, Scott, Kennedy, Mersar, Balnevis, and Henryson already discussed, new names appear: Sempill (perhaps the author of *The Gude and Godly Balletis*) with three poems on the harlots of Edinburgh (96, 231, 246); Fleming with an obscurely mixed satire (37); Stewart with a rebellious lover poem and a defense (302, 67a); Sir John Moffet's warning against love (41); Montgomery's three rebellious lover poems (146, 362, 376); Allanis Subdert's attack on adulterating ale-wives (368); and Weddirburne's four poems—a general satire, two attacks on false men, and a renunciation of love (205, 101, 110, 224). There are many anonymous rebellions and "contemptis of Blyndit luve" (see Index III). At least seven poems are attributed to Chaucer, all without foundation, though Bannatyne can share the responsibility with William Thynne, whose edition he probably had seen (21, 49, 54, 118, 229, 306, 345). Of the many short "epigrams" a good number are excerpts from longer poems (100, 118, 173, 207, 242, 267, 284, 310). Bannatyne was especially fond of lying-songs or "ballatis of vnpossibiliteis" which ridiculed woman's lack of faith (69, 116, 353, 354, 357). An obscene lament of a forsaken maiden is discreetly attributed to "ane Inglisman" (43). Four songs on wanton ladies are based on elaborate double talk: one uses the terms of music (209), another those of colors (231), and two are nautical in their analogies (96, 216).

With this brief catalogue of our terminal anthology specific remarks on the history of Scots and English satire must end, for with Bannatyne's collection the book of Chaucer's Jankin is brought to its most significant revision.[45] Our history on the whole has dealt with literary externals: matters of continental influence; outstanding figures like Chaucer, Lydgate, Dunbar,

---

[45] For the later Elizabethan and Jacobean representatives of the controversy see Wright, *Middle-Class Culture*, pp. 473-507; *CBEL*, I, 716; and Joachim Heinrich, *Die Frauenfrage bei Steele und Addison*, Leipzig (Palaestra, CLXVIII), 1930.

Turbervile, and Scott; set *querelles* like those of Christine and the *Scholehouse of Women;* and the contribution made by scribes and printers to our corpus. The full analysis of woman's place in the history of ideas and of social forces demands further documentation than that provided here, and shall be reserved for a more propitious time. But some appraisal of the special renaissance contribution to the controversy seems desirable.

In spite of all we have said about the survival of medieval currents in the sixteenth century (and to the present day) the Renaissance has something new to offer. It is not merely a numerical increase in the words devoted to woman's praise, for the period has lost in large part the essence of the courtly tradition which fostered medieval defense. It is not merely the abandoning of the ascetic ideal, for Puritanism can be as devastating about "carnality" as any monastic order. It is not merely the substitution of a monogamous ideal for the warring codes of courtly adultery and churchly celibacy; for medieval clerics, practical confessors, and wise doctors of the church were perfectly aware of these twin perils to the world's future. It is all these things and more: by the end of the sixteenth century the sexual pattern has arrived at a balance which is essentially "modern," no matter how details might displease social reformers like Mill, Ellis, and Russell.

Humanism, in short, had much to offer to the emancipation of women, as much as or more than that attributed to the very different reforms of early Christianity. We have already witnessed how the great names connected with the history of human enlightenment take part in our controversy: Jean de Meun, Chaucer, Pierre and Gontier Col, Jean de Montreuil, Vives, Erasmus, More, and Rabelais. So long as we continually remind ourselves that a movement such as this does not develop *ex nihilo,* we may credit the sixteenth century with originating four factors which aided in the breakdown of older theories about woman's inferiority: a great stress on individualism, the beginnings of relativism in morals and in the assessment of character, a revolution in the ideals of woman's education, and a confirmation of the monogamous ideal which was to preserve it even after marriage lost its position as a sacrament of the Church.

Of individualism—the Man and Woman of the Renaissance— we need say little; everyone will recognize how men's inner

contemplation was turning from thoughts of heaven to thoughts
of themselves, and how, despite self-consciousness and melancholy, they were on the whole not too displeased with what they
saw. Nowhere is this more apparent than in the English substitution of the worship of the Virgin Queen for that of the
Virgin Mother—exaltation of a living genius with all her faults
for the older symbol of divine perfection.[46] A great institution,
the medieval Church, was losing its worldly catholicity; and a
woman was supreme in England over what remained. Only in
this century, when absolute monarchies were developing, when
the divine right of kings was being urged as an alternative to
the City of God, could the controversy over woman's fitness to
rule, which we associate with the names of Knox and Montaigne,
have taken on such universal significance. Elizabeth is as much
a symbol as her heavenly predecessor; Machiavelli's Prince never
lived, but many a prince tried to live in accordance with the
symbol. The courtly lady, *la belle dame sans merci* who dominated the groveling lover,[47] gave way to half-real and half-
symbolic women like Victoria Colonna, Jane Colte and her
daughter Margaret More, Marie de Gournay (adopted daughter
of Montaigne), Marguerite de Navarre, Catherine de Medici,
Mary Herbert (Countess of Pembroke), and Elizabeth herself—
some of them noblewomen and some commoners, but all learned
and all emancipated, and all with a very different place in the
scheme of things than that of Eleanor of Aquitaine. These
women are important in the history of civilization, and an age
which could produce their myth and their reality was bound to
have some effect on the attitudes of men toward their sex.

But as real people became heroes and heroines, as tragedy
was transformed from a fall from high place to a testimony to
the dignity of the human spirit with all its flaws and all its blind
spots, the old rigid notions of good and evil were of necessity
altered, and it was no longer possible for men of great or even
of little genius to separate women and men into goatland and
sheepfold. Even the Middle Ages had been doubtful just where
to place Helen of Troy; Chaucer's conversion of Cleopatra
to a good woman and Christine's citation of Xanthippe as a

[46] In many cases the symbolic transformation was quite conscious. See Elkin C.
Wilson, *England's Eliza*, Cambridge, Mass., 1939, pp. 166-229.
[47] Lord Henry Howard's defense of woman rulers against Knox is an interesting
attempt to re-employ the old terms of chivalry for this novel purpose (see **64**).

noble dame demonstrate the difficulties experienced even then. Throughout the Renaissance the old catalogues of good and evil women continue, but there seems to be a growing embarrassment in their use (see **6, 298**)—realization, in short, that an argument which may be used so glibly on both sides of the question may also be of little worth to either. Defense becomes a matter not of citation, but of appeal to nature and reason and toleration and truth and real virtue, fallible but humanely satisfying. And so it becomes harder and harder for serious satirists to maintain their position: the woods are full of apologies, qualifications, paradoxes, and of such self-conscious artifices as Pyrrye's *The Praise and Dispraise of Women* (**94, 113, 210**). Andreas, Chrétien, Chaucer, even Dunbar, could write satire and palinode without blushing, but Pyrrye could not. It is not only because he is a lesser figure; the temper of the times has converted his attempted impartiality into absurd contradiction. And so the medieval genres of satire and defense begin to blur around the edges. In spite of Swetnam the Woman-Hater, Stephen Gosson, Thomas Heywood, and a mass of pamphleteers who keep the controversy alive in the next fifty years, we may justly say that the true heirs to the masters who had participated in it during the Middle Ages are not these formal satirists and defenders, but rather such universal minds as Spenser and Shakespeare, who combine discordant elements into one poem like the *Faerie Queene* or into characters like Beatrice, Ophelia, and Katherine.

Once the capacities of women for action good or evil were recognized, the opportunity for their education had to be widened.[48] This phenomenon is not merely one of feminism, of course; the Renaissance was a time of novel educational theory for men as well. Nor must we say that the high-born lady of the Middle Ages had been deprived of learning; it may well be that she had a better opportunity for it than her hunting and warring brother.[49] Too many treatises devoted to the instruction of women exist during that period to permit us to assume that women could not read.[50] But, except for the late figure of Chris-

[48] For general treatments of this subject see Foster Watson, *Vives and the Renascence Education of Women*, New York, 1912; and Mary A. Cannon, *The Education of Women during the Renaissance*, Washington, D. C., 1916.

[49] See, for instance, Dow, *Varying Attitude toward Women*, pp. 96–98.

[50] See the 114 titles listed from several European languages by Alice A. Hentsch, *De la Littérature Didactique du Moyen Age s'Adressant Spécialement aux Femmes*, Cahors, 1903.

tine de Pisan, the Middle Ages had no bluestockings to compare
with the many-tongued Elizabeth, with Lady Jane Grey, Mary
Tudor, Marguerite of Navarre, Marie de Gournay, or those
précieuses whom Molière was to ridicule. In the persons of Vives,
Erasmus, Elyot, and More, humanism recognized as Plato had
done that our feminine guardians need education as well as men
do. For, in every age when horizons expand, women share the
hunger for widening knowledge and succeed in obtaining some
part in the new movements sweeping the world. That men
satirize them more in these times than others is merely a sign
of uneasiness.

The final element in the renaissance re-evaluation of woman's
position is the strengthening of the monogamous ideal, a compromise which many reformers today feel has not gone far
enough, but which seemed complete enough to the sixteenth
century, and which with its unfriendliness to celibacy succeeded
in placing a higher value on the sex without which the world
could not be served. No longer, we feel, can the older compromise of St. Jerome, which classified heavenly merits as accruing
thirty-fold to chaste marriage, sixty-fold to chaste widowhood,
and a hundred-fold to untainted virginity, appeal to even a few
minds.[51] The rare sixteenth-century praise of virginity embodies
a continual qualification, revealed most clearly in the very crudity
of the following lines:

> It is allowed as you may reade,
> And eke auowed by *Paul* indeede,
>   *Virginitie* is accepted,
>   a thing high in Gods sight:
> Though marriage is selected,
>   a thing to be most right:
>   yet must I praise *Virginitie*,
>   For I would faine a Virgin be (**98**).

Most similar panegyrics in this period are mere counsels to
beware of seducers, lest a maid's value be diminished not in
heaven but in earthly marriage (see **144** and **300**).

The *Franklin's Tale* is often called the first attempt to idealize
marriage by merging the usually adulterous courtly code with
the laws of Church and State. But Chaucer was not alone: he

[51] For the idea see Lea, *History of Sacerdotal Celibacy*, I, 37–38, and Cockayne,
ed., *Hali Meidenhad*, p. 32. The complexity of the problem is shown by the Wycliffean
Of Weddid Men and Wifis, which repeats the traditional view that chastity is the
highest state and at the same time urges that priests be permitted to marry (Thomas
Arnold, ed., *Select English Works of John Wyclif*, Oxford, 1869-71. III. 189-91).

was joined by Gower, who believed that marriage was not incompatible with love, and that the true end of courtship was wedding.[52] Before them Jean de Meun had put depth into the courtly vilification of the *Jaloux* by demanding equality in marriage:

> Compainz, cist fos vilains jalous,
> Don la char seit livree a lous,
> Qui si de jalousie s'emple,
> Con ci vous ai mis en essemple,
> *Ese fait seigneur de sa fame,*
> *Qui ne redeit pas estre dame,*
> *Mais sa pareille e sa compaigne,*
> *Si con la lei les acompaigne,*
> *E il redeit ses compainz estre,*
> *Sens sei faire seigneur ne maistre.*

This is admittedly an ideal, he continues, for nowadays the lover vows servitude to his mistress and turns the table on her when marriage ensues. It is no longer as it was in the Golden Age.[53] Thus even Jean, Wikked Tunge himself, wishes to reconcile Court and Church. In the heyday of the ideal of *cortoisie* its exponent, the Nightingale, refuses to accept the adulterous pattern. He rebukes the Owl:

> þu liest iwis, þu fule þing!
> þ[urh] me nas neauer ischend spusing.
> Ah soþ hit is ich singe & grede
> þar lauedies beoþ & faire maide;
> & soþ hit is of luue ich singe:
> for god wif mai i[n] spusing
> bet luuien hire oʒene were,
> þane awe[r] hire copenere;
> an maide mai luue cheose
> þat hire wurþschipe ne forleose.[54]

Since Usk, the Knight of La Tour-Landry, and Dunbar all utter similar sentiments,[55] we must not apply too widely the peculiar

---

[52] See Quixley's translation of Gower's *Traitié pour essampler les amants marietz*, ed. H. N. MacCracken, *Yorkshire Archeological Journal*, XX (1908-1909), 33-50; *Confessio Amantis*, v, 6145-6492; vii, 4215-5438; W. G. Dodd, *Courtly Love in Chaucer and Gower*, Boston, Mass., 1913, pp. 83, 89-90. Donnel van de Voort, *Love and Marriage in the English Medieval Romance*, Nashville, Tenn., 1938, argues that the adulterous tradition was absent from the usual English romance, *Troilus* is an exception, and thus Chaucer gives artistic expression to both sides of the question.

[53] *Roman de la Rose*, 9421-9500 (ed. Langlois, III, 121-24).

[54] *The Owl and the Nightingale*, 1335-44 (ed. J. W. H. Atkins, Cambridge, 1922, pp. 112, 114).

[55] Usk's *Testament of Love*, ed. Skeat, *Chaucer*, VII, 40-41; *The Book of the Knight of La Tour-Landry*, ed. Thomas Wright, London (EETS, XXXIII), 1868, pp. 179–81; "Sen that I am a Presoneir," *Poems of William Dunbar*, ed. Small, II, 164–67.

conditions of Provence or Aquitaine. Courtly praise of adultery
did exist, and the poets of Medieval Latin, Provençal, and Old
French, like those of any age, hymned the joys of sense; but
again as always there was a restraining attitude provided by sober
thought and external law.

The praisers of modernity too often assert that adulterous
love was a sort of compromise by which the Church avoided the
responsibilities arising from forced and loveless marriages. We
will not say that there were no medieval men who took that
view, but in the serious clerical writing that preceded the Renaissance the ideal of partnership in marriage was more conventional
than not. Robert Mannyng of Brunne and others are violently
opposed to forced marriages.[56] The husband was nominally head
of the household (one person is usually the head in any household), but the statement of principle was generally accompanied
by a counsel for leniency which may force us to repudiate the
common caricature of the medieval wife-beater. The qualification is as old as St. Paul, whose "Wives, submit yourselves unto
your own husbands, as unto the Lord" is balanced by "Husbands,
love your wives, even as Christ also loved the church, and gave
himself for it . . . He that loveth his wife loveth himself."[57] It
is found in the *Ancren Riwle:*

> Hwonne a mon haueð neoweliche wif iled him, he nimeð ȝeme all softe-
> liche of hire maneres. Þauh he iseo bi hire ei þing þet him mispaie, he
> let þe ȝet iwurðen, & makeð hire ueire cheres, & is vmbe eueriches
> weis þet heo him luuie inwardliche in hire heorte: and hwon he
> understond wel þet te luue is treouliche iuestned touward him: þeonne
> mei he, sikerliche, chasten hire openliche of hire unðeawes, þet he er
> uorber ase he ham nout nuste: makeð him swuðe sterne, & went to
> þene grimme toð uorte uonden ȝete ȝif he muhte hire luue touward
> him unuesten. A last, hwon he understont þet heo is al wel ituht,—
> þet for none þinge þet he deð hire, heo ne luueð hine neuer þe lesse,
> auh more & more, ȝif heo mei, urom deie to deie: þeonne scheaweð
> he hire þet he hire luueð sweteliche, & deð al þet heo wule, ase þeo
> þet he luueð & iknoweð,—þeone is al þet wo iwurðen to wunne.[58]

Modern feminists will be disconcerted by portions of this picture
of ideal marriage, just as they are by the tale of Griselda or
Chrétien's *Erec and Enid;* but we must admit that we have here

---

Handlyng Synne (EETS, CXXIII), pp. 345–47; see also Lydgate's *Temple of Glas,*
ed. J. Schick (EETSES, LX), pp. 8–9; G. R. Owst, *Literature and Pulpit in Medieval
England,* Cambridge, 1933, pp. 381-82.
Eph. 5:22-28.
Ed. James Morton, London (Camden Society, LVII), 1853, p. 218.

an attitude with its share of common sense, far from the courtly and satirical opinion that all marriages are likely to turn out badly. Even today some moralists may agree that domestic love needs breaking in, whatever the initial passion or whoever may be the dominant figure in the relationship.

In both sober treatise and in literature, therefore, the Renaissance had the ground prepared for it. Such a generalization as the following goes too far:

> Domestic happiness was not a subject which attracted the attention of the literary or scholastic class in Chaucer's time. Philosophers did not reason about it; poets did not sing it; priestly writers sneered at the life which nourished it as distinctly inferior to celibacy.[59]

It is true, however, that there was a progressive attention to the praise of marriage as the aristocratic element in literature declined. Lewis shows us such an evolution in Lydgate, the *Kingis Quair* (the first real allegory of marriage in England), Neville, and Hawes.[60] And Gower and Chaucer certainly helped to make marriage respectable material for *belles lettres*.

What really happens in the Renaissance is not the creation of a new ideal, but the pouring of old wine into new bottles. In the Middle Ages, after the polemic *De Matrimonios* of the early Fathers are over, we are likely to find serious (as distinct from satirical) treatments of marriage imbedded in encyclopedic works which treat marriage in its place as one of many elements in the framework of society. But in the sixteenth century the world was out of kilter, and reformers concentrated on one thing at a time. Instead of a *Summa* or a *Speculum Morale* we have a host of separate treatises on marriage, on woman's education, or on whether priests should marry. This application of a magnifying glass to one problem at a time naturally shed new light on certain subjects. Because there was a spirit of inquiry in the air we may too readily conclude that the attitudes of modern feminism have been reached. When Martin le Franc attacks husbands for adultery and claims that he who suffers from infidelity deserves to pay his wife back in the same coin, he is scarcely advocating a single standard of morality. Martin is by no means urging either the codes of Greenwich Village or those of Victorian chastity; he merely reveals his heritage of Gallic wit and of

---

[59] T. R. Lounsbury, *Studies in Chaucer*, London, 1892, I, 115.
[60] *Allegory of Love*, pp. 237, 255.

courtly love.[61] And in the same way the Puritans invented nothing new; they adapted the old ideal of virginity to continence in marriage, and their violent insistence on sexual regularity recalls the heretics of old time who departed from the universalizing morality of the Church by concentrating on a segment of human experience. "Immorality" comes to mean sexual immorality, since, to oversimplify a bit, it can no longer mean usury. A better balance is found in Spenser, "the man who saved us from the catastrophe of too thorough a renaissance," whose Garden of Adonis is the abode of the romantic marriage of Britomart and Artegall, enemies alike to monkish asceticism and courtly immorality.[62] Spenser is both behind his time and ahead of it; his literary encyclopedia combines Protestant reform, the chaster kind of humanism (Vives rather than Rabelais), the medieval tribute to marriage, and the romanticism of Malory. The blend is new but the ingredients are old enough. Thus in one of its rarer spirits the Renaissance did bring marriage into greater honor, because it brought it out of rivalry with celibacy. Whatever the jesting Chaucer might say to cloud the issue, we can estimate the distance which has been traveled by contrasting the central ideals of Dante and of Spenser.

With all this ferment of individualism, of educational reform, of moral relativity, and of the exaltation of marriage, how could the Spensers and the Shakespeares any longer hold to the old false dichotomy between Eve and Mary? Only the hacks like Gosynhill and Pyrrye could stomach it any longer. The very flood of satires and defenses in the last twenty years before our story ends is evidence that what was once a jest for cleric, courtier, and sophisticate has descended to the less literate masses, in the same fashion that courtly romance has become a chapbook and the *chanson d'aventure* a nursery rime. The quantity of renaissance controversy on our subject does not argue rejuvenation; it means merely that the better poets have moved on to a realm which incorporates the old jest into a larger whole, and leaves the serious aspects of the woman question to the specialist. That is why we may feel that we have completed the task we have set ourselves, no matter how many survivals we could list from that time to our own.

[61] See Richardson, *Forerunners of Feminism*, p. 41. Nor is the doctrine new in Robert Vaughan, as Wright, *Middle-Class Culture*, p. 468, suggests.
[62] Lewis, *Allegory of Love*, pp. 297-360.

ANALYTICAL INDEX

ANALYTICAL INDEX

AN ANALYTICAL INDEX TO POEMS AND PROSE WORKS IN ENGLISH AND SCOTS WHICH RELATE TO THE ARGUMENT ABOUT WOMEN AND WHICH WERE COMPOSED BEFORE THE END OF THE YEAR 1568

The three numbered indexes list poems and prose works written during the Middle Ages and Early Renaissance whose major subject matter is the eternal *querelle des femmes,* or which, despite the intrusion of other matters, have played a major part in that *querelle.* The total corpus of satirical charge and counter-charge is extensive, and awaits further analysis; but the first step in clearing up the bibliography of the subject is to classify the works formally and specifically concerned with the problem of woman's worth, and to record as compactly as possible the evidence about such matters as date, authorship, source, textual authority, genre, and literary intention. Occasionally I have departed from the basic principle of including works primarily devoted to the argument about women. No one will, I believe, question the inclusion of such major contributions to the *querelle* as the *Romaunt of the Rose* and Chaucer's Marriage Group, which a literal application of the basic rule might exclude. A few other departures will be explained under their respective entries.

INDEX I

Index I attempts to list all of the satires, defenses, and debates concerning women to the end of 1568 under first lines in the case of poems, and titles in the case of prose. The plan of the individual entry as as follows:

1. **First line** (or title if prose)
2. Author where known; problems of authorship
3. *Title* and alternative *titles*
4. Burden or other specious first lines
5. Authorities (MSS. and early editions); modern editions
6. Date
7. Classification, summary, discussion of sources and parallels.

1. *First line (or title).*—Verse first lines, which provide the basic entry, are in boldface type, and each is numbered. Since

it is impossible to obtain a prose first line (an *Incipit* would be confusing), I have placed the most common title in bold face and followed it with the bracketed word "prose." Alphabetical order is determined by the modern spelling. *Masteres,* for instance, will be found entered as *Mistress,* and *Quhan* as *When*; where this practice might lead to confusion I have used a cross reference. In first-line entries initial *A, An,* or *The,* being integral parts of the line which do not vanish in modern citation, have been preserved. In title entries I follow the common practice of beginning with the first word following these articles or their French equivalents. First lines and titles have been quoted from the best modern edition where one exists; in case of important variants a cross reference has been provided. Acephalous poems have been entered under the first extant line unless a true first line exists in another authority; in this case cross reference is made for the line which begins the beheaded version. When, with a few poems which I have not seen, I am uncertain of the exact first line or title, I have entered what I have within square brackets. Such brackets surround the whole entry in the case of six poems from Collier's *Extracts,* where no convincing MS. authority has been identified and there exists a suspicion that the poem is a fabrication of the nineteenth-century editor.

2. *Author and problems of ascription.*—Since the larger number of pieces are anonymous, item two is frequently omitted. Where the author is known his name is briefly indicated. Where some argument exists about his identity the facts are briefly presented. At times (as in **292**) the question of authorship is a crucial matter for us and I have been able to offer new and significant data; in such cases space has been no consideration. More often we may dismiss problems of ascription with allusion to the works of such editors as have made special study of the canon. On the whole I have attempted to exclude farfetched conjecture and, while presenting important suggestions, have ignored such shadowy figures as Huchown of the Awle Ryale and a certain Francis Bacon. On the other hand, the recording of an ascription without MS. authority should not be taken to mean that the compiler would defend it.

3. *Title.*—The titles of prose works supply the basic entry. Alternative titles, or titles of poems, have been collected as item three. In many cases the title is the product of a modern editor.

Expansion of references elsewhere in the entry will make it possible to ascertain the authority for the title when that problem concerns the reader.

4. *Burden, salutation, verse title, and the like.*—A special problem exists with carols and a few other poems, when the true first line does not begin the piece in MSS. or modern editions. Here the entry has been made under true first line, and the burden, verse title, or salutation has been entered as a cross reference and included also as item four.

5. *Authorities.*—Many, but not all, of the MSS. have been consulted. In a few cases there is confusion on the part of editors, and I have done my best to present the obtainable evidence. Some of these problems will no doubt be further elucidated after the war by firsthand consultation of such authorities as I have been unable to see. A detailed list of MSS. and early editions will make it easy to ascertain the relative popularity of a piece in its own time. In the case of a few books often reprinted, such as the editions of Chaucer, the reference to one or two early printed authorities has been deemed sufficient. But where, as in the case of Skelton's poems, modern textual work is sorely needed, the early editions have been listed in greater detail. When one or more recent editions exists, a reference to the best has been a desideratum, and the authorities on which the modern text is based have been specified wherever possible. Since my major purpose has been to enable the user of the Index to obtain a good text of the piece under discussion, I make no claim to completeness with regard to modern editions. I have consciously refrained from duplicating standard bibliographies like Wells' *Manual* or Hammond's *Chaucer*.

6. *Date.*—Problems of dating, like those of authorship, have been conservatively treated. Often it is impossible to suggest more than the upward limit provided by the approximate date of the earliest authority in which the piece appears. Occasionally the efforts of an editor to fit a poem into his scheme of the author's development and chronology have been recorded; but it has been recognized that the only certainty will be found in the vital statistics of the author, which themselves are not always securely fixed. When an undoubted allusion exists I have acknowledged its evidence for date; but I have attempted to avoid stretching this method beyond the breaking point. As with authorship, I

have rested in the main upon prior work; but usually the evidence has been reviewed, and pieces which occupy a special importance in the tradition have been treated with some detail. Obvious bibliographical evidence, such as that of device or title-page border, has been called upon; but the more complex problems of type font and script have been relegated to the expert. It is hoped that a presentation of the evidence may in many cases lead to further work on the subject.

7. *Classification, summary, discussion of sources and parallels.* —I have usually classified a piece under the special rhetorical, poetic, or subject type to which it belongs, but where the genre is obscured through the author's originality or through his ineptness, I have tried to avoid vicious pigeonholing. At times a summary is necessary for the purpose of revealing tone, unusual or typical content, and matters of historical importance. At other times the briefest remarks suffice to reveal the nature of an undistinguished poem. At still others, when treating, for instance, the members of Chaucer's Marriage Group, extended summary would be a work of supererogation. The mention of major sources and analogues has been restricted to poems deprived of significant treatment elsewhere; once more Chaucer has been slighted as a tribute to his greatness. But it has always been felt a special duty and a bibliographical economy to make cross reference to other entries in the Index.

INDEX II

Index II, which lists titles of poems and alternative titles of prose, is, like the Index of Authorities (III), a mere appendage to the first index. An Index of Authors, Scribes, and Printers has been incorporated along with other proper names into the General Index at the end of the book, which serves the introductory essay and Index I as well. Titles or authorities mentioned in Indexes II and III are not repeated in the General Index. In Index II I have often sought to avoid confusion by alphabetizing the title under more than one key word; I have ignored French or English articles as in Index I. At times a significant word rather than the conventional and meaningless *Ballad* or *Treatise* is the basis of the entry; a cross reference will prevent the entry from being overlooked.

INDEX III

Index III, which lists the authorities, is provided as an aid to cataloguers or to others working at firsthand with MSS. or early editions. A glance should tell whether the compiler has included a promising satire, defense, or debate from the authority being examined. I shall be grateful if omissions are called to my attention. Index III also offers graphic evidence of the collections which contain more than their share of pieces relating to the *querelle*. For the Bannatyne MS. I have followed the order of the scribal editor, and arranged references under his own interesting classifications. The fact that George Bannatyne felt a poem to be a "Ballat of the remedy of luve" or a "Ballat of the reproche of fals vicius men And prayiss of guid wemen" is of considerable historical value in our study of genre. Printed books have been arranged under their number in the *Short Title Catalogue* for several reasons. In the first place, I have wished to abstain from elaborate repetition of a bibliographical description of the title page. Such brief titles as are supplied are for the convenience of the reader, and make no claim to bibliographical precision. In the second place, major American libraries will in the next ten years be provided with a complete set of microfilm in accordance with the Edwards Brothers' project of books printed before 1600, and the key to classification will be the *STC* number. Finally, although an arrangement of books under localities would be convenient, it would either demand extensive verification or be a mere duplication of the *STC,* which can be easily consulted. Several MSS. or editions which I have been unable to identify are placed separately; I should be grateful for further information on any of them.

A, a, a, a, yet I loue wherso I go (130).

1. Ane doolie sessoun to ane cairfull dyte.
> By Robert Henryson.
> *The Testament of Cresseid.*
> (1) [Lost from MS. Asloan].
> (2) St. John's College Cambridge L. 1.
> (3) Edinburgh, University, MS. Ruthven (stanzas 1-3 only).
>   Apparently neither of the MSS. has been edited in recent
>   times.
> (4) Thynne (1532) and later editions of Chaucer (616 lines,
>   in rime-royal and nine-line stanzas); reproduced in Skeat's
>   *Facsimile*, p. 457.
> (5) Henry Charteris (1593) (first separate printing); ed. G.
>   Gregory Smith, *The Poems of Robert Henryson*, Edin-
>   burgh, (STS, LV, LVIII, LXIV), 1906-1914, III, 3; ed. with
>   collations from (2) W. M. Metcalfe, *The Poems of Robert
>   Henryson*, Paisley, 1917, p. 143. Often reprinted (in early
>   editions as sixth book of Chaucer's *Troilus and Criseyde*);
>   for extensive bibliography see Hammond, *Chaucer*, p. 457;
>   Smith, I, xlv; Brown and Robbins, *Index*, no. 285.

Late XV cent. Skeat, *Chaucer Canon*, p. 106, says about 1460.

Narrative warning to women against inconstancy; a moralizing
sequel to *Troilus and Criseyde*. The Scots appear to have had a fondness
for making a lesson of a fictional heroine; see Gavin Douglas' treatment
of Dido in **381.**

2. A harlatt. a hunter and a hore [prose].
> (1) Rawlinson C. 813. I have transcribed it for publication.

MS. time of Henry VIII; according to Bolle, *Anglia*, XXXIV
(1911), 274, most of the contents late XV cent.

Satire on woman's lasciviousness. A comic definition.

3. A horsse chuying on the brydle.
> *A Ballyt* (called by Böddeker "Thorheit der Liebe").
> (1) Cotton Vespasian A. 25 (5 ten-line stanzas); ed. Böddeker,
>   *JbREL.* XIV (1874), 218.

MS. dated by Böddeker 1578, but some poems have been identified with earlier broadsides. Rollins, *Analytical Index,* suggests this may be the ballad "loue" licensed 1562-63 to Thomas Colwell.

Highly rhetorical and antagonistic description of love as folly. Contrast with **170** and **171.** For what must have been a rather celebrated comparison of a horse and a lover see John Heywood's *The Play of Love* (printed in 1534 and again in [1582?]), ed. Alois Brandl, *Quellen des Weltlichen Dramas vor Shakespeare,* Strassburg (Quellen und Forschungen, LXXX), 1898, pp. 204-205. In addition to title and comparison the play shares with the ballad a similar bout of rhetoric: the ballad has a long catalogue of alliterating adjective-participle pairs; the play has a series of alliterating superlative adjectives (Brandl, p. 171).

4. A levedy ad my love leyt, the bole bigan to belle.

(1) College of Arms, Arundel 37 (formerly E.D.N. 27) (11 long lines alliterated and in irregular rime); ed. Wright and Halliwell, *Reliquiae Antiquae,* II, 19.

The editors date the MS. time of Edward II. Oakden, *Alliterative Poetry* [1930], p. 104, assigns the piece on linguistic grounds to NEMl of about 1300, not later than 1320.

Text obscure. Possibly a lying poem involving a rebellious lover and the suggestion that women be allowed the mastery until they are won.

5. A lytyll tale I will you tell.

Strife in the House.
Burden: "'Alas,' sayd the gudman, 'this ys an hevy lyff!'
And 'All ys well that endyth well,' said the gud wyff."

(1) Balliol College Oxford 354 (two-line burden and 14 four-line stanzas); ed. Dyboski, *Songs, Carols* (EETSES, CI), p. 110; Flügel, *Anglia,* XXVI (1903), 271; Greene, *Early English Carols,* p. 273 (no. 408).

MS. composed *ca.* 1530-40; many of the contents much earlier.

Satire on women's shrewishness; a fight for the breeches.

6. A Man may liue thrise Nestors life.

Ascribed to William Gray by Dormer, but the MS. copy bears the signature of [Thomas] Norton (Rollins, II, 309).

Against women either good or badde.

(1) Cotton Titus A. 24 (14 lines); ed. Norman Ault, *Elizabethan Lyrics,* London, 1925, p. 30.

(2) *Tottel's Miscellany* (in all editions); ed. with collations from (1) by Rollins, I, 201. For imitations see II, 309.

1557 or before.

General satire on women; both the Helens and the Penelopes bring a man trouble. Answered by **298.**

7. A man that lovyth fyscheng and fowlyng bothe.

Piers of Fulham.

(1) Bodleian James 43 (143 couplets); ed. with corrections from (3) by Hazlitt, *Remains*, II, 1. I am preparing an edition.

(2) Cambridge University Library Ll. 4. 14 (143 couplets).

(3) Rawlinson C. 86 (184 couplets).

(4) Trinity College Cambridge R. 3. 19 (184 couplets); ed. C. H. Hartshorne, *Ancient Metrical Tales*, London, 1829, p. 117.

Middle of XV cent.

Mainly satire on woman's inconstancy and desire for the mastery. A rubric calls the poem "vayne conseytes of folysche love vndyr colour of fyscheng and fowlyng." For extensive parallels to this convention see Introduction, pp. 45-46.

8. A newe songe anewe.

(1) Rawlinson C. 813 (4 four-line stanzas); ed. Padelford and Benham, *Anglia*, XXXI (1908), 328.

MS. time of Henry VIII; according to Bolle, *Anglia*, XXXIV (1911), 274, most of the contents late XV cent.

Rebellious lover with a lingering courtly tone, but generalized in the end as a warning to lovers.

9. A Philosophre, a good clerk seculer.

Halliwell, p. 27, and J. H. Lange, *ESt*, XXX (1902), 346, ascribe it to John Lydgate. MacCracken, *Minor Poems of Lydgate*, I, xlviii, wishes to assign it to Thomas Hoccleve, but admits that "there were certainly more poets at work in this period than we know about."

The Prohemy of a Mariage, or *Advice to an Old Gentleman who Wished for a Young Wife.*

(1) Harley 372 (72 rime-royal and envoy of 2 ballade stanzas); ed. Halliwell, *Selection from the Minor Poems of Dan John Lydgate*, p. 27.

Early (?) XV cent. Spurgeon, *Five Hundred Years of Chaucer Criticism*, I, 36, assigns it to [1430].

Warning against December's marrying July. A transparent and very successful attempt to repeat the theme of Chaucer's *Merchant's Tale*. Unmistakable references to the Marriage Group (Spurgeon notes only one of the many allusions). Tatlock, *MP*, XXXIII (1936), 377-79, observes that the January and May convention appears to have begun with Chaucer. We may recall, however, that Gower uses a very similar contrast:

> It sit a man be weie of kinde
> To love, bot it is noght kinde
> A man for love his wit to lese:
> For if the Monthe of Juil schal frese
> And that Decembre schal ben hot,
> The year mistorneth, wel I wot.

Confessio Amantis, vii, 4297-4302; ed. Macaulay, II, 355. These lines take on special meaning when we consider Gower's own pose of the old lover on the verge of renunciation. For further treatments of the theme see **17** and **24**.

10. A Schollar skillde in Vergils verse.

By George Turbervile.
A pretie Epigram of a Scholler, that having read Vergils Aeneidos, maried a curst wyfe.
(1) Turbervile's *Epitaphes, Epigrams, Songs and Sonets* (1567) (7 quatrains); ed. Collier [1867], p. 129; also in Chalmers, II, 617.
1567 or before.

Satire on shrewish wife; word-play on *arma virumque*. Adapted from the Greek Anthology, ix, 168 (where the joke is furnished by a student of the *Iliad*); according to Lathrop, *MLN*, XLIII (1928), 225, Turbervile took it from Janus Cornarius, who credits it to Ausonius. For another epigram showing that scholarship and marriage do not agree see **11**.

11. A Student at his boke so plast.

Hazlitt thought it might be by Sir Thomas More, but later editors have not followed his suggestion. See Rollins, II, 271.
Of a new maried Student.
(1) *Tottel's Miscellany* (all editions) (8 lines); ed. Rollins, I, 150, and Padelford, *Early Sixteenth Century Lyrics*, p. 94.
1557 or before.

Marriage destroys scholarship and advancement; see **10** and **75a**.

12. A thousand sythes [var. times] have I herd men telle.

By Geoffrey Chaucer.
The Legend of Good Women (2723 lines in Robinson).
(1) British Museum Additional 9832 (lines 1-1985 only).
(2) British Museum Additional 12524 (lines 1640-end).
(3) British Museum Additional 28617 (nine fragments).
(4) Bodley 638.
(5) Bodleian Fairfax 16; "F-Prologue" edited from this as base with corrections from all authorities by Robinson, *Chaucer*, p. 565. The "G-Prologue" is printed parallel from its

unique authority (7), on which the text of the legends is also based. For further material on MSS., editions, and commentary see Robinson, pp. 952, 1031; Hammond, *Chaucer*, p. 378; Griffith, *Chaucer*, p. 121; Martin, *Chaucer*, p. 70; Brown and Robbins, *Index*, no. 100; and the current bibliographies.

(6) Cambridge University Library Ff. 1. 6 (*Thisbe* only).
(7) Cambridge University Library Gg. 4. 27 (with the unique "G-Prologue," 2489 lines in all).
(8) Magdalene College Cambridge, Pepys 2006 (lines 1-1377).
(9) Rawlinson C. 86 (*Dido* only).
(10) Arch. Selden B. 24.
(11) Tanner 346.
(12) Thynne (1532).
(13) Trinity College Cambridge R. 3. 19.

Assigned by most critics to the period just before the *Canterbury Tales* were begun. Robinson, p. xxv, places it between 1380 and 1386. The "G-Prologue" may be later.

Defense: Cupid's Martyrs; a catalogue and palinode. Translations of its two major sources appear in this Index; see Ovid's *Heroides* (**280**) and Boccaccio's *De Claris Mulieribus* (**236**). For congeners and imitations see **80, 247,** and **46.** Certain of the supposed revisions in the "G-Prologue" may be the result of a semi-satirical corrective to Chaucer's early courtly love doctrines. See Robert M. Estrich, "Chaucer's Maturing Art in the Prologues to the *Legend of Good Women*," *JEGP*, XXXVI (1937), 326-37.

13. A woman most haue iij propretes [prose].
(1) Rawlinson C. 813; I have transcribed it for publication.
MS. time of Henry VIII; according to Bolle, *Anglia*, XXXIV (1911), 274, most of the contents are late XV cent.
General satire in form of typical medieval triad.

14. A woman thatt ys wylfull ys a plage off the worste.
Proverbs.
(1) Copied according to the editors "from an ancient set of ten fortune cards in the Chetham Library at Manchester"; ed. Wright and Halliwell, *Reliquiae Antiquae,* II, 195 (10 couplets).
Early XVI cent.?
A group of satirical characters of women used in a dicing game. One or two may apply to men as well. On this type of medieval and renaissance sport see **201.**

A yong wyf and an arvyst gos (298a).

15. Adew, my prety pussy.

>(1) Ashmole 48 (6 twelve-line stanzas); ed. Wright, *Songs and Ballads,* p. 209.

Rollins dates the MS. *ca.* 1557-65 in *MLN,* XXXIV (1919), 349, on the basis of broadside contents.

Rebellious lover with hints of the lying-song (see **69**). The tone is light and the beloved appears to be a wanton tavern-wench who has ended as the vicar's wife. Possibly alludes to that perennial subject of controversy, the marriage of the clergy, on which see **361**. For an imitation see **16**.

16. Adewe, sweete harte, adewe!

>(1) William Griffith (1569) (3 twelve-line stanzas); ed. Lilly's *Collection,* p. 222.

1569 or before. May be too late for this handlist. But according to Duff, Griffith began printing in 1552 and changed to the sign of the Falcon, mentioned in the colophon of this broadside, in 1556 (*Century,* p. 61). William R. Parker has informed me that *STC* entries (see nos. 1655 and 11436) of Griffith's books extend from 1553 to 1571. The latest record of Griffith at the Falcon is 1567 (see *STC* nos. 12787 and 19917). The use of **15** suggests printing before 1569.

The lover promises to return to his lady; the ballad-maker suggests that his promises will be kept like that of Sir Launcelot's return. In any event the wanton lady is scarcely worth returning to. Overtones of the lying-song. Rollins, *MLN,* XXXIV (1919), 347, makes clear that this is a close imitation of **15**.

Avyse youe, wemen, wom ye trust (147).

17. After playes, sportes, and daunces of solace.

By Robert Copland, whose name appears in an acrostic in the envoy.

The complaynte of them that ben to late maryed.

>(1) Wynkyn de Worde (n.d.) (53 rime-royal stanzas). The *STC* (no. 5728) lists only two extant copies: one at Huntington Library complete, the other at British Museum with only two leaves. Ed. J. P. Collier, *Illustrations of Early English Popular Literature,* London, 1863-64, I, 3. The *British Museum Catalogue,* XVI (1886), lists two editions by John [Baron] Somers: *A Fourth Collection of Scarce and Valuable Tracts,* London, 1753, vol. II; and *A Collection of Scarce and Valuable Tracts,* London, 1809-1815, vol. VIII.

The *STC* dates [1535?] and H. R. Plomer dates about 1534;

both appear to be influenced by the known date of the companion piece, **67**, which was printed, possibly for the first time, in 1535. According to Plomer Copland's activity as a translator spanned the years 1496-1547. See his "Robert Copland," *Transactions of the Bibliographical Society,* III (1895-96), 211-25; and his *Wynkyn de Worde & his Contemporaries,* London, 1925, pp. 75-76, 99-100. Duff, *Century,* p. 32, objects to the common tendency of assuming that books with introductory verses by Copland, "the boke prynter," and issued by de Worde, are merely reprints of editions first issued by Copland and now lost. He believes that others like de Worde may have issued them, but that Copland printed them (his dates as a printer are from 1515 to 1534-35). For further bibliographical details see Collier's introduction to his reprint and to his edition of *The Pain and Sorrow of Evil Marriage,* London (Percy Society I), 1840, pp. v, ix; Wright, *Middle-Class Culture,* p. 471; and Beatrice Wright, "Two Tracts on Marriage by Robert Copland," *Huntington Library Bulletin,* I (1931), 205. The *Stationers' Register* entry to William Copland in 1563-64 of "the lamentation of an olde man for maryinge of a yonge mayde" (Arber, I, 232) may reflect a desire on the part of Robert's heir to repeat the success of *To Late.*

The old husband, who spent his youth in riotous living and is now impotent, is sorry he did not marry sooner. Early marriage is thus defended, and the attack is on the *senex amans* rather than women. The complainant reminds us in several ways of Chaucer's January. Unquestionably *To Late* is a companion to *A complaynte of them that be to soone maryed* (**67**), and appears to be a sequel; but the exact relationship between these two translations of Copland and their French originals is not yet clear. The similarity of the two titles has caused confusion. Plomer attributes the original of *To Late* to "J. Gringoir" ("Robert Copland," pp. 222-23). Actually it is by Pierre Gringoire, and appeared as *La Complainte de trop tard marié* with a colophon naming Pierre and dated October 1, 1505 (*Catalogue général des livres imprimés de la Bibliothèque Nationale,* LXIV [1916], col. 782). The *British Museum Catalogue* lists four XIX cent. editions of *Trop Tard;* the only one I have been able to verify is an edition of *Trop Tôt.* Montaiglon, *Recueil des Poésies Françoises,* III, 130, promises an edition of *Trop Tard;* but his *Oeuvres Complètes de Gringore* (ed. with Charles d'Hericault), Paris, 1858-77 (2 vols. published), was never completed.

After that hervest Inned had his sheves (28).

After this story tellith also (75).

A Robyn, joly Robyn (202).

Airlie (see **Early**).

18. Alas! how should I sing?

(1) Kilkenny, Red Book of Ossory, ed. St. John Seymour, *Anglo-Irish Literature, 1200–1582*, Cambridge, 1929, p. 98 (5 lines); for other editions see Brown and Robbins, *Index*, no. 1265.

XIV cent. hand. See Wells, *Manual*, pp. 1176, 1222, 1411, 1632, for date and further bibliography.

Fragment of a *chanson de mal mariée*, in which a lass bewails her marriage to an old man and the loss of her lover. Robbins, *MLN*, LIII (1938), 241, has reconstructed the poem as "the first English carol."

"Alas," sayd the gudman, "this ys an hevy lyff" (5).

19. Allace so sobir is the micht.

By "Mersar."

(1) Advocates' Library 1. 1. 6 (4 eight-line stanzas); ed. Ritchie, *Bannatyne Manuscript*, IV, 48; for further editions see Hunterian Club *Bannatyne*, I, cvii.

1568 or before. If this is the "Merseir" of Dunbar's *Lament for the Makaris* (1508 or before; see Small, *Poems of William Dunbar*, I, clxiii; II, 50), he was dead in 1508.

Defense: warning to women against false men.

20. All that I may swynk or swet.

A Hen-pecked Husband's Complaint.
Burden: "Care away, away, away,
    Care away for euermore."

(1) Bodleian Eng. poet. e. 1 (two-line burden and 5 four-line stanzas); ed. Greene, *Early English Carols*, p. 272 (no. 406); W. H. Auden, *Oxford Book of Light Verse*, Oxford, 1938, p. 63; J. E. Masters, *Rymes of the Minstrels*, p. 9; H. M. Fitzgibbon, *Early English Poetry*, London, 1887, p. 179; Chambers and Sidgwick, *Early English Lyrics*, p. 208; Wright, *Songs and Carols* (Percy Society), p. 26.

XV cent.

Satire on women's drunkenness and shrewishness; a *chanson de mal marié*. The first line of the burden is repeated in the burden of **93**.

21. All tho þat lyste of women euyl to speke.

Thynne attributes to Chaucer. Skeat, *Chaucer Canon*, p. 111, suggests that it may be by Lydgate, and be the poem "In pris of women" promised in *Temple of Glas*, lines 1378-92. He errs in saying that no other poem of this title is known; see Index II. McCracken, *Minor Poems of Lydgate*, I, xlix, denies the attribution. *In Praise of Women.*

(1) Thynne (1532) (25 rime-royal stanzas); reproduced in
Skeat's *Facsimile*, p. 650; ed. in early Chaucer texts up to
Bell, for which see Hammond, *Chaucer*, p. 447.

(2) Advocates' Library 1. 1. 6; ed. Ritchie, *Bannatyne Manuscript*, IV, 64; see also Hunterian Club *Bannatyne*, I, cvii.

Before 1532.

Defense: men falsely defame women and deceive these gentle creatures, who have given us birth and nurture and inspiration, and one
of whom was Christ's Mother.

22. All wemein Ar guid noblle And excellent.

Ascribed to Richard Hattfield in (1).

(1) British Museum Additional 17492 (two copies punctuated
differently, each with 3 rime-royal stanzas); ed. Flügel,
Neuenglishes Lesebuch, p. 39; Padelford, *Early Sixteenth
Century Lyrics*, p. 94.

(2) Magdalene College Cambridge, Pepys 2553 (1 rime-royal
stanza); ed. Craigie, *Maitland Folio Manuscript*, I, 433.

(3) "Harington MS." (at Arundel Castle); to be edited by
Professor Ruth Hughey.

(4) Marquis of Bath, Longleat 258.

Early XVI cent.

Satire under the guise of ironic praise. Punctuated one way it
praises women in exaggerated fashion; punctuated another it reviles
them with similar excess. Such poems are used with humorous success
in *Ralph Roister Doister* (III. iv. 33) and in *Midsummer Night's Dream*
(V. i. 108). The type has been discussed by James R. Kreuzer, *RES*,
XIV (1938), 321, and by Rossell Hope Robbins, *RES*, XV (1939), 206.
The examples given in these articles indicate that the favorite subjects
for such satire are women, the law, and the clergy. A similar device is
found in MS. Jesus College Oxford 88: "There was a coye maid in
Anglesey named Ann, which was sought after and sued by divers that
thought themselves noe meane babyes, who caused these rymes [*in
Welsh*] folowing to be made in her commendacion, etc. which may be
understood in her discommendacion by joyning of the first syllable."
See Henry O. Coxe, *Catalogus Codicum MSS. qui in Collegiis Aulisque
Oxoniensibus Hodie Adservantur*, Pars II, Oxford, 1852 (Jesus College),
p. 32. Compare **143**. No doubt the punctuation poem is a superficial
form of a much more subtle type of poetic ambiguity (see William
Empson, *Seven Types of Ambiguity*, London, 1930, pp. 62-129).

All women have vertues noble & excelent (22).

22a. Also use not to pley at the dice ne at the tablis.

An extract from Peter Idley's *Instructions to His Son*, ed. Charlotte d'Evelyn, Boston and London (MLA Monograph Series, VI),
1935, p. 124 (IIA, 1028-55); see also her discussion, p. 61.

Extracts Illustrating Costume.
(1) Laud 416 (4 rime-royal stanzas). From this MS. abridgement of Idley's Book II Wright and Halliwell, *Reliquiae Antiquae*, II, 27, have given independent existence to these stanzas and to **41a** and **93a**. For six other MSS. of the whole poem see Miss d'Evelyn's edition.

On the authority of the scribe, John Newton, Miss d'Evelyn dates the Laud MS. October 25, 1459. The *Instructions* are securely dated between 1438 and 1459, more narrowly according to Miss d'Evelyn between 1445 and 1450.

The extract is from a discussion of the third commandment (against Sabbath-breaking). A brief attack on sports, tavern-haunting, secular songs, and mayflower gathering leads to the remark that these are the pitfalls for a maiden's virtue. The difference between a damsel and a maid is that maids wear silken "calles" and damsels kerchiefs. Wives parade their finery in church and envy that of other women. The stumbling irony is continued with a flat denial that women jangle in church (see **329**). The first lines are from Robert Mannyng's *Handlyng Synne;* the remainder appears to be Idley's own.

23. Among dame natures workes such perfite lawe is wrought.

That nature which worketh al thinges for our behofe, hath made women also for our comfort and delite.
(1) *Tottel's Miscellany* (all editions) (19 couplets); ed. Rollins, I, 174.
1557 or before.

Defense on the basis of a strong new argument, "nature." Fire, frost, sun, moon, serpents, and women all have their seamy side, but all work as well for men's good. Feigning men say women were made to give men pain, "Yet sure I think they are a pleasure to the mynde."

24. Amang foleis ane greit folie I find.

By Sir Richard Maitland.
The Folye of ane auld Man.
(1) Magdalene College Cambridge, Pepys 2553 (5 rime-royal stanzas); ed. Craigie, *Maitland Folio Manuscript*, I, 61, with variants from (2) and (3); for other editions see II, 64.
(2) Magdalene College Cambridge, Pepys 1408; ed. Craigie, *Maitland Quarto Manuscript*, p. 39.
(3) Cambridge University Library Ll. 5. 10 ("Reidpeth MS.").
Maitland Folio composed 1570-85.

Warning against the marriage of an old man and a young lass. Clear reference to Chaucer's *Merchant's Tale;* fresh May and cold January do not agree upon a song in June.

25. Among other things profiting in our tongue.

By John Heywood.

A dialogue conteynyng the number of the effectuall prouerbes in the Englishe tounge, compact in a matter concernynge two maner of maryages.

(1) T. Berthelet (1546). The *STC* (no. 13291) mentions only one copy, at Huntington Library. The following list of editions is based on *STC*, nos. 13285-89, 13291-94.

(2) T. Berthelet [1549].

(3) T. Powell (1556).

(4) (Printer unnamed), London (1561).

(5) T. Powell (1562); ed. John S. Farmer, *The Proverbs, Epigrams, and Miscellanies of John Heywood,* London, 1906, p. 1 (about 1400 couplets).

(6) H. Wykes (1566).

(7) T. Marsh (1576).

(8) T. Marsh (1587).

(9) F. Kingston (1598).

1546 or before.

This tremendously popular XVI cent. work is less a satire on marriage than a collection of proverbs which Heywood has, with a keen eye to his public, tied to conversations about marriage between a young man and his friend, and between wives and husbands. For summaries see Robert W. Bolwell, *The Life and Works of John Heywood,* New York, 1921, pp. 131-33; and R. de la Bère, *John Heywood, Entertainer,* London, 1937, pp. 88-93. Proverb-lore was not a bad method of revealing the folk attitude toward women. There is additional satirical matter scattered throughout Heywood's various collections of epigrams, which were printed along with the *Dialogue* in editions from 1562 on. To include each of these couplets, quatrains, and the like as a separate satire on women would swell this handlist beyond all proportion; we must therefore be content to consider the various "hundreds" of epigrams as loosely bound together longer works which contain some incidental satire. Actually they are just that; they are very similar in purpose and content to the *Dialogue.*

26. Ane aigit man twyss fourty ʒeiris.

By Walter Kennedy.

Against Mouth-Thankless.

(1) Advocates' Library 1. 1. 6 (6 eight-line stanzas); ed. J. Schipper, "The Poems of Walter Kennedy," *Denkschriften der kaiserlichen Akademie der Wissenschaften* [Vienna], *Philos.-Hist.-Classe,* XLVIII. 1 (1902), 12, with collations of (2) and record of earlier editions; also ed. Ritchie,

Bannatyne Manuscript, IV, 46; see Hunterian Club *Bannatyne,* I, cvii.

(2) Magdalene College Cambridge, Pepys 2553; ed. Craigie, *Maitland Folio Manuscript,* I, 364. For notes see F. Holthausen, "Kennedy-Studien," *Archiv,* CX (1903), 360.

According to the *DNB* Kennedy died in or about 1508.

Lament of an aged Franciscan for his youth misspent in lechery. Once the *double-entente* is unriddled the poem is seen to be full of rather startling realism.

27. An aged trot and tough.

By George Turbervile.

Of a contrarie mariage.

(1) Turbervile's *Epitaphes, Epigrams, Songs and Sonets* (3 four-line stanzas); ed. Collier [1867], p. 150; also in Chalmers, II, 623.

1567 or before.

Aged woman marries a young man and an aged man a girl; both suffer serious discomforts and a fruitless marriage. Lathrop, *MLN,* XLIII (1928), 225, points out that the epigram is ultimately from the Greek Anthology, xi. 70, possibly via Janus Cornarius.

28. And, endyd my 'complaynt' in this manere.

By Thomas Hoccleve.

Dialogus cum Amico.

(1) Durham Cathedral III. 9 (258 rime-royal stanzas and a prose moralization of the tale); ed. Furnivall, *Hoccleve's Works, I. The Minor Poems,* p. 110, with variants from (2).

(2) Arch. Selden supra 53; ed. in part by Hammond, *English Verse,* p. 69.

(3) Laud 735.

(4) Bodley 221.

(5) [In a lost Coventry MS., once belonging to King Henry VIII School?] For this information see Hammond, *English Verse,* p. 57. This list of MSS. is based on a comparison of Hammond with Brown and Robbins, *Index,* no. 299. Hammond's descriptions are not wholly clear, since she is describing the whole "Series" of which the *Dialogus* is but a part.

The "Series" was composed around 1420 at intervals.

Hoccleve's "Series" (no better name for this hodge-podge is known) contains a Complaint, this Dialogue, two Stories from the *Gesta Romanorum,* and Learn to Die. The bibliography and text still need careful study, which may reveal more underlying unity than is apparent on the

surface. I include in this handlist the part edited in Furnivall's text, pp.
110-78, which comprises the Dialogue, *Jereslaus' Wife,* a short verse link,
and a prose moralization. Despite the rambling nature of his "Series"
Hoccleve was attempting a kind of palinode to his early attacks on
women (one of which, strangely enough, is his translation of Christine
de Pisan's *Letter of Cupid*). After a long prologue on various subjects,
including his weak brain, false coining, his relations with Humphrey
of Gloucester, friendship in general, and learning to die, he seeks a new
subject for verse. His friend suggests an apology for his satire on
women, and after some rather ambiguous remarks on the sex in general
and his wife in particular, he translates *Jereslaus* from the *Gesta Romanorum.* This tale of a patient wife is a remote analogue of Chaucer's
Man of Law's Tale and *Clerk's Tale.* Hoccleve is obviously aware of
the Marriage Group and *Legend of Good Women;* he makes specific
reference (p. 135) to the Wife of Bath.

29. And I war a mayden as many one ys.

> (1) British Museum Additional 31922 (8 lines, the first two five
> times repeated); ed. Flügel, *Anglia,* XII (1889-90), 250.
First half XVI cent.

Forsaken maiden's lament; but she has been somewhat wanton
with courtiers since fifteen years of age. The exact tone is somewhat
difficult to discover.

30. And whan they had resceyvede her charge [beginning im-perfect].

> *Why I Can't Be a Nun.*
> (1) Cotton Vespasian D. 9 (392 extant lines); ed. F. J. Furni-
> vall, *Early English Poems and Lives of Saints,* Berlin (Ap-
> pendix to *Transactions of the Philological Society* 1858),
> 1862, p. 138.
XV cent. (early, according to Eileen Power, *Medieval English
Nunneries,* Cambridge, 1922, p. 545).

Elaborate development of the *chanson de nonne,* which involves
allegorical satire on the failings of a convent, and considerable personal
feeling as well. A summary and interpretation will be found in Power,
p. 545, where it is compared to passages in Gilles li Muises, John Gower,
Erasmus, and Sir David Lyndsay. W. H. Schofield, *English Literature
from the Norman Conquest to Chaucer,* New York, 1906, p. 373, suggests it has been influenced by *Pearl.* Since women make up nunneries,
their vices are exposed; but in the main the poem is a satire on the men
whose activities discredit the monastic ideal.

Ane (see A, An, or One).

Apon (see Vpon).

31. As I cowth walke be-cause of recreacioun.

Dialogue between a Clerk and a Husbandman.
(1) British Museum Additional 38666 (7 eight-line stanzas);
ed. Brown, *MLN*, XXXIII (1918), 415.
Middle of XV cent.

The Clerk defends love and women on the basis of the well-known
refrain "Quia amore langueo"; the Husbandman counters with the
satirical "Turn vp hyr haltur and let hyr goe" (see **104**). The clerk has
the best of it, or at least the last word.

32. [As I was walking forth of late.]

a man that his wyfe ys master.
(1) British Museum ballad collection, pressmark C. 22. f.
14(66). See Rollins, *Analytical Index*, no. 1655.

Equated by Rollins tentatively with the broadside with this
title licensed 1562-63 to John Cherlewood; but Rollins also suggests
that Cherlewood's broadside may be **245**.

Not seen. Appears to be either a henpecked husband's complaint
or a fight for the breeches.

33. As many as match themselves with shrowes.

Burden: "Tom Tiler, Tom Tiler,
More morter for Tom Tiler."
(1) *Tom Tyler and his Wife* ("second Impression" 1661) (20
lines, including burden); for editions see **193**.

This lyric may be later than 1568, since the date of the first
impression and of the play's composition is unknown. But possibly
it may be identified with broadsides such as that mentioned by
Rollins, *Analytical Index*, no. 2664.

Gossips' song on the power of shrews over their husbands, no
matter how stout and strong.

34. As Menelaus did lament.

By George Turbervile.
*The forsaken Lover laments that his Ladie is matched with an
other.*
(1) Turbervile's *Epitaphes, Epigrams, Songs and Sonets* (1567)
(3 ten-line stanzas); ed. Collier [1867], p. 209; also in
Chalmers, II, 632.
1567 or before.

Rebellious lover. Uses classical allusion to illustrate his lady's fickleness, bad taste, and greed. The new lover will soon find out which side
his bread is buttered on.

35. At Breyntforde, on the west of London.
By Robert Copland.
Gyl of Braintfords Testament.

(1) William Copland [1560?]; never reprinted or thoroughly
collated. I have examined microfilm of the apparently
unique copy at Huntington (*STC*, no. 5730). Furnivall
was not sure where Collier had seen this edition; in a note
appended to Furnivall's remark Corser says it was in
Collier's own possession. Collier, *Bibliographical and Critical Account,* I, 189, gives a selected collation of (1) and (2)
and extracts from (2). The exact status of the texts before
Collier is obscured by occasional modernization and by the
running feud between Collier and Furnivall. Certainly
the divergences between Furnivall's text of (2) and the
Huntington copy of (1) are great. Some of Collier's variants
do not correspond to either text which I have seen; so
a third text may be involved, though *STC* lists only two.
Furnivall feels (2) is the earlier edition; Collier favors (1).

(2) William Copland [1562?]; ed. F. J. Furnivall, *Jyl of Breyntfords Testament,* Printed for Private Circulation, London,
1871, p. 7 (two separate quatrains appended to cuts on
verso of title page and 336 lines in couplets, rime-royal,
triplets, and ballade stanzas). Furnivall used the Bodleian
copy. The *STC* (no. 5731) lists this and another at Huntington; but according to Mr. Herman R. Mead no copy
of this edition is owned by Huntington.

Composed, and possibly printed, some time before the extant
copies. The latest known date in Robert Copland's life is 1547; his
satirical work appears to have been done by 1535 (see Plomer, "Robert Copland," pp. 211-25). The colophon of (1) is "Imprinted at
London by me William Copland"; of (2) "Imprented at London in
Lothbury ouer agaynst Saint Margarytes church by me Wyllyam
Copland." William presumably inherited from Robert Copland
about 1548 (Duff, *Century,* p. 32). According to Duff, William
printed at Robert's sign of the Rose Garland and also at a shop on the
"Three Crane Warfe in the Vintree" during the early portion of
his career, and moved in 1562 to Lothbury; (1) therefore might well
have been printed at some earlier address anywhere between 1548
and 1562, and (2) anywhere from 1562 to 1568-69, when William
died. But of course it is not impossible that the unlocated colophon
of (1) was also printed at Lothbury. Only a more thorough collation of the editions than any yet attempted would be likely to give
finality to the evidence of the colophons.

A combination of mock-testament and ale-wife poem, which involves both specific satire of the Eleanor Rumming type and general satire on a host of fools who show no proper sense in the affairs of life. For parallels to the mock-testament see Furnivall, p. 6. Jill's actual bequest is identical with that in Chaucer's *Summoner's Tale*. For Jill's continued popularity see Rollins, *Analytical Index*, no. 960; and H. C. Hart, ed., *The Merry Wives of Windsor*, London (The Arden Shakespeare), 1904, pp. xlvii-l.

At my commyng the ladys euerychone (82).

Avyse (see Advise).

36. **Be it right or wrong, these men among.**
   The Notbrowne Mayde.
   (1) Arnold's *Chronicle*, according to *STC*, no. 782 [1503?] (30 eighteen-line stanzas); ed. with emendations from (2) by Hazlitt, *Remains*, II, 271. Hazlitt dates [1502?].
   (2) Arnold's *Chronicle* (1521).
   (3) Balliol College Oxford 354; ed. Hales and Furnivall, *Bishop Percy's Folio Manuscript*, III, 174.
   (4) British Museum Additional 27879 (the Percy Folio MS.) (incomplete, 20 twelve-line stanzas); ed. Hales and Furnivall, III, 174. (This poem has been extensively reprinted, usually on the basis of (1). I have given key editions only; see them for other editions. For further bibliography see W. W. Skeat, *Specimens of English Literature*, 3rd ed., Oxford, 1880, p. 96; L. L. Tucker and A. R. Benham, *A Bibliography of Fifteenth Century Literature*, Seattle, 1928, pp. 140-41; Chambers and Sidgwick, *Early English Lyrics*, p. 334; Brown and Robbins, *Index*, no. 467.)
   Certainly before 1502 or 1503; Hazlitt believes it is late XV cent.; Hales and Furnivall believe it was old when incorporated by Arnold into his *Chronicle*.

Debate on women's worth is the frame, but the charm of the poem seems to rest in its narrative kernel, in which an outlaw pretends to despise women and to spurn the love of the Nut-Brown Maid. In the end he reveals himself as the son of the Earl of Westmorland, fully satisfied with women's fidelity as manifested in the Maid. The poem is more than a combination of the outlaw ballad, the courtly debate (as old as Andreas Capellanus), and the *querelle des femmes;* it contains elements from all these and transmutes them. Its exquisite tone and composite character are certainly the result of conscious artistry; yet it has the freshness of folk song. For some French parallels see Paul Meyer, *Romania*, XXXVII (1908), 224: *Jourdains de Blaivies* (see Chambers and Sidgwick, p. 335). For German parallels see Hazlitt, *Remains*, II, 272; and Flügel, *Neuenglisches Lesebuch*, I, 447-48. For

English parallels see the ballad *Child Waters* (Child, no. 63); *De Clerico et Puella* (ed. Brown, *English Lyrics of the XIIIth Century*, p. 152); for a late courtly love-dialogue *Tottel's Miscellany*, ed. Rollins, I, 76. Seldom considered is the parallel with Chaucer's Marriage Group, with which it shares a debate over women and an exemplum in evidence of women's patience in great trials set for her as a pitfall by a man who loves her. The poem was popular in the sixteenth century; John Kynge was fined for printing it as a broadside without license in 1558-59 (Rollins, *Analytical Index*, no. 1983). It was also honored by pious parody: *The New Notbroune Mayd vpon the Passion of Cryste* (ed. Hazlitt, *Remains*, III, 1).

37. Be mirry bretherene ane and all.

> By "Flemyng."
>> (1) Advocates' Library 1. 1. 6 (12 eight-line stanzas); ed. Ritchie, *Bannatyne Manuscript*, III, 76; see Hunterian Club *Bannatyne*, I, xcii.
>
> 1568 or before.

Begins with the theme "be merry and praise the Lord for rich and poor alike will die." The unity of the poem seems to be furnished by the command to hoard up no riches, since they cannot be taken to heaven. Instead they will fall into the hands of your wife, who has given you sorrow all your days and will hurl your money away on other men when you are dead. A strange combination of satire on women's shrewishness, infidelity, and extravagance, of epicureanism and of Christian rejoicing (compare, for instance, Psalm 96 and the *Te Deum*).

37a. Bytwene a þousend men may on y kouþe.

> *On Woman's Lack of Discretion.*
>> (1) Cambridge University Library Gg. 3. 8 (two long couplets)? So catalogued by Brown and Robbins, *Index*, no. 514. But the Cambridge *Catalogue*, III, 66, lists Gg. 3. 7-14 as eight folio volumes, XVII cent., of a commentary on Aeschylus by Thomas Stanley, which seems an unlikely place for such a scrap. Perhaps the reference should be to the XV cent. Wycliffean New Testament (Gg. 6. 8) or, better, to the XV cent. *Evangelisterium* (Gg. 2. 8), which has at least one verse scribble in its pages (see Brown and Robbins, no. 1151).
>
> MS. before 1500?

Satire, apparently, on woman's caprice or "cold counsel." I have not examined the verses.

38. Blessid mot be oure heuen quene.

> By John Audelay.
> *Of Virginity.*

Burden: "For the loue of a maydon fre
        I haue me choson to chastite."
(1) Bodleian Douce 302 (two-line burden and 6 four-line stan-
    zas); ed. Greene, *Early English Carols*, p. 264 (no. 397);
    for other editions see p. 430.
MS. composed in the first half of the XV cent.
Praise of chaste women by witness of Mary. Compare **98, 144,
147, 384.**

Blow ye horne hunter & blow ye horne on hyt (271).

39. **Bo pepe! what have I spyed?**
    By Charles Bansley.
    *A Treatyse Shewing and Declaring the Pryde and Abuse of
    Women Now A Dayes.*
    (1) T. Raynalde (n.d.) (59 four-line stanzas). The *STC* (no.
        1374) lists only one copy, then in the possession of J. L.
        Clawson. Is this identical with that described in *Hunting-
        ton Library Supplement*, p. 14? Presumably this copy was
        used as the basis for J. P. Collier's anonymously issued
        edition for the Percy Society (vol. XXXI of the series,
        London, 1847), in which this is one of the "two pieces
        printed, but suppressed by the Society." Reprinted by Haz-
        litt, *Remains*, IV, 227.
    Dated by Hazlitt and Collier and the *STC* as about 1550 because
    of a reference to Edward VI and because of Raynalde's dates (he
    printed 1540-52). Of the author nothing is known save a hint that
    he has been in "Many straunge regions." Collier, *Extracts*, I, 28,
    suggests comparison with a "ballett Called the prayse of the vayne
    beauty of women" licensed to John Sampson in 1560 (Rollins,
    Analytical Index, no. 2165, makes no comment).
    Satire on women's vainglory and exaggerated fashions. The theme
    is old in the Middle Ages (see, for instance, **232**); but our author
    attributes the pride of women to "popyshe ydolatry" and threatens that
    "reformacyon wyll come shortlye." His language is neither moderate
    nor euphemistic. The poem contains a reference to "the scole house of
    women," which is probably **292.**

40. **brief and pleasant discourse of duties in Mariage, called the
    Flower of Friendshippe, A** [prose].
    By Edmund Tilney, later Master of the Revels.
    (1) Henry Denham, 1568. *STC* (no. 24076) lists copies at
        British Museum, Bodleian, and Huntington. I have exam-
        ined microfilm of the third. According to *CBEL*, I, 728,
        and Mary A. Scott, there were two editions in this year—
        a statement I have been unable to verify.

(2) Henry Denham, 1571. *STC* (no. 24077) lists a single copy
   at Bodleian.
(3) Henry Denham, 1577. *STC* (no. 24077*a*) lists a single copy
   at Bodleian.
Entered 1567-68 and dedicated to "the Noble and most Uertu-
ous Princesse, Elizabeth."
  The first part describes the duties of a good husband, the second of
a good wife. Essentially a skillfully written matrimonial treatise, it merits
a place in the *querelle* by virtue of one character, the merry Master
Gualter of Cawne, whose cynicism about women is firmly rebuked by
the others. The sharp-tongued Lady Isabella also indulges in a bit of
satire on husbands. The frame, avowedly borrowed from Boccaccio
(the *Filocolo*?), is a courtly meeting in a springtime garden. The
treatise is probably influenced also by Castiglione's *Courtier*, translated
by Sir Thomas Hoby in 1561. In the first part Master Pedro de Luxan,
the continuator of the model courtly romance, *Amadis of Gaul*, is chosen
master of ceremonies; in the second part he relinquishes his post to
Lady Julia. Two other distinguished authorities on marriage, Erasmus
and Vives, appear as participants. *Exempla* are used with art anticipating that of Elizabethan prose fiction. For summaries see Frederick S.
Boas, *Queen Elizabeth, the Revels Office, and Edmund Tilney* (Annual
Elizabeth Howland Lecture), London, 1938, p. 12; Collier, *Bibliographical and Critical Account*, IV, 156; Mary A. Scott, *Elizabethan Translations from the Italian*, Boston, Mass., 1916, p. 20.

41. Bruþir be wyiss I reid ȝow now.
   By Sir John Moffett.
   (1) Advocates' Library 1. 1. 6 (9 five-line stanzas); ed. Ritchie,
      Bannatyne Manuscript, IV, 26; see also Hunterian Club
      Bannatyne, I, cv.
   1568 or before. See **133**.
   Women destroy youth, strength, and wisdom.

41a. But and the wyf oons happe to go astray.
   An extract (IIA, 1782-1825) from Peter Idley's *Instructions to
His Son*, ed. Charlotte d'Evelyn, Boston and London, 1935, p. 137;
see also p. 61.
   Extracts Illustrating Costume.
   (1) Laud 416 (2 lines and 6 rime-royal stanzas). From this
      MS. abridgement of Idley's Book II Wright and Halliwell,
      Reliquiae Antiquae, II, 27, have given independent existence
      to these stanzas and to **22a** and **93a**. For six other MSS. of
      the whole poem see Miss d'Evelyn's edition.
   Between 1438 and 1459. See **22a**.
   This satire on woman's lust and malice is from a passage on the
sixth commandment (against adultery). A wife who once goes astray

cannot be cured. She has no shame; lures men with her "horns"; demands new finery each day. Boccaccio tells of many contrary to their husbands, among them incestuous Semiramis. Yet most women are good, obedient, and chaste; although some men will say I lie. Idley, who usually follows Mannyng's *Handlyng Synne*, here borrows in large part from Lydgate's *Fall of Princes*. Stanzas 4 and 5 rework *Fall of Princes*, i, 6630-43, with such revisions as are necessary to incorporate Idley's refrain, "With hir crokyd instrument encrese and multeplie." Stanza 6 catches the sense of Lydgate's ironic apology, without preserving significant verbal echoes. The basis of the refrain is Biblical, but possibly Idley was aware of the Wife of Bath's enthusiasm for the text (*Wife of Bath's Prologue*, III, 28).

42. **Bot fals men make her fingres feld** [beginning imperfect].
   Praise of Women.
   (1) Advocates' Library 19. 2. 1 (Auchinleck MS.) (30 ten-line extant stanzas); ed. [John Leyden], *The Complaynt of Scotland*, Edinburgh, 1801, p. 161; David Laing, *A Pennyworth of Witte*, Edinburgh (Abbotsford Club), 1857, p. 107; Eugen Kölbing, *ESt*, VII (1884), 101, with notes by Julius Zupitza, *ESt*, VIII (1885), 394; F. Holthausen, *Archiv*, CVIII (1902), 288, and CX (1903), 102. Not in Wright's *Political Songs* as implied *CBEL*, I, 270. For further bibliography see Wells, *Manual*, p. 799.
   MS. first quarter XIV cent.

Defense in ABC form: the example of Mary is repeated at least thirteen times. A French original is found in MS. Harley 2253; Holthausen prints the two poems parallel. Kölbing's opinion (p. 102n.) that the poem is not ironical is, I believe, correct; although the mention of the Virgin does not in itself prove the case, since many satires do use her name. See, for instance, **192, 274, 340**, and a satirical passage in *Originals and Analogues of Chaucer's Canterbury Tales*, London, 1872-87, p. 288. Wells says, however (*Manual*, p. 234): "One feels sometimes that the English poet is overdoing, and suspects that the whole is ironical." But usually the medieval devices for ironic praise are crude and obvious enough. Hyperbole was too common in serious work to be readily available for parody; the usual methods were to call on false translation (Chaucer's Chantecleer), a destroying burden (see **136**), or obvious impossibility (see **69**). Such a stanza as that beginning "Eiȝen gray & browes bent" seems to me to involve honest chivalry and natural piety. Brown, *English Lyrics of the XIIIth Century*, p. 228, has some interesting remarks on medieval irony in connection with another poem (**340**).

43. **Be chance bot evin this vþer day.**
   By "ane Inglisman."
   Of ane wench w' chyld.

(1) Advocates' Library 1. 1. 6 (10 eight-line stanzas); ed. Ritchie, *Bannatyne Manuscript*, II, 336; see also Hunterian Club *Bannatyne*, I, lxxxvii.

1568 or before.

Humorous forsaken maiden's lament, with the refrain "O lord my littill finger." Ends with a warning against men.

44. By force I am fixed my fancie to write.

By Leonarde Gybson.
Prefatory couplet:
> "Leaue lightie loue, Ladies, for feare of yll name,
> And true loue embrace ye, to purchace your Fame."

A very proper Dittie: To the tune of Lightie Loue.
(1) Richard Jones (n.d.) (prefatory couplet and 13 eight-line stanzas); ed. Lilly's *Collection*, p. 113.

May be too late, although most of Lilly's reprints are from the period before 1568. The *STC* (no. 11836) identifies it tentatively with a *Stationers' Register* entry for 1570-71. McKerrow, *Dictionary*, p. 159, gives Jones's dates as 1564-1602. The colophon of this broadside locates Jones at "his shop, ioyning to the South-weste Dore of Saint Paules church," a location for which McKerrow's first date is 1571. He was at the Lottery House, at the west door of St. Paul's in 1569 (*STC*, no. 24935), which argues, though not finally, against inclusion here. Not mentioned in Rollins' *Analytical Index;* but see his no. 1501, "Light of Loue or the young mans resolution," entered in 1638 to Francis Coles, which may be a late imitation or reprint.

Women are flirtatious and deceitful and cause "poore fisshes their freedom to lose." They are like Helen, not chaste like Diana, Thisbe, or Cleopatra; they are schooled not by Penelope but by Cressed. Lovers suffer like Troilus and Menander (Leander). The rebellious lover will have no more to do with women until they leave "lightie love" and embrace true love. For the "lightie loue" tradition see Lilly's extensive note, p. 294.

45. By west of late as I dyd walke.

Ane Ballat of Matrymonie, or The Honey Moon.
(1) Cotton Vespasian A. 25 (11 eleven-line stanzas); ed. Böddeker, *JbREL*, XIV (1875), 220; David Laing, *Early Popular Poetry of Scotland*, rev. W. C. Hazlitt, London, 1895, II, 74 (and other editions there listed).

MS. dated 1578 by Böddeker, but some poems have been identified with earlier broadsides. Rollins, *Analytical Index*, no. 1740, says it is probably to be equated with "A merye newe ieste of a wife that threst her husband with a fflealle" licensed 1590 to Thomas Scarlet.

Chanson de mal marié, with a lively fight for the breeches. See Introduction, p. 41, and Sandison, *Chanson d'Aventure,* pp. 50-51, 131. The young wife refuses to work; they fight, and he gets the worst of it. Well-meaning neighbors rush in and save the tyrannous wife from her husband's wrath.

Care away, away, away (20 and 93).

46. Cyte of Ladyes, The Boke of the [prose].

Christine Pisan's *Le Livre de la Cité des Dames,* translated by Bryan Anslay.

(1) H. Pepwell (1521); never reprinted (*STC,* no. 7271). I have examined the Edwards Brothers film 221 (Case I, carton 2), from British Museum pressmark C.13.a.18. For summaries of the original see Rose Rigaud, *Les Idées Féministes de Christine de Pisan,* 1911, p. 75 and *passim;* Richardson, *Forerunners of Feminism,* pp. 26-32; A. Jeanroy, *Romania,* XLVIII (1922), 93.

Christine's version was composed somewhere between December, 1404, and April, 1405; the translation was made in 1521 or before.

Derived from Boccaccio's *De Claris Mulieribus,* this is a defense based on examples of noble women. Christine's guides in her dream-vision are Reason, Ryghtwysnesse, and Justyce (all ladies). The first book treats of women who have excelled in martial valor and other masculine virtues, the second of faithful wives and women martyred by faithless lovers, and the third of feminine saints and martyrs. One of Christine's noblest attempts to undo the evil work of Jean de Meun and Matheolus. The argument by example occasionally leads to odd results, as when Xantippe is offered as a type of wifely virtue.

Comparing togither, good huswife with bad (126).

47. Cruell and vnkind whom mercy cannot moue.

Against a cruell woman.

(1) *Tottel's Miscellany* (in all editions) (3 eight-line and 1 seven-line stanzas); ed. Rollins, I, 170.

1557 or before.

Rebellious lover; a violent attack, the merest shreds of courtliness remaining, on an unfaithful woman.

48. Cuckold, my freinde, wilt mee beleive.

(1) Ashmole 48 (4 couplets); ed. Wright, *Songs and Ballads,* p. 208.

Rollins dates the MS. 1557-65 in *MLN,* XXXIV (1919), 349, on the basis of broadside contents.

The life of a cuckold is sad whether his horns be visible or not.

49. Cupido, unto whos comaundëment.

By Thomas Hoccleve, an adaptation of Christine de Pisan's *L'Epistre au Dieu d'Amours* (for which see Maurice Roy, ed., *Oeuvres Poétiques de Christine de Pisan*, Paris [SATF], 1886-96, II, 1).

Letter of Cupid to Lovers his Subjects; Lettre of Cupide, god of Loue; or *Litera Cupidinis, dei Amatoris, directa subditis suis amatoribus.*

> (1) Fairfax 16 (68 rime-royal stanzas); ed. with variants from (2)-(6) by Furnivall, *Hoccleve's Works. I. The Minor Poems*, p. 72 (with extracts from Christine on p. 243); ed. with variants from (2)-(9) by Skeat, *Chaucer*, VII, 217.
>
> (2) Bodley 638.
>
> (3) Tanner 346. Brown and Robbins, *Index*, no. 666, say that Urry used this authority for his *Chaucer* (1721), p. 534.
>
> (4) Arch. Selden B. 24.
>
> (5) Huntington Library HM 744 (formerly Ashburnham Appendix 133); ed. Sir Israel Gollancz, *Hoccleve's Works. II. The Minor Poems*, p. 20.
>
> (6) Digby 181.
>
> (7) Trinity College Cambridge R. 3. 20.
>
> (8) Thynne (1532) and later editions of Chaucer; reproduced by Skeat, *Facsimile*, p. 769; see Hammond, *Chaucer*, p. 434, and Hammond, *English Verse*, p. 58, for further material.
>
> (9) Cambridge University Library Ff. 1. 6.
>
> (10) Advocates' Library 1. 1. 6; ed. Ritchie, *Bannatyne Manuscript*, IV, 49; see also Hunterian Club *Bannatyne*, I, cvii.
>
> (11) Durham Cathedral V. ii. 13.
>
> (12) [Lost from MS. Longleat 258], see Hammond, *English Verse*, p. 57.

Christine's poem was written in 1399, as the final lines indicate. Hoccleve changed the date to 1402.

Cupid's defense of women. His letter warns against false men's wooing and slander. The usual charges against women are answered one by one. Christine's attacks on Ovid and Jean de Meun are supplemented by Hoccleve's reference to "my Legende of Martres," which Skeat identifies with Chaucer's *Legend*. Hoccleve retains the tone and mood of Christine, but departs in some respects rather widely from his original.

50. Dayly in England mervels be found.

Of the Tyranny of Women.

Burden: "Nova, noua, sawe yow euer such?
        The most mayster of the hows weryth no brych."

(1) Bodleian Eng. poet. e. 1 (two-line burden and 9 rime-royal stanzas); ed. Greene, *Early English Carols,* p. 272 (no. 407); Wright, *Songs and Carols* (Percy Society), p. 64; J. E. Masters, *Rymes of the Minstrels,* p. 14.

MS. written second half XV cent.

General satire on women, with emphasis on woman's shrewishness and desire for the mastery. The burden, with its appeal to "strange news," appears to have been derived from poems on Christ's Nativity (see Greene, carol no. 73, p. 45); it had a long history in lying-songs (see Greene, carol no. 472, p. 317). Although this poem does not make the usual appeal to nonsense found in the lying-song, its theme and burden make it akin to that genre. See **69.**

51. Danger me hath vnskilfuly.

(1) Cambridge University Library Additional 5943 (formerly belonged to Lord Howard de Walden) (7 lines); ed. L. S. M[ayer], *Music, Cantilenas, Songs etc. from an Early Fifteenth Century Manuscript,* Privately Printed, 1906, sig. g.

MS. composed about 1417-25.

Text obscure, but appears to be a final rebellion on the part of a lover.

52. deceyte of women, The |prose|.

Stein, *Library,* Series 2, XV (1934-35), 40, suggests that the translator and compiler may have been Laurence Andrewe, who worked for the conjectured printer of the first edition. His argument, which is offered with some hesitancy, rests on too many assumptions to be accepted more than very tentatively.

(1) Since the two extant editions both are described on their title pages as "newly corrected," Stein suggests an earlier edition, possibly by Jan van Doesborgh, who printed at Antwerp from about 1508 to 1523-24 (Duff, *Century,* p. 40). The earlier edition may of course have been by Vele or Copland, but these two printers revived at least two other works originally printed by van Doesborgh, *Frederyke of Iennen* and *Howleglas.*

(2) W. Copland for J. Wyght. The *STC* (no. 6452) dates this edition [1561?], but Brie believes it was the first of the two extant editions. Since it was printed in Fleet Street, Copland's first address, it may be dated somewhere between 1548 and 1560. See Duff, *Century,* pp. 32-33 (Brie's 1543-58 seems to be an error). Stein further narrows the date to 1551-58 on the grounds that Wyght began his career about 1551 and Copland left the Rose Garland in Fleet Street in

1558. I am not sure of the exact evidence for the narrower date. Wright, *Middle-Class Culture,* p. 471, tentatively accepts the *STC* date. The only extant copy is at Huntington (formerly Britwell).

(3) A. Vele. The *STC* calls it the first edition [1560?], but Brie considers it the second and edits it: "The Deceyte of Women: älteste englische Novellensammlung (1547)," *Archiv,* CLVI (1929), 17. It is extant in a single copy at the British Museum (*STC,* no. 6451). William R. Parker informs me that Vele appears as a printer only between the years 1550-51 and 1557 (*STC,* nos. 12442 and 21600). Brie places Vele in Paul's Churchyard at the Sign of the Lamb, where this edition is located, from the years 1563 to 1581, on what evidence I do not know. Duff, *Century,* pp. 161-62, says that Vele gave up his printing office to William How in 1566, and was alive until at least 1586. On the basis of *STC* entries, Parker finds evidence of books printed *for* Vele in 1560 and again from 1569 to 1586, which confirms Duff rather than Brie. Stein believes that the type of this edition belonged to Copland, and therefore suggests that Copland was the printer and Vele the publisher or bookseller, in spite of the evidence of the colophon. The edition therefore appears to have been printed between 1550 and 1557 if Vele was the printer, or between 1548 and 1569 (see Duff, pp. 32-33) if Copland was the printer. Collation might establish further evidence of the priority of either (2) or (3).

Though Brie confidently dates the collection 1547 in his title, he gives no apparent reason for his decision. I have not seen the article by Brie of which that in *Archiv* is a revision: *Stephaniskos: Ernst Fabricius zum VI. IX. MDCCCCXXVII gedruckt,* Freiburg im Breisgau, 1927, p. 5. **52** was certainly written before 1568-69, when J. Allde entered it in the *Stationers' Register* (Arber, I, 389), and probably before 1560, the terminal date of (2). John W. Spargo dates it "[about 1550?]" in *Virgil the Necromancer,* Cambridge, Mass., 1934, p. 342. For further bibliographical material see Spargo; and Rollins, *Analytical Index,* no. 934. Stein, who suggests that (1) was printed by van Doesborgh in the first quarter of the century, believes that it was revived by Copland, Vele, and Wyght in "the 1550's."

A collection of tales revealing woman's faithlessness. They are alternately old, from the Bible and the classics, and new, from *Les Cent Nouvelles Nouvelles* (*ca.* 1435).

53. Defence of Good Women, The [prose].

By Sir Thomas Elyot.

(1) T. Berthelet (1540); for this single extant copy of the first edition see *Huntington Library Supplement,* p. 45 (*STC* lists only the 1545 edition). Reprinted by Edwin J. Howard, Oxford, Ohio, 1940, with variants from (2).

(2) T. Berthelet (1545); selections in Foster Watson, *Vives and the Renascence Education of Women,* New York, 1912, p. 211.

Watson dates between 1531 and 1538. A preface to Anne of Clèves is omitted in the second edition, presumably because her marriage to Henry VIII, which took place January 6, 1540, was declared null and void on July 9 of the same year.

Platonic (or Erasmian) dialogue between Caninius, the opponent of women, and Candidus, their defender. Plato is the master of Candidus, Aristotle the master of Caninius; and this authentic opposition is a definite sign of the author's humanism. In the end the martial queen Zenobia appears and confirms the arguments of Candidus.

54. Devyce / proves / and eik humilitie.

Attributed to Chaucer in both MSS., but not in the accepted canon (see Hammond, *Chaucer,* p. 342). Perhaps enough weight has not been put on the double ascription; but Bannatyne is a worthless authority (see Spurgeon, *Five Hundred Years of Chaucer Criticism,* I, 102), and he may have derived his information from the earlier MS. The problem is not simplified by the comment in Hunterian Club *Bannatyne,* I, cvi: "Not in Chaucer; perhaps by Lydgate." MacCracken does not mention the poem in his discussions of the Lydgate canon.

(1) Arch. Selden B. 24 (7 stanzas rime-royal); I have transcribed it for publication.

(2) Chapman and Myllar [dated 1508? by *STC*]; ed. George Stevenson, *Pieces from the Makculloch and the Gray MSS. together with The Chepman and Myllar Prints,* Edinburgh (STS, LXV), 1918, p. 217.

(3) Advocates' Library 1. 1. 6; ed. Ritchie, *Bannatyne Manuscript,* IV, 34; see also Hunterian Club *Bannatyne,* I, cvi.

The Arch. Selden MS. was composed after 1486 (Hammond, *Chaucer,* p. 341).

Satire: maidens are virtuous but they become vicious when they are married. Eve, a wife, brought the world to confusion; wives destroyed Solomon, Samson, and David. But the Blessed Virgin redressed Eve's sin.

55. Doctrina et Consilium Galienis [prose].

(1) Harley 78; ed. Furnivall, *Jyl of Breyntfords Testament,* London, 1871, p. 39.

Furnivall dates "?ab. 1455"; this portion of the composite MS. was copied by John Shirley (1366?-1456). See Hammond, *Chaucer,* pp. 328, 515.

Semi-satirical counsel on how to rule one's wife.

56. Dust is lighter then a fether.

(1) I have been unable to identify this quatrain's textual authority, but it may be from the same broadside or manuscript as **343**. See Lilly's *Collection,* p. 193. The brevity of the piece suggests its use as "filler" in a broadside.

Most of Lilly's pieces are before 1569; but there is no certainty about this piece.

Woman's fickle mind is lighter than feather, dust, or wind.

Airlie on Als Wodnisday (251).

57. Eche man folwith his owne fantasye.

By John Lydgate.

Amor Vincit Omnia, Mentiris Quod Pecunia, or *A Demawnde by Lydgate.*

(1) Harley 2251 (17 eight-line stanzas); ed. with collations of (2) and (3) by MacCracken, *Minor Poems of Lydgate,* II, 744.

(2) British Museum Additional 29729.

(3) Ashmole 59.

Early XV cent.

Primarily a satire on women's inconstancy and greed, with the refrain "Love is sette bakke, gold goth byfore, and mede." But it rambles on to other subjects, and ends with the conclusion that the proverb "Amor vincit omnia" is true of heavenly love alone.

Ek ye wymmen whiche been enclynd (230).

58. Experience, though noon auctoritee.

By Geoffrey Chaucer.

The Wife of Bath's Prologue and Tale.

(The following list of authorities has been compiled from Sir William McCormick and Janet E. Heseltine, *The Manuscripts of Chaucer's Canterbury Tales,* Oxford, 1933. Minor imperfections in the appropriate section of the MSS. are not noted. *WBProl* and *WBT* begin the D fragment of the *Canterbury Tales* and consist of 1264 lines in all.)

(1) British Museum Additional 5140.

(2) British Museum Additional 35286 (formerly Ashburnham Appendix 125).
(3) Bodley 414.
(4) Bodley 686.
(5) Bodleian Barlow 20.
(6) Christ Church College Oxford 52.
(7) Cardigan (now Brudenell Estate).
(8) Corpus Christi College Oxford 198.
(9) Caxton's first edition (*ca.* 1478).
(10) Caxton's second edition (*ca.* 1484).
(11) Cambridge University Library Dd. 4. 24. Succeeding editions by de Worde, Pynson, Thynne, Stow not listed here.
(12) Delamere (now owned by Boies Penrose III) (imperfect).
(13) Duke of Devonshire, Chatsworth (McCormick's Ds¹).
(14) Ellesmere (now Huntington El 26. C 12); ed. Robinson, *Chaucer,* p. 91, with corrections and collations from the other MSS.; ed. John M. Manly and Edith Rickert, *The Text of the Canterbury Tales,* University of Chicago Press, 1940, III, 234, with the same. See also Robinson, p. 801; Hammond, *Chaucer,* p. 297; Griffith, *Chaucer,* p. 93; Martin, *Chaucer,* p. 55; and the current bibliographies.
(15) Egerton 2726.
(16) Egerton 2863.
(17) Fitzwilliam Museum McClean 181 (formerly Ashburnham Appendix 127).
(18) Cambridge University Library Gg. 4. 27.
(19) Hunterian Museum (Glasgow) V. 1. 1.
(20) Harley 1239 (*Tale* only).
(21) Harley 1758.
(22) Harley 7334.
(23) Harley 7335.
(24) Helmingham Hall, Suffolk (Lady Tollemache).
(25) National Library of Wales Hengwrt 154 (or Peniarth 392D).
(26) Holkham Hall, Norfolk (Earl of Leicester) 667.
(27) Bodleian Hatton Donat. 1.
(28) Cambridge University Library Ii. 3. 26.
(29) Lansdowne 851.
(30) Lichfield Cathedral 2.
(31) Laud 600.
(32) Laud 739.
(33) Lincoln Cathedral 110.
(34) John Rylands Library (Manchester) Eng. 113.

(35) Pierpont Morgan Library 249 (formerly Ashburnham Appendix 124).
(36) McCormick (formerly Ashburnham Appendix 126, now at University of Chicago).
(37) Cambridge University Library Mm. 2. 5.
(38) New College Oxford D. 314.
(39) Duke of Northumberland 455.
(40) Phillipps 8136 (now Rosenbach).
(41) Phillipps 8137 (now Rosenbach).
(42) Bibliothèque Nationale fonds anglais 39.
(43) Petworth (Lord Leconfield).
(44) College of Physicians (London) 13.
(45) Rawlinson Poetry 141.
(46) Rawlinson Poetry 149.
(47) Rawlinson Poetry 223.
(48) Royal 17. D. 15.
(49) Royal 18. C. 2.
(50) Arch. Selden B. 14.
(51) Sion College (London) Arch. L. 40. 2. E.
(52) Sloane 1685.
(53) Sloane 1686.
(54) Trinity College Cambridge R. 3. 3.
(55) Trinity College Oxford 49.
(56) [Lost from British Museum Additional 25718.]
(57) Egerton 2864.
(58) [Lost from Harley 7333.]
(59) Trinity College Cambridge R. 3. 15.
Usually dated very late in Chaucer's career; perhaps about 1394-96 (see Robinson, p. 801).

Confession of an "archwife," who by masterly irony is made the vehicle of satire even as she is defending her sex and her own lusty personality. Begins the Marriage Group, and therefore masquerades as a defense of women although it is derived from the greatest satires of women in the Middle Ages: Jerome's *Against Jovinian*, Deschamps' *Miroir de Mariage*, and Jean de Meun's portion of *La Roman de la Rose*. The paradox is continued in *The Clerk's Tale*, in which the story of a patient wife becomes the vehicle for attack on women. Chaucerian "ambiguity" at its best, in which the sharpness of type satire is rounded off by realistic observation and artistic sympathy.

59. [Faine would I have a vertuous wife.

The Vertuous Wife; "a ballet intituled fayne wolde I have a vertuous wyfe adourned with all modeste both mylde and meke of quyett lyf esteemynge chef hyr chastetye" (Rollins, *Analytical Index,* no. 820).

(1) "From the Editor's MS." in Collier's *Extracts*, I, 162 (8 six-
line stanzas, instead of the *abab* quatrain which one would
expect from the entry in the *Stationers' Register*).

This title and (probable) first stanza was licensed in 1566-67 to
Richard Jones. Collier is believed to have created the poem to fit an
entry in the *Stationers' Register*. See Rollins, ed. *Handful*, p. 100,
and his note in *JEGP*, XVIII (1919), 53. Collier's "ballad manuscript" has recently turned up in the Folger Library, too late to be
of use here. See Introduction, p. 80.

The ballad entry refers to a moralization of "Fain would I have a
pretty thing," preserved in *Handful*, ed. Rollins, p. 57; it probably
was based on Proverbs 31, like **283**. Collier's piece injects a strongly
satirical note by describing the virtuous wife in terms revealing the
shortcomings of most women. If it is spurious it is still interesting
evidence of the knowledge of the facts and the temper of Elizabethan
times possessed by a remarkable though unprincipled student.]

60. Fane wald I luve, bot quhair abowt?

By William Dunbar? Included in the dubious portion of
Small's edition; excluded in MacKenzie's *Poems of William Dunbar*. Ascribed in the MS. to "[Maister Johne] Clerk," but the
ascription is in a lighter ink than the poem.
Counsale in Luve, or *Advyce to Luvaris*.
(1) Advocates' Library 1. 1. 6 (7 five-line stanzas); ed. Small,
Poems of William Dunbar, II, 308; Ritchie, *Bannatyne
Manuscript*, IV, 13; Hunterian Club *Bannatyne*, I, civ.
Certainly before 1568. Dunbar and Clerk appear to have been
contemporaries (see T. F. Henderson, *Scottish Vernacular Literature*, 3rd ed., Edinburgh, 1910, pp. 132-33); if this poem is by either
of them it would be late XV or early XVI cent.

Rebellious lover, with general satire on women and the excesses of
lovers; heavenly love preferred to earthly.

61. Farewell, Loue, and all thy lawes for euer.

By Sir Thomas Wyatt.
A renouncing of loue.
(1) Egerton 2711 (14 lines—a sonnet); ed. Foxwell, *Poems of
Sir Thomas Wiat*, I, 19, with collation of (2) and (3).
(2) British Museum Additional 17492.
(3) *Tottel's Miscellany* (in all editions); ed. Rollins, I, 69, with
collation of (1).
Foxwell would date shortly after 1528 (II, 33).

Rebellious lover. Love with its "rotten boughes" is abandoned to
"younger hertes" by the author, who is called away by Senec and Plato.

62. Farewell thou frosen hart and eares of hardned stele.

The louer forsaketh his vnkinde loue.

(1) *Tottel's Miscellany* (second edition, 1557, and all later editions) (17 long couplets); ed. Rollins, I, 256.

1557 or before.

Rebellious lover; vicious attack on woman's wantonness with the use of hunting and hawking terms (see **7**). The lover "rather asketh present death, then to beholde thy face."

63. ffavour is fair in luvis lair.

By Alexander Scott.

(1) Advocates' Library 1. 1. 6 (6 quatrains); ed. Cranstoun, *Poems of Alexander Scott*, p. 64; Donald, *Poems of Alexander Scott*, p. 41; Ritchie, *Bannatyne Manuscript*, IV, 5; for further editions see Cranstoun, p. 159.

Cranstoun dates Scott's work 1545-68.

Rebellious lover; happy is the man at liberty who can hold him so.

64. First Blast of the Trumpet against the monstruous regiment of Women [prose].

By John Knox.

(1) Printed at Geneva by J. Crespin (1558); ed. Edwin Arber, *The English Scholar's Library of Old and Modern Works*, II, Southgate (London), 1878; for further editions see p. vii.

Laing believes the book was written toward the end of 1557 (Arber, p. xvi).

A learned treatise on the imperfections and inferiority of women, written as Knox contemplated the feminine menace which threatened to engulf Christendom: Catherine de Medici, Queen of France; Marie de Lorraine, Queen Regent of Scotland, whose sole heir was Mary, afterwards Queen of Scots; Mary Tudor; and the heir apparent Princess Elizabeth. Knox's argument that women are incapable of rule is particularly directed against the Catholic Mary Tudor. For Knox's apologies after the Protestant Elizabeth came to the throne see Arber, p. 57. The only answer to Knox written before 1568 is John Aylmer's *Harborowe for faithfull and trewe subjects* (**84**). Others, including the unprinted MS. defense of Lord Henry Howard (1590), are listed by Arber, pp. vii-viii. See "John Knox and His Relations to Women," in Robert Louis Stevenson's *Familiar Studies of Men and Books*, New York, 1923, p. 283; James E. Phillips, "The Background of Spenser's Attitude toward Women Rulers," *Huntington Library Quarterly*, V (1941-42), 5-32; and "The Woman Ruler in Spenser's *Faerie Queene*," *ibid.*, pp. 211-34. For another angelic *Trumpet*, published by Robert Crowley in 1549, see **296**. On French aspects of the controversy over women rulers, which involved Montaigne and François Hotman, see Richardson, *Forerunners of Feminism*, pp. 126-31.

65. Fleshly lustys and festys.

(1) From the primatial register of John Swayne, Archbishop of Armagh (1418-39); reprinted from Cotton's *Fasti Ecclesia Hiberniae*, III, vi, by St. John D. Seymour, *Proceedings of the Royal Irish Academy*, Section C, XLI (1932-33), 209 (2 six-line stanzas).

(2) Corpus Christi College Oxford 274 (8 lines); ed. Coxe, *Catalogus*, p. 117; Thomas Wright, *Political Poems and Songs*, London (Rolls Series), 1859-61, II, 252.

Found among entries of the first half XV cent.; Miss Mabel Day would date then or late XIV cent.

Satire on women's fashions ("horns" and "tails"). The Armagh version shares a line or two with **309**. The Corpus Christi version differs greatly after the first two lines; its satire is directed against courtly fashion and hypocrisy without regard to sex.

66. For as moche as ydelnesse is rote of all vyces.

By William Walter, with envoy by Robert Copland.

The spectacle of louers. . . . a lytell contrauers dyalogue bytwene loue and councell / With many goodly argumentes of good Women and bad.

(1) Wynkyn de Worde (n.d.). Never reprinted. According to the *STC* (no. 25008) there are only two extant copies, one of them (Bodleian) fragmentary and the other (Huntington Library) complete. I have examined a microfilm of the latter (117 rime-royal stanzas).

The *STC* dates the extant edition [1520?], on what evidence I am unaware. The device on sig. D4ᵛ appears to be McKerrow's no. 21, and in a later stage of deterioration than McKerrow's exemplar, reproduced from Fisher's *Treatise concerning. . . . the Seven Penitential Psalms*, published by de Worde on August 13, 1529. McKerrow does not list Walter's poem; his latest record of the use of the device is in the Stanbridge *Accidentia* of 1534. The extant edition therefore would seem to have appeared between 1529 and 1535, the date of de Worde's death. The poem itself was probably written close to 1520. Walter is described on the title page as "seruaunt vnto syr Henry Marnaye knyght Chauncelour of the Duchye of Lancastre"; and Marnaye died in 1523. On Marnaye and Walter see Herbert G. Wright, *Early English Versions of the Tales of Guiscardo and Ghismonda and Titus and Gisippus from the Decameron*, London (EETS, CCV), 1937, pp. liv-xc. *The spectacle of louers* is described by Collier, *Bibliographical and Critical Account*, IV, 211.

Consultor (the author) is walking in the fields of a morning and encounters an unhappy lover. A dialogue ensues, in which the lover, however melancholy, defends the love of women against Consultor's attacks on carnal love and the evil nature of women. Consultor advances the usual examples from the Bible and the classics. Amator defends love and marriage and the mothers who bear us; he appears to win the argument. The author in an envoy claims to have written the piece in no spirit of malice and with no hatred of women; he presents the dialogue as an example of men's vicious words against women. If he is to be maligned for speaking dispraise he should be thanked for speaking praise. Although the subject matter and the title are similar the piece has no connection with Myll's *Spektakle of Luf* (**271a**). The title suggests a Latin source with some such name as *Speculum Amoris;* but Walter is said to have "newly compyled" the poem. Walter's other books were translations from the Italian. Similar titles appear in broadsides: "A looking glasse for Disdaynefull lovers" was entered in 1594 to John Danter; "A lookinge glasse for Lovers" in 1576 to John Cherlewood (Rollins, *Analytical Index*, nos. 1536, 1538).

67. For as moche as many folke there be.

By Robert Copland, whose name appears in an acrostic in the envoy.

A complaynt of them that be to soone maryed.

(1) Wynkyn de Worde (1535) (1 rime-royal and 50 eight-line stanzas). Never reprinted; I have examined the single extant copy at Huntington by means of microfilm. Described by Beatrice White, "Two Tracts on Marriage by Robert Copland," *Huntington Library Bulletin,* I (1931), 206; Wright, *Middle-Class Culture,* p. 471; and others cited under **17**. There is no query about the date of this edition, as implied by the *STC* (no. 5729).

Copland says that this is his "fyrst werke," and Collier accepts the statement without comment. Plomer (*Wynkyn de Worde & his Contemporaries*, London, 1925, pp. 75-76) believes Copland was contributing prologues to books as early as 1495, and therefore interprets "fyrst werke" as "first attempt at an extended book" or "first translation." A verse colophon dates the extant edition 1535:

Fynyssed and done the yere of our lorde
A thousand CCCCC, and .xxxv. at London.

Although Copland's meter is none too regular, it is basically a four- or five-stress line, and if we read "A thousand, five hundred, and seven [or eight, nine, ten] in London" we would seem to have a better line than that extant. This suggests a prior edition now lost. The printer's device on sig. B4ʳ (McKerrow, no. 11) was used as early as 1499 and as late as 1530. By the state of the device Plomer (*Wynkyn de Worde,* pp. 75-76) would date shortly before Stephen Hawes' *Conversion of Swerers* (1509).

Satire on woman's shrewishness and sloth. It is better to be a friar or a hermit than a husband. The author blames not marriage, which was instituted by God, but evil wives. The first domestic battle in the author-speaker's married career comes when he takes his wife on his knee and says that, now that eight days are past, the honeymoon is over, and feast and idleness must give way to thrift and hard work. With vitriolic words both wife and mother-in-law turn on him. Cousins, gossips, and neighbors eat them out of house and home. Hence poverty is the usual end of marriage. For the short honeymoon see **45**; for the problem of poverty in marriage **70**. *To soone maryed* is a free translation of *La Complainte du Trop Tôt Mariée*, reprinted under the title *La Complainte du Nouveau Marié* by Anatole de Montaiglon, *Recueil de Poésies Françoises*, IV, 5. For the sequel, *The complaynte of them that ben to late maryed*, see **17**; and for a merging of the two see *La Resolution de Ny Trop Tost Ny Trop Tard Marié* in Montaiglon, III, 129.

For tell a woman all your cownsayle (136).

For the loue of a maydon fre (38).

67a. ffor to declair þe he magnificens.

>   By "Stewart."
>   (1) Advocates' Library 1. 1. 6 (8 eight-line stanzas); ed. Ritchie, *Bannatyne Manuscript,* III, 256; see Hunterian Club *Bannatyne*, I, xcv.
>   (2) Advocates' Library 1. 1. 6 (another copy with important variants); ed. Ritchie, IV, 71.
>   1568 or before.

Defense: my pen is unworthy, yet I must answer old dotards who defame women, the bringers of peace, beauty, and felicity. Witness of Mary. The last stanza employs the convention of **118**, "Gif all the erth war perchmene scribable."

68. For to revoke to pensiue thought.

>   By George Turbervile.
>   *The Lover abused renownceth Loue.*
>   (1) Turbervile's *Epitaphes, Epigrams, Songs and Sonets* (1567) (11 eight-line stanzas); ed. Collier [1867], p. 206; and Chalmers, II, 638.
>   1567 or before.

Rebellious lover. Women's love is like a snare. There is a dramatic shift in the poem: the lover beseeches the lady to hear him; when she refuses he charges her with having been suckled by a cruel tiger, refuses to be one of Circe's swine, and revolts from Cupid's banner on Plato's recommendation.

69. ffurth ouer the mold at morrow as I ment.

By "Stewart."

Ballat of vnpossibiliteis.

(1) Advocates' Library 1. 1. 6 (8 rime-royal stanzas); ed. Ritchie, *Bannatyne Manuscript,* IV, 40; see Hunterian Club *Bannatyne,* I, cvi.

1568 or before.

Satire: *chanson d'aventure* setting for a lying-poem uttered by "Pandarius" with the refrain "Than ladyis to thair luvaris salbe leill." As usual the subject is woman's inconstancy; compare **4, 116, 203, 292, 351, 353, 354, 357.** The finest transmutation of this folk-genre is "Go and catch a falling star" (H. J. C. Grierson, *The Poems of John Donne,* Oxford, 1912, II, 11); note especially the emphasis on "news" or "strange wonders." Lying-songs do not necessarily involve women; a good illustration is our childhood "The barefoot boy with shoes on/ Stood sitting in the grass." For extensive parallels from modern folk-literature and continental sources see G. L. Kittredge, "Notes on a Lying Song," *JAFL,* XXXIX (1926), 195-99; on the *Lügenlied* see also Archer Taylor, *Problems in German Literary History,* New York, 1939, p. 81; and his *Literary History of Meistergesang,* New York, 1937, p. 101. Professor Taylor has generously furnished me with a supplementary reference, to Karl Goedeke, *Grundrisz zur Geschichte der Deutschen Dichtung,* 2nd ed., Dresden, 1884—, II, 559. For a French pair involving the *querelle* see *Le Loyauté des Hommes* and *Le Loyaulté des Femmes,* both of the XV cent., in Anatole de Montaiglon, *Recueil de Poésies Françoises,* Paris, 1855-78, I, 227; II, 35. For a Welsh lying-song see Grace Rhys, *A Celtic Anthology,* London, 1927, p. 292. In its popular form the lying-song is akin to the tall tale; see Antti Aarne, *The Types of the Folk-Tale,* rev. and tr. Stith Thompson, Helsinki (FF Communications, 74), 1928, nos. 1875-1961; Jonas Balys, *Lietuviu Pasakojamosios Tautosakos Motyvu Katalogas,* Kaunas (*Tautosakos Darbai,* II), 1936, pp. 161-64. See also Nicholas Breton, *Strange Newes* (1622). For further English parallels see "Benedicite what dremyd I this nyȝt," ed. Bernhard Fehr, *Archiv,* CVI (1901), 55; *Newes,* beginning "Now, gentlemen, if you will hear," ed. Ritson, *Ancient Songs,* rev. Hazlitt, p. 366; "Herkyn to my tale that I schall to yow schew" (two versions) ed. Wright and Halliwell, *Reliquiae Antiquae,* I, 81, 86; and "The mone in the mornyng merely rose," *ibid.,* I, 84; Greene, *Early English Carols,* pp. 317, 319 (nos. 471, 472, and 474); George Milburn, *The Hobo's Handbook,* New York, 1930, pp. 61-62, 85-91; Chambers and Sidgwick, *Early English Lyrics,* pp. 178, 362; "When trout swim down Great Ormond Street," in Conrad Aiken, *Modern American Poets,* New York, 1927, p. 329. The origin of this widespread form must be complex. Often it purports to be the results of drunkenness or the love-malady. In connection with the latter compare the Provençal "enigma" (Barbara Smythe, *Trobador Poets,* London, 1929, p. 2) and the French *fatrasie* (see **201**). The type may also owe something to popular proverb (see

T. F. Thisleton-Dyer, *Folk-Lore of Women*, London, 1905, pp. 185-86; and John M. Manly, ed., *Canterbury Tales*, New York, 1928, p. 531) and to literary metaphor (see *Testament of Mr. Andro Kennedy*, lines 63-64, in Small, ed., *Poems of William Dunbar*, II, 56; and *Troilus and Criseyde*, iv, 1548-53, ed. Robinson, *Chaucer*, p. 537). The lying-song seems to be enjoying a revival among contemporary poets. See, in addition to Aiken's poem already cited, William Butler Yeats' *The Fool by the Roadside*, in *Collected Poems*, New York, 1933, p. 254.

70. Frend, where we met this other day.

By Thomas Tusser.
Dialogue betweene two Bachelers, of wiuing and thriuing by Affirmation and Obiection.

(1) Tottel's 1570 edition of *A hundreth good pointes of husbandrie* is the first extant version to contain the *Dialogue* (four-line prologue, beginning "Man minded for to thriue," 27 six-line stanzas and one seven-line stanza); ed. W. Payne and S. J. Herrtage, *Fiue Hundred Pointes of Good Husbandrie, by Thomas Tusser*, London (English Dialect Society, XXXI), 1878, p. 152.

Not in the 1557 edition of Tusser. The *Stationers' Register* lists the following entry under 1561-62 (Arber, I, 179): "Recevyd of Thomas hackett for his lycense for pryntynge of a Dyaloge of Wyvynge and thryvynge of TUSSERS with ij lessons for olde and yonge. . . . iiijd." According to Payne and Herrtage, an edition may have appeared in 1562 with the *Dialogue* (p. xxiii). What looks like a parody, *An hundreth poyntes of evell huswyfrye*, was licensed to J. Allde in 1565-66. See **126.**

Debate for and against woman's thriftiness and desire for the mastery. The author is very careful to take no sides, and to indicate that the debate mingles jest and earnest.

71. Fra raige of ʒowᵗ the rynk hes rune.

By Alexander Scott.
Luve suld be vsit with prudens.

(1) Advocates' Library 1. 1. 6 (7 eight-line stanzas); ed. Cranstoun, *Poems of Alexander Scott*, p. 76; Donald, *Poems of Alexander Scott*, p. 51; Ritchie, *Bannatyne Manuscript*, IV, 79; for further editions see Cranstoun, p. 166.

Cranstoun dates Scott's work 1545-68.

Defense of women and of temperate love.

72. Ful longe I haue a seruant be.

By John Lydgate.
The Servant of Cupyde Forsaken, or Complaynt Lydegate.

(1) British Museum Additional 16165 (9 eight-line stanzas); ed. MacCracken, *Minor Poems of Lydgate*, II, 427.
Early XV cent.

Semi-allegorical complaint on woman's doubleness; directed in the envoy against all women. Shirley writes in the margin of the envoy "Be stille daun Johan, suche is youre fortune."

73. [Full merilie singes the cuckoo.
The Cuckoe's Song.
(1) Said by Collier to be in a MS. "in possession of the editor," "and that at least half a century after the date of the entry"; printed in *Extracts*, I, 122 (5 eight-line stanzas).

Probably spurious, created by Collier to fit an entry with such a title licensed to Wylliam Griffith in 1565-66 (see Rollins, *Analytical Index*, no. 936, who suggests an identification of the entry with a ballad sung in Barry's *Ram Alley* [1611]). On these Collier poems see **59**.

Collier's piece cleverly sits the cuckoo on five trees, the beech, the oak, the ash, the alder, and the aspen, and makes him sing of his perennial subject, the horns of a cuckold.]

Gif (see **If**).

74. Glad was the Sonne of frowning Beldams death.
By George Turbervile.
Of the Cruell Hatred of Stepmothers.
(1) Turbervile's *Epitaphes, Epigrams, Songs and Sonets* (1567) (1 five-line stanza); ed. Collier [1867], p. 189; and Chalmers, II, 633.
1567 or before.

Stepmothers are malicious even in death. See also **295**. From the Greek Anthology, ix. 67; according to Lathrop, *MLN*, XLIII (1928), 225, via the Latin of Janus Cornarius.

75. Glory vnto God, laude and benysoun.
Translated by John Lydgate (not by Robert Copland, as suggested in Wright, *Middle-Class Culture*, p. 471) from the French or Latin of *De Coniuge non Ducenda*.
The Payne and Sorow of Evyll Maryage.
(1) Digby 181 (16 rime-royal stanzas); ed. MacCracken, *Minor Poems of Lydgate*, II, 456; with variants from (2)-(4); and by Thomas Wright, *The Latin Poems Commonly Attributed to Walter Mapes*, London (Camden Society, Series I, No. 16), 1841, p. 295, with variants from (4).
(2) Harley 2251 (6 stanzas, plus **387**); see Hammond, *Anglia*, XXVIII (1905), 21. Begins "After this story tellith also."

(3) Cambridge University Library Ff. 1. 6 (1 extra stanza).
(4) Wynkyn de Worde (n.d.) (5 extra stanzas); ed. J. P. Collier, London (Percy Society, I), 1840, from the unique copy
now at Huntington; ed. Hazlitt, *Remains,* IV, 73. *STC*
(no. 19119) dates the print [1509?]. See Plomer, "Robert
Copland," p..222.
Early XV cent.

Satire warning against marriage. The author, "in purpoce for to
take a wiff," was saved by a vision of three of God's angels, John
Chrysostom, Peter of Corbeil, and "Laurentius" (appears in French and
Latin only; Laurence of Durham?), who among them revealed the
evil nature of women. The extra stanzas in de Worde's print, possibly
supplied either by printed Latin versions or by de Worde's translator
Copland, add counsel to those already caught in the snare. The ultimate
source of both French and English is the XII or XIII cent. *Golias de
Coniuge non Ducenda,* also called *De tribus angelis qui retraxerunt a
nuptiis; Dissuasio nubendi Goliae; Naufragium Nubentium secundum
Goliam;* or *Apocalypsis Goliae de Naufragio Nubendi.* The first line
parodies the Palm Sunday Processional of Theodulfus of Orleans:
"Gloria, laus et honor tibi sit, rex Christe, redemptor" (for the Processional see F. J. E. Raby, *A History of Christian-Latin Poetry,* Oxford,
1927, p. 174; and John Julian, *A Dictionary of Hymnology,* London,
1915, p. 426). *De Coniuge* is attributed variously to "Golias," Gilbertus,
Gauterus (Walter Map?), and Galwinus or Gawain. Along with the
English Wright edits the Latin and the French (pp. 77, 292). To his
list of eight Latin MSS. in English libraries other scholars have added
thirty others in England and the Continent: five in Paris, five in Cambridge, three in Munich, two (or three?) in Vienna, two in Venice,
and one each in Oxford, Dublin, Berne, Troyes, Tours, Geneva, Madrid,
Jena, Eisleben, Berlin (the *editio princeps*), Melk (Austria), Padua, and
Florence. See Wattenbach, *Zeitschrift für deutsches Alterthum,* XV
(1872), 501; [Hauréau,] *Bibliothèque de l'École de Chartes,* XLVII
(1886), 95; Esposito, *English Historical Review,* XXXII (1917), 400;
and Ludwig Bertalot, *Humanistisches Studienheft eines Nürnberger
Scholaren,* Berlin, 1910, pp. 74-75. We may add three more from England: Lansdowne 564, Lambeth Palace 486, and Digby 166. Wright
lists one French copy, to which may be added Bodleian Douce 210. For
additional material see F. J. E. Raby, *A History of Secular Latin Poetry,*
Oxford, 1934, II, 222; Wulff, *Die Frauenfeindlichen Dichtungen,* pp.
36-40; Paul Lehmann, *Die Parodie im Mittelalter,* Munich, 1922, pp.
165-68. Lehmann notes the attempts which have been made to tie the
poem to the Lateran Council of 1215, when one of many efforts was
made to promulgate celibacy; but he observes that *De Coniuge* never
refers to the specific problem of clerical marriage. He also opposes
the identification of "Laurentius" with Laurence of Durham. Just why
the author chose these three particular "angels" has never been settled.
Pierre de Corbeil, Archbishop of Sens (died 1222), may well owe his

selection to the so-called *Missel des Fous* of Sens, which he revised for the Feast of the Circumcision, a day of merry-making for choir-boys and inferior clergy. On the *Missel* see E. K. Chambers, *Mediaeval Stage,* I, 281-87; and Henri Villetard, ed., *Office de Pierre de Corbeil (Office de la Circoncision), Improprement Apellé "Office des Fous,"* Paris (Bibliothèque Musicologique, IV), 1907. Pierre is a logical candidate for the role of chief angel on several grounds: (1) the satirical nature of the *Missel* and of *De Coniuge,* both of which involve liturgical parody; (2) a tradition that he wrote "Satires contre les maris et les tribulations du mariage" (Villetard, p. 55); (3) the connection of Pierre and the *Missel* with the goliards (Villetard, p. 58; Chambers, I, 281; Lehmann believes that the goliards were his enemies because he revised their favorite feast); (4) certain allusions in the *Missel* to the virtues of chastity; (5) the similarity of the opening lines of *De Coniuge* to those of the climactic trope of the *Missel* "Laus, honor, uirtus Deo nostro"; (6) the connection of Pierre with England as coadjutor of Lincoln (Chambers, I, 281), a point made important by the strong possibility that *De Coniuge* was composed in England; (7) Pierre's fitness as a champion of celibacy and adviser to youth, since he had composed the office for the feast of the younger ecclesiastics.

75a. Gooe feede thie fylthie lustes.

(1) Written in margin of the Rosenbach copy of *Tottel's Miscellany* (second edition, second setting); ed. Rollins, II, 271 (8 lines).

After July 31, 1557, the date of this edition of *Tottel's*. Rollins says it is in "a hand about as old as the copy itself."

Satire on love or marriage, the enemies of study. An answer to **11.**

Go ye beffore, be twayne and twayne (107).

God honoured women in His life (145).

76. God spede you, maysters, everychone!

By John Heywood, according to all recent editors. Charles W. Wallace ascribed it to William Cornish; but this ascription is not accepted by Robert W. Bolwell, *The Life and Works of John Heywood,* New York, 1921, p. 114, or by R. de la Bère, *John Heywood, Entertainer,* London, 1937, p. 87.

A Mery Play betwene Johan Johan, the Husbande, Tyb, his Wyfe, and Syr Johan, the Preest.

(1) William Rastell, 1533 (678 lines); ed. Joseph Quincy Adams, *Chief Pre-Shakespearean Dramas,* Boston, 1924, p. 385; by J. S. Farmer, *The Dramatic Writings of John Heywood,* London, 1905, p. 65; by de la Bère, p. 233; and by Alois Brandl, *Quellen des Weltlichen Dramas in Eng-*

land vor Shakespeare, Strassburg (Quellen und Forschungen, LXXX), 1898, p. 259.

1533 or before. On the basis of the type W. W. Greg believes it was set up in 1532-33 rather than in 1533-34 (*A Bibliography of the English Printed Drama to the Restoration*, London, 1939, I, 88). De la Bère believes this play is "the best and probably the latest of Heywood's farces," four of which were published by Rastell (Heywood's brother-in-law) with the imprint 1533.

A domestic farce satirizing the shrewishness and inconstancy of women, aided and abetted by the parish priest. In the end the worm turns; after untold humiliations Johan Johan gives his wife a good beating. Bolwell (p. 114) believes that the play may be based on a French farce adapted from a fabliau, and notes analogies to the *Farce nouuelle trèsbonne et fort joyeuse de Pernet qui va au vin* ("nouvellement imprimé" in 1548). Because Heywood was a good Catholic, some have been disturbed by the satire on the priest. Actually Heywood would have felt no more disloyalty to his Church than if he were an American poking fun at a "bureaucrat." A later broadside writer appears to have tried to capitalize on the success of *Johan Johan* and *Tom Tyler* (**193**), if one may so interpret the ballad entered in 1562-63 called "Tyb will playe the Tome boye" (Rollins, *Analytical Index*, no. 2780). Tib and Tom were rustic counterparts, as shown by a couplet in **375**:

> No! No! torne tibb to tom,
> Tibbes owne dear countreman.

77. God wote grete cause these wyffys haue a-mong.

(1) British Museum Additional 22718 (5 triplets, each with the brief refrain, "In besenysse"); ed. Curt F. Bühler, "The Dictes and Sayings of the Philosophers," *Library*, Series 2, XV (1934-35), 318.

MS. late XV cent.

Satire: husbands must give way to woman's desire for the mastery.

78. Good awdience, harken to me in this cace.

By John Wallys.

(1) Ashmole 48 (15 eight-line stanzas); ed. Wright, *Songs and Ballads*, p. 129.

Rollins, *MLN*, XXXIV (1919), 349, dates the MS. 1557-65 on the basis of broadside contents.

Satire: ironic treatment of a widow's sorrow at her husband's death, with the basic refrain "I wat not wher for to have a newe." In a *chanson d'aventure* setting the author overhears a conversation between a widow and her gossip. Akin to **336**.

Gode gosyp . . . (107).

79. gospelles of dystaues, The [prose].

The translator, who gives his initials as "H. W.," probably was Henry Watson, apprentice to de Worde, who printed and translated other works. See Duff, *Century*, pp. 166-67.

(1) Wynkyn de Worde (n.d.). Never reprinted. There is a fragmentary copy at the Bodleian and a single complete copy at Huntington Library, both of which I have examined by means of microfilm.

The *STC* (no. 12091) makes no attempt to date. The device is McKerrow 23*a* in its pristine, unworn state. McKerrow's exemplar is reproduced from *The Book of Good Manners*, dated Dec. 10, 1507. A second example in McKerrow, *Stans Puer ad Mensam*, shows a worn state of the device and was printed in 1515. Hence the book must have been printed in 1515 or before, perhaps as early as 1507.

A deft and vigorous piece of Gallic irony, which purports to reveal "the grete noblesse of ladyes / and the grete goodnes that from them procedeth." Actually it is a parody of the Gospels, with book, chapter, and glose. The Evangelists are six old wives, and their subject old wives' tales. They impress the author into service, and he cannot escape until he has sat through a week of boring secretarial labor. Although the Evangels primarily consist of superstitions, there are many boasts of the glory of women and the way in which husbands may be ruled. The original, *Les Evangiles des Quenouilles,* was printed at Bruges by Colard Mansion about 1475, and reprinted at least eight times during the later XV and early XVI cent. See the edition of [P. Jannet], Paris (Bibliothèque Elzevirienne), 1855.

80. Grete Rayson Cleopatre is þy Kyndenesse.

Not by Chaucer, as implied in title (see Hammond, *Chaucer,* p. 416). By the scribe, John Shirley?

þe Cronycle made by Chaucier.

(1) Ashmole 59 (9 eight-line stanzas); ed. F. J. Furnivall, *Odd Texts of Chaucer's Minor Poems*, London (Chaucer Society, Series I, Nos. XXIII, LX), 1868-80, Appendix, p. vi; Otto Gaertner, *John Shirley, sein Leben und Wirken*. Halle, 1904, p. 66.

The scribe and possible author lived from 1366 (?) to 1456. The MS. was composed late in life, perhaps after 1447 (Hammond, *Chaucer,* p. 333).

Defense: Cupid's Martyrs. Shirley heads it "Here nowe folowe þe names of þe nyene worshipfullest Ladyes þat in alle cronycles . and storyal bokes haue beo founden of trouþe of constaunce and vertuous or reproched womanhode. by Chaucier." The heroines treated are identical with Chaucer's in the *Legend*, except that Alceste is confused with

"Alcyone" and Philomela is omitted. This piece should not be confused
with *The Nine Ladies Worthy* (**247**), which is apparently also an imitation of the *Legend*.

81. Grisilde is deed, and eek hire pacience.

> By Geoffrey Chaucer.
> *Envoy to the Clerk's Tale.*
> (1)–(64) For MSS. see **261**. These 6 rime-royal stanzas appear
>   in all MSS. of the *Clerk's Tale* except Harley 5908, a frag-
>   ment from which it was apparently lost. For its position,
>   which sometimes varies, see McCormick and Heseltine,
>   *Manuscripts of Chaucer's Canterbury Tales, passim.*

Perhaps composed later than *The Clerk's Tale*, to fit the Marriage Group. This would place it in the last decade of the XIV
cent. or thereabouts.

Satire: ironic exhortation to "archewyves" to eschew the example of
Patient Griselda "Lest Chichevache yow swelwe in hire entraille!" As
for husbands, "lat hym care, and wepe, and wrynge, and waille!"
Alludes to the fabulous beasts later treated by Lydgate (**227**).

82. Half in a dreme, not fully wel awaked.

> Translated from Alain Chartier by Sir Richard Ros. The trans-
> lator's name is provided only by (2).
> *La Belle Dame sans Mercy;* called by Bale (1548) *Carmen
> Facetum* and (1557) *Super impia Domina* (see Hammond, *Chaucer,*
> p. 432).
> (1) Bodleian Fairfax 16 (8 rime-royal and 100 eight-line
>   stanzas).
> (2) Harley 372; ed. Furnivall, *Political, Religious and Love
>   Poems* (1st ed., 1866), p. 52; Otto Gröhler, *Ueber Richard
>   Ros' mittelenglische Uebersetzung des gedichtes von Alain
>   Chartiers La Belle Dame sans Mercy,* diss. Breslau, 1886.
> (3) Cambridge University Library Ff. 1. 6; ed. with variants
>   from (2) and (4) by Furnivall (2nd ed., 1903).
> (4) Trinity College Cambridge R. 3. 19.
> (5) Marquess of Bath, Longleat 258 (see Hammond, p. 432).
> (6) Sloane 1710 (lines 93-764). Not mentioned by Hammond.
>   This version, which begins "At my commyng the ladys
>   everychone," is treated as an independent poem by Padel-
>   ford, "Transition English Song Collections," *CHEL, II,* 442.
> (7) Pynson's *Chaucer* (1526), with added 6 rime-royal stanzas,
>   "Lenvoy de limprimeur," warning against carnal lust and
>   all love except honest marriage. These stanzas ed. Ham-
>   mond, p. 432.

(8) Thynne (1532) and later editions of Chaucer. Reproduced in Skeat's *Facsimile*, p. 598; ed. from Thynne with variants from (1)-(3) in Skeat's *Chaucer*, VII, 299.

Dated by Skeat, *Chaucer*, VII, lii, between 1450 and 1460; in his *Chaucer Canon*, p. 106, "ab. 1450." According to Bédier and Hazard, *Histoire de la Littérature Française Illustrée*, Paris, 1923, I, 91, Chartier wrote *La Belle Dame* in 1424. Since Chartier was in England the following year, Skeat's date may perhaps be pushed back.

Ros sets Chartier's garden-poem in a dream-vision frame by means of eight added stanzas at beginning and end. The essential tone is courtly, and if it had not been for subsequent history the poem might not have been regarded as even in part satirical. But the dramatic sharpness of the Merciless Beauty's answers to her groveling lover, however much a part of the courtly tradition, gave rise to as great a controversy as Jean de Meun had done. See the extensive series of poems discussed by Arthur Piaget, *"La Belle Dame sans Merci* et ses Imitations," *Romania*, XXX (1901), 22-48, 317-51; XXXI (1902), 315-49; XXXIII (1904), 179-208; XXXIV (1905), 375-428, 559-602. The force of the satirical reputation of Chartier's poem is seen in Pynson's *Envoy*, in Bale's titles, and in the metamorphosis of La Belle Dame into an eternally feminine creature of the otherworld at the hands of that seeker after remembered beauty, merciless or otherwise, John Keats.

83. Hange I wyl my nobyl bow vpon the grenewod bough.

Accompanied in the MS. by music composed by Dr. [Robert] Cooper, and therefore presents the usual ambiguity of early XVI cent. musical pieces, since sometimes the author and composer were identical. According to Greene (p. 451) the burden may be from an older folk song, such as **97**.

The Old Forester.

Burden: "I haue bene a foster long and many a day;
Foster wyl I be no more;
No lenger shote I may;
Yet haue I bene a foster."

(1) British Museum Additional 31922 (four-line burden and 5 three-line stanzas); ed. Greene, *Early English Carols*, p. 313 (no. 465); Flügel, *Anglia*, XII (1889), 244.

The MS. is early XVI cent. and contains music by King Henry VIII and by his court musicians. Cooper lived from about 1474 to about 1529.

The happy old forester of the greenwood is here transformed by rather crude double meaning to an impotent old bachelor who cannot be loved. In a sense it is a bachelor's rejoicing, although the tone is vastly different from that of its congeners, **97** and **364**.

84. [harborowe for faithfull and trewe subjects agaynst the late blowne blaste concerning the gouernment of wemen, An] [prose].

By John Aylmer, afterwards Bishop of London.

(1) Strassburg [J. Daye, London], 1559. Never reprinted. The *STC* (nos. 1005-1006) lists copies owned by British Museum (two), Bodleian, Cambridge University Library, Sir R. L. Harmsworth, and Huntington Library. One of the British Museum copies contains an additional preface.

Composed in 1558 or 1559.

An answer to Knox's *First Blast of the Trumpet against the monstruous regiment of Women* (**64**). Not examined. It defends women as sovereigns fit to rule by a long list of examples taken from Jewish, pagan, and Christian history. For summaries and extensive quotations see John Strype, *Historical Collections of the Life and Acts of the Right Reverend Father in God, John Aylmer,* Oxford, 1821, pp. 11, 147-61; see also the articles by James E. Phillips referred to under *First Blast.*

He wil my corse all beclip et clap [me] to his breist (336).

85. Her commys Holly, that is so gent.

In Praise of Holly.

Burden: "Alleluia, alleluia,
Alleluia, now syng we."

(1) Bodleian Eng. poet. e. 1 (two-line burden and 4 three-line stanzas); ed. Greene, *Early English Carols,* p. 94 (no. 137); for further editions see his notes, p. 380; and Brown and Robbins, *Index,* no. 1195.

MS. second half XV cent.

The holly-half of a debate, which threatens Holly's antagonists with serious punishments. Holly's intent is plainly "To please all men." For the ivy-half see **291**. The sexual and satirical implications of holly-ivy poems are discussed under **86**. One must be careful in making any positive statement about this murky subject. But we are reminded by one pair of lines of Virgil in the basket (see John W. Spargo, *Virgil the Necromancer,* Cambridge, Mass., 1934, pp. 62-68, 137-97); by another of Chaucer's Marriage Group, in which the Clerk's "And lat hym care, and wepe, and wrynge and waille" is picked up by the Merchant "Wepyng and waylyng, care and oother sorwe/ I knowe ynogh." (*Canterbury Tales,* IV, 1212-14.) Surely no really educated clerk of the fifteenth century who heard this carol would fail to recall two of the most famous repositories of medieval satire on women? But there is one fly in the ointment. Virgil and the Merchant were both men; in "Her commys Holly" women are to pay the forfeits. Is this poetic justice?

Hey howe! / sely men, God helpe ʒowe (305).

Hey derie, hoe derie, hey derie dan (328).

Hey Robyn Joly Robyn tell me (202).

Herfor, and therfor, and therfor I came (275).

Hit (see It).

86. **Holver and Heyvy mad a gret party.**

    (1) Bodleian Eng. poet. e. 1 (4 three-line stanzas); ed. Greene, *Early English Carols,* p. xcix; Wright, *Songs and Carols* (Percy Society), p. 44; Chambers and Sidgwick, *Early English Lyrics,* p. 237.

MS. second half XV cent., but the tradition is certainly much older. Rollins, *Analytical Index,* no. 1131, mentions a broadside called "holly and hyve &c" entered in 1561-62.

Since Holly is masculine and Ivy feminine, this and the other holly-ivy songs become a contention over what the Wife of Bath most desired, the mastery. In **86** Holly submits like a good courtier. The origin of the strife between these two varieties of Christmas greenery appears to be connected with some survival of fertility custom and belief. See Chambers and Sidgwick, *Early English Lyrics,* pp. 374-75. But in the later Middle Ages it had become a courtly game, in which one of the features was the exclusion of Ivy from the hall. It merged with the carol tradition, also associated with Yuletide, and in its heyday in the XV and early XVI centuries. The Green Knight's "holyn bobbe" (*Sir Gawain and the Green Knight,* ed. Sir Israel Gollancz, London [EETS, CCX], 1940, line 206) may be an allusion, especially when we consider the underlying theme of the poem (the testing of chivalry and chastity), the time of the year in which it is set, and the hall-games between the sexes which set the scene (lines 64-70). Note the element of forfeits in both *Sir Gawain* and **85.** Another favorite medieval game was the telling of fortunes by casting lots. Several collections of individual fortunes remain, and there is a great deal of the controversy over women in most of them. *Ragman Roll* (**201**) is especially directed against women, and purports to be written by "kynge Ragman holly, which dyde the make many yeres ago." There is also a relationship between the *estrif* and the holly-ivy ritual (see Chambers and Sidgwick, p. 374). In *Annot and Johon* (Brown, *English Lyrics of the XIIIth Century,* p. 137) we find this allusion to the bird-debate: Annot is "þrustle pryuen in þro þat singeth in sale." Compare **273.** The Owl was proverbially connected with ivy; see *The Owl and the Nightingale* (ed. Atkins, Cambridge, 1922, lines 27, 617); Greene, p. cii; and Taylor's review of Greene, *MPh,* XXXIV (1936-37), 200. The holly-ivy strife reminds us of the medieval flower-cults, such as that which gives impetus to Chaucer's *Legend.* Many of the post-medieval survivals are clearly satirical. Greene cites a XVII cent. volume, *The Twelve Months,* which says "Great is the contention of holly and ivy, whether master or dame wears the breeches"; he mentions also an Oxfordshire tradition that a man must supply a maid with ivy lest she steal his breeches. A satirical ballad reported by Collier mingles "Madge Howlet," ivy, and satire on women. The fullest modern account will be found in Greene, pp. xcviii-ciii; for further notes see Dyboski, *Songs, Carols* (EETSES, CI), p. 190; and Flügel, *Anglia,* XXVI (1903), 279. The other holly-ivy songs in this index are **85, 87, 88, 243,** and **291.**

87. Holy berith beris, beris rede ynowgh.

Holly Against Ivy.

Burden: "Nay, nay, Ive, it may not be, iwis,
        For Holy must haue the mastry, as the maner is."

(1) Balliol College Oxford 354 (two-line burden and 4 four-line stanzas); ed. Greene, *Early English Carols,* p. 94 (no. 136B); see his notes, p. 380, and Brown and Robbins, *Index,* no. 1226, for other editions.

MS. early XVI cent., many of the contents much earlier.

Praises "Holy with his mery men" who sit on thrones of gold while "Ivy and her jentyll women" sit outside with kibed heels in the cold. The "thristilcok," the "popyngay," and the "woode-coluer" are partisans of Holly; Ivy has no fowls to champion her but the "sory howlet." On the satirical meaning of this holly-ivy game and on its connection with bird-debates see **86.**

88. Holy stond in the hall, fayre to behold.

Holly Against Ivy.

Burden: "Nay, Iuy, nay, hyt shal not be, iwys;
        Let Holy hafe the maystry, as the maner ys."

(1) Harley 5396 (two-line burden and 7 two-line stanzas); ed. Green, *Early English Carols,* p. 93 (no. 136A); see his notes, p. 380; and Brown and Robbins, *Index,* no. 1226, for other editions.

MS. dated about 1456.

Praises Holly who sits within the hall while Ivy freezes without. Differs verbally from **87,** but burden and contents are very similar.

89. [Hough for the batchelor! mery doth he live.

The Batchelor.

(1) Said by Collier to be in "the Editor's MS. (not older than the reign of James I)"; printed in *Extracts,* I, 43 (8 rime-royal stanzas).

Probably spurious, created by Collier to fit an entry with such a title licensed to Jno. Wally in 1561-62 (see Rollins, *Analytical Index,* no. 117). On these Collier poems see **59.**

A bachelor's rejoicing over his freedom to drink, make love, and go to fairs; with satire on the sorrows of the married man with his

horns, his shrewish wife, and his noisy children. If Collier is responsible for this poem he has at least caught the spirit of other satires of
the period; see, for instance, **97**.]

How hey, it is [non] les (401).

How shold y with that olde man (18).

90. I am a fol, i can no god.

> *Amor Fatuus,* or *Foolish Love.*
> (1) Harley 7322 (8 lines); ed. Furnivall, *Political, Religious
> and Love Poems* (1866), p. 238.
> MS. dated by Furnivall end XV cent.

Those that love foolish love shall burn hard and die; I slew a wise
king and shall slay more. The speaker is *Amor fatuus;* probably the
poem was originally attached to a portrait in a fashion similar to the
Danse Macabre or to Spearman Death (see Brown, *Register,* no. 841).

I am a joly foster (364).

91. I am a poor Tyler in simple aray.

> Burden: "The Proverb reporteth, no man can deny,
>   That wedding and hanging is destiny."
> (1) *Tom Tyler and his Wife* ("second Impression" 1661) (two
> line burden and 5 five-line stanzas); ed. separately by Nor-
> man Ault, *Elizabethan Lyrics,* London, 1925, p. 35; for
> editions of the whole play see **193**.

This lyric may be later than 1568, since the dates of the play's
composition and first impression are unknown. But possibly **91**
may be identified with broadsides such as Rollins, *Analytical Index,*
nos. 2216 and 2664 (licensed respectively 1558-59 and 1562-63).

Tom's wife is a spendthrift and a shrew; it would not have been
pleasant to have been hanged instead of married, but at least it would
be over with. On the proverbial burden see **233a**.

92. I am as I am and so will I be.

> By Sir Thomas Wyatt (signed "T. V." in the earliest MS.).
> (1) British Museum Additional 17492 (10 four-line stanzas);
> ed. Foxwell, *Poems of Sir Thomas Wiat,* I, 354; and E. M.
> W. Tillyard, *The Poetry of Sir Thomas Wyatt,* London,
> 1929, p. 126.
> (2) Advocates' Library 1. 1. 6; ed. Ritchie, *Bannatyne Manu-
> script,* IV, 2; see also Hunterian Club *Bannatyne,* I, ciii.

Wyatt's dates are 1503?-1542. Good evidence of the need for
assuming certain poems in Bannatyne to be much earlier than 1568,
since Wyatt's poem appears there without ascription.

According to Tillyard (p. 174) the "poem seems to be a piece of personal moralizing, Stoic in tone, written at a time when Wyatt was or had been in danger from his enemies." But Bannatyne included it in his anthology of "Ballatis of remedy of luve . . . And to the reproche of evill wemen"; and it is not impossible to take it as a severe and unspecific example of the Rebellious Lover type. The "Stoic" quality makes it akin to **61**.

I am as lyght as any roe (322).

93. I am sorry for her sake.

> *A Lover's Sad Plight.*
> Burden: "Care away, away, away,
>   Murnyng away!
>   Y am forsake, another ys take;
>   No more murne yc may."
> (1) Gonville and Caius College Cambridge 383/603 (four-line burden and 3 four-line stanzas); ed. Greene, *Early English Carols,* p. 317 (no. 470).
> Middle of XV cent. MS.

Parody of a courtly love poem. My love has brought me into such torment that when I sleep I may not wake and when I have good wine I drink no ale. Greene (p. 452) offers some parallels, among them **168**, with which some lines are shared. He does not note the parallel with the third part of *Merciles Beaute,* **403**. **93** shares a line of burden with an outspoken satire on women, **20**.

93a. I can fynd no man now that wille enquere.

> An extract (IIA, 2197-2210) from Peter Idley's *Instructions to His Son,* ed. Charlotte d'Evelyn, Boston and London, 1935, p. 143; see also p. 61.
> *Extracts Illustrating Costume.*
> (1) Laud 416 (2 rime-royal stanzas). From this MS. abridgement of Idley's Book II Wright and Halliwell, *Reliquiae Antiquae,* II, 29, have given independent currency to these stanzas and to **22a** and **41a**. This is the only extract separately catalogued by Brown and Robbins (*Index,* no. 1287). For six other MSS. see Miss d'Evelyn's edition.
> Between 1428 and 1459. See **22a**.

This satire on marriage with the refrain, "Tylle the world be turnyd into another shap," is from a passage on the sixth commandment. Men no longer seek the Dunmow flitch of bacon. Miss d'Evelyn's note (p. 229) provides a valuable bibliography of this famous and little-claimed prize for a peaceable year of marriage. Idley's imbedded refrain-lyric, truncated by Wright and Halliwell, contains four stanzas. Miss d'Evelyn (p. 56) believes that the heavy irony of this section of Idley may be borrowed from Chaucer.

94. I chaunced once to come in place.

By C. Pyrrye. See **210**, to which this is an answer.
The prayse of VVomen.
(1) William How (n.d.). I have examined the unique copy
at Huntington Library by means of microfilm (204 four-
line stanzas, 5 eight-line stanzas, and a concluding four-
line stanza).
On the date, from about 1563 to 1571, see **210**.

Once I came across a book which abused womankind. How could
the author teach his pen to write so? He could not have been of man's
seed and written such slander against defenseless creatures. Perhaps
one woman displeased him, and so he vilified all the rest. He forgot
what women do for us as infants, when we are ill, and in the ordinary
course of domestic management. Women make peace and give good
counsel. They do not waste words in idle talk; they listen to wisdom,
hate lechery, lies and oaths, obey us in all things, use friendly advice
to mend our guilt, indulge in godly meditation, work unremittingly,
joy with the joyous and weep with the sorrowful, tell no secrets and
slander nobody, eschew flirtation, dress neatly but not gaudily, eat and
drink with moderation, and acquaint themselves with all manner of
virtue. These characteristics are illustrated by a long catalogue from
the classics and the Bible. Men who defame women do it to their own
shame. Eve transgressed but Mary redressed her guilt. It is dangerous
to generalize from a few examples of evil women. Paul tells us that
there is no greater sin than to misjudge others. What creature slanders
the feminine of his own kind but man alone? In concluding stanzas of
a different meter the poet sums up with unadulterated panegyric. It is
not impossible that Pyrrye's defense is in part based on Gosynhill's
Mulierum Pean (**347**).

95. I haue a lady where so she bee.

Ascribed to Chaucer by Stow; rejected by Francis Thynne in
his *Animadversions* (see Hammond, *Chaucer,* p. 428).
The Discriuing of a Faire Lady, or *A Balade Pleasaunte.*
(1) Trinity College Cambridge R. 3. 19 (7 rime-royal stanzas).
(2) Leyden Vossius 9. Described F. N. Robinson, "On Two
Manuscripts of Lydgate's Guy of Warwick," [Harvard]
Studies and Notes, V (1896), 188, 193.
(3) Stow's *Chaucer* (1561) and many later editions; see Chalmers, I, 563; and for others Hammond, *Chaucer,* p. 428.
Hammond believes that Stow used (1) as the basis for
his text.

According to Brown, *Register,* I, 239, 518, the Trinity MS. is late
XV or early XVI cent. and the Leyden MS. XV cent. Skeat
(*Chaucer Canon,* p. 123) remarks: "The author says that when he
was fifteen years old, he saw the wedding of queen Jane; and that

was so long ago that there cannot be many such as himself still
alive. As Joan of Navarre was married to Henry IV in 1403, he was
born in 1388, and would have been sixty-two in 1450. This gives
us a likely date for these precious productions." But Skeat is wrong;
it is the *lady* who was fifteen in 1403. If the poem were composed
in 1488, say, she would then be a hundred. That would not impair
the joke.

Parody of a courtly panegyric. For a discussion of this type, which
catalogues a lady's uglinesses instead of her charms, see **226**. In most of
these the lady is not merely ugly and excessively amorous; she is old as
well.

96. I haiff a littill fleming berge.

By [Robert?] Sempill, on whom see T. F. Henderson, *Scottish
Vernacular Literature*, 3rd ed., Edinburgh, 1910, p. 275.

*The ballat maid vpoun Margret fleming callit the flemyng bark
in Edinburt.*

(1) Advocates' Library 1. 1. 6 (8 eight-line stanzas); ed. Ritchie,
   Bannatyne Manuscript, II, 327; see also Hunterian Club
   Bannatyne, I, lxxxviii.

Robert Sempill, the reformer, lived 1530?-1595 according to
DNB. If this scarcely puritanical poem is his, it is to be dated
between about 1545 and 1568, the date of the MS.

Somewhat enthusiastic description of the wanton ways of a harlot
called Margaret Fleming; an elaborate piece of *double entente* in which
the lady is compared to a ship which all may board. For similar *tours
de force*, not half so witty, see **7, 209, 216**. Two other poems on wanton
women, **246** and **231**, follow **96** in the MS. immediately; both are
ascribed to Sempill and the last specifically to Robert. All such poems
are ambiguous; one is not sure whether one is reading the praise of a
tavern wench or a satire on a court lady who has repulsed the author,
and who must suffer the false accusations of a lover scorned. As far as
type-satire is concerned, the use of specific names further clouds the
issue. We are reminded of Chaucer's Dame Alisoun, who is apologist
for women as well as a satirical type and a portrait from life, or of
Dunbar's Kind Kittok (**195**), who diverges considerably from the ale-
wife type. Despite their medieval conservatism, Scottish poets had a
peculiar talent for transforming type-satire into individual portrait.

97. Y haue ben a foster long and meney day.

(1) British Museum Additional 5665 (2 four-line stanzas); ed.
   Greene, *Early English Carols*, p. 451; Chambers and Sidg-
   wick, *Early English Lyrics*, p. 247; for other editions see
   Greene, p. 451, and Chambers and Sidgwick, p. 376.

MS. first quarter XVI cent.

The old foster will retire but will wed no wife. See **83** and **364**. 83 incorporates the first line of **97** into its burden; and **364** uses the significant variation "I am a joly foster." Perhaps any of the three can be classed as an Aged Bachelor's Rejoicing, although the tone of each differs.

I haue bene a foster long and many a day (83).

98. I Iudge and finde, how God doth minde.

The ioy of Virginitie: to, The Gods of loue.
(1) *A Handful of Pleasant Delights*, Richard Jones (1584); ed. Rollins, *Handful*, p. 42 (42 lines).

Rollins dates the poem about 1566, since it is a moralization of William Elderton's "The Gods of Love," printed in 1562, and since many moralizations and imitations of Elderton's poem were in print before 1566, the date of the lost first edition of *A Handful*.

A praise of virginity, which is brought into our sphere by the proverbial last line: "But hard it is, I saie no more, / To finde an hundreth in a score." In general this handlist does not include mere treatises on celibacy unless there is some such reason. Mention should be made, however, of the excessively realistic homily of the XIII cent., *Hali Meidenhad*, rev. F. J. Furnivall from Oswald Cockayne's edition, London (EETS, XVIII), 1922, which woos young women to the cloister by a violent description of the miseries of marriage, above all the horrors of pregnancy and childbirth. It is by no means typical of the Church's position on celibacy then or now. For the tradition see many of the pieces described in Alice A. Hentsch, *De la Littérature Didactique du moyen âge s'addressant spécialement aux femmes*, Cahors, 1903.

99. I lothe that I did loue.

Ascribed to Thomas, Lord Vaux by George Gascoigne and in MSS. (1) and (2) (see Rollins, *Tottel's Miscellany*, II, 284-85).

The aged louer renounceth loue.
(1) Ashmole 48 (13 four-line stanzas); ed. Wright, *Songs and Ballads*, p. 34.
(2) Harley 1703 (14 four-line stanzas).
(3) British Museum Additional 38599 (13 four-line stanzas).
(4) British Museum Additional 26737 (32 lines only).
(5) British Museum Additional 4900.
(6) *Tottel's Miscellany* (all editions); ed. Rollins, I, 165, with collations from (1), (2), and (3). For further printings see II, 285.

MS. Ashmole is dated by Rollins *ca.* 1555-65; and the poem was registered for publication as a ballad in 1563-64 (see Rollins, *Tottel's Miscellany*, II, 285, and his *Analytical Index*, no. 48). The other authorities are later.

Farewell in age to love and lusty youth. Its fame and popularity in the mid-XVI cent. were climaxed by its use by Shakespeare and Goethe (Rollins, *Tottel's Miscellany*, II, 285-86). For a parallel see **154**.

100. I luve and I Say not.

(1) Advocates' Library 1. 1. 6 (1 six-line stanza); ed. Ritchie, *Bannatyne Manuscript*, IV, 22.

1568 or before.

Rebellious lover tells us to beware woman's wiles and "wrinkis."

101. I marvell of thir vane fantastik men.

By "Weddirburne" according to the MS. There were three Scottish poets by this name who flourished in the first half of the XVI cent.: James (1495?-1553), John (1500?-1556), and Robert (1510?-1557?); for their biographies see *DNB*.

The ballat of the prayis of Wemen.

(1) Advocates' Library 1. 1. 6 (34 rime-royal stanzas); ed. Ritchie, *Bannatyne Manuscript*, III, 327; see Hunterian Club *Bannatyne*, I, ci.

1568 or before.

Defense of women against the malicious remarks of men; made up mostly of examples classical and scriptural of good women. In presenting the poor case of his malicious adversaries he manages to list most of the bad women of satirical tradition. Women "ar lyk the sillie scheip / Among þe wolffis quhilk dois þame kill & bytt." Had I the riches of Darius and the valor of Hannibal I should "be all wemenis campione" and go to the Holy Land with the token of "ane womanis richt hand gluve" fastened to my spear.

102. I muse and mervellis in my mynd.

By Alexander Scott.

Of Wemenkynd.

(1) Advocates' Library 1. 1. 6 (13 six-line stanzas); ed. Ritchie, *Bannatyne Manuscript*, IV, 11; Hunterian Club *Bannatyne*, I, civ; Cranstoun, *Poems of Alexander Scott*, p. 68; Donald, *Poems of Alexander Scott*, p. 58.

Cranstoun dates Scott's work 1545-68.

Women are the opposite of what they seem to be: they tolerate no disloyal man but themselves deceive, pretend to be secret yet tell all, crave service but give no reward, and the like. Good women will not blame me for what I say; crabbed ones are here given "quytclame."

103. I ne wot quat is love.

In John Grimestone's MS., probably by a Franciscan.

(1) Advocates' Library 18. 7. 21 (2 four-line stanzas); ed. G. R. Owst, *Literature and Pulpit in Medieval England,*

Cambridge, 1933, p. 21. I owe this reference to Dr. Rossell Hope Robbins.

The MS. was apparently completed in 1372; see Brown, *Religious Lyrics of the XIVth Century*, p. xvi.

I do not know what love is since I never loved; but well I know that he who loves burns hard in youth. A renunciation of love with a strong undercurrent of desire. For the pseudo-Ovidian lines, "Nescio quid sit amor," on which this poem is based, see Brown, *Religious Lyrics of the XVth Century*, p. 328; and for the companion "Dicam quid sit Amor" see **106a**.

104. I not what I shall syng nor say.
> *Turne up hur halter and lat hur go.*
>> (1) Harley 5396 (11 eight-line stanzas); ed. Wright and Halliwell, *Reliquiae Antiquae*, I, 75; I have transcribed it for publication.

This portion of the MS. is mid-XV cent.

Rebellious lover, using fowling figure. The refrain is a popular tag; see **31** and **365**, and also "Cast of þe bridel, and liȝtly lete hem go," in Lydgate's *Troy-Book*, ed. Henry Bergen, London (EETSES, XCVII, CIII, CVI), 1906-1910, II, 520. The falconry metaphor is used also in **7, 108**, and in such later poets as Alexander Scott, Allan Ramsay, and Robert Burns (see Louis B. Salomon, *The Devil Take Her*, Philadelphia, 1931, pp. 210-11).

I pray youe, maydys that here be (144).

105. I se where is but little truste.
>> (1) Sloane 554 (1 rime-royal stanza, badly faded); I have transcribed it for publication.
>> (2) Cambridge University Library Kk. 6. 30.

Appears on a flyleaf of John Walton's *Boethius*, and therefore later than 1410 (see Hammond, *English Verse*, p. 39). Brown, *Register*, I, 372, fails to date (1). (2) is dated XV cent. by the Cambridge *Catalogue*.

There is little trust in woman's words. Probably the author, doubly unfortunate as lover and as poet, never got beyond his first inarticulate scribble.

106. I serue wher I no truyth can ffynde.
>> (1) British Museum Additional 18752 (2 five-line stanzas); ed. Reed, *Anglia*, XXXIII (1910), 366.

This portion of the MS. written in early XVI cent.

Rebellious lover: parody of a courtly complaint. The surprise is carefully saved for the last line; up to that time the poem is simply a somewhat excessive description of lover's melancholy.

106a. Y shall say what ynordynat loue ys.

Translated from John of Garland?
Inordinate Love Defined.
(1) Copenhagen, Royal Library 29264 (MS. Thott 110) (1
eight-line stanza); ed. Brown, *Religious Lyrics of the XVth
Century*, p. 287.
MS. of XV cent.

The marvelous madness of excessive love. This poem, like **170** and
171, is based on oxymoron; but it is less friendly to love than either
of them. It is preceded in the MS. by its Latin source. "Dicam quid
sit Amor." Elsewhere (see Brown, *English Lyrics of the XIIIth Century*,
p. 170) this popular Latin quatrain is ascribed to "Jean de Garlande,"
and although its canonicity is in doubt, it appears in XIII cent. MSS.,
contemporary with the great Anglo-Parisian scholar. For a palinode,
ascribed to "Ouidius," see **103**.

107. I shall you tell a full good sport.

How Gossips Myne; or *Lytyll Thank;* or *The Gossips.*
Burden: "Hoow, gossip myne, gossip myn,
　　　　Whan will we go to the wyne?
　　　　Good gossipes [myn]."
(1) Balliol College Oxford 354 (three-line burden and 23 six-
line stanzas); ed. with (3) and variants of (2) by Greene,
Early English Carols, p. 280 (no. 419A); Flügel, *Anglia*,
XXVI (1903), 208 (with valuable comparative material);
for other editions see Greene, p. 436, and Brown and
Robbins, *Index*, no. 1362.
(2) Bodleian Eng. poet. e. 1 (omits several lines of Balliol but
adds two extra stanzas); ed. Wright, *Songs and Carols*
(Percy Society), p. 91; modernized by G. G. Coulton, *Life
in the Middle Ages*, New York, 1935, III, 141; and by Edward Arber, *The Dunbar Anthology,* London, 1901, p. 108.
(3) Cotton Titus A. 26 (fragment of a burden and 20 four-
line stanzas); ed. Greene, p. 283 (no. 419B); Wright, p. 104;
Dyboski, *Songs, Carols* (EETSES, CI), p. 187; J. E.
M[asters], ed. *The Gossips*, Shaftesbury (Dorset), 1926; for
other editions see Greene, p. 436.
Bodleian, the earliest MS., is second half XV cent. The variants
are considerable enough to suggest oral transmission.

A roystering ale-wife poem, which satirizes in dramatic fashion
woman's drunkenness, sloth, infidelity, gossip, and domestic strife. Greene
(p. 437) compares the *Gossips' Song* in the Chester *Deluge* play, *Four
Wittie Gossips* in the Pepys collection. Flügel adds *The Tunnyng of
Elynour Rummyng* (**277**), which may have some verbal echoes. See

79, 172, 193, 195 for parallels. Conviviality as well as satire is the purpose of this and other poems of the tradition. Its use by minstrels is suggested by the introduction of Frankeleyn the harper in version (3).

108. I Smile to se how you deuise.

Rollins is not convinced by Bond's hesitant attribution to John Lyly.

A proper sonet: Intituled: I smile to see how you deuise. To anie pleasant tune.

> (1) *A Handful of Pleasant Delights,* Richard Jones (1584) (10 four-line stanzas); ed. Rollins, *Handful,* p. 52; R. W. Bond, *The Complete Works of John Lyly,* Oxford, 1902, III, 440, 468; for another partial edition see Rollins, p. 112.

"No evidence for dating this ballad can be found except that it appears to be an answer to no. 19 and, in that case, probably followed it immediately" (Rollins, p. 111). No. 19 (our **316**) was probably in print by 1566, and both were therefore likely to have been in the lost first edition (1566) of *A Handful.*

Rebellious lover poem, using the falconry image (see **104**). Violent attack on the lady's infidelity and a promise that the new lover will soon learn where the shoe pinches.

109. I That Vlysses yeres haue spent.

Attributed to "H.S." by the MS. and therefore identified by Padelford as by the Earl of Surrey; see Rollins, II, 322. Eleanor Hammond in *MLN,* XXXVII (1922), 505, observes that the initial letters of the stanzas form the acrostic IAWTT, and suggests Sir Thomas Wyatt as the possible author. Rollins, II, 323, is doubtful of the credence which should be given to this type of signal. William R. Parker has remarked to me that the poem makes good sense if stanza 3 is transposed to the beginning, which would lead to the more tempting acrostic WIATT. But this is no definite evidence of authorship. It is possible that the acrostic, if not a mirage, is actually a compliment or dedication by Surrey to Wyatt. The one certain case where Wyatt used an acrostic himself involves not his name but SHELTUN, which is a clear reference to his friend Mary Shelton. Miss Hammond also cites "When raging loue" with the acrostic WIATT, and this poem is assigned to Surrey by Tottel. Another poem in *Tottel's Miscellany* has an acrostic, and Rollins (II, 277) favors the compliment or dedication theory in that case. Compare also **323**, where both dedication and authorship seem to be involved in an acrostic composed very near to Wyatt's time.

The louer disceiued by his loue repenteth him of the true loue he bare her.

> (1) Harley 78 (4 six-line stanzas); ed. Padelford, *Early Six-*

teenth Century Lyrics, p. 41; and his *Poems of Henry Howard, Earl of Surrey,* University of Washington Press, 1920, p. 57.

(2) *Tottel's Miscellany* (second and succeeding editions only); ed. Rollins, I, 230 (5 six-line stanzas), with variants of (1).

Certainly before July 31 (the first setting of the second edition), 1557; if by Surrey before 1548; if by Wyatt before 1543.

Rebellious lover, citing classical and medieval examples of woman's infidelity. Now that he has left the perilous seas he is glad of his anchorage; Ulysses has come home, but not to Penelope.

110. I think thir men Ar verry fals and vane.

According to the MS. by "Weddirburne," on whom see **101**.

(1) Advocates' Library 1. 1. 6 (14 rime-royal stanzas); ed. Ritchie, *Bannatyne Manuscript,* IV, 76; see also Hunterian Club *Bannatyne,* I, cviii.

1568 or before.

Defense: malicious men should not spit against the wind by defaming women, for I can list a host of men more evil than women ever were. This type of defense goes back ultimately to Boccaccio and Lydgate; see *Fall of Princes,* ed. Bergen, III, 783-96.

111. I thought, good faith, and durst have gagde my hand.

By George Turbervile.

To his Friend T. having bene long studied and well experienced, and now at length loving a Gentlewoman that forced him naught at all.

(1) Turbervile's *Epitaphes, Epigrams, Songs and Sonets* (1567) (18 four-line stanzas); ed. Collier [1867], p. 135; also in Chalmers, II, 619.

1567 or before.

Horatian advice to a supposedly wise man who is about to be made a fool by love. Women are unfaithful, and wisdom does not preserve a man from their cruelty and guile. Beware by my own experience. Remember how Ulysses stuffed his ears with wax to avoid being turned like his men into a swine by Circe.

112. Ich was in one sumere dale.

Of the various candidates for authorship the best case has been made for Nicholas of Guildford; but his major rival John of Guildford is still in the running. For this vexed problem see Atkins, pp. xxxviii-xlvi; Gratton and Sykes, pp. xx-xxii.

The Owl and the Nightingale; called in the Jesus College MS. *altercacio inter filomenam et Bubonem.*

(1) Cotton Caligula A. 9 (896 couplets); ed. with the parallel

text of (2) by J. E. Wells, Boston, 1907; J. W. H. Atkins, Cambridge, 1922; and J. H. G. Grattan and G. F. H. Sykes, London (EETSES, CXIX), 1935. See all of these editions for earlier printings and for extensive commentary and bibliography.

(2) Jesus College Oxford 29 (deposited in the Bodleian); for editions see (1).

The date is still a problem. According to Grattan and Sykes (p. xx) the majority opinion would place the earliest possible date of composition in 1189. Atkins (p. xxxviii) feels the latest possible date to be 1216, and would place the poem in the reign of King John (1199-1217); but Grattan and Sykes throw some doubts in the way of his argument (pp. xx-xxi).

The third major problem of the poem is its exact tone and meaning. Certainly it is a debate; certainly its references to love and women and its kinship to other bird-debates on woman's worth cause it to merit a place in this handlist. W. P. Ker (*English Literature—Medieval*, New York and London, 1912, pp. 181-83) makes it clear that its ambiguity rests on the skill of the artist, who refuses to limit his argument to one issue, and makes each party share something of the other's mind. "The Owl wishes to be thought musical; the Nightingale is anxious not to be taken for a mere worldling." The many suggestions are perhaps best summarized by R. M. Wilson, *Early Middle English Literature*, London, 1939, p. 161: "Is it the old conflict between pleasure and asceticism, between an active and a contemplative life, between a monastic and a secular life, or between art and philosophy? Possibly they all enter into it, though if any single formula must be applied the suggestion that the contest is between the older didactic and religious poetry and the newer lyric is probably the best." One thing is sure; it is a contention between two medieval and universal birds, the owl and the nightingale; the various issues spring from their traditional nature; and both in the end agree that woman is a worthy thing. For an interesting treatment of the folk-background see references mentioned under **86**. For valuable collections on the contrast between earthly and heavenly love see Will Héraucourt, *Die Wertwelt Chaucers*, Heidelberg, 1939, pp. 315-25.

113. I will not knit before I knowe.

Probably by C. Pyrrye. See **210**.

A fruytful short dialogue vppon the sentence, knovve before thou knitte.

(1) *The praise and Dispraise of Women*, William How (n.d.). I have examined the unique copy at Huntington Library by means of microfilm (8 four-line stanzas).

On the date, from about 1563 to 1571, see **210**.

This dialogue on the choice of a wife follows two poems on the Praise and Dispraise of Women. "W." wishes to marry; "C." in alternate single lines gives him advice on choosing well and avoiding repentance. The author is not exactly a master of stichomythia; his dialogue is often unclear. Just who the participants in the dialogue are is not certain. They may be "Wooer" and "Counsel" or "Consultor"; or they may be *C.* Pyrrye, whose name is on the title page of the volume, and *W.* How, the printer.

113a. I winked, I winked, whan I a woman toke.

> (1) Lansdowne 762 (3 lines); ed. Wright and Halliwell, *Reliquiae Antiquae*, I, 289.

This portion of the MS. appears to be of the XV cent.; see Brown and Robbins, *Index*, no. 1392.

I closed my eyes when, more than ever, I should have kept them open. Imbedded in a collection of Latin, English, and macaronic verses, mnemonic and proverbial. A Latin distich immediately following warns against marriage to widows; a Latin line preceding compares virginity to wax. The English is verbally close to the second stanza of **179**.

I wyll you tell a full good sport (107).

114. I Wold I found not as I fele.

> *Of womens changeable will.*
> (1) *Tottel's Miscellany* (all editions but the first); ed. Rollins, I, 243 (3 four-line stanzas).

Before July 31, 1557 (the date of the first setting of the second edition).

Would that reason preserved me from the fickleness of woman and of fortune. Rebellious lover, with some sparks of the old fire left.

115. I wolde no man wear anggré, but all women pleasyde.

> By John Wallys.
> (1) Ashmole 48 (13 eight-line stanzas); ed. Wright, *Songs and Ballads,* p. 149.

Rollins in *MLN,* XXXIV (1919), 349, dates the MS. 1557-65 on the basis of broadside contents.

I would put the controversy about women to rest by having all men as good as women are. A *tour de force* of alliterative adjectives in derogation of men and in praise of women. See **229**.

116. I ȝeid the gait wes nevir gane.

> (1) Advocates' Library 1. 1. 6 (12 four-line stanzas); ed. Ritchie, *Bannatyne Manuscript,* III, 66; see also Hunterian Club *Bannatyne,* I, xci.
> 1568 or before.

A lying poem with a number of new and witty impossibilities. Climaxed by the lines: "Quhen all thir tailis are trew in deid / All wemen will be trew." On the type see **69**.

Ich (see **I**).

117. Yff a ʒong woman had a c. men take.

A good medesyn yff a mayd have lost her madened to make her a mayd ageyn; called by the editors *Burlesque Receipt.*

    (1) From a flyleaf of a copy of Caxton's *Mirrour of the World* (1481) in the British Museum (press mark C. 21. d. 7), according to the editors, Wright and Halliwell, *Reliquiae Antiquae,* I, 250 (34 lines in irregular stanzaic pattern, the predominant one being *aabccb*).

Certainly after 1481; the editors say that it was "written by some owner of the book in the year 1520."

A burlesque formula for restoring a wanton woman's chastity, which satirizes both women and folk-medicine. Among the ingredients are "the kreke of a henne," "the lyʒthe of a glaweworme in the derke," "the mary of a wheʒstone," and "the lenthe of Judas gerdylle." Akin to the lying-song, for which see **69**. For a similar burlesque formula see "A maiden of late," from d'Urfey's *Pills to Purge Melancholy,* reprinted in Denys K. Roberts, *Straw in the Hair,* London, 1938, p. 6; for a set of parody "practysis of medecyne" see Ritchie, *Bannatyne Manuscript,* III, 28.

118. Gif all the erth war perchmene scribable.

Ascribed to Chaucer in the MS. It is stanza 35 of **255**, *The Remedy of Love,* which Thynne erroneously assigned to Chaucer.

    (1) Advocates' Library 1. 1. 6 (1 rime-royal stanza); ed. Ritchie, *Bannatyne Manuscript,* IV, 23; Hunterian Club *Bannatyne,* I, cv.

Skeat dates **255** "about 1530."

If all the earth were parchment and all the sea ink and every man a scribe, they would not all suffice to write the cursedness of women. The formula is used for satirical ends in **310**, which precedes **118** in the Bannatyne MS.; and in **166**, another member of the Chaucerian apocrypha. It is adapted to the defense of women in **67a**, and to the praise of the Virgin in a poem by Walter Kennedy (*Poems,* ed. J. Schipper, *Denkschriften der kaiserlichen Akademie der Wissenschaften* [Vienna], Philos.-Hist.-Classe, XLVIII, 1 [1902], 19). For a heavily documented study of the formula's history see Irving Linn, "If All the Sky Were Parchment," *PMLA,* LIII (1938), 951-70. To his references may be added a Spanish folk-song in Mark Van Doren, *An Anthology of World Poetry,* New York, 1928, p. 652; and material on the English nursery-rime in *Concert Bulletin of the Boston Symphony Orchestra,*

LIV (1934-35), 542. Swetnam the Woman-Hater and Matheolus also use the formula against women; see F. P. Wilson, ed. *The Batchelars Banquet*, Oxford, 1929, p. xvii.

119. [If ever I marry, I'le marry a maid.

Maides and Widowes.

(1) "In a MS. of the reign of James I, in the possession of the Editor," according to Collier, *Extracts*, I, 9 (6 four-line stanzas). Norman Ault, *Elizabethan Lyrics*, London, 1925, p. 34, reprints the piece from Collier with "modernization."

Probably spurious (see **59**)—created by Collier to fit entries with such a title licensed to John Wally and Mrs. Toy in 1557-58 and to William Pekering in 1564. See Rollins, *Analytical Index*, nos. 1214-15. The lines which Rollins quotes from John Hilton's *Catch as Catch Can* (1652) do not correspond to Collier.

Maidens are simple, but a widow knows too much. For several reasons a woman who has never known a man is preferable. "But to marry with anie, it asketh much care; / And some batchelors hold they are best as they are." The battle over the respective merits of maid and widow is continued in a broadside entered 1557-58 to John Wally and Mrs. Toy, called "I will have a Wydow yf ever I marye," also entered in 1564 to William Pekering (Rollins, *Analytical Index*, nos. 1203-1204).]

120. If I be wanton I wotte well why.

Burden, chorus, or refrain begins: "My wanton ware
                                        shall walk for me."

(1) Harley 7578 (burden of 8 lines and 6 couplets as stanza); ed. Bernhard Fehr, *Archiv*, CVII (1901), 58.

This part of the MS. of early XVI cent.

The speaker of the stanzas is a wanton wench whose aim is to lure men into marriage or what-not. The musical arrangement suggests a song in two parts, and the burden or chorus may have been sung by a man as a method of introducing the girl. Probably sung in a tavern on convivial occasions.

121. Yf love wear all lost for lacke of lybartye.

By J[ohn] W[allys].

(1) Ashmole 48 (9 eight-line stanzas); ed. Wright, *Songs and Ballads*, p. 140.

According to Rollins, *MLN*, XXXIV (1919), 349, the MS. can be dated 1557-65. In *Analytical Index*, no. 2167, and in the article just cited (p. 345) he suggests identification with "the prayse of Women," entered in 1563-64 to Thomas Colwell. See Index II for the many poems which have gone under such a title.

There is enough extravagant praise in the poem to justify its being classed as a defense of women on the basis of their virtue, their motherhood, and the Virgin Mary. But at times the specific details of what women are not almost gives the case away, as when Wallys says "Synce my nativitie I never harde non so namyde, / That with wynkys nor wythe wyllys wold give ther husbandes glose." Taken together with the somewhat ambiguous refrain, "Youe shall not fynde me contrary, axe them yf I lye," these summaries of the case of the opposition are either ironic or else a black mark on the author's reputation for wit. Perhaps the mixture of serious praise and oblique blame may suggest the XVI cent. medleys *In Praise and Dispraise of Women*. See **210** and (in the Ashmole MS.) **386**. The refrain of the latter is very close to **121**.

122. If that thy wicked wife had spon the thred.

Attributed to William Gray [of Reading] by Dormer, his editor. Rollins feels that the probabilities are against it (II, 308), even if **159** "was not a death-bed production."
An aunswere [to **159**].

(1) Lansdowne 98 (5 four-line stanzas), ed. F. J. Furnivall, *Notes and Queries*, 4th Series, IV (1869), 194.
(2) *Tottel's Miscellany* (in all editions); ed. with variants from (1) by Rollins, I, 201; for further editions see Rollins, II, 308.

1557 or before.
If your wicked wife was the cause of your death you are doubly happy, since she is now spared you and you her. An epigram on an ill-matched couple.

123. Yf the turtle doue.

By Edward More?
(1) Title-page motto for More's *Defence of Women* (6 lines); see **125**.

1560 or before.
Miniature satire, oddly enough prefaced to a defense. If the turtle dove is both true and stupid, what shame then that man has wit and hates a woman?

123a. If thow art young then mary not ekit.

(1) Harley 3835 (2 couplets); ed. Henry Littlehales, *The Prymer or Lay Folks' Prayer Book*, London (EETS, CV, CIX), 1895-97, p. xlix.
A scribble at the end of a XV cent. primer.

Marry not when young; when old you'll be too wise. Young men's wives are unteachable; old men's wives good for nothing.

124. Iff thow canst not leive chast.

A Songe.

(1) Advocates' Library 1. 1. 6 (14 three-line stanzas); ed. Ritchie, *Bannatyne Manuscript,* IV, 330; Hunterian Club *Bannatyne,* I, cxiv.

Perhaps too late for this Index, since it is written in a later hand on the last leaves of the MS.

Satire on marriage and counsel to beware of cuckoldry. The third line of each stanza is a Latin tag: "tempus est," "bonum est," and the like.

125. If thy name were knowen that wrytest in this sorte.

By Edward More.

A Lytle and bryefe treatyse, called the defence of women, and especially of Englyshe women, made agaynst the Schole howse of women.

(1) J. Kynge (1560), ed. from the defective Douce copy by [Edward V. Utterson], *Select Pieces of Early Popular Poetry,* London, 1817, II, 99 (prose preface and 313 couplets). The *STC* (no. 18067) lists four copies, at the British Museum, Huntington Library, Bodleian, and in the Clawson collection. Stein notes that the last is now owned by Mr. Pforzheimer. I have examined the Huntington copy by means of microfilm. Described by Utterson, II, 53, 96; Wright, *Middle-Class Culture,* p. 470; Collier, *Extracts,* I, 14, 26; Hazlitt, *Remains,* IV, 100; Harold Stein, "Six Tracts About Women: A Volume in the British Museum," *Library,* Series 2, XV (1934-35), 43.

The Preface is dated July 20, 1557, when More (grandson of Sir Thomas) was "a bachyler and prynkokes but of twenty yeares of age or lytle more." This apparently is the basis for the *DNB* birth date (1537). The date of the Preface squares with the entry in the *Stationers' Register* to Kynge in 1557-58 (Arber, I, 19). Only one edition, that of 1560, is known; it was in that year that Kynge published four tracts about women. The delay may have had something to do with Queen Mary's death and Elizabeth's succession on November 17, 1558. A new license was issued to Tysdale in 1562-63 (Arber, I, 213); apparently the poem was never reprinted. There is no need to identify it with the "Defence agaynst them that commonlye Defame women" entered in 1560 to John Allde (Rollins, *Analytical Index,* no. 531).

An answer to *The Scholehouse of Women* (**292**), which along with *Mulierum Pean* (**347**) is alluded to by More. In his Preface he urges young men to repent and marry. He calls on Venus and on classical rhetoricians to aid his youthful work. Adam and Lucifer, not Eve, were responsible for the Fall of Man; and Jesus was born "of Mary vyrgyn mylde." (More presumably was a Catholic, and flourished in the reign of Queen Mary, although he lived on until 1620.) In any event English women are much better than those of Rome. And even Rome had Lucretia and Ovid's wife. Other examples are catalogued from Scripture and from modern times, including false men like Aeneas, and Virgil in the Basket. In most vices men are worse than women.

126. Ill huswiferie lieth.

By Thomas Tusser.
A comparison betweene good huswiferie and euill.
Prefatory verses: "Comparing togither, good huswife with bad,
The knowledge of either, the better is had."
(1) Tottel's 1570 edition of *A hundreth good pointes of hus-bandrie* is the first extant version to contain material on "huswiferie," including this poem (prefatory couplet, 16 four-line stanzas, and concluding couplet); ed. W. Payne and S. J. Herrtage, *Fiue Hundred Pointes of Good Husbandrie, by Thomas Tusser,* London (English Dialect Society, XXXI), 1878, p. 184.
Not in the 1557 edition of Tusser. The entries of additional material for 1561-62 may include this piece; which also may be related to *An hundred poyntes of evell huswifrye,* licensed to J. Allde in 1565-66. See **70.**
In praise and dispraise of women, for the didactic purpose of showing the virtues of the good housewife. Incorporates much of the usual satirical material. Tusser as usual refuses to commit himself on the woman question.

127. ymage of Loue, The [prose].

By John Ryckes.
(1) Wynkyn de Worde (n.d.). The *STC* (no. 21472) lists only one copy, that in the Bodleian. Never reprinted.
(2) Wynkyn de Worde (1525). The *STC* (no. 21473) lists only one copy, that in the Huntington Library, which I have examined by means of microfilm.
A late hand in the Huntington copy inserts the author's name and his death date: "1536." Written in 1525 or before.
A prose treatise on the advantages of heavenly love over earthly. The author offers the book as his New Year's Gift. He visited dame Nature and she showed him goodly images, of natural love, including friendship, of worldly love, of carnal love, and of Christ himself or divine love. The earlier sections contain attacks on women sufficient to allow inclusion of this book here. Many such treatises are less specific

about women and therefore are only remotely connected with the feministic controversy. See Miles Hogarde, *A mirrour of loue*, R. Caly, (1555); *A lytell treatise cleped La conusance damours*, Richard Pynson (n.d.); and *This tretyse is of loue*, Wynkyn de Worde (1493). I have examined these three from microfilm and find none of them a candidate for this handlist. *La conusance* tells as an example of the power of love the tale of Pyramus and Thisbe; its descriptions of the torments of love are in the courtly tradition. The other two are religious and didactic; love is essentially the Christian *caritas* in its broadest sense, and has little to do with the woman-problem. *Caritas* (the margarete of virtue or the pearl of price) and the consolations of philosophy are the major themes of Thomas Usk's *Testament of Love* (1387?) which contains in Book II, chapter 3, a debate on woman's worth (Skeat, *Chaucer*, VII, 53). And in John Heywood's *Play of Love* (printed in 1534 and [1582?]) we have a contention between Lover loved, Lover not beloved, Neither lover nor loved, and the Woman beloved not loving, in which the *coup de grace* is administered by Lover not beloved, who favors the heavenly variety (see the edition by Alois Brandl, *Quellen des Weltlichen Dramas in England vor Shakespeare*, Strasburg [Quellen und Forschungen, LXXX], 1898, p. 159).

128. In a comly closset, when the tyme was.
> By "T. S. P."
> (1) Ashmole 48 (33 four-line stanzas); ed. Wright, *Songs and Ballads*, p. 64.

In *MLN*, XXXIV (1919), 349, Rollins dates the MS. *ca.* 1557-65 on the basis of broadside contents.

Rebellious lover poem; an unskillful medley of opposing commonplaces. Begins as the usual lover's complaint, and the tone of injured masculinity and use of "swete face" throughout would bar this poem from our tradition if it were not for the finality of the stated rebellion, the religious turn in the renunciation of love, and the many generalizations about woman's inconstancy. The satirical interpretation is confirmed by a Latin proverb at the end, "Amare et sapere vix deo conceditur."

129. In a mornyng of May, as I lay on slepyng.
> *The Misogynic Nightingale.* On the analogy of other bird-debates, might well be renamed *The Clerk and the Nightingale*.
> (1) Cambridge University Library Ff. 5. 48 (though printed as 26 long couplets, should really be 13 quatrains *abab*); ed. J. B. Halliwell, *Nugae Poeticae*, London, 1844, p. 37.
> MS. second half XV cent.

Debate over woman's worth. The Clerk, a lover suffering the usual torments, defends women; the Nightingale attacks them with Biblical examples and the charge that all a woman wants is a man's money. For another lover and misogynistic bird see **313**. The Nightingale is

usually the champion of women, because he is the bird of love; but at
times he becomes the exponent of heavenly love, which causes a shift
in his attitude toward women. See **139** and Otto Glauning, ed., *Lydgate's Minor Poems. The Two Nightingale Poems*, London (EETSES,
LXXX), 1900, for this kind of Nightingale; and **112** and **273** for the
friend of women. I have been unable to examine the *Disputacio inter
Clericum et Philomenam*, which appears in acephalous form in MS.
Rawlinson poetry 34, f. 5 (*Summary Catalogue*, III, 291). Its first line,
"And a woman of hauntynge moode," does not correspond to anything
in **129**, nor does its verse-pattern, as described by Brown and Robbins,
Index, no. *5.

130. In all this warld [n]is a meryar life.

The Wandering Bachelor.
Burden: "A, a, a, a,
　　　　Yet I loue wherso I go."
(1) Bodleian Eng. poet. e. 1 (two-line burden and 4 four-line
　　stanzas); ed. Greene, *Early English Carols*, p. 278 (no.
　　414); Wright, *Songs and Carols* (Percy Society), p. 27;
　　Chambers and Sidgwick, *Early English Lyrics*, p. 210; J. E.
　　Masters, *Rymes of the Minstrels*, p. 7; Albert S. Cook,
　　A Literary Middle English Reader, Boston, 1915, p. 430;
　　see also Brown and Robbins, *Index*, no. 1468.
MS. second half XV cent.

Bachelor's rejoicing; there are maidens everywhere to love a young
peddler (or friar). For parallels to this picaresque carol see Greene,
nos. 415-17.

131. In all this warld no man may wit.

(1) Advocates' Library 1. 1. 6 (10 eight-line stanzas); ed. Rit-
　　chie, *Bannatyne Manuscript*, IV, 19; see also Hunterian
　　Club *Bannatyne*, I, cv.
1568 or before.

Rebellious lover. A lingering hint or two of love remains, but the
charges against woman's inconstancy and greed are strong enough to
link this poem to the satirical tradition.

132. In an arber of honor, set full quadrant.

By John Wallys.
(1) Ashmole 48 (13 rime-royal stanzas); ed. Wright, *Songs and
　　Ballads*, p. 136.
Rollins dates the MS. 1557-65 in *MLN*, XXXIV (1919), 349,
on the basis of broadside contents.

Satire on woman's lascivious desire. The poet is walking amidst
a typical love-vision or *chanson d'aventure* setting, and finds a woman
hunting for "A goodly erbe withe braunchis thre." There is consider-

able gross discussion of what women most desire, and the use of the "Sum sayd" formula recalls the *Wife of Bath's Tale* and its analogues. In view of John Donne's attachment to the satirical tradition the allusions in this poem to the mandrake are worthy of record.

133. In awchtirmwchty thair dwelt ane man.

> Assigned in a later hand to [Sir John?] "Mofat."
> *The wyf of auchtirmwchty.*
> (1) Advocates' Library 1. 1. 6 (15 eight-line stanzas); ed. with variants from (2) by David Laing, *Early Popular Poetry of Scotland*, rev. W. C. Hazlitt, London, 1895, II, 52. For other editions see Laing, II, 47; Ritchie, *Bannatyne Manuscript*, II, 320; Hunterian Club *Bannatyne*, I, lxxxvi.
> (2) The editors mention and give variants from a "MS. A" which is "written in a hand not much later than the year 1600." I have been unable to identify it.

The editors suppose the author to have flourished "about the year 1520," on what grounds I do not know. Certainly the poem is 1568 or before.

The classic story about the couple who dispute whose work is the hardest. So husband and wife change tasks, and soon learn that the man is best at the plough and the wife at home. For an English version see **149a**. A Latin version of the jest from the *Silva Sermonum jucundissimorum* (1568) is printed by Laing, II, 48.

134. In Bocas an Guydo I rede and fynde.

> *But I wyll say nothinge.*
> (1) Ashmole 48 (12 four-line stanzas); ed. Wright, *Songs and Ballads*, p. 163.

Rollins dates the MS. *ca.* 1557-65 in *MLN*, XXXIV (1919), 349, on the basis of broadside contents. In *Analytical Index*, no. 1207, he identifies it with the ballad "I will say nothyng," entered in 1564-65 to Thomas Colwell.

Satire on woman. Lists in vigorous fashion all the usual charges: greed, hypocrisy, lasciviousness, shrewishness, and the like, and employs the ambiguous destroying refrain "But I wyll say nothinge." Calls upon the Troy story (Guido delle Colonne and Boccaccio) as authority.

135. In bowdoun on blak monunday.

> By "Clappertoun."
> *Wa worth Maryage.*
> (1) Magdalene College Cambridge, Pepys 2553 (10 five-line stanzas); ed. W. A. Craigie, *Maitland Folio Manuscript*, I, 243; see II, 105, and Helen E. Sandison, *The "Chanson d'Aventure,"* no. A20.

MS. composed during the years 1570-85.

Chanson de mal mariée. A wanton maid laments her marriage to a shrew and churl. She dare not dress well or "Scantlie . . . gif ssir Iohne ane kis." In view of the rarity of this type in English it is worthy of note that the piece is immediately followed in the MS. by another example, **333**.

136. In euery place ye may well see.

Women are Excellent—or the Contrary.
Burden: "Of all creatures women be best,
   Cuius contrarium verum est."
(1) Balliol College Oxford 354 (two-line burden and 10 four-line stanzas); ed. with variants from (2) by Greene, *Early English Carols*, p. 266 (no. 399); Dyboski, *Songs, Carols* (EETSES, CI), p. 112; without variants by Flügel, *Anglia,* XXVI (1903), 275.
(2) Bodleian Eng. poet. e. 1; ed. Wright, *Songs and Carols* (Percy Society), p. 88.
MS. Eng. poet. was written in the second half of the XV cent.

Ironic defense. Specific praise through denial of the usual charges against women, with each stanza followed by a "destroying burden." On this device, which is an essential part of the popular French satire, *Évangile aux Femmes* (ed. George C. Keidel, Baltimore, 1895), see Greene, p. 431, and **334**. The phrase appears as a scribal gloss to satirical passages in Lydgate's *Reson and Sensuallyte* (see Lewis, *Allegory of Love*, p. 277); and in the XVI cent. *Scholehouse of Women* (**292**). Huizinga, *Waning of the Middle Ages,* pp. 282-83, discusses the heavy-handed nature of this sort of irony. For a XVII cent. exchange of poems between lover and mistress, each with destroying refrain, see F. J. Furnivall, *Love Poems and Humourous Ones,* Hertford (Ballad Society), 1874, p. 7. MS. Corpus Christi College Cambridge 168 (XVI cent.) contains the following distich: "The black shepe is a perylous beast, / Cujus contrarium falsum est" (see M. R. James's *Catalogue,* I, 380). Another destroying burden is "Doll thi ale, doll; doll thi ale, dole; / Ale mak many a mane to haue a doty poll" (Greene, *Early English Carols,* no. 423). Greene (p. 438) is surprised at "the vigorous disapproval expressed in this carol of the nearly universal English beverage . . . especially in view of the convivial associations of carol-singing"; and suggests that it was written by "a moralizing religious, probably . . . a friar." But surely "Doll [*warm, mull*] thy ale" is a burden which destroys the sting of the serious charges in the stanzas proper, which go to the extreme length of threatening the ale-drinker with the gallows. The first line of the burden of **136** recalls an appeal to all mothers by the Virgin Mary, beginning "Off alle women þat euer were borne"; see Brown, *Religious Lyrics of the XVth Century,* p. 13.

137. In evyn ther sitte a lady.

> Burden: "Women ben good for lo[ve]
> . . . . . . that sit above."
>
> (1) St. John's College Cambridge S. 54 (two-line burden and
>   5 three-line stanzas, badly damaged); ed. Greene, *Early
>   English Carols*, p. 322 (Appendix, no. vi); James and
>   Macauley, *MLR*, VIII (1913), 85.
>
> MS. second half XV cent.
>
> Defense: witness of Mary. On the burden compare **384** and **385**.

138. In June the jem.

> By Alexander Scott.
>
> (1) Advocates' Library 1. 1. 6 (5 ten-line stanzas); ed. Ritchie,
>   *Bannatyne Manuscript*, IV, 15; Cranstoun, *Poems of Alex-
>   ander Scott*, p. 71; Donald, *Poems of Alexander Scott*, p. 43.
>   For other editions see Cranstoun, p. 162.
>
> Cranstoun dates Scott's work 1545-68.
>
> Rebellious lover. If he ever loves in the future he will pay women
> back in their own guileful coin.

139. In May as that Aurora did vpspring.

> By William Dunbar.
> *The Merle and the Nychtingaill; or The twa Luves erdly and
> devyne.*
>
> (1) Advocates' Library 1. 1. 6 (15 eight-line stanzas); ed. with
>   variants of (3) by Small, *Poems of William Dunbar*, II,
>   174; Ritchie, *Bannatyne Manuscript*, IV, 87; MacKenzie,
>   *Poems of William Dunbar*, p. 134. For other editions see
>   Small, III, 263.
> (2) [Lost from MS. Asloan].
> (3) Magdalene College Cambridge, Pepys 2553; ed. W. A.
>   Craigie, *Maitland Folio Manuscript*, I, 188 (lacks two
>   stanzas).
>
> According to the *DNB* Dunbar's dates are 1465?-1530?. Mackay
> in his introduction to Small (I, cxxxvii) would date this and other
> moralizing poems late in his life, but such dating by subject matter
> is risky. Mackay says "probably written after 1513."
>
> Debate over earthly and heavenly love. Fairly courteous in tone
> toward women; but deserves a place here because of other bird-debates.
> The Merle speaks to the refrain "A lusty lyfe in luves scheruice bene";
> the Nightingale to "All luve is lost bot vpone God allone." In the end
> both their voices join in praise of heavenly love. The conventional
> nightingale is the wanton symbol of love, one of the "smale foweles
> . . . That slepen al the nyght with open ye" in order to sing of woman's

worth. See **273** and Flügel, *Anglia*, XII (1889-90), 262; Flügel, *Neu-englisches Lesebuch*, I, 139, 435; Padelford, *Early Sixteenth Century Lyrics*, pp. xxxv-xxxvi; Boccaccio, *Decameron*, Fifth Day, Fourth Novella; and Albert R. Chandler, *Larks, Nightingales and Poets*, Columbus, Ohio, 1937. Chandler, p. 7, notices the subsidiary position of the "pious" nightingale, who appears in Latin poems of Alcuin and John Pecham, and Lydgate's adaptation of the latter. For another unorthodox nightingale see **129**.

140. In may hit murgeþ when hit dawes.
    A Defence and a Warning.
    (1) Harley 2253 (4 twelve-line stanzas); ed. Brown, *English Lyrics of the XIIIth Century*, p. 146; for other editions see p. 230, and Wells' *Manual*, p. 846.
    Late XIII cent. MS.
    Defense: women are noble and men treacherous.

141. In May, when floures swetely smel.
    By "T. W. T."
    A mery balade, how a wife entreated her husband to haue her owne wyll.
    (1) Alexander Lacy, (n.d.) (12 eight-line stanzas); ed. Lilly's *Collection*, p. 129.
    The *STC* (no. 23631), on the basis of an apparent entry to Lacy, 1567-68, dates [1568]. Lilly (p. 296) and Duff, *Century*, pp. 87-88, observe that Lacy apparently no longer printed after 1571.
    Chanson d'aventure setting. The author overhears a dialogue between a young man and his wife. She wishes to have her will and leave the house once in a while. He permits her to go to church and market but not to ale-houses or to visit her gossips. She wishes gay clothes that gentlewomen will call on her. He will have her neat but not gay. She wishes other liberties, and he urges her rather to be thrifty. In all cases her "Good husband, let me haue mine owne wyll" is countered with "Doe good, and therein take your owne wyll." At last she laments and wishes she might have married John Goosequill, who would have been kinder to her. In the concluding stanza the author reveals his purpose to be counsel to good wives and a rebuke to shrews.

In soro and car he led hys lyfe (400).

In villa, in villa, quid vidistis in villa? (180).

142. In womanhede as auctours do all write.
    By John Lydgate.
    A Ballad, Declaring that Womens Chastity Doth Much Excell All Treasure Worldly; or Chastity.
    (1) Trinity College Cambridge R. 3. 19 (9 rime-royal stanzas).

(2) Stow's *Chaucer* (1561) and later Chaucer editions; see Chalmers, I, 565, and for further discussion and bibliography Hammond, *Chaucer,* p. 415.

Skeat, *Chaucer Canon,* p. 120, says "it is much later than the time of Lydgate." But MacCracken, *Minor Poems of Lydgate,* I, xvi, identifies it as part of the *Fall of Princes.* It corresponds to Book iv, 2374-87, and Book iii, 1373-1421 (ed. Bergen, II, 538, 366). I have been unable to identify the appended and unconnected tenth stanza mentioned by Hammond as in (1). According to Bergen (I, ix-x) the *Fall of Princes* was probably begun soon after May, 1431, and perhaps finished in 1438 or 1439.

The thing most commended in women is chastity, which once lost can never be recovered. Hence wicked men who despoil virgins, wives, or widows steal something very precious from them. May be ranked as a didactic defense using the argument of evil men. There are many such extracts from the *Fall of Princes* (see Brown and Robbins, *Index,* no. 1168; Bergen, IV, 123; and MacCracken, I, xvi). I have not examined them all; some, however, merit a place here. See **185, 220, 317,** and **350**.

143. In women is rest peas and pacience.

(1) Cambridge University Library Hh. 2. 6 (1 eight-line stanza); ed. R. H. Robbins, "Punctuation Poems—a Further Note," *RES,* XV (1939), 206.

MS. of the early XV cent.

Satire under the guise of ironic praise. Punctuated one way it praises women; punctuated another it satirizes them. See **22**.

144. In word, in dede, in wyl, in thoght.

By John Audelay.

The Treasure of Virginity.

Burden: "I praye youe, maydys that here be,
         Kepe your state and your degre."

(1) Bodleian Douce 302 (two-line burden and 7 four-line stanzas); ed. Greene, *Early English Carols,* p. 265 (no. 398); for further editions see p. 430.

Audelay's MS. was composed in the first half of XV cent.

Advice to maids to beware wicked men and to preserve the treasure without which you cannot be married.

145. In worschupe of þat Mayden swete.

Of Women cometh this Worldes Weal.

(1) Bodleian Eng. poet. a. 1 ("Vernon MS.," numbered 3938 in *Summary Catalogue*) (10 twelve-line stanzas); ed. Brown, *Religious Lyrics of the XIVth Century,* p. 174;

F. J. Furnivall, *The Minor Poems of the Vernon MS.*, London (EETS, CXVII), 1901, p. 704; four stanzas modernized by Mary G. Segar, *A Mediæval Anthology*, London, 1915, p. 109 (arranged 6, 9, 8, 10, and beginning "God honoured women in His life").

(2) British Museum Additional 22283 ("Simeon MS.").

Brown, *Register*, I, 49, 395, dates Simeon late XIV cent. and Vernon about 1385.

In worship of Mary I greet all good women. Those who defame them are like those that crucified Christ, who harm their own parent. I counter those who cite the evil examples of women who misled Adam, Samson, and Solomon with the evil men "Macabeus," Judas, "Ion," and Alexander. Wicked men seduce women to vice. Whence gentry if not through our mothers back to Eve? The poem is bound together by the refrain-title "Of wimmen comeþ þis worldes welle," which is also line 85 of **21**. These two are among the best of the early defenses.

146. Irkit I am with langsum luvis lair.

By [Alexander?] Montgomerie. See under date.
A Regrate of his Vnhappie Luve.
(1) Advocates' Library 1. 1. 6 (9 six-line stanzas); ed. James Cranstoun, *The Poems of Alexander Montgomerie*, Edinburgh (STS, IX-XI), 1885-87, p. 217; and Ritchie, *Bannatyne Manuscript*, IV, 9; for other editions see Cranstoun, p. 379, and Hunterian Club *Bannatyne*, I, civ.

Cranstoun, who believes that Alexander Montgomerie lived from 1545? to 1615?, chose the birth date in order to permit time for the creation of this poem by 1568. But the first incontrovertible record of his life is in 1577, and if Alexander, the well-known author of *The Cherrie and the Slae*, also wrote this poem, he was either a remarkable prodigy or a long-lived man. The *DNB* gives his birthdate as 1556. Montgomerie was a common enough name in Scottish court circles during the XV and XVI cent.

Rebellious lover, with clear generalizations on the subject of woman's cruelty and inconstancy.

147. Hit is ful heue chastity.

By John Audelay.
Of the Decadence of Marriage.
Burden: "Avyse youe, wemen, wom ye trust,
        And beware of 'had-I-wyst.'"
(1) Bodleian Douce 302 (two-line burden and 7 five-line stanzas); ed. Greene, *Early English Carols*, p. 276 (no. 411); for further editions see p. 434.

Audelay's MS. was composed in the first half of XV cent.

Warning to women against wicked men and adultery. Audelay makes a clear allusion to the fashionable courtly love of the time, and to the worldly damage it does to the bloodstream of nobility. Those who marry should be equal in birth, wealth, and age. For the burden see Greene, p. 434, and Hyder E. Rollins, ed., *The Paradise of Dainty Devices,* Cambridge, Mass., 1927, p. 182. Audelay lifted stanzas 2-7 bodily out of another poem of his, and made them into a carol by the addition of a burden and initial stanza (see Greene, p. 434).

148. Hit is no right alle oþer lustes to leese.

By Geoffrey Chaucer? So ascribed by John Shirley in (1). Some weight is given to the ascription by Furnivall, Hammond, and Brusendorff. Robinson, *Chaucer,* p. 981, says "The language of neither poem is positively incompatible with the theory that Chaucer was the author. But both are so unlike his acknowledged works in tone and subject, and . . . so inferior in style and technique, that the present editor has not even admitted them to the limbo of 'Doubtful Poems.'"

Balade of a Reeve.
(1) British Museum Additional 16165 (3 rime-royal stanzas); ed. F. J. Furnivall, *Jyl of Breyntfords Testament,* London, 1871, p. 34; Eleanor P. Hammond, "Omissions from the Editions of Chaucer," *MLN,* XIX (1904), 38; Aage Brusendorff, *The Chaucer Tradition,* London and Copenhagen, 1925, p. 280.
(2) Harley 7578; ed. Brusendorff, p. 280.

Shirley, the scribe of (1), died in 1456. Whether or not the poem is by Chaucer, it is noteworthy that none of the Chaucerian scholars who have discussed it have objected to a date before 1400 on linguistic grounds.

Rebellious lover. I have had my troubles, but in May one must gamble anew, must hunt in a new chase; "þus holde I bett þan labour as a reve." In other words, there are plenty of fish in the sea.

149. It makes me laugh a good to see thee lowre.

By George Turbervile.
Of the straunge countenaunce of an aged Gentlewoman.
(1) Turbervile's *Epitaphes, Epigrams, Songs and Sonets* (1567); ed. Collier [1867], p. 77; also in Chalmers, II, 603 (1 six-line stanza).

1567 or before.

Satire on an ugly old woman, who smiles when she tries to frown. Ugly age is sometimes attacked for its own sake in the Middle Ages (see **226**), but the stark simplicity of this poem has a classical appearance. We are reminded of Martial, Horace, or the Greek Anthology.

Ivy, chefe off treis it is (291).

149a. Jhesu that arte jentylle, ffor joye of thy dame.

Ballad of a Tyrannical Husband.

(1) Manchester, Chetham Library 8009 (28 four-line stanzas, ending imperfectly); ed. Wright and Halliwell, *Reliquiae Antiquae*, II, 196.

MS. of the time of Henry VII.

Another version of the tale told in **133**, the wife and husband who exchange tasks with one another. In this case more of the satire applies to husband than to wife.

150. Knight of La Tour-Landry, The Book of the [prose].

Translated (1) by an unknown author and (2) by William Caxton from the French original of Geoffrey de la Tour-Landry.

(1) Harley 1764; ed. Thomas Wright, London (EETS, XXXIII), 1868; revised with collations from (2) by Furnivall *et al.*, 1906; ed. with collations from (2) G. S. Taylor, London, 1930.

(2) William Caxton, [1484] (*STC*, no. 15296); ed. G. B. Rawlings, London, 1902.

Geoffrey began the original in April, 1371, and completed it in 1372, according to Wright, p. x. Translation (1) is "in a good formal writing of the reign of King Henry VI"; Caxton's translation was finished June 1, 1483, and printed in the following January (Wright, p. xiv).

Didactic work for instruction of Geoffrey's three daughters; an elaborate collection of exempla on good and evil women, and of warnings against wicked men and the courtly code. Although Geoffrey is primarily a teacher, the book was a treasure house for satirists and defenders, and thus merits inclusion. For an excellent summary see Hentsch, *De la Littérature Didactique*, pp. 127-35.

151. [Know er thow knytte, / Prove er thow preyse yt.]

(1) Digby 196 (10 lines). Never printed. Described G. D. Macray, *Catalogi Codicum Manuscriptorum Bibliothecae Bodleianae, Codices . . . Digby*, Oxford, 1883, p. 212.

MS. dated XV cent. by Macray.

Described as "Versus decem Anglice de matrimonio caute contrahendo." Apparently a counsel of careful choice in marriage. Compare "I will not knit before I knowe" (**113**).

152. Ladeis, be war, þat plesand ar.

By Alexander Scott.

(1) Advocates' Library 1. 1. 6 (6 four-line stanzas); ed. Ritchie, *Bannatyne Manuscript*, IV, 70; Cranstoun, *Poems of Alex-*

ander Scott, p. 75; Donald, *Poems of Alexander Scott,* p. 60; for further editions see Cranstoun, p. 165.

Cranstoun dates Scott's work 1545-68.

Warning to women to beware wicked men.

Langour (see **Longer**).

Leaue lightie loue, Ladies, for feare of yll name (44).

153. Leif, Luve, and lat me leif allone.

By Alexander Scott.

(1) Advocates' Library 1. 1. 6 (6 seven-line stanzas); ed. Ritchie, *Bannatyne Manuscript,* III, 349; Cranstoun, *Poems of Alexander Scott,* p. 58; Donald, *Poems of Alexander Scott,* p. 37; for further editions see Cranstoun, p. 156.

Cranstoun dates Scott's work 1545-68.

Rebellious lover; Reason has helped him to leave Cupid and his merciless lady. This rebellion only mildly generalizes, but it merits inclusion because of the philosophical appeal and the echo of **154.**

154. Leiff luif, my luif, no langir I it lyk.

By Walter Kennedy.

Pious Counsale.

(1) Advocates' Library 1. 1. 6 (2 eight-line stanzas); ed. Ritchie, *Bannatyne Manuscript,* II, 185.

(2) Advocates' Library 1. 1. 6 (another copy of the poem); ed. Ritchie, IV, 82.

(3) Magdalene College Cambridge, Pepys 2553; ed. J. Schipper, *The Poems of Walter Kennedy,* in *Denkschriften der kaiserlichen Akademie der Wissenschaften,* Philos.-Hist. Classe, XLVIII .1 (1902), p. 10, with variants from (1), (2), (4), and notes on further editions. See also F. Holthausen, "Kennedy-Studien," *Archiv,* CX (1903), 359; W. A. Craigie, *Maitland Folio Manuscript,* I, 342 (an edition), II, 117 (variants of (4)).

(4) Cambridge University Library Ll. 5. 10 ("Reidpeth MS.").

According to Schipper (p. 3) Kennedy was born in 1460 and died perhaps by 1507, certainly by 1530.

A very serious renunciation of love, addressed in common to himself and his lady.

155. Leave off, good Beroe, now.

By George Turbervile.

To an olde Gentlewoman that painted hir face.

(1) Turbervile's *Epitaphes, Epigrams, Songs and Sonets* (1567)

(3 four-line stanzas); ed. Collier [1867], p. 148; see also Chalmers, II, 622.

1567 or before.

Satire on an ugly old woman who still adorns herself as though she were young. You can't make Hecuba into Helen. For the type see **226**. According to Lathrop, *MLN*, XLIII (1928), 224, the poem was translated from the Greek Anthology, xi, 408, by Sir Thomas More and by Janus Cornarius. Turbervile probably used Cornarius.

Le[nten] is comen wiþ loue to toune (273).

156. **[Letter sent by the Maydens of London to the vertuous Matrones and Mistresses of the same, in the defence of their lawfull Libertie, (A). Answering the Mery Meeting by us Rose, Jane, Rachell, Sara, Philumias and Dorothie** (prose).]

Collier, *Bibliographical and Critical Account*, II, 268, believes it remotely possible that the author was Edward Hake. See further discussion below.

(1) Printed by Henry Binneman for Thomas Hacket in 1567, according to Collier, II, 267. Described with copious quotations by Collier there and in his *Extracts*, I, 167, 172, and in de Vocht and Edmonds as cited below (they appear to have based their comments on Collier). In the *Bibliographical and Critical Account*, II, 271, Collier speaks of "the unique copy which we discovered in a library remarkable for the preservation of several other tracts of an ephemeral kind, that exist in no other collection, public and private." This description would fit Lambeth Palace Library, and in *Extracts*, I, 172, he says that the book "exists only, as far as our research has gone, in the Library at Lambeth." S. R. Maitland, *An Index of Such English Books, Printed before the Year MDC., As are Now in the Archiepiscopal Library at Lambeth*, London, 1845, p. 75, lists the book as xxx. 8. 8 (4.) and calls it a 12mo (he is followed by Lowndes in this collation). Collier called the copy he used an 8vo. The title is not listed in the *STC*, and, puzzled by this and other discrepancies, I wrote to Lambeth. Miss Irene J. Churchill has kindly supplied me with the following information: "The pamphlet . . . exists in the volume listed in S.T.C. under *Glaucus* 11920, though it has been missed itself. In this case Collier's representation of the title seems, from a note which I made independently some time ago, to be accurate. The volume is unfortunately inaccessible for the duration of the war."

According to Collier, the maidens date their letter November
13, 1567. The *Stationers' Register* has this entry in 1565-66: "Recevyd
of Thomas hackett for his license for pryntynge of *a letter sente by
the maydes of London to the vertuous matrons and misteres[ses] of
ye same Cetie . . . iiijd.*" (Arber, I, 357).

Collier believes that this is an answer to Hake's lost *Mery metyng
of Maydens in London,* which had apparently demanded that servant
girls be banned the right to gad about and go to plays and feasts and
interludes on Sunday. The title of the two tracts suggests the old strife
between maidens and wives (see for instance, **54**). The bibliographical
picture is complicated by several other recorded items:

1. The original book to which this purports to be an answer is lost.
The *Stationers' Register* reads "Recevyd of henry Denham for his
lycense for pryntinge of a boke intituled *a mery metynge of maydes in
London, &c . . . iiijd*" (Arber, I, 355).

2. We have record of the title of a poem written by Edward Hake
which shares with *A mery metynge of maydes* only one word, but which
has nevertheless been widely identified with it. In the dedicatory poem
to Edward Hake's *Newes out of Powles Churchyarde* (1579) (ed.
Charles Edmonds, London, 1872, sig. A5ᵛ), one John Long, minister of
London, says:

> A great conquest of sinne hath made
>   a Student Edward Hake.
> O London learne for to beware,
>   from sinne arise and wake.
> *Of wanton Maydes* he did also,
>   *the slights* a late detect:
> Learne to be wise, and looke to them,
>   The worst always suspect.

3. Turbervile apparently alludes to Hake in *A Plaine Path to Perfect Vertue* (the quotation is from Collier, *Bibliographical and Critical
Account,* I, 105):

> I neither write the Newes of Poules,
>   Of late set out to sale,
> Nor Meting of the London Maides,
>   For now that fish is stale.

This leads Collier to identify *A mery metynge* with Long's "the slights
of wanton Maydes" on the ground that Hake was certainly the author
of the "Newes of Poules" and that Turbervile is probably punning on
his name when he describes the fish as being stale. His argument is
accepted by Edmonds (p. xxi) and by Henry de Vocht, ed., *The Earliest
English Translations of Erasmus' Colloquia,* Louvain, 1928, (p. lxv),
although both of them are disturbed by the next item. See also Wright,
Middle-Class Culture, p. 473.

4. The picture is further confused by a *Stationers' Register* entry
of "A mooste Delectable conference betwene the wedded lyf and the

syngle by master Henry Hake," licensed in 1566-67 to William Griffith (Arber, I, 330). Edmonds (p. xxii) thinks that Henry is a mere mistake by the clerk for Edward, and that Turbervile may be alluding to this piece.

5. De Vocht suggests that the E.H. who in 1566 published his translation of Erasmus' *Diversoria* (preserved only in John Rylands Library—see *STC*, no. 10456) may be Edward Hake, and that the translation may be identical with item 4, since William Griffith is the printer of both.

6. Possibly *A mery metynge of maydes* may be connected in authorship, text, or at least in subject matter with a broadside called *The Wiving Age or A great complaint of the maidens of London* against the widows, who with their money lure all the young men to marriage. For the text of this ballad see Hyder E. Rollins, *A Pepysian Garland,* Cambridge, 1922, p. 234. Rollins' ballad is rather late, although it may be a reprint.

157. Lysten friendes, and holde you still.

At the end, "Finis quoth Mayster Charme her." This pseudonym, which means "silence her" or "shrew-tamer," may hide a name like Chalmers or Chambre. But see below.

A merry Ieste of a Shrewde and curste Wyfe lapped in Morrelles skin.

(1) Hugh Jackson (n.d.) (1120 lines: 2 couplets, 3 quatrains, and 138 eight-line stanzas); ed. W. C. Hazlitt, *Remains,* IV, 179; and his *Shakespeare's Library,* London, 1875, part I, vol. IV, 416. For further editions see Francis J. Child, *The English and Scottish Popular Ballads,* Boston, 1882-98, V, 104.

Jackson's edition is dated [1580?] by the *STC* (no. 14521). William R. Parker informs me that Jackson's earliest printing is recorded as 1576. But that the poem was written before that date seems evident from its mention in Laneham's 1575 Letter from Kenilworth as part of Captain Cox's repertoire. Collier thought that the poem was composed about 1550 or 1560, and a similar date was favored by Hazlitt, *Shakespeare's Library,* part I, vol. IV, 416; and by R. Warwick Bond, ed., *The Taming of the Shrew,* London (The Arden Shakespeare), 1929, p. l. But Brown and Robbins, *Index,* no. 1884, list it, implying a date before 1500.

The tale tells how to charm a shrewish wife. Wrap her in the salted hide of old Morel, your horse, and beat her till the blood comes. A long and less subtle variant of the Child ballad, no. 277, which has lived on in Scotland and the United States. Both are remote analogues of *The Taming of the Shrew.* For some forerunners see Routh, *CHEL,* III, 102. It has not, I believe, been observed that the humorous *raison d'être* for the ballad and for **157** rests on the double function of the animal hide—as a cure and as an appropriate medium for flogging. The wife's shrewishness is thus *charmed* away (see the author's pseudonym); but whether the cure is natural or supernatural remains a question. Sir Walter Scott was wrapped in a sheep's hide as a cure for lameness (John G. Lockhart, *Memoirs of the Life of Sir Walter Scott,* Boston, 1901, I, 13-14; see also George L. Kittredge, *Witchcraft in Old and New England,* Cambridge, Mass., 1929, pp. 46-47).

158. lytle treatyse called ye Image of Idlenesse, conteininge certeyne matters moued betwen Walter Wedlock and Bawdyn Bacheler, (A). Translated out of the Troyane or Cornyshe tounge into Englyshe, by Olyuer Oldwanton, and dedicated to the Lady Lust [prose].

> (1) William Seres (n.d.). *STC* (no. 25196) lists only one copy, at the British Museum. There is also a copy at Huntington, which I have examined by means of microfilm. No modern edition.
>
> (2) William Seres (1574). *STC* (no. 25197) lists only one copy, at the British Museum. Wright, *Middle-Class Culture,* p. 469, notes that this edition is "Newly corrected and augmented."

STC dates (1) [1558?] and observes it was entered 1558-59. The *CBEL* (I, 728) dates it [1559].

A series of letters in which Bawdin Bacheler, who considers himself a paragon of love and a brilliant counselor to husbands, attempts to woo himself a wife. Unfortunately, he is too frank to the seven or so candidates he courts, and none of his suits speeds well. Though the surface tone is that of woman's praise, he continually slips into damaging admissions, such as the counsel to rule a woman by letting her have her own will, since the sex is by nature shrewish. Wright, who calls it a burlesque of the books in praise of women, believes it "faintly forecasts the epistolary novel," and this fictional element leads *CBEL,* I, 728, to group it under "Original Works of Fiction." One feels a certain kinship between the wooing techniques of Bawdin and Panurge (Rabelais, *Works,* Book II, ch. 21). When in his tenth chapter Bawdin says that marriage and war are not compatible, except when a man would rather die than remain married, we are reminded that Panurge's search for a wife began as a means for exemption from military service (Book III, ch. 6—but a common source might be Deut. 20:5-7 and 24:5). If "Cornysshe" in the title is not mere nonsense, it probably alludes to the visible badge of cuckoldry. Rabelais is very fond of this particular pun, though it is by no means peculiar to him. According to Lefranc, Book II (*Pantagruel*) appeared in 1532, Book I (*Gargantua*) in 1534, and *Le Tiers Livre* in 1546. This would allow plenty of time for the author of *The Image of Idlenesse* to become aware of Rabelais. Huntington Brown, *Rabelais in English Literature,* Cambridge, Mass., 1933, p. 33, dates the first certain allusion in English 1577. Oscar J.

Campbell, *Huntington Library Quarterly*, II (1938), 53-58, observes that the name Pantagruel appears in English as early as 1533, but this is a mere translation of the first edition of Antoine de Marcourt's *Le Livre des Marchands* (Neuchatel, 1533). If our piece can on more careful comparison of the texts be established as an imitation of Rabelais, it will therefore be the first in English.

159. Lo here lieth G. vnder the grounde.

By William Gray of Reading. See Rollins, *Tottel's Miscellany*, II, 306.

An Epitaphe.
 (1) Lansdowne 98 (4 four-line stanzas); ed. F. J. Furnivall, *Notes and Queries*, 4th series, IV (1869), 194.
 (2) Sloane 1207 (20 four-line stanzas); ed. Furnivall, *Ballads from Manuscripts*, London, 1868-73, I, 435. For further editions see Rollins, II, 306, who observes that Furnivall erroneously called this MS. "Sloane 1206."
 (3) *Tottel's Miscellany* (all editions); ed. Rollins, I, 200 (same 4 stanzas as Lansdowne), with variants of (1) and (2).
 (4) According to Rollins, II, 308, the last 4 stanzas of (2) are chiseled "on a stone slab beneath an old mural monument in the parish church of Sonning."

1557 or before.

Here lies G., slain by the spiteful tongue of a wicked wife. Answered by **122**. The extra stanzas in (2) have nothing to do with women, but discuss the vanity of worldly things and the evils of the Roman Catholic Church. Rollins believes that they were suppressed by the editor, who was cautious about such attacks.

160. Lo, what it is to love!

By Sir Thomas Wyatt, according to Miss Foxwell (signed "Tho." in MS. Egerton). Erroneously ascribed to "Scott" in MS. Bannatyne.

A Roundel of Luve, according to Cranstoun.
 (1) Egerton 2711 (a trilogy, each part containing 5 eight-line stanzas and an indication of repetition of the first stanza); ed. Foxwell, *Poems of Sir Thomas Wiat*, I, 165.
 (2) Advocates' Library 1.1.6 (the first part of the trilogy only); ed. Ritchie, *Bannatyne Manuscript*, IV, 95; Cranstoun, *Poems of Alexander Scott*, p. 81; Donald, *Poems of Alexander Scott*, p. 47. For further editions see Cranstoun, p. 157.

Wyatt's dates are 1503?-1542. "About 1539," according to Miss Foxwell.

The trilogy involves a dramatic development. Part I calls love a fervent fire and an uncertain cast of dice, which cannot live together with wisdom. Part II defends love, and Part III casts the blame on feigning lovers. According to Miss Foxwell (II, 118) this is Wyatt's contribution to "the *querelle des dames*" raging in Lyons when Wyatt visited Spain. She dates the Lyons controversy from 1537 to 1545, but its keystone, Héroet's *La Parfaicte Amye*, was published in the year of Wyatt's death. See my Introduction, p. 68.

161. Lang heff I maid of ladyes quhytt.

By William Dunbar.

Of Ane Blak-Moir, or *On ane Blak moir Ladye.*

(1) Magdalene College Cambridge, Pepys 2553 (5 five-line stanzas); ed. Small, *Poems of William Dunbar,* II, 201, with variants of (2); ed. W. A. Craigie, *Maitland Folio Manuscript,* I, 416; see II, 128, for variants of (2); MacKenzie, *Poems of William Dunbar,* p. 66. For further editions see Small, III, 286.

(2) Cambridge University Library Ll. 5. 10 (the "Reidpeth MS.").

According to the *DNB* Dunbar's dates are (1465?-1530?). Mackay in his introduction to Small (I, cii, clxiv) believes the poem was written on the occasion of a tournament held in June, 1507, for Elen More, or Black Elen, an African girl captured from a Portuguese ship by one of the Bartons and presented to James IV.

Parody of a courtly love panegyric, with the refrain "My ladye with the mekle lippis." Such parodies were frequent enough (see **226**); **161** differs from the tradition by having a clearly identifiable subject. No doubt the slave girl would not have been insulted too greatly, since her command of Scots would scarcely equal that of the court which heard this broadly humorous lyric.

162. Long you with greedie minde to bleare mine eie.

By George Turbervile.

The Aunswere, for taking a Wyfe (see **163**).

(1) Turbervile's *Epitaphes, Epigrams, Songs and Sonets* (1567) (8 four-line stanzas and a couplet); ed. Collier [1867], p. 131; also in Chalmers, II, 618.

1567 or before.

Answers the charges against women and marriage in **163** by showing that every cloud has its silver lining. Turns the satire against the misogynist in the end by "But if you thinke so yll to take a wyfe, / Let others wed, leade you the single lyfe."

163. Long you with greedie minde to leade a lyfe.

Included in Turbervile's works, but may be by another. The answer, **162**, is signed "(qd) G. T."; there is no signature after the original poem. Many a poet could, however, take both sides in this controversy.

To a yong Gentleman, of taking a Wyfe.

(1) Turbervile's *Epitaphes, Epigrams, Songs and Sonets* (1567) (4 four-line stanzas); ed. Collier [1867], p. 130; also in Chalmers, II, 618.

1567 or before.

Take my advice and eschew marriage, for all alternatives in choice are bad. An ugly wife is foul to behold, a fair wife is alluring to other men, a wanton girl is proud, an aged trot no pleasure, a wife who brings you children brings you care, a barren wife brings you disappointment. Marry a shrew in haste and repent in leisure. For this type of contrasting choices see **343, 259**; Chaucer, *Wife of Bath's Tale*, III, 248-72; references collected by Robinson, p. 803; and Introduction, pp. 28, 49.

164. Langour to leive, allace!

By Alexander Scott.

(1) Advocates' Library 1. 1. 6 (12 four-line stanzas); ed. Ritchie, *Bannatyne Manuscript*, IV, 4; Cranstoun, *Poems of Alexander Scott*, p. 62; Donald, *Poems of Alexander Scott*, p. 40; for other editions see Cranstoun, p. 158.

Cranstoun dates Scott's work 1545-68.

The rebellious lover will be as false as his lady, hypocrite that she is, and will not love again for a long time.

165. Loke, er thin herte be set.

Against Hasty Wedding.

Burden: "Man, bewar of thin wowyng,
      For weddyng is the longe wo."

(1) Sloane 2593 (two-line burden and 4 four-line stanzas); ed. Greene, *Early English Carols*, p. 270 (no. 403); also in Wright, *Songs and Carols*, (Warton Club), p. 27; Bernhard Fehr, *Archiv*, CIX (1902), 49.

MS. first half XV cent.

Warning against marriage with maid, wife, or widow. The variable refrain, "Knet vp the heltre, and let here goo," recalls **104** and other poems there mentioned. The first line of the burden is derived from a didactic commonplace popular in the Peasant's Revolt of 1381, and present in the burden of two other carols, one by John Audelay (Greene, nos. 325, 355; see his Introduction, p. cxliv). The oldest form of "be war or him be wo" is as line 860 of the Jesus MS. of **112**; see also the proverbial *Quatrain on the Wise Man*, Brown, *Register*, no. 700; Greene, p. 420; Wright and Halliwell, *Reliquiae Antiquae*, II, 120. "Man, bewar, the way ys sleder" appears in the text of two carols (Greene, nos. 356, 382). This warning is specifically applied to wedding in **179** and in the Towneley *Second Shepherds' Play* (see Greene, p. 432); it is also used more generally in *Think on Yesterday* (Brown, *Religious Lyrics of the XIVth Century*, p. 144). The second line of the burden of **165** is found also in *A Disputison bitwene a God Man and the Deuel,* ed. Carl Horstmann, *The Minor Poems of the Vernon Manuscript,* Part I, London (EETS, XCVIII), 1892, p. 345. Since the contrast between maids, wives, and widows is also proverbial, the poem is a rather remarkable pastiche.

166. Loke wel aboute, ye that lovers be.

Ascribed in (1) and (4) to Chaucer; rejected by Tyrwhitt, Skeat, and all modern editors. Skeat (*Canŏn,* p. 124, and *Chaucer,* VII, 1) follows Tyrwhitt in ascribing to Lydgate because of its appearance in (3), which they thought a Shirley codex, and in which it directly follows another satire on women by Lydgate, **232**. MacCracken, *Minor Poems of Lydgate,* I, xlix, rejects it because no early authority actually assigns it to Lydgate, and because certain rimes violate Lydgate's practice. But in view of a possible allusion in *A Reproof to Lydgate* (**186**) he is hesitant about making his rejection too final.

A Balade: Warning Men to Beware of Deceitful Women; or *Beware.*

> (1) Trinity College Cambridge R. 3. 19 (6 rime-royal stanzas); ed. with variants from (2) and (3) by Skeat, *Chaucer,* VII, 295.
> (2) Trinity College Cambridge O. 9. 38 (7 rime-royal stanzas).
> (3) Harley 2251. Though Skeat and others believed this MS. to be in Shirley's hand, Foerster and Hammond (see her *Chaucer,* p. 329) show it to be in another's hand and only in part derivative from Shirley.
> (4) Tanner 407.
> (5) Stow's *Chaucer* (1561) and later Chaucer editions. See Hammond, *Chaucer,* p. 412. Skeat believes that (1) was Stow's authority.

According to Hammond, *English Verse,* p. 77, Lydgate died in 1448 or 1449. If the poem is not his, we must resort to the date of the earliest authority, which Brown, *Register,* I, 315, dates "Time of Edw. IV" (1461-83).

Women deceived wise Solomon and strong Samson. They laugh and love not, they shave nearer than razors, their gall is hidden under honey. Deceit, spinning, and weeping are their three properties. If all the earth were parchment and the sea ink their faithlessness could not be set down on paper. A skillful use of proverbial libels. For the refrain, "Bewar therfore; the blinde et many a fly," see **239**; references in Skeat, *Chaucer,* VII, 516; and a XVII cent. broadside in Rollins, *Analytical Index,* no. 212. Deceit, spinning, and weeping goes back to the Latin "Fallere flere nere tria sunt hec in muliere," which glosses the stanza in (2), and also to *The Wife of Bath's Prologue* (see Manly and Rickert, *Text of the Canterbury Tales*, III, 500). For its use by "Puttenham" see my Introduction, pp. 3-4. See **118** for the parchment-ink formula. Version (2) contains an additional stanza based on the distich "Vento quid levius? fulgur; quid fulgure? flamma. / Flamma quid? mulier. Quid muliere? nichil." The interpolation shows how easily a proverbial satire on women could be expanded. The distich was also used by Chaucer (see Skeat, *Chaucer*, VII, 516, on this and other proverbial matter in the poem). Some gallant reader of MS. Harley 2251, who throughout marked his favorite pieces "Reade thys," on this occasion rebelled and wrote "Do not Reade thys / but hyde your eye." The scribe of this MS. may have picked up such marginalia from a Shirley codex (see **185**).

167. Lord god my hairt is in distres.

> *Commonyng betuix the mester and the heure.*
> (1) Advocates' Library 1. 1. 6 (8 eight-line stanzas); ed. Ritchie, *Bannatyne Manuscript*, IV, 38; see also Hunterian Club *Bannatyne*, I, cvi.

1568 or before.

The author reports a rather free-spoken dialogue with his wanton mistress, in which she postpones all his demands with "Byd quhill the court be of the toun." In the end he takes another love. If the "mester" of the title is authentic the poem reveals an amorous rivalry between scholar (clerk) and courtier which is at least as early as the XIII cent. See Charles Oulmont, *Les Débats du Clerc et du Chevalier*, Paris, 1911; Lewis, *Allegory of Love*, p. 19; Paul Lehmann, *Die Parodie im Mittelalter*, Munich, 1922, pp. 156-59, 169-72; and H. Walther, *Das Streitgedicht in der Lateinischen Literatur des Mittelalters*, Munich, 1920, pp. 150, 248. See also **301**.

168. Lord, how shall I me complayn.

> *The Disconsolate Lover.*
> (1) Balliol College Oxford 354 (8 eight-line stanzas); ed. Flügel, *Anglia*, XXVI (1903), 284; with variants from (2) Dyboski, *Songs, Carols* (EETSES, CI), p. 119; modernized and combined with (2) Chambers and Sidgwick, *Early English Lyrics*, p. 217. Extensive notes in Dyboski, p. 190.
> (2) Lord Harlech, Brogyntyn, Oswestry; MS. Porkington 10; ed. J. O. Halliwell, *Early English Miscellanies*, London (Warton Club, II), 1855, p. 6.

The oldest authority, MS. Porkington, was written in the third quarter of the XV cent.

Parody of a courtly love poem, with the heterodox refrain "That when I slepe, I can not wake." I smart as when my shoe pinches my little toe; I eat no meat till I rise; I drink no ale at all if I can get good wine; I grow fatter every day. Greene, *Early English Carols*, p. 452, believes that the author of this poem was reworking **93**.

169. Lord þat lenest vs lyf ant lokest vch-an lede.

On the Follies of Fashion; or The Luxury of Women; or Satire Against the Pride of the Ladies.

(1) Harley 2253 (5 seven-line stanzas); ed. Brown, *English Lyrics of the XIIIth Century*, p. 133; F. W. Fairholt, *Satirical Songs and Poems on Costume*, London (Percy Society, XXVII), 1849, p. 40 (with a translation). For other editions see Brown, p. 224, and Wells, *Manual*, pp. 799, 1709.

Oakden places the poem in the time of Edward I (1272-1307); see his *Alliterative Poetry* [1930], p. 110.

Satire on woman's love of extremes in dress, which start as a method of honoring ladies and then are imitated by every strumpet and shrew. Several obscure fashions are attacked, among them the boss or ram's horn (akin to the "horns" of **232** and to "le bossu" of the *Dit des Cornetes*, for which see Fairholt, p. 30), the "bout" and the "barbet" (perhaps a chin-covering such as survived in the dress of widows and nuns). Wells (*Manual*, p. 230) remarks: "Driven by intense moral feeling, and filled with disgust, the author attacks the offenders with bitter, passionate invective, expressive of the attitude of the clergy of the day toward the excesses of fashion, and anticipates what one would expect of an especially narrow Puritan of the middle seventeenth century. One feels that the humor of a gleeman would have accomplished more, in the situation, than would this abusive onslaught."

170. Loue is a selkud wodenesse.

Love's Madness.

(1) Bodleian Douce 139 (a four-line stanza); ed. Brown, *English Lyrics of the XIIIth Century*, p. 14; for further editions see p. 169; and Brown and Robbins, *Index*, no. 2005.

The MS. contains several fragments bound together, which E. W. B. Nicholson in his most recent opinion dates about 1270 (Brown, p. 169).

Love is a marvelous madness which leads the idler into wilderness; there he thirsts for pleasure and drinks sorrow, and his joy is mixed with frequent sadness. Accompanied by a French and a Latin version, the poem recalls definitions of love by Richard de Fournival, by a quatrain assigned to John Garland, and by the *Roman de la Rose*. See also **3, 106a, 171**. In a sense definitions of this sort are satires and renunciations of the love of women; in another sense they exalt its glory and power. They reduce the paradox of courtly love to its simplest terms, and deliver it over to the ascetic satirist. Like the figure behind most of them, oxymoron, these poems are intentionally ambiguous, and anticipate the packed and dramatic ironies of the contemporaries of John Donne. There is a similar conflict of feeling in **103**.

171. Loue is sofft, loue is swet, loue is goed sware.

The MS. heading, *Ci comence la manere quele amour est pur assaier*, is translated by Brown *What Love is Like*.

(1) Digby 86 (28 lines in irregular monorimed stanzas, the most frequent of which is *aaaa*); ed. Brown, *English Lyrics of the XIIIth Century*, p. 107; Wright, *Anecdota Literaria*, p. 96; J. J. Conybeare, *The Romance of Octavian*, Oxford, 1809, p. 58.

The MS. was composed in the time of Edward I, probably between the years 1272 and 1283 (see Wells, *Manual*, p. 422, and the corrected issue of Brown, p. xxviii). In his *Register* Brown dates it "*Ca*. 1275."

A packed example of the antithetical definition of love, which is described in terms of joy and strength and fire and destruction. Like other poems of this type its conflict is insoluble and its function as praise or blame of women ambiguous (see **170**). In the end it breaks out of the antithetical pattern:

> Were loue also londdrei as he is furst kene,
> Hit were þe wordlokste þing in werlde were, ich wene.
> Hit is I-said in an song, is I-sene,
> Loue comseþ wiþ kare and hendeþ wiþ tene,
> Mid lauedi, wid wiue, mid maide, mid quene.

The specific mention of women does not help to tell us whether the point of view is for or against them. *Mid* is once more ambiguous; it may mean "for" (man's love for lady, wife, maid, and queen) or "among" (love brings sorrow to lady, wife, maid, and queen—the theme of the forsaken maiden, or man's wickedness to women). Brown (p. 208) gives a number of parallel definitions extracted from longer Middle English poems; and R. M. Wilson, *Early Middle English Literature*, London, 1939, p. 262, calls it a derivative of the Provençal *reversaris*.

172. Leve, lystynes to me.

A Talk of Ten Wives on Their Husbands' Ware.

(1) Lord Harlech, Brogyntyn, Oswestry: MS. Porkington 10 (20 six-line stanzas); ed. F. J. Furnivall, *Jyl of Breyntfords Testament*, London, 1871, p. 29.

MS. third quarter of XV cent.

After a *chanson d'aventure* opening, which links the poem to the *chanson de mal mariée*, the author describes the conversation of ten ale-wives on the amorous equipment of their husbands. Needless to say, none is satisfied. The poem recalls Dunbar's Wedow (**336**), Chaucer's Wife of Bath (**58**), and Skelton's Elynour Rummyng (**277**). Furnivall remarks (p. 6), "A near relative of mine, a few years since, was greatly astonished to see a like question to that discust by the Wives, experimentally settled on some clean plates, for a bet, by a party of Welsh farmers after a market dinner at an inn on the borders."

Luve þat is het can no skill (173).

173. Love þat is powre it is with pyne.

> *Off Luve*, or *What Love Is*.
>> (1) Pierpont Morgan Library, Printed Book 775 (4 couplets on last printed page of *De consolatione philosophiae*, William Caxton, *ca.* 1478); ed. Curt F. Bühler, *MLN*, LIII (1938), 246.
>> (2) Advocates' Library 1. 1. 6; ed. Ritchie, *Bannatyne Manuscript*, IV, 40; see also Hunterian Club *Bannatyne*, I, cvi (where it is erroneously merged with **267**). The order of lines differs from that in (1); the Bannatyne version begins "Luve þat is het can no skill."

Bühler dates the hand in the Morgan copy "probably in the first half of the sixteenth century"; Brown and Robbins, *Index*, no. 2013, imply by their inclusion that the poem is before 1500. Neither was aware of the Bannatyne copy.

Denunciation, with antithetical repetition, of false love, and praise of true. The contrast seems to be of heavenly love against earthly.

174. Luvaris, lat be the frennessy of luve.

> By Alexander Scott.
> *The slicht Remeid of Luve*.
>> (1) Advocates' Library 1. 1. 6 (7 eight-line stanzas); ed. Cranstoun, *Poems of Alexander Scott*, p. 16; Donald, *Poems of Alexander Scott*, p. 53; Ritchie, *Bannatyne Manuscript*, II, 325; for further editions see Cranstoun, p. 123.

Cranstoun dates Scott's work 1545-68.

Leave love, you lovers, for if you knew the veritable nature of women you could not remain so true. But if you must love I'll tell you what to do to keep your lady and obtain your desires. The revelations which follow are probably meant as satirical attacks. The title suggests that the author had Ovid's *Remedia Amoris*, with its ambiguous message, specifically in mind.

175. Madame, for your newefangelnesse.

By Chaucer? Modern scholars are considerably divided on the question. Skeat (*Chaucer*, I, 88, 409; *Canon*, p. 62) is the most noteworthy exponent of its genuineness; he observes that the rimes are satisfactory, the idea borrowed from Machaut ("Chaucer's favorite author. . . . It has not been shown that any one but Chaucer was acquainted with Machault"), and in (2) and (3) the MS. location is close to that of several genuine poems. Yet Stow was the first to actually ascribe it to Chaucer, and Robinson therefore includes it among his "Minor Poems of Doubtful Authorship." Koch (see

Hammond, *Chaucer,* p. 441) has defended it; it is rejected by Tyrwhitt, Furnivall, and Brusendorff (see his *Chaucer Tradition,* p.
441).

A balade which Chaucer made agaynst women vnconstaunt; or
Newfangleness.

(1) Bodleian Fairfax 16 (3 rime-royal stanzas).
(2) Cotton Cleopatra D. 7; ed. with variants from (1), (3), and
(4) by Skeat, *Chaucer,* I, 409; and Robinson, *Chaucer,* p. 636.
Both editors correct Cotton by (1), which Robinson calls
"superior." For other editions see Hammond, *Chaucer,* p.
440; Griffith, *Chaucer,* pp. 21, 127; Martin, *Chaucer,* p. 66;
and the current bibliographies.
(3) Harley 7578.
(4) Stow's *Chaucer* (1561) and later Chaucer editions. Brusendorff (p. 441) says Stow derived it from (2).

Fairfax, apparently the earliest MS., is first half XV cent.; Harley
7578 is about 1450 (Brown, *Register,* I, 356). Since it has not been
denied to Chaucer on linguistic grounds it may be before 1400.

Rebellious lover. His lady cannot love half a year in one place;
she turns like a weathercock; she is as fickle as Dalilah, Criseyde, or
Candace. The refrain, "In stede of blew, thus may ye were al grene,"
recalls a ballade of Machaut (Robinson, p. 981), where fickle green is
likewise opposed to true blue. The same color symbolism appears in
194. It seems to have conflicted with a more complimentary sense of
green in the XV cent. "Ordre de l'Escu Vert à la Dame Blanche"; see
Huizinga, *Waning of the Middle Ages,* pp. 43, 107.

176. Madame, ye ben of al beauté shryne.

Accepted as Chaucer's by Skeat, Robinson, Koch and most
modern editors, since it follows *Troilus* in the MS. and like that
poem is signed "Tregentil - - - Chaucer." But Brusendorff, *Chaucer
Tradition,* p. 439, observes that the colophon is later than the poem
itself and probably an imitation of the colophon of *Troilus.*

To Rosemounde.

(1) Rawlinson Poetry 163 (3 eight-line stanzas); ed. Skeat,
Chaucer, I, 389; Robinson, *Chaucer,* p. 627. For further
editions see Robinson, p. 1036; Hammond, *Chaucer,* p. 460;
Griffith, *Chaucer,* pp. 20-21, 132; Martin, *Chaucer,* p. 75;
and the current bibliographies.

MS. in several hands, all of the XV cent. Brusendorff dates the
copy of this poem last third of the century. Robinson (p. 974)
remarks that "the general temper of the poem is recognized as
suitable to the period of the *Troilus* (1380-88)."

A very skillful parody of a courtly complaint, where a few delicate shifts of tone do the trick. The lover weeps a "tyne" full of tears, and wallows in love like a "pyk . . . in galauntyne." He boasts of being "trewe Tristam the secounde" though his lady will do him "no daliaunce." Lewis, *Allegory of Love*, p. 171, does not believe the parodic intent to be quite clear, but the poem seems to me to be an excellent example of expression intentionally too low for the avowed matter.

177. Madame, зour men said thai wald ryd.

By William Dunbar.

To the Quene.

(1) Magdalene College Cambridge, Pepys 2553 (7 five-line stanzas); ed. Small, *Poems of William Dunbar*, II, 203; and W. A. Craigie, *Maitland Folio Manuscript*, I, 417 (both with variants from (2)); MacKenzie, *Poems of William Dunbar*, p. 59. For further editions see Small, III, 287.

(2) Cambridge University Library Ll. 5. 10 ("Reidpeth MS.").

According to the *DNB* Dunbar's dates are (1465?-1530?). Mackay in his introduction to Small (I, clxii) places it among the poems written between 1503 and 1513. He observes that it was written for Fastern's Eve (Shrove Tuesday), probably some time after Margaret Tudor's marriage to James IV in 1503.

A boisterous and ribald description of how the Queen's courtiers behave on Carnival Night, the day before Lent. Wives apparently had to struggle to keep them home and "lib tham of the pockis." Whether Dunbar's mild satire is directed most at the unsuccessful wives, their unsatisfied and riotous husbands, or the harlots who were the cause of all the trouble is difficult to discover. The tone is as incomprehensible to the modern mind as the *mores* of a court which would permit the poet laureate to grace his queen with such a piece of comic obscenity. But perhaps the modern mind does not understand the carnival spirit.

178. Maddamys alle as зe bee.

(1) "From a Psalter of the fourteenth century, discovered in a farmhouse in Leicestershire, by J. Stockdale Hardy" according to the editors, Wright and Halliwell, *Reliquiae Antiquae*, II, 117 (4 couplets). Brown and Robinson, *Index*, no. 2033, have not located the present owner.

Wells, *Manual*, p. 235, accepts the date given to the MS. by the editors.

A piece of didactic scribbling, intentionally or unintentionally obscure, but apparently warning women to beware unchaste conduct. The poem is preceded by a French scrap called *Les aprises qe ly sages aprent à ces enfaunz*, and the use of the phrase "Scho that haw wyll to play the chylle" suggests that our inarticulate poet was referring to the French text, which applies presumably to either sex.

179. Man, be war, or thou knyte the fast.

(1) Bodleian Eng. Poet. e. 1 (3 quatrains); ed. Wright, *Songs and Carols* (Percy Society), p. 34; J. E. Masters, *Rymes of the Minstrels,* p. 17.

The MS. is of the second half of the XV cent.

Warning to beware in the choice of a wife, for "poverte partyth company." Wink when you take a wife and stare after. Wives are "rekeles," children unnatural, and executors covetous. For the proverbial first line see **165**. A fourth quatrain printed by Wright, beginning "I saw iij. hedles playen at a ball," seems to have no connection with the poem; but it may involve a lost jest or riddle which bears on the preceding stanzas, which are loosely enough bound together as it is. Brown and Robbins, *Index,* nos. 1354, 2049, 2056, 3919, treat Wright's "poem" as four independent quatrains. This is probably correct, but in defense of Wright it should be observed that all appear on one page in the MS., and that the first three share the theme of woman's malice in marriage. The second stanza is paralleled by **113a**; and the third belongs to the widespread tradition of the Evils of the Age.

Man, have this in thi mynd (179).

Man minded for to thriue (70).

180. Many a man blamys his wyffe, perde.

Women Will Have their Word.

Burden: "In villa, in villa,
          Quid vidistis in villa?"

(1) Balliol College Oxford 354 (two-line burden and 14 four-line stanzas); ed. with variants of (2) by Greene, *Early English Carols,* p. 275 (no. 410) and by Dyboski, *Songs, Carols* (EETSES, CI), p. 109; Flügel, *Anglia,* XXVI (1903), 269.

(2) Bodleian Eng. Poet. e. 1; ed. Wright, *Songs and Carols* (Percy Society), p. 86; J. E. Masters, *Rymes of the Minstrels,* p. 24.

MS. (2), the earliest authority, belongs to the second half of the XV cent.

None of the editors appear to have observed that the poem is in need of a series of quotation marks. The burden has an introductory value; it sets the stage for an overheard dialogue akin to the *chanson d'aventure.* One speaker praises women: a man who blames his wife is worse than she, women are right liberal and speak only to defend themselves, their husbands cruelly keep them indoors, and the like. The other believes that women's tongues are seldom lame, that they call their husbands by evil names, and that in general they deserve all that is said about them. The last three stanzas are probably given to the

misogynist, who advises men to give wives their own way, since it is
hard to strive against the stream, and the penalty of opposing them is
to have one's hair grow through one's hood. This final threat, according
to Greene, means that the husband shall go in rags; according to Dyboski, that the husband shall be luckless. There is another possibility: that
his wife will make him wear horns. For an early example of the torn
hood of wisdom as a sign of misery, frustration, and despair see "Will
and Wit," in Brown, *English Lyrics of the XIIIth Century,* p. 65. It is
also possible that the last three stanzas are sung in chorus by the two
speakers, who have come to an agreement about the wicked ways of
women. The burden is probably a parody of the Easter Prose *Victimae
Paschali Laudes* (see Greene, p. 434, and on the Prose, F. J. E. Raby,
A History of Christian-Latin Poetry, Oxford, 1927, p. 218, and F. Brit-
tain, *The Medieval Latin and Romance Lyric,* Cambridge, 1937, p. 95).
Greene comments on the numerous proverbs in the poem.

181. Many men sayn that in sweveninges.

Since Chaucer is known to have translated all or part of the
Roman de la Rose, and since this is the only extant Middle English
version, it has long been ascribed to him. The problem is too complex for full discussion here. Robinson (*Chaucer,* pp. 988-89) sum-
marizes present opinions: "Kaluza assigned fragments A and C
to Chaucer, and held B to be by another poet. Skeat's final opinion
was that fragment A alone was Chaucer's. The authenticity of the
entire poem was defended by Lounsbury, whose arguments were
answered in detail by Professor Kittredge. At the opposite extreme
from Lounsbury stands Professor Koch, who would deny Chaucer
any part of the work. . . . Brusendorff recognized only two fragments,
. . . both of them, in their original form . . . by Chaucer." Robinson himself feels that A "accords well enough with Chaucer's
usage in language and meter" and that "it seems more reasonable
to assign B and C to a second translator, perhaps a Northern Chaucerian, than to explain them as works of Chaucer corrupted in transmission." See the references collected by Robinson and also Hammond, *Chaucer,* p. 450; Griffith, *Chaucer,* p. 130; Martin, *Chaucer,*
p. 75; and the current bibliographies.

    The Romaunt of the Rose.
    (1) Hunterian Museum, Glasgow, MS. V. 3. 7 (in Robinson
        7696 lines in couplets); ed. Robinson, *Chaucer,* p. 664; for
        further editions see references under authorship.
    (2) Thynne's *Chaucer* (1532) and later Chaucer editions (see
        Hammond, *Chaucer,* p. 450). Thynne reproduced in
        Skeat's *Facsimile,* p. 273. This authority provides a number
        of lines not in (1) for Robinson's text.
    The date is inextricably bound up with the authorship. Brusen-

dorff (*Chaucer Tradition,* p. 296) dates the MS. "from the first quarter of the XV century or so"; he feels that Skeat's "towards 1440" is certainly too late. As for Chaucer's translation, which these fragments may or may not represent, Robinson remarks "It must have preceded the *Prologue to the Legend* (*ca.* 1386), and is usually assigned to the earliest years of his literary production." Brusendorff would date it near 1380. According to Ernest Langlois, *Le Roman de la Rose,* Paris (SATF), 1914-24, I, 2, Guillaume de Lorris composed the first portion of the original between 1225 and 1240, and Jean de Meun completed it over forty years later, perhaps between 1265 and 1280.

In view of the prominent role played by the *Roman* in the *querelle,* we may depart from our rule of including in this Index only works wholly devoted to the controversy. Even under the more rigid rule we might accept it on the grounds that it blends the courtly love of Guillaume with the misogyny of Jean, and that Jean's digressions into other subjects are that and nothing more. The Middle English corresponds to the French as follows: *Romaunt* 1-1705 (A)=*Roman* 1-1670; *Romaunt* 1706-5810 (B)=*Roman* 1671-5154; *Romaunt* 5811-7696 (C)=*Roman* 10679-12360 (line numbers from Robinson and Langlois). Guillaume's portion ends with line 4058 of the original (4432 of the translation). Thus only a small portion of Jean's continuation is represented by the translation. Those archetypes of satire, Le Jaloux and La Vieille, are conspicuously missing from the Middle English. But there is enough of Meun to catch the flavor of his non-courtly attitude. The following is a brief summary of the portion of the translation which corresponds to Meun's original. Guillaume's Lover was about to fall into wanhope when the poem broke off. The fresh and rebellious spirit of Jean bursts out at the very beginning of his continuation: "Allas, in wanhope? nay, pardee! For I wole never dispeired be." Nevertheless he laments the fickleness of hope and the loss of Love's gifts of grace, Swete-Thought, Swete-Speche, and Swete-Lokyng. But soon Dame Resoun appears on the scene to have a talk with the Lover. She reveals the disadvantages of taking Love as master, and presents us with one of those antithetical definitions of love which were so popular in the later Middle Ages (see **170**). After many further revelations of the folly of love the Lover interrupts Reason with a philosophical shift of position: "Is it your will algate / That I not love, but that I hate / Alle men, as ye me teche?" Reason replies that there are many kinds of love, which leads to a discussion of various matters, friendship, the evils of love for gain, the advantages of poverty, and the wickedness of some priests. Fragment B ends with an attack on women who sell their bodies for gain. The intervening portion of the original introduces, among other matters, Le Jaloux, with his wicked attack on women, used to such advantage in their favor by the Wife of Bath. The allegory proper begins again, with the Lover determining to rescue Fair-Welcome from his bondage.

Cupid and his barons are discussing the plan of attack when Fragment C opens. Fals-Semblaunt is chosen as one of the band of Love, which leads to a long discourse on the sins of monks and friars. The Lover's friends make ready for the attack, and Fals-Semblaunt pretends to be a friar in order to dispose of one of the major enemies in the path, Wicked-Tonge. It is here that Fragment C ends, with La Vieille, the Duenna whose revelations in part inspired those of the Wife of Bath, still to appear. This summary will indicate that, although some of the most brilliant passages of Jean de Meun's satire on women are not in the Middle English, there is enough to reveal that Jean was somewhat heterodox in his search for the Rose of love. On the controversy engendered by the *Roman de la Rose* see the Introduction, p. 56. "Few books," says Huizinga (*Waning of the Middle Ages*, p. 96), "have exercised a more profound and enduring influence on the life of any period."

Mastres; Masteres (see **Mistress**).

182. **Maist thou now be glade, with all thi fresshe aray.**
Called by Brown *A Mirror for Young Ladies at Their Toilet*. The poem is headed in the MS.: *Cest le myrroure pur lez Iofenes Dames a regardir/aud maytyne pur lour testes bealment adressere."*
(1) Harley 116 (two-line title with 3 five-line stanzas); ed. Brown, *Religious Lyrics of the XVth Century*, p. 241.
According to Brown (p. 340) the MS. must have been composed after 1454.

A *memento mori* for vain and beautiful women. Although it is not accompanied by a picture in the MS., the speaker is Death with his mace, and recalls such illustrated poems (see, for instance **90**, and Brown's *Register*, no. 841). The text of the poem might apply to any frivolous person, but the title limits it to young women. The French original has not yet been identified. Of the many *Miroirs des dames* of which we have record the most likely candidate seems to me to be a poem ascribed to Frère Jehan de Castel, *L'example des dames et damoiselles et de tout le sexe feminin,* which is listed by Arthur Langfors, *Les Incipit des Poèmes Francais*, Paris, 1917, I, 219, as beginning "Mirez vous cy, dames et demoiselles," and which appears at the end of the XV cent. printing of Castel's *Spécule des pécheurs,* from which it was edited in 1904 by Werner Söderhjelm. I have been unable to compare it with the English, however. Langfors also lists three MSS., two in the Bibliothèque Nationale and one in Fitzwilliam Museum (no. 164). Hentsch, *De la Littérature Didactique*, p. 163, adds another MS. in the Bibliothèque Nationale; she was unaware of the three cited by Langfors, or of the authorship. According to M. R. James, *A Descriptive Catalogue of the Manuscripts in the Fitzwilliam Museum,* Cambridge, 1895, pp. 363-65, the poem is in quatrains and is accompanied by a picture of "Eight ladies seated in a garden: to left a corpse of a woman with shroud, decaying, stands." Langfors and Arthur Piaget, ed., *Le Miroir aux Dames* [attributed to Alain Chartier], Paris, Neuchatel, 1908, connect the Castel poem with the feminine *Danse macabre* beginning "Mirez vous icy, mirez femmes." Besides Chartier's supposed poem (the authorship of which is denied by Piaget), Hentsch lists three others with similar titles, one a translation of Durand de Champagne's Latin, another by Ysambert de Saint-Léger, and another by Philippe Bouton. We may also recall the *Speculum Virginum* of Mathais Laurentius, a Swedish translation from the Latin (ed. Robert Geete, Stockholm, 1897-98; see also Arthur Watson, "The *Speculum Virginum* with Special Reference to the Tree of Jesse," *Speculum*, III [1928], 445-69); and Guilelmus Parfeius, *Speculum iuvenum uxores impetuose affectantium*, ex. off. J. Herfordi, 1547 (*STC*, no. 19195). The French title, with its figure of virtuous counsel as a headdress, reminds us of the tradition represented by **388**. For Barnaby Rich's *My Ladies Looking Glasse* (1616) see Wright, *Middle-Class Culture*, p. 483. The stanzaic form of **182**, which is skillfully placed on two rimes throughout, deserves remark.

183. Meaning of Marriage, The [prose].

> (1) Sloane 1983B; ed. F. J. Furnivall, *Jyl of Breyntfords Testament*, London, 1871, p. 40.

This may be too late for our purposes, but since it accompanies late XV and early XVI cent. pieces in Furnivall's volume, I have included it here. Furnivall assigns it no date.

The young wife is forced to call in the parish priest to teach her old husband the meaning of marriage. The story, which is in essence a "noodle" jest, purports to be translated from the Irish. It illustrates the dangers of a January and May marriage. A similar but not identical jest will be found in Poggio (no. 5; see Pierre des Brandes, ed. and tr., *Les Facéties de Pogge Florentin*, Paris, n.d., pp. 14-15).

184. Mery Dialogue, Declaring the Propertyes of Shrowde Shrewes and Honest Wyues, A [prose].

An anonymous translation of Desiderius Erasmus' *Uxor Mempsigamos* or *Coniugium;* called by Bailey *The Uneasy Wife*.

> (1) Anthony Kytson (1557). Ed. from a unique copy in the British Museum (*STC*, no. 10455) by Henry de Vocht, *The Earliest English Translations of Erasmus' Colloquia, 1536–1566*, Louvain, 1928, p. 55. For later translations of the *Coniugium* see de Vocht, pp. lxx-lxxix.
>
> (2) Abraham Vele (1557)? De Vocht (p. xxxiii) found record of this additional edition in Dibdin-Ames and Herbert, but I was unable to locate a copy. It is not mentioned in *STC*.

According to Preserved Smith (*A Key to the Colloquies of Erasmus*, Cambridge [Harvard Theological Studies, XIII], 1927, p. 15), *Coniugium* was added to the *Colloquies* for the first time along with four others on love and marriage in Froben's edition of August, 1523. The translation may have been made at any time, therefore, between 1523 (or a little later) and 1557.

The dialogue takes place between Xantippe, a complaining wife, and her friend Eulalia, who is a model of conjugal wisdom. Amid a good deal of banter on the failings of both sexes we are introduced to Eulalia's counsels on how to keep a husband happy and to make a true partnership of marriage. The dialogue is climaxed by a number of modern instances, among them an allusion to Jane Colte, the wife of Sir Thomas More. For a very similar dialogue see **337**. The extant edition appends to the colloquy the famous jest of *The Man Who Married a Dumb Wife* (**352**) taken in de Vocht's opinion (p. xxxiv) from *A. C. mery Talys,* published by John Rastell about 1525. It is possible that the names Eulalia and Xantippe, used for the good and evil mothers of the interlude *Nice Wanton* (John Kynge, 1560), were borrowed from **184**.

185. Myn auctour Bochas rejoysed in his lyve.

> By John Lydgate.
> *A chapitle of Bochas discryuyng þe malis of wommen.*
> (1) Harley 2251 (32 rime-royal stanzas). Never separately edited. Discussed with extracts by Brusendorff, *Chaucer Tradition,* p. 462.

This is an extract from *Fall of Princes,* Book i, 6511-6734 (preceded by other selections), which was probably begun soon after May, 1431, and perhaps finished in 1438 or 1439 (Bergen's edition, I, ix-x; for the selection see I, 184-190).

One of the best examples of Lydgate's passing off the blame of his satire on women onto his authorities. Following the story of Dalilah Boccaccio had written his famous and virulent attack *In Mulieres.* This in turn was translated by Laurence de Premierfait, who slightly expanded Boccaccio's concessions at the end to good women who were not subject to his charges. Lydgate leaves out many of the wicked examples and spends about as much time on woman's virtues as on her vices. The specific charges which remain are against the vanity of old women with regard to jewels and cosmetics, their crocodile tears and flattery and slights. The examples which remain are those of Hercules, Agamemnon, Dalilah, Amphiorax, Scylla, and Semiramis. Speaking in his own person (as if there had never been a disclaimer in Boccaccio) Lydgate says it wearies him to rehearse such examples of evil women when there are so many who are good. Many a woman has lived all her life in chastity. Though Boccaccio abused bad women good women need not heed this chapter, for only a galled jade winces. For the French and Latin versions, which deserve careful comparison with Lydgate as an evidence of his ambiguous method, inherited in part from greater artists like Chaucer and Boccaccio, see Bergen's edition of *The Fall of Princes,* IV, 161-70. The Harley MS. was in part copied from John Shirley, who appears to have been more than a mere scribe, and who often uses a familiar tone toward Lydgate. The frequent marginalia beside **185** are in the chivalrous vein, and are probably Shirley's (taken over by the scribe of Harley from one of his MSS.). When Lydgate mentions crocodile tears our annotator writes "Lat hem compleyne that neode have"; when Lydgate contrasts Samson's fidelity to Dalilah's lack of faith he rises to "Be pees or I wil rende this leef out of your booke"; when Lydgate asserts that Boccaccio's book contains no harm toward good women he boils over with "There is no goode woman that wilbe wroth / no[r] take no quarrell agenst this booke as I suppose." On these marginalia see Brusendorff, *Chaucer Tradition,* pp. 462-65. For other extracts from *The Fall of Princes* see **142**.

186. Myn hert ys set and all myn hole entent.

MacCracken suggests the author was William de la Pole, fourth Earl and first Duke of Suffolk, and intimate friend of Charles of Orleans, whose courtly poems appear in translation in the same MS. Miss Hammond is skeptical, and suggests the author is more likely to be someone like Shirley, who was in the habit of writing marginalia in opposition to Lydgate's satires (see **185**). The subject is reopened by Robert Steele, ed., *The English Poems of Charles of Orleans,* London (EETS, CCXV), 1941, pp. xxi-xxiii.

A Reproof to Lydgate; or *Praise of the Flower;* or *How þe louer ys sett to serve the floure.*

    (1) Bodleian Fairfax 16 (12 rime-royal stanzas); ed. H. N. MacCracken, "An English Friend of Charles of Orleans," *PMLA,* XXVI (1911), 168; and by Hammond, *English Verse,* p. 200.

According to Hammond, certainly before Lydgate's death in 1448 or 1449. If, as she also feels, it is in direct answer to extracts from *The Fall of Princes* (see **142**), it must have been written during the last ten years of his life. The latest date in the MS. is 1450. Suffolk died in that year, and Shirley in 1456.

The poet's heart is set to serve the flower (symbolic, like Lorris' rose and Chaucer's daisy, and perhaps an emblem of some courtly order). He cannot address Chaucer, who is dead, and so he turns to the Monk of Bury for inspiration. But he proceeds to rebuke Lydgate for saying love is but dotage, that women are untrue, and that they can laugh and love not (see **166**). The erring Monk is accused of envy, told to cry "mea culpa," and offered the services of our poet as attorney. We can well imagine the whole poem as part of a court entertainment in which Lydgate was himself a participant. One wonders whether Suffolk, who was busy in his last years with another symbolic flower, the red rose of Lancaster, would have had time or patience to address this mild, jesting reproof to the protegé of his bitter enemy, Humphrey of Gloucester,

187. Masteres anne, I am your man.

Ascribed to John Skelton by Brie and Henderson, in view of
the "Mistress Ann" who is addressed in **383** and in *The Garland of
Laurel*. Bale also attributes *Cantilenas de magistra Anna* to Skelton.
Lloyd is doubtful about the attribution.

(1) Trinity Cambridge R. 3. 17 (5 five-line stanzas, with some
corrections, said to be Skelton's own by Henderson and
Brie, but Lloyd denies it); ed. Walter W. Skeat, *The Ro-
mans of Partenay*, London (EETS, XXII), 1866, p. ii; F.
Brie, "Skelton-Studien," *ESt*, XXXVII (1906-1907), 29;
L. J. Lloyd, "A Note on Skelton," *RES*, V (1929), 304.

(2) Trinity College Cambridge O. 2. 53? Henderson, *Complete Poems of John Skelton*, p. 36, says his edition is based
on this MS.; but M. R. James, *The Western Manuscripts in
the Library of Trinity College Cambridge*, Cambridge,
1900-1904, III, 174, does not mention it in his description of
O. 2. 53 (he has, however, some unspecified English verses
on f. 74ᵛ). James (II, 67) confirms the presence of the
poem in R. 3. 17. Lloyd, who discusses O. 2. 53 in another
connection, does not appear to have seen this poem in that
MS. The confusion is not mitigated by Lloyd's erroneous
designation of (1) as R. 3. 27 and Henderson's designation
of the same as "K. 347." Brown and Robbins, *Index*, no.
2195, list only Trinity R. 3. 17 (James 597); but they are
unaware of the Skelton attribution and of any edition other
than that of Skeat.

Skelton's dates are 1460?-1529. Brie dates the "Mistress Anne"
poems 1490-98. The R. 3. 17 verses are in a XVI cent. hand (James,
II, 67).

Rebellious lover, warning his somewhat wanton mistress that if
she doesn't give up her habit of consorting with every knave that comes
by he'll have to renounce her. Compare Skelton's *Manerly Margery
Mylk and Ale* (a wanton song which is similar but which does not
qualify as a satire).

188. Masteres your maners are hard to know.

(1) Royal 17. D. 18 (2 rime-royal stanzas); I have transcribed
it for publication.

The MS. (including this poem on the flyleaf) is mid-XV cent.

Attack on woman's inconstancy; with the refrain "Slypper is to
grype one whome is no holde." It is not impossible that the invocation
is to "Masters," but the tone and the fact that "mistress" could be
spelled similarly (see **187**) seem sufficient to justify this as a satire
against women.

189. modest meane to Mariage, pleasauntly set foorth, A [prose].

Translated by Nicholas Leigh.

(1) Henry Denham (1568). The *STC* lists one copy only, owned by Captain Jaggard; the *Huntington Library Supplement* assigns the *STC* number (10499) to its copy with a query. I have examined the Huntington copy by means of microfilm.

The original colloquies of Erasmus which Leigh translated (*Pamphilus* and *Adolescens et Scortum*) appeared for the first time in Froben's edition of August, 1523. Leigh speaks of having written his translations as a school exercise. If we accept his reminiscent tone as authentic this would seem to have been many years before he wrote his dedication (to Master Francis Rogers, a Gentleman Pensioner of the Queen). But a young author might well put on world-weary trappings.

A modest meane to Mariage, the title of the book, presumably applies to *Pamphilus,* or *A Lover and a Maiden.* The Lover woos in the exaggerated terms of malady and death, and is rebuked by his clever mistress, who feels he is not like to die at once. Mingling high philosophy and homely figures, the wooing proceeds to a discussion of chaste wedlock and to a rebuttal of satires against marriage. The maiden coyly accepts him, but refuses to bind the bargain with a kiss lest the little soul he has left jump out of him. Brilliantly conceived in the spirit of the new humane approach toward marriage. For the second dialogue in the volume see **238.** Preserved Smith (*A Key to the Colloquies of Erasmus,* Cambridge [Harvard Theological Studies, XIII], 1927, p. 13) is "tempted to see [in *Pamphilus*] a reminiscence of an early flirtation of the humanist himself." De Vocht, the student of these early translations (*The Earliest English Translations of Erasmus' Colloquia,* London, 1928), appears to have been unaware of Leigh's work.

190. Moost noble Prynce, with support of Your Grace.

By John Lydgate.

A Mumming at Hertford.

(1) Trinity College Cambridge R. 3. 20 (127 couplets); ed. E. P. Hammond, *Anglia,* XXII (1899), 364; and with variants from (2) by MacCracken, *Minor Poems of Lydgate,* II, 675; see also W. A. Neilson and K. G. T. Webster, *Chief British Poets of the Fourteenth and Fifteenth Centuries,* Boston, 1916, p. 223.

(2) British Museum Additional 29729.

Neilson and Webster date first quarter XV cent., but Chambers (*Mediæval Stage,* I, 398) would place a bit later. The mumming was held at the King's "feest of Cristmasse in þe Castel of Hertford," and was "devysed by Lydgate at þe request of the Countre

Roullour Brys slaune at Loviers." Miss Hammond's attempts to identify the King Henry or to date a Christmas visit to Hertford are unavailing. Chambers, following Rudolph Brotanek, *Die Eng-lischen Maskenspiele,* Wien and Leipzig, 1902, p. 306, observes that Louviers was taken by the French in 1430 and besieged in 1431. Certainly the poem is before 1448-49, when Lydgate died.

This early dramatic piece consists of three parts: the supplication of certain rustics to the King, the answer of their wives, and the King's judgment. The rustics complain that their wives waste their money and time in drink, and nag them, and beat them. "Þeos holy martirs, preued ful pacyent," beseech the King to grant them protection and to modify the "Olde Testament" of wives' rule. The wives answer that they have won their husbands by teaching them patience, that they were not meant by nature to be silent, and that they wash and wring for—and wring—their husbands. They therefore demand confirmation of the "statuyt of olde antiquytee." The King says he will be guided by Reason and postpone a decision at this time. For the next year women shall be the masters; as for men, let them "be-ware þer-fore or þey be bounde" in wedlocke.

191. Mourning, mourning.

(1) Harley 2252 (6 six-line stanzas, with 3 lines at the end of another, unfinished); ed. Chambers and Sidgwick, *Early English Lyrics,* p. 78; for further editions see p. 344.

MS. (and probably poem) are from the time of Henry VIII.

Dialogue between two forsaken lovers, one of whom seeks a new love, while the other admits woman's fickleness but vows heroically to remain constant. Very likely a gay and musical irony is flickering beneath the sentiments of the "true" lover. For a similar *débat* see Alfred Jeanroy, *Les Origines de la Poésie Lyrique en France au Moyen Age,* Paris, 1925, pp. 53, 470. See also A. Langfors, A. Jeanroy, and L. Brandin, *Recueil Général des Jeux-Partis Français,* Paris (SATF), 1926, I, 7.

192. My darlyng dere, my daysy floure.

By John Skelton.
Burden: "With lullay, lullay, lyke a chylde,
        Thou slepyst to long; thou art begylde."

(1) *Dyuers Balettys and dyties solacyous deuysed by Master Skelton Laureat,* [Richard Pynson] (n.d.); ed. Dyce and Child, *Poetical Works of Skelton,* I, 27; Philip Henderson, *Complete Poems of John Skelton,* p. 27; Greene, *Early English Carols,* p. 310 (no. 459) (two-line burden and 4 rime-royal stanzas).

Greene dates Pynson's volume about 1520(?). According to Duff, *Century,* p. 126, Pynson began to print about 1486-90 and died in 1530. Skelton died in 1529.

When the lover goes to sleep in his lady's lap, she steals away to find another lover. Wake up, you fool! The burden, borrowed from the lullaby tradition, alludes to the tenderness of motherhood and especially to that of the Blessed Virgin for her Infant Son. Skelton is therefore demonstrating his usual sprightly malice and irreverence when he parodies the tradition to woman's dispraise. For lullaby carols see Greene, nos. 142-55, and notes. For other songs on woman's wantonness, similar but too sympathetic to include in the Index, see Greene, nos. 447, 450-58, 460-61.

193. My dutie first in humble wis fulfill'd.

According to Greg's preface to his edition (p. vii) the ascription by Winstanley to William Wager or Wayer "hardly deserves discussion." William R. Parker, who discusses a number of early play-lists in a forthcoming article, has pointed out to me that Winstanley's attribution is simply copied from Phillips, who misunderstood the 1661 and 1671 lists of Kirkman, in which *Tom Tyler* follows a play correctly ascribed to Wager. The *DNB* and the British Museum *Catalogue* perpetuate the error.

Tom Tyler and His Wife.

(1) "An Excellent Old Play, as It was Printed and Acted about a hundred Years ago," London [Francis Kirkman?], 1661 (875 lines). Facsimile by G. C. Moore Smith and W. W. Greg, Malone Society Reprints, 1910; ed. Schelling, *PMLA*, XV (1900), 253; J. S. Farmer, *Two Tudor Shrew Plays*, London, 1906; J. S. Farmer, *Six Anonymous Plays (Second Series)*, London (Early English Drama Society), 1906, p. 289; and as one of the Tudor Facsimile Texts, 1912.

That the "second Impression" of 1661 is no forgery is made evident by the mention in Edward Archer's 1656 play-list (Greg, *A List of Masques*, London, 1902, p. cxii). The date of the first edition is unknown, and conjecture has ranged all the way from about 1530 to a few years before 1661. For discussions see Schelling, pp. 254-58; Farmer, *Six Anonymous Plays*, p. 460; and Greg and Moore, pp. vi-vii. Literal acceptance of the remark on the title page would place it within our period, and other considerations confirm a date before 1568: the linguistic evidence mentioned by Schelling (which needs more careful study); the association in tone, theme, and external allusion with Heywood's *Johan Johan* (**76**; for allusion in *Stationers' Register* see Rollins, *Analytical Index*, nos. 2664, 2780); similarities to the early morality drama (Tom's wife is called Strife and her gossip Sturdie); and the testimony of **290**, itself hard to date accurately, but probably *ca.* 1560. But, as Greg remarks, the only bibliographer to claim direct knowledge of the first edition was Chetwood, and he specifically dates it 1598. The *NED* accepts

Chetwood's date. An allusion in the final song, "God preserve our
Noble Queen," almost certainly places the play as now constituted
within the reigns of Mary or Elizabeth.

The burly Tom Tyler cannot control his wife, who beats him and
nags him and spends the rest of her time gossiping, singing, eating,
and tippling. So Tom Taylor (of the timid profession) disguises himself
as Tom Tyler and beats her well. For a while she is filled with love
for her strong-willed husband, until he with his usual naiveté betrays
the truth. She turns on him, and it takes Patience the Parson to reconcile the married couple. Some of the satirical lyrics in this play are
separately listed, since they may have led an independent existence as
broadsides: see **33**, **91**, **327**, **328**.

194. My fayr lady, so fressh of hewe.

Ascribed to Lydgate in the MS. MacCracken, *Minor Poems of
Lydgate,* I, xxxi-xxxii, rejects on the grounds of its "abominable
filth," and "in spite of my reverence for him who penned the *Explicit
quod Lydgate."* This is scarcely MacCracken's usual caution. Koep-
pel, in *ESt,* XXIV (1898), 292, accepts Lydgate's authorship.

*A Satirical Description of his Lady; or Whan She Hathe on
hire Hood of Grene.*

(1) Harley 2255 (21 eight-line stanzas); ed. J. O. Halliwell, *A
   Selection from the Minor Poems of Dan John Lydgate,*
   London (Percy Society, II), 1840, p. 199.

Brown, *Register,* I, 322, does not date MS.; but from his *Religious Lyrics of the XVth Century,* no. 39, it is clear he considers
some part of it XV cent. If **194** is Lydgate's it must have been
written before 1448-49.

Parody of a courtly panegyric ; a catalogue of his mistress' uglinesses "Whan she hath on hire hood of green." For the type see **226**;
and for the color symbolism **175**. In one way this varies from the usual
parody panegyric; the lover dramatically admits that his insults spring
from his jealousy.

195. My Gudame wes a gay wife, bot scho wes rycht gend.

By William Dunbar.
The Ballad of Kynd Kittok.

(1) Chapman and Myllar (3 thirteen-line stanzas); among the
   fragments beginning with **336**, dated [1508?] by *STC.* Ed.
   with variants of (2) Small, *Poems of William Dunbar,* II,
   52; George Stevenson, *Pieces from The Makculloch and the
   Gray MSS.,* Edinburgh (STS, LXV), p. 262; MacKenzie,
   Poems of William Dunbar, p. 169; for further editions
   see Small, III, 95.

(2) Advocates' Library 1. 1. 6; ed. Ritchie, *Bannatyne Manu-*

script, III, 10; see also Hunterian Club *Bannatyne*, I, lxxxviii.

According to *DNB* Dunbar's dates are (1465?-1530?). Mackay in his introduction to Small, I, clix, would place it before 1503, the date of the marriage of Margaret Tudor and James IV, on the grounds of the usually accepted date of the Chapman and Myllar print; the alliteration, used by Dunbar especially in his early works; and the allusion to Falkland Fells, a place frequented by the King before his marriage (a definite visit recorded in August-September, 1495).

Perhaps the most gentle and charming of the ale-wife satires. Ugly Kittok died of thirst, they say. She went to an eldritch well and picked up a ride to heaven on a snail. She stopped at an alehouse near heaven, drank her fill, and slept till noon. The gates of heaven were fastened, but she crept past St. Peter. "God lukit et saw hir lattin in, et lewch his hert sair." She became Our Lady's hen-wife and squabbled with St. Peter. One day when the ale of heaven was sour she went out to get a drink, and when St. Peter saw her coming back he hit her with a club. So she went back to the alehouse to pour and brew and bake. "Gif ʒe be thristy or dry, / Drink with my Guddame, as ʒe ga by, / Anys for my saik." The portrait is good enough to be from life. Its peculiar daftness is that of Scottish burlesque, of *The Droichis Pairt of the Play*, *The Gyr-Carlyng*, *King Berdok*, and *The Fenʒeit Freir of Tungland*. Kittok's feud with St. Peter reminds us of that gem of *fabliaux*, *Le Vilain qui Conquist Paradis par Plait*, and of the blundering Peter of folk-lore; see the indices under "Petrus" in Oskar Dähnhardt, *Natursagen*, Leipzig, 1907-1912, I, 372, and II, 314. Compare also *The Wanton Wife of Bath*, ed. J. W. Ebsworth, *The Roxburghe Ballads*, London (Ballad Society), 1871-97, VII, 212.

196. My hart I gaue thee, not to do it pain.

By Sir Thomas Wyatt (signed in MS.).
The louer forsaketh his vnkinde loue.
(1) Egerton 2711 (a fourteen-line sonnet); ed. Foxwell, *Poems of Sir Thomas Wiat*, I, 20, with variants from (2).
(2) *Tottel's Miscellany* (in all editions); ed. Rollins, I, 69, with variants from (1).

Foxwell, I, 389, dates approximately 1528-32. Wyatt lived from 1503? to 1542.

Rebellious lover; satire on woman's inconstancy and desire. Adapted from a poem by Serafino (see Rollins, II, 200).

197. My hairt is gone / confort is none.

(1) Advocates' Library 1. 1. 6 (10 four-line stanzas); ed. Ritchie, *Bannatyne Manuscript*, IV, 45; see also Hunterian Club *Bannatyne*, I, cvii.

1568 or before.
Rebellious lover; he will hold all women "fals of fay" from this time on.

198. My hairt is quhyt / and no delyte / I haif of ladeis fair.

(1) Advocates' Library, 1. 1. 6 (5 six-line stanzas, with elaborate internal .rime); ed. Ritchie, *Bannatyne Manuscript,* IV, 18; see also Hunterian Club *Bannatyne,* I, cv.

1568 or before.

When a youth I raged; now to earthly love I say "ffairwell now feildis fair."

My harte of golde as true as stele (203).

199. My hartis tresure, and swete assured fo.

By William Dunbar.
To a Lady, Quhone He List to Feyne.
(1) Magdalene College Cambridge, Pepys 2553 (7 rime-royal stanzas); ed. Small, *Poems of William Dunbar,* II, 245; W. A. Craigie, *Maitland Folio Manuscript,* I, 386; Mackenzie, *Poems of William Dunbar,* p. 99; for further editions see Small, III, 331.

According to the *DNB,* Dunbar's dates are 1465?-1530? In his introduction to Small Mackay would place the poem between 1503 and 1513 (I, clxiv). He appears to take it seriously as a final renunciation of love, and to assume that such an event can be considered a landmark in Dunbar's intellectual and emotional development. But see my Introduction, p. 48.

Parody of a courtly poem. After highly exaggerated accounts of his torments and his lady's cruelty, Dunbar suddenly reverses the field with "And syne, Fair weill, my hartis Ladie deir!" This, with the MS. colophon "Quod Dumbar quhone he list to feyne," makes the intent of the piece unquestionable. Yet Pinkerton misread it (see Craigie, II, 123), and with Olympian calm remarked "A ballad of Dunbar, but worth nothing. . . . It is all one cry to his mistress for mercy." There is no reason to feel with H. B. Baildon (*The Poems of William Dunbar,* Cambridge, 1907, p. 250) that the last stanza is an afterthought.

200. My jornay lat as I dyd take.

By Harry Sponare.
(1) Ashmole 48 (17 seven-line stanzas); ed. Wright, *Songs and Ballads,* p. 97.

Rollins dates the MS. about 1557-65 in *MLN,* XXXIV (1919), 349, on the basis of broadside contents. See next section.

After a *chanson d'aventure* opening the author overhears a dialogue between a husband and his mother on his wife's shrewishness, her idleness, drunkenness, and adultery. Mother agrees to everything; even if the priory did not lie in ruins John would not qualify for the bacon of Dunmowe. The conscious antiquarianism of the piece should place it after the closing of the monasteries and probably near our end-date.

201. My ladyes and my maistresses echone.

Wynkyn de Worde says the poem's faults are due to "kynge Ragman holly." See **86** and W. C. Hazlitt, ed., *A Select Collection of Old English Plays Originally Published by Robert Dodsley,* London, 1874, I, 242.

Ragman Roll; or *The rolles of Kynge Ragman.*

(1) Bodleian Fairfax 16 (26 eight-line stanzas); ed. Wright, *Anecdota Literaria,* p. 83; Hazlitt, *Remains,* I, 69; for other editions see Hammond, "The Chance of the Dice," *ESt,* LIX (1925), 1.

(2) Bodley 638.

(3) Wynkyn de Worde (n.d.). Hazlitt, *Remains,* IV, 358, dates it about 1533 because of an allusion by John Heywood. I have been unable to find this fragmentary print, of which one leaf only is known, in the *STC;* Hazlitt refers us to "Rodd's Catalogue for 1825." Hazlitt prints the printer's envoy in *A Select Collection,* I, 242.

The MS. was composed about 1450. One stanza, **366**, exists separately in a MS. dated about 1442.

A set of characters for a fortune-telling game. All are about women, and they run the gamut from extreme praise to ruthless satire (but the poem is not "a satire on women" as implied in *CHEL,* II, 561). The best possible evidence that entertainment is one of the major uses of satire and defense, these stanzas illustrate the range of tone, from courtly to obscenely comic, possible in a lady's bower or in a baronial hall at this time. Above all they help us to understand what moved Chaucer, Lydgate, and Dunbar to disagree with themselves so violently from poem to poem on the subject of women, and warn us away from the twin dangers of reconstructing sociological or biographical currents on the basis of contradictory poems. The title *Ragman Roll* applies equally to a legal document and to the game, since both consisted of a long roll with seals attached to ribbons. In the game the seal would be accepted blindly and the ribbon followed to the verses which revealed the player's character. Miss Hammond has discussed the type along with a similar set of verses called *The Chance of the Dice,* where a cast led an individual to his "fortune." *The Chance* has not been included here because it applies to both sexes, but some of the fortunes, if separated, would rank as miniature satires of women. Miss Hammond's study emphasizes the fact that in such contrasting portraits we have true ancestors of Renaissance character portrayal, long before the Theophrastians began their work; see *ESt,* LIX (1925), 1-4. A French satire,

Ragemon le Bon, is printed from MS. Digby 86 by Wright, *Anecdota Literaria,* p. 76. According to Johann Vising, *Anglo-Norman Language and Literature,* London, 1923, p. 49, Ragemon is the Devil, and the French poem is therefore a kind of bestourné, fatrasie, or nonsense poem about "the Good Devil." On the type see Gaston Paris, *La Littérature Française au Moyen Age,* Paris, 1913, pp. 204, 318; Hermann Suchier, *Oeuvres Poétiques de Philippe de Remi Sire de Beaumanoir,* Paris (SATF), 1884-85, I, cxxiii. Its connection with the Devil reminds us of the useful imp who records the chatter of women or the syllables priests slide over in saying mass, and who, running out of paper, attempts to stretch his recording roll until he falls off the rafters (see **329**). The popularity of the fortune-game is indicated in allusions by *Piers Plowman,* Gower, Dunbar, Skelton, and Heywood. For these, for parallels in other literatures, and for the vexed problem of the etymology of *ragman,* see Hammond's article as cited and her *English Verse,* p. 526; W. W. Skeat, ed., *The Vision of William Concerning Piers the Plowman,* Oxford, 1924, II, 238; Dyce and Child, *Poetical Works of Skelton,* III, 351; Hazlitt, *Remains,* I, 68; Small, *Poems of William Dunbar,* III, 77. In addition to *The Chance of the Dice* (in MSS. Bodleian Fairfax 16 and Bodley 638), the unprinted *Book of Fate* (in MS. Douce 241; see Hammond, *ESt,* LIX [1925], 2), and *The Casting of Dice* (in MS. Brome, owned by the Hon. Mrs. R. Douglas Hamilton, Diss, Norfolk, and in MS. Sloane 513—printed from Brome with corrections from Sloane by Lucy T. Smith, *A Common-place Book of the Fifteenth Century,* London, 1886, p. 15), we may cite as parallel the fortune cards included in this Index as **14** and **308**. For an addition to Hammond's examples of continental dicing treatises see Antithetus Faure, *Le Livre du Passe-Temps de la Fortune des dez* (1528). Another dicing-poem (for political prophecy) is listed by Brown and Robbins, *Index,* no. 4018; see also their index under "Dice."

202. My lady is unkynd, perde!

By Sir Thomas Wyatt (signed "Wyat" in MS. Egerton).
Burden: "A Robyn [*or* Hey Robyn]
     Joly Robyn
     Tell me how thy leman doeth
     And thou shalt knowe of myn."

(1) Egerton 2711 (four-line burden and 5 four-line stanzas); ed. with variants and corrections from (2) and (3) by Foxwell, *Poems of Sir Thomas Wiat,* I, 106; with variants and corrections from (2), (3), and (4) by Padelford, *Early Sixteenth Century Lyrics,* p. 10; with corrections from (3) by E. M. W. Tillyard, *The Poetry of Sir Thomas Wyatt,* London, 1929, p. 90.

(2) British Museum Additional 17492, f. 22ᵛ ("a fragment" followed by an additional verse bearing Mary Shelton's

signature); the Shelton stanza will be found in Foxwell, I, 107, and in Padelford, p. 12.

(3) British Museum Additional 17492, f. 24 (the "complete" poem, burden plus 6 four-line stanzas).

(4) British Museum Additional 31922 (burden and first two stanzas set to music by William Cornysshe); see the facsimile in Foxwell, I, facing pp. 62-63.

Miss Foxwell places this among the poems written between 1528 and 1536 by Wyatt. According to the *DNB* Cornysshe died by 1524. We are faced by two alternatives: the poem was either written earlier in Wyatt's career or the three quatrains set to music by Cornysshe are an earlier poem which Wyatt adapted. Wyatt died in 1542.

Robin, *"Le Plaintif,"* is asked how his mistress fares. She is unkind, he says, and loves another better than him. *Response* finds no such doubleness in woman. Robin says woman's love is but a blast and turns like the wind. *Response* (supplied from (3)): even if that be true, you'll fare better with women if you curb your tongue. Robin: all I get in love is tears. *Response*: the best remedy is to warm yourself at other fires. In spite of her insertion of a stanza from (3), Miss Foxwell's version still offers rather disjointed and contradictory dialogue. For another dialogue-poem on woman's inconstancy and a lover's rebellion see **191**. One wonders, by the way, why the poem has not been classified by Greene as a carol.

203. My lady went to Caunterbury.

> Burden: "My harte of golde as true as stele,
> As I me lened to a bough,
> In fayth, but yf ye loue me well,
> Lorde, so Robyn lough!"

(1) *Christmas carolles newely imprynted,* Richard Kele (n.d.) (four-line burden and 8 four-line stanzas); ed. Greene, *Early English Carols,* p. 318 (no. 473). Its popularity even in modern times is shown by such reprints as W. H. Auden, *The Oxford Book of Light Verse,* Oxford, 1938, p. 87; and Denys K. Roberts, *Straw in the Hair,* London, 1938, p. 190. For further editions see Greene, p. 453.

Around 1550 or before. Dated [154—?] by *Huntington Library Supplement,* p. 35. Several of the carols in Kele's collection appear in XV cent. MSS.

A charming nonsense carol, with enough glimpses of the moon to show that a lady's inconstancy has something to do with the poet's fantastic state of mind. For other lying-songs of this type see **69**.

My lawtie (see **My loyalty**).

204. My lytell prety one my prety bony one.

> (1) British Museum Additional 18752 (4 five-line stanzas); ed.
> Edward B. Reed, *Anglia,* XXXIII (1910), 352. For other
> editions see Hazlitt, *Remains,* IV, 234.

This portion of the MS. is in a hand of the time of Henry VIII.

The poem has the usual character of a tavern song about a "jolly
wanton," with the refrain "nou doute she ys a love of all that euer I see."
The irony is gentle, and there is a touch of parody on the conventional
farewell poem. The gay tone and first line recall "The lytell prety
nyȝhtyngale," Flügel, *Anglia,* XII (1889-90), 262; and the poem is
obviously related to a carol with the burden "My lady is a prety on"
(Greene, *Early English Carols,* no. 445).

205. My luve was fals and full of flattry.

By "Weddirburne" according to the MS. On the various candidates see **101.**

> (1) Advocates' Library 1. 1. 6 (9 rime-royal stanzas); ed.
> Ritchie, *Bannatyne Manuscript,* IV, 28; see also Hunterian
> Club *Bannatyne,* I, cv.

1568 or before.

Rebellious lover. Satire on woman's inconstancy, cruelty, hypoc-
risy, and greed. Definitely generalized with examples: Pirance and
Meridiane, Virgil, Aristotle, Chaucer's Absolon and Alisoun (from the
Miller's Tale), and the Troilus of Chaucer and Henryson (see Caroline
Spurgeon, *Five Hundred Years of Chaucer Criticism,* IV, 37).

206. My loving frende, amorous Bune.

*A lettre sende by on yonge woman to a-noder, whiche aforetyme
were felowes to-geder.*

> (1) Rawlinson C. 813 (23 couplets); ed. Padelford and Benham,
> *Anglia,* XXXI (1908), 320; for textual notes and emenda-
> tions see W. Bolle, *Anglia,* XXXIV (1911), 301.

The MS. is of the time of Henry VIII; according to Bolle, p.
274, most of the contents are late XV cent.

This purports to be a letter from one young woman to another,
and employs exceedingly catty and (to mix essential metaphors) fish-
wife-like language. If, as one suspects, it is really a masculine compilation, it may be taken as a satire on woman's wantonness and jealousy.

207. My lawtie garris me be lichtleit allaik.

> (1) Advocates' Library 1. 1. 6 (1 eight-line stanza); ed. Ritchie,
> *Bannatyne Manuscript,* IV, 22; see also Hunterian Club
> *Bannatyne,* I, cv.

1568 or before.

Rebellious lover (among a group headed by Bannatyne "Schort
Epegrammis Aganis Women"). "Als gud luve cumis as gangis."

208. My maister Bukton, whan of Crist our kyng.

By Geoffrey Chaucer.

Lenvoy de Chaucer a Bukton; or The counceyll of Chaucer touchyng Maryag.

(1) Bodleian Fairfax 16 (4 eight-line stanzas); ed. Robinson, *Chaucer,* p. 635, with variants from the others. For further editions see Robinson, p. 979; Hammond, *Chaucer,* p. 366; Griffith, *Chaucer,* p. 115; Martin, *Chaucer,* p. 67; and the current bibliographies.

(2) Julian Notary (1499-1501).

(3) Thynne (1532) and later Chaucer editions. On the two earliest prints see Hammond, p. 366.

Most authorities agree that allusions in the poem support the date 1396.

When Christ was asked "What is truth?" he said nothing, and implied "No man is al trewe." Therefore I dare write of marriage no wickedness, "Lest I myself falle eft in swich dotage." I will not say it is the chain of Satan on which he ever gnaws in order to escape; but God let such a man as would rather be in prison than free have his fill of woe! Better to marry than to burn, but if you marry you become your wife's thrall, and it would have been better, you'll find, to have been captured in Frisia. I send you this "lytel writ, proverbes, or figure" and counsel you to turn to the Wife of Bath for more advice. Chaucer was not afraid to advertise his wares.

209. My mistress is in Musik passing skilfull.

(1) Advocates' Library i. i. 6 (5 six-line stanzas); ed. Ritchie, *Bannatyne Manuscript,* III, 239-41 (broken up by MS. headings).

1568 or before.

Satire on his lady's insatiability, under the cover of musical terminology. Perhaps there is some connection with the ballad controversy over whether women should be taught to play music. See Rollins, *MLN,* XXXIV (1919), 341.

210. My penne prolong no longer time.

By C. Pyrrye. See discussion below.

The Dispraise of VVomen.

(1) *The praise and Dispraise of Women, very fruitfull to the well disposed minde, and delectable to the readers therof. And a fruitfull shorte Dialogue vppon the sentence, know before thou knitte. C. Pyrrye. . . . Imprinted at London in Fleetstreete, by William How* (n.d.) (**210** is in 98 four-line stanzas). I have examined the unique copy at Huntington by means of microfilm (*STC,* no. 20523).

Collier, *Extracts,* I, 83, notes the entry of "[a] ballett intituled the prayse and Dysprayse of Women very fruthfull to the Well Dispoysed mynde" in the *Stationers' Register* for 1563-64 to Rychard Serlle, which he and the *CHEL* (III, 553) identify with this book. For the entry see Arber, I, 234. Rollins, *Analytical Index,* no. 2156, records Collier's conjecture without comment. The *STC* identifies it rather with the entry of 1568-69 to William How of "the prayse and Dysprayse" (see Arber, I, 383), and therefore dates the extant edition [1569?], a conclusion followed by *CBEL,* I, 716. By itself the title of 1563-64 might be ambiguous, since there is extant a broadside of about that time (see **386**) with a similar title. But the broadside is otherwise accounted for, and the addition in the *Register* entry of the words "very fruthfull to the Well Dispoysed mynde" argues that Pyrrye's tract or an earlier version of it was in the hands of Serlle in 1563-64, although it may not have been printed until later. We may perhaps conjecture that the title of **386** was borrowed in the next year from whatever Serlle possessed. The device on the title page (McKerrow, no. 142) was first used in England by R. Hall, according to McKerrow, who does not list Pyrrye's tract. How's first recorded use of the device is conjectured for [1570], and the first certain date is 1571. Duff, *Century,* p. 77, says How was admitted as a freeman in 1556 and continued to print up to 1590. His first registration of ballads was in 1565; and William R. Parker informs me that his first recorded books (seven or more) are dated 1569. The composition of Pyrrye's tract seems therefore to lie somewhere between 1563 and 1571.

The tract consists of a Latin address in 20 lines *Ad Candidum Lectorem;* a prose address to the reader, in which the dedicator says that he writes dispraise to warn good women away from crimes and praise to confirm them in virtue; and three poems, *The Disprayse of VVomen* (**210**), *The prayse of VVomen* (**94**), and *A fruytful short dialogue vppon the sentence, knovve before thou knytte* (**113**). If the title page is to be trusted, Pyrrye wrote all three poems; but one becomes slightly suspicious when his name is inserted beneath the title of the second poem (on sig. [B]5, wrongly designated as "Av"). Does this mean that he only wrote the second poem? Our suspicion of the unity of authorship is increased by the separate entries in the *Stationers' Register,* discussed under date. **210** begins with the usual disclaimer: the author's words do not defame good women, and only those who are pricked need feel the sting. He will describe a Monster Womankind, beautiful without and with strong poison within. She is proud, servile, cruel, flaunts all law and reason; she is slothful, capricious, immoderate in joy and sorrow, bold and wanton, inconstant, garrulous, greedy, impatient, drunken, vain, prone to anger, ungrateful, hypocritical, shrewish, slanderous, deceitful. These charges are substantiated by examples from

Ovid, Virgil, and the Bible. Take heed, then, and shun this monster as a bird would a hawk or wolf. Her tears are crocodile. Strong men of old who slew other monsters were tamed by this one: Hercules, Samson, David, Lot, and Solomon. The monster has a thousand arts and ruses and vain adornments. A good woman is rarer than a coal-black swan. Believe what I say and you will lead a peaceful life. The poet packs into a small compass most of the conventional charges, and attains unity by his allegory of the Monster. There is a parallel in title between Pyrrye's book and Jean de Marconville's *De la bonté et mauvaistié des femmes* (1564—see Richardson, *Forerunners of Feminism*, p. 116), but in spite of this correspondence and the closeness in date, I have found no conclusive relationship between them.

My wanton ware (120).

Nay, Iuy, nay, hyt shal not be, iwys (88).

Nay, nay, Ive, it may not be, iwis (87).

211. Ne be þi wimpil nevere so jely ne so stroutende.

(1) From the margin of Cotton Cleopatra C. 6 (2 couplets); ed. Wright and Halliwell, *Reliquiae Antiquae*, II, 15.

The MS. is of the XIII cent. I have been unable to ascertain whether these marginal verses are in a later hand or not. The assimilation of an intitial þ to a preceding dental (*That tu; And tou; as tou*) and the retention of the *-ende* participial ending suggest SEMl of the XIII cent.

However imposing your wimple, however long your fine train ("tail"), at even you shall be left in tatters and go to bed as naked as you were born. A satire on woman's fashions.

212. Ne no thyng ys to man so dere.

By Robert Mannyng of Brunne.
Praise of Women.

(1) Harley 1701 (5 couplets); ed. Frederick J. Furnivall, *Robert of Brunne's "Handlyng Synne,"* London (EETS, CXIX, CXXIII), 1901-1903, p. 68; and separately by John W. Hales and F. J. Furnivall, *Bishop Percy's Folio Manuscript,* London, 1868, III, 545; Sir Arthur Quiller-Couch, *The Oxford Book of English Verse,* Oxford, 1939, p. 13; Henry S. Pancoast and John D. Spaeth, *Early English Poems,* New York, 1911, p. 140. Furnivall collates with (3) and (4).

(2) Cambridge University Library Ii. 4. 9.

(3) Dulwich College XXIV.

(4) Bodley 415.

Mannyng began his poem in 1303.

A selection from *Handlyng Synne,* which has led a separate exist-

ence in modern anthologies (for other medieval extracts, this apparently
not among them, see Brown, *Register,* nos. 340 and 583). Mannyng
says that nothing is so dear to man as woman's love. "A gode womman
ys mannys blys" (we recall Chantecleer's translation of "Mulier est
hominis confusio"). There is no solace under heaven like a good
woman who is true in love, or nothing dearer in God's eyes than a chaste
woman with lovely speech. This selection is important in reminding
us that a fourteenth century monk in a religious manual could give
high praise to women. Nor is he unusual, although it is noteworthy that
he modifies the tone of his original, William of Waddington's *Manuel
des Péchiez.* William had been much less flattering; like Proverbs 31
he had found such paragons rare.

213. Next þe derke nyght þe grave morewe.

> The MS. attributes to "Impingham" (see below).
> *Proverbes.*
> (1) Harley 7333 (13 couplets); I have transcribed it for
> publication.

The MS., which Furnivall thought to have been copied by
Impingham from John Shirley, has been dated about 1450 by the
Chaucer Society. It contains many pieces by Chaucer and Lydgate,
and the *Proverbes* contains an allusion to Chaucer's *Merchant's Tale.*

Begins with one or two general proverbs, but after "Wyn and
women make men folis" (compare **387**) proceeds to a group of attacks
on woman's garrulousness, shrewishness, vanity, waywardness, crocodile
tears. A man must marry his equal; for "may and Janyuer" are always
at war. There is a cancellation in the piece which suggests compilation
on the spot by the scribe, presumably Impingham. For a bibliography of
Middle English proverb collections, which often contain a large group
of unfriendly remarks about women and love, see Sanford B. Meech,
"A Collection of Proverbs in Rawlinson MS D 328," *MPh,* XXXVIII
(1940), 113.

214. [Nobility of Women, The (prose?)]

> By William Bercher or Barker.
> (1) From a Magdalen College Oxford MS., ed. R. W. Bond
> and C. B. Marlay, 2 vols., Roxburghe Club, 1904-1905.
> The work is dated 1559 by the editors.

I have been unable to consult this work, which was translated "from
Lodovico Domenichi, but based on Agrippa" according to the *CBEL*
(I, 809). The same source lists three other translations of Cornelius
Agrippa's *De Nobilitate et Praecellentia Foeminei Sexus* (1529), one of
them David Clapham's *Of the Nobilitie and Excellencie of VVoman-
kynde* (see **237**).

Nowell, nowell, ell, ell! (243).

Nova, noua, sawe yow euer such (50).

Now cumis aige quhair ȝewth hes bene (215).

215. **Now culit is dame Venus brand.**

By William Dunbar.

Of Luve erdly and divine. With prefacing title, burden, or refrain: "Now cumis aige quhair ȝewth hes bene,
And trew luve rysis fro the splene."

(1) Advocates' Library 1. 1. 6 (printed as two-line title and 15 six-line stanzas, but see below); ed. Small, *Poems of William Dunbar*, II, 179; Ritchie, *Bannatyne Manuscript*, IV, 91; MacKenzie, *Poems of William Dunbar*, p. 101; for further editions see Small, III, 266, and Hunterian Club *Bannatyne*, I, cix.

According to the *DNB* Dunbar's dates are (1465?-1530?). Mackay, in his introduction to Small (I, clxx) says it was "probably written after 1513," since it is written in old age. It should be remembered that "aige" came a good deal sooner in the Middle Ages than it is said to come today.

Now that the fire of Venus is burned out I have a truer love which does not subject me to the torments of my youth. One of the more convincing renunciations of earthly love. On Greene's definition (*Early English Carols*, pp. xxiii, cxxxiii-cxxxiv) this poem could surely be qualified as a carol consisting of a quatrain *aaab* and a "burden" *BB*. The "burden" precedes the whole poem and is repeated or abbreviated after each stanza. Dunbar's possible connections with the carol-form deserve investigation, especially in view of his temporary assumption of the Franciscan habit.

Now farewell love and thy lawes for ever (61).

216. **Now gossop I must neidis begon.**

(1) Advocates' Library 1. 1. 6 (25 lines in irregular pattern); ed. Ritchie, *Bannatyne Manuscript*, III, 238; see also Hunterian Club *Bannatyne*, I, xciii.

These appear to be in a later hand than that of the MS. proper, and may therefore have been written after 1568.

Request to his friend to take care of his wanton mistress; erotic *double entente* in nautical terminology. This may be too late for our index, but it is very similar to **96**.

217. **Now I do know you chaungyd thought.**

(1) British Museum Additional 18752, f. 77ᵛ (6 four-line stanzas); ed. Edward B. Reed, *Anglia*, XXXIII (1910), 353.

(2) British Museum Additional 18752, f. 139ᵛ (another version with several variants); ed. Reed, p. 368.

THE CROOKED RIB

The poems in the MS. are in an early XVI cent. hand.

Rebuke to his "new ffangled" mistress; he reveals her wantonness and inconstancy.

Now I perceue you chaungyd thought (217).

218. Now lesten a whyle, and let hus singe.

> *Women will haue their Will;* or *I hold you a groate the wyfe will haue yt;* or *A merry new ballad;* or *A mery Ballett.*

(1) Cotton Vespasian A. 25 (5 eight-line stanzas); ed. Böddeker, *JbREL,* XIV (1875), 224.

The MS. is dated by Böddeker 1578, but some poems have been identified with earlier broadsides. Rollins, *Analytical Index,* nos. 3010-11, equates it with two broadsides entered in 1605 to Simon Stafford. These may well be a late reprint (compare **386**).

Satire on marriage. Whenever it comes to a dispute about the mastery, "Y hold a grote, the wyfe wyll hayte." (As Rollins indicates, *hayte* is a contraction of "have it," and not, as Böddeker says, "order, command.") Such is now the case, but husbands wrangle about it. God grant that marriage may mend, and that every husband will learn to "graunt his wyffe to haite." The author's ironical counsel about how to rule a wife and have peace in the family is similar to that of Bawdin Bacheler in **158**.

219. Now of wemen [var. Off women now] this I say for me.

By William Dunbar. Accepted as Dunbar's on the testimony of both MSS.; questioned only by Pinkerton, who said of it: "A paltry piece in praise of women. *Non defensoribus istis* . . . The point of it is that Christ had a woman for mother, but no man for father. It is subscribed, *quod Dunbar in prays of woman,* but I dare say he is innocent of it" (see Craigie, II, 118).

> *In Prays of Woman.*

(1) Advocates' Library 1. 1. 6 (17 couplets); ed. Small, *Poems of William Dunbar,* II, 170, with variants of (2); ed. Ritchie, *Bannatyne Manuscript,* IV, 75; MacKenzie, *Poems of William Dunbar,* p. 83; see for further editions Hunterian Club *Bannatyne,* I, cviii, and Small, III, 261.

(2) Magdalene College Cambridge, Pepys 2553; ed. W. A. Craigie, *Maitland Folio Manuscript,* I, 345.

According to the *DNB* Dunbar's dates are (1465?-1530?). Mackay in his introduction to Small (I, clxix) believes this is a palinode to Dunbar's *Ballade against Evil Women* (**282**), and that it was probably written shortly after. Of the *Ballate* itself he remarks "Of uncertain date, but probably between 1508 and 1513." Mackay's whole argument is based on a somewhat outmoded type of conjecture, the "period" and the autobiographical fallacy; and in any event the *Ballate* is probably not Dunbar's.

There is nothing better on earth than women. He who defames them defames himself, "Sen that of wemen cumin all ar we." "Wemen ar wemen and sa will end and de." Shame to the fruit that would put the tree to nought. They conceive us with pain, and feed us within their breasts, and suffer marvellous woe in bringing us to birth. "Than meit and drynk to feid ws get we nane, / Bot that we soik out of thair breistis bane." They are all our comfort here on earth; no man is half so dear to us. A man who slanders them should be exiled from all good company. Christ, the well of all goodness, whose majesty rings through heaven and earth, had a human mother; but a man was not his father. Hence all women should be served and loved and honored. It will be seen from the summary that, in spite of Pinkerton, the poem bids for an emotional appeal over and above the worship of the Virgin. Logic, "enlightenment," or the religious convictions of a critic are scarcely the proper tests for any poem.

220. O fayre Dido! most noble in constaunce!

By John Lydgate (an extract from *The Fall of Princes*, Book ii, 2171-2233, with the third and fourth stanzas transposed; see Bergen, *Fall of Princes*, I, 261).

The Moral of the Legend of Dido; or *L'Envoy of Dydo, Quene of Cartage.*

(1) Harley 2251 (9 rime-royal stanzas); ed. Halliwell, *Selection from the Minor Poems of Dan John Lydgate*, p. 69.

The Fall of Princes is dated by Bergen (I, ix-x) between the years 1431 and 1439.

Four stanzas commend the chaste and faithful Dido, who slew herself for love. The praise of Dido, a perennial example in defense of women from Ovid to Chaucer, is found in Lydgate's sources, Boccaccio and Laurence de Premierfait. But Lydgate, who had pretended in **185** to be shocked at Boccaccio's satire on women, proceeds to add five stanzas headed *Lenvoye direct to wydowis of the translatour,* which are hardly gallant. Noble matrons, beware lest such folly as Dido's assail you! To slay yourselves were too great a penance. God preserve you with your fickleness! Pretend sobriety and steadfastness. Never be "withoute purueiaunce" of lovers; no single man is safe, and with many you may increase your wealth. Make your servants obedient and humble, and when you are inconstant, enjoy yourselves "Contraire to Dido, that was queen off Cartage." Lydgate was unquestionably remembering the way in which Chaucer's Clerk turned his praise of Griselda into an attack on women in general. "Purueiaunce" was a bit of technical jargon much used by the Wife of Bath; it brought her many lovers and much wealth. For other extracts from the *Fall of Princes* which appear as independent poems see **142.**

221. O fresch floure most plesant of pryse.

Salutation: "To you dere herte variant and mutable
Lyk to Carybdis whych is vnstable."
(1) Rawlinson Poetry 36 (two-line saluation, 8 rime-royal
    stanzas, and a concluding couplet according to Robbins);
    ed. Rose Cords, *Archiv*, CXXXV (1916), 297; R. H. Rob-
    bins, *MLR*, XXXVII (1942), 416.
MS. second half XV cent.

Man's answer to a comic valentine from a girl (see **335**). The
tone is indicated by the salutation. You have sent me a letter of derision
which is written in a style modeled on neither Chaucer nor Cicero. He
then proceeds to a most virulent catalogue of uglinesses (see **226**), and
concludes by commending her to "the pyp and þe pose" and a somewhat unconventional place in heaven. The couplet at the end indicates
that the real reason for his satire is her love for another. (The "earylew"
of Miss Cords' transcript might be the curlew, unstable like the waves;
see **7**. But Robbins reads "Carybdis.")

222. O gallandis all I cry and call.

MS. (1) attributes to "balnevis," MS. (2) to "Johnne balnavis."
Advice to Gallandis.
(1) Advocates' Library 1. 1. 6 (28 four-line stanzas); ed. Ritchie,
    Bannatyne Manuscript, III, 18; see also Hunterian Club
    Bannatyne, I, lxxxix.
(2) Magdalene College Cambridge, Pepys 2553; ed. W. A.
    Craigie, *Maitland Folio Manuscript*, I, 355, with variants
    from (1) in II, 119.
1568 or before.

Warning to young men against the perils of sensuality. A great deal
of counsel buried under obscure hunting metaphors. See **7**.

223. O man more then madde, what ys þi mynde?

(1) Rawlinson C. 813 (8 rime-royal stanzas); ed. Padelford
    and Benham, *Anglia*, XXXI (1908), 393.
According to Bolle, *Anglia*, XXXIV (1911), 274, the MS. is of
the time of Henry VIII, but most of its contents are late XV cent.
Satire on woman's inconstancy, falsehood, and greed.

224. O man transformit and vnnaturall.

By "Weddirburne," on whom see **101**.
(1) Advocates' Library 1. 1. 6 (18 rime-royal stanzas); ed.
    Ritchie, *Bannatyne Manuscript*, IV, 98; see also Hunterian
    Club *Bannatyne*, I, cix.
1568 or before.

Warning to old men to avoid lust and sensuality. The author employs Jesus, son of Sirach, and "The devyne prudent plato."

225. O mestres whye / Owtecaste am I.

> (1) Harley 2252 (4 eight-line stanzas); ed. Wright and Halliwell, *Reliquiae Antiquae*, I, 255; Flügel, *Neuenglisches Lesebuch*, I, 140; Chambers and Sidgwick, *Early English Lyrics*, p. 76. Flügel erroneously merges it with the following "Som do entende" (**266**).

MS. of the time of Henry VIII. There are some XV cent. pieces in the MS., but the metrical form and language of this poem suggest that it is early XVI cent. Brown and Robbins would seem to imply a date before 1500, since they include it in their *Index* as no. 2518.

Rebellious lover. Sad as he is, he will leave his lady and "have free chayse."

226. O mossie quince hanging by your stalke.

Ascribed by Stow to Chaucer; rejected by Tyrwhitt and all recent editors (see Hammond, *Chaucer*, p. 442).

> (1) Trinity College Cambridge R. 3. 19 (2 rime-royal stanzas; 1 eight-line stanza; and an interpolated rime-royal stanza discussed as **387**).
> (2) Stow's *Chaucer* (1561) and later Chaucer editions (without the interpolation); see Chalmers, I, 564, and Hammond, *Chaucer*, p. 442.

MS. late XV or early XVI cent.

Satirical panegyric to his lady, with a catalogue of uglinesses instead of the usual catalogue of charms (on the normal convention see Hammond, *English Verse*, p. 405). One is reminded of the almost contemporary friends of Villon, Grosse Margot and La Belle Heaumière (see Louis Dimier, ed., *Oeuvres Complètes de Villon*, Paris, 1927, pp. 106-110, 180-82). But this type of satire is at least as old as Horace, *Epodes* 8 and 12. Turbervile and Wyatt revive the classical epigram; see **149, 155**, and **395**. "O mossie quince," which is a parody of the medieval courtly praise of one's mistress, is associated in both authorities with **95**, a member of the same genre; for others see **161, 221**, and **335**. Dunbar's Kind Kittok is likewise an ugly old woman, but Dunbar is essentially sympathetic with her (**195**). His Gaelic fancy recalls the Loathly Lady of Celtic tradition and the *Wife of Bath's Tale*. In some respects Kittok also reminds us of Skelton's Elynour Rummyng (**277**). A special development of this kind of parodic praise is found in poems by Chaucer and Hoccleve (**235** and **325**), where the heroine is Lady Money, who is as cruel as the usual courtly mistress. By implication the malice of most of these poems comes from the anger of a rebuffed lover. It is strange that Shakespearean editors have not observed these traditional prototypes of Sonnet cxxx, "My mistress' eyes are nothing like the sun." Donne's *The Anagram* also belongs to the tradition.

227. O prudent folkes, takeþe heed.

> By John Lydgate.
>
> *Bycorne and Chychevache;* or *þe couronne of disguysinges con-trived by Daun Iohan Lidegate;* or *þe maner of straunge desguys-inges;* or *þe gyse of a mummynge* (the last three are running titles in Trinity R. 3. 19 inserted by John Shirley).
>
> > (1) Trinity College Cambridge R. 3. 20 (19 rime-royal stanzas with prose descriptions of the accompanying tapestries); ed. Hammond, *English Verse,* p. 115; MacCracken, *Minor Poems of Lydgate,* II, 433; for other editions see Hammond, p. 115, and MacCracken, I, xiii.
> >
> > (2) Trinity College Cambridge R. 3. 19.
> >
> > (3) Harley 2251 (according to Hammond, pp. 114-15, this is derived from (1)). See Hammond, and Brown and Robbins, *Index,* no. 2541, for several editions.
> >
> > (4) British Museum Additional 29729.
>
> The oldest MS. (1) is by John Shirley, who died in 1456. Lydgate diverges from his French analogues by saying that Chichevache has sought for Griselda "more þane thritty Mayes," and this has been taken as an allusion to the *Clerk's Tale,* which is certainly echoed elsewhere in the poem. There is some disagreement as to whether Lydgate meant over thirty years after Chaucer's death or the same lapse of time from the composition of the *Clerk's Tale.* If we accept these two dates as variant limits we can assign *Bycorne* approximately to the years 1420-35.
>
> Satire on woman's shrewishness. A group of poems to accompany " a peynted or desteyned clothe for an halle a parlour or a chaumbre / deuysed by Iohan Lidegate at þe request of a werþy citeseyn of London." Various actors on the tapestry are given lines to speak. The poet introduces Bycorne and Chichevache, the former fed on patient men and the latter on good women. Bycorne then describes how fat he is and how his poor wife (Chichevache) suffers from a lack of food. A company of patient men warn their fellows of how Bycorne lies in wait for them. A woman projecting from the mouth of Chichevache warns her fellows against humility. Chichevache herself has looked for more than thirty Mays and has found but one Griselda. An old man beats Chichevache and complains that she has stolen his rare bird of a patient wife. The *locus classicus* for this story in English is the *Envoy* to Chaucer's *Clerk's Tale* (see **81**), where he warns noble wives against such humility as may lead to fame in a clerk's tale "Lest Chichevache yow swelwe in hire entraille!" This line and many others are directly borrowed by Lydgate. It is usually assumed, however, that Lydgate had also a French source, such as those discussed by Hammond, p. 113. For additional extensive material on these fabulous beasts from England, France, Germany, and Italy see Johann Bolte's articles in *Archiv,* CVI

(1901), 1; CXIV (1905), 80; and R. J. Menner, *MLN*, XLIV (1929), 455.

228. O Temerous tauntres that delights in toyes.

Assigned in (2) to [Thomas] Lord Vaux.
Against an vnstedfast woman.
(1) "Harington MS." at Arundel Castle (1 six-line stanza); to be edited by Professor Ruth Hughey.
(2) British Museum Additional 28635.
(3) *Tottel's Miscellany* (in all editions); ed. Rollins, I, 169, with variants from (2).
Baron Vaux died in 1556.
Rebellious lover complains of woman's cruelty and inconstancy.

229. O wicket wemen wilfull and variable.

Ascribed by Bannatyne to "chauceir." The Hunterian Club *Bannatyne* (I, cvi) says "Not in Chaucer; perhaps by Lydgate." MacCracken, *Minor Poems of Lydgate*, I, v-l, does not even mention the poem, and it is not an extract from *The Fall of Princes*. Several words, *dowgit, dour, laitis, standfra, taiclit, skald,* and *but* for "without," clearly point to Scots provenance.
(1) Advocates' Library 1. 1. 6 (3 rime-royal stanzas); ed. Ritchie, *Bannatyne Manuscript*, IV, 35.
1568 or before. Brown and Robbins, *Index*, no. 2580, imply a date before 1500, on what grounds I do not know. The attribution to Chaucer makes it likely that Bannatyne knew it was not by a contemporary; but how old was his original it is impossible to ascertain. Thynne, however, who with Stow and Bannatyne built the Chaucer apocrypha, appears to have attributed a poem nearly contemporary with himself to Chaucer; see **255**.
Satire on woman in all her wicked aspects. A *tour de force* in alliterating adjectives. Compare **115**, an English defense; **170**, a set of definitions of love; and the Latin analogues in Wulff, *Die Frauenfeindlichen Dichtungen*, p. 44.

230. O ye wymmen, which been enclyned.

The last stanza of **307**, by Lydgate. Ascribed by Stow to Chaucer.
(1) Royal Library Naples xiii. B. 29 (1 rime-royal stanza); ed. Wright and Halliwell, *Reliquiae Antiquae*, II, 70; for edition and facsimile see Tarquinio Vallese, *La Novella del Chierico di Oxford*, Naples, 1939, p. 77 (Vallese erroneously transcribes the first word as "Ek"). On this interesting far-wanderer of a MS., the scribe of which appears to

have been Harry More, see Manly and Rickert, *Text of the Canterbury Tales,* I, 376-78.

(2) Fragments from the binding of Ashmole 39; ed. W. H. Black, *A Descriptive . . . Catalogue of the Manuscripts Bequeathed . . . by Elias Ashmole* (Bodleian Quarto, X), Oxford, 1845, cols. 61-62.

Lydgate died in 1448-49. The Naples MS. was completed in 1457, but some scraps like this may be slightly later.

You women inclined by nature to be true should arm yourselves in the strong armor of doubleness. When the scribe of Naples appended this last verse of Lydgate's *Doublenesse* to the *Clerk's Tale,* he was obviously aware of the military imagery it shared with the Clerk's *Envoy.* Lydgate's poetry was especially susceptible to extracting in the XV and XVI centuries (see **142**).

Of all creatures women be best (136).

Of alle thynges that God ... (385).

231. Off cullouris cleir // quha lykis to weir.

By "robert semple."

The ballat . . . of Ionet Reid ane violet and ane quhyt Being slicht wemen of lyf & conversatioun and tavernaris.

(1) Advocates' Library 1. 1. 6 (13 eight-line stanzas); ed. Ritchie, *Bannatyne Manuscript,* II, 333; for other editions see Hunterian Club *Bannatyne,* I, lxxxvii.

1568 or before. See **96**.

This song, which discusses the advantages of three lasses of wanton character, one violet, one red, and one white, is obscured by a heavy mass of local allusion and of double meanings with the use of metaphors from colors and cloth-making. It was made "In Iedburgh at the Iustice Air. . . . abone glasss," which I assume means written in a tavern. There is considerable allusion to the wanton habits of "court-men"; compare **301**.

232. Off god and kynde / procedith al bewte.

By John Lydgate.

Horns Away!; or *Of Women's Horns;* or *Ballad on the Forked Headdresses of Women;* or *A Dyté of Womenhis Hornys.*

(1) Harley 2255 (9 eight-line stanzas); ed. Hammond, *English Verse,* p. 112; for other editions see Hammond, p. 111.

(2) Laud 683; ed. with variants from the other authorities by MacCracken, *Minor Poems of Lydgate,* II, 662; for other editions see Hammond, p. 111.

(3) Harley 2251 (4 stanzas only).

(4) British Museum Additional 34360 (4 stanzas only).

(5) Cambridge University Library Hh. 4. 12; ed. with variants from (1) by Furnivall, *Political, Religious and Love Poems* (1866), p. 45; for other editions see Hammond, p. 111.

(6) Jesus College Cambridge 56 (lacks Envoy).

(7) Ashmole 59 (7 stanzas only).

(8) Trinity College Cambridge R. 3. 19.

(9) Rawlinson C. 86 (8 stanzas only).

(10) Leyden University Vossius 9? "MS. Voss. Lugd. 359" is mentioned as an authority by Halliwell, *Selection from the Minor Poems of Dan John Lydgate,* p. 46 (his own text is based on Laud). MacCracken, I, xviii, has instead "Leyden Voss. 9," and Miss Hammond does "not find justified" the listing of this MS. The issue is further confused by MacCracken's notes (II, 662) beneath his text, where he refers once more to "Leyden Univ. Voss. 9" as MS. *L,* and then designates Laud by the same sigla. The piece is not mentioned in Robinson's description of Leyden Vossius 9 in [Harvard] *Studies and Notes,* V (1896), 187-94.

The poem may be dated between about 1390, since it alludes to the "arche wyves" of Chaucer's *Clerk's Tale,* and 1448-49, when Lydgate died. Attempts to date this and other works on the basis of allusion to "horns" are dangerous, since the term was applied to various fashions, from the "boss" or "ram's horn," a kind of covered puff of hair over the ears much like the fashion of the early 1920's, which is attacked in the XIII cent. *Dit des Cornetes* and in **169**, to the doublepeaks which Anne of Bohemia is said to have brought to England in 1381. See Hammond, p. 111; Mendal Frampton, *PMLA,* L (1935), 635-38.

Satire on fashions with the variable refrain "Bewte wyl shewe / thouh hornys wer away." Horns were given by God to beasts, not to women. In the envoy Lydgate addresses noble princesses with the plea to cast these ugly headdresses away, and to remember that the Virgin Mary had but a kerchief to cover her head when Christ was born. For similar satires see **169, 211, 65, 309,** and **369.** The subject of woman's dress was as perennial a subject of pulpit rhetoric as today, and the preacher's advice seems to have been about as well heeded.

Of hondes and body and face are clene (384).

233. Off ladies bewties to declair.

(1) Magdalene College Cambridge, Pepys 2553 (9 eight-line stanzas); ed. W. A. Craigie, *Maitland Folio Manuscript,* I, 66; for variants of (2) and further editions see II, 65.

(2) Cambridge University Library Ll. 5. 10 (the "Reidpeth MS.").

Maitland Folio, the earliest authority, was composed 1570-85.

Women seem beautiful, but the man who trusts their outward appearance will be beguiled as Adam was by Eve. Our Lords today are ruined by the extravagant clothes women put upon their backs; the same process is destroying our lairds and our "Iakmen."

233a. Of life and deth nowe chuse the.

(1) Lansdowne 762 (2 couplets); ed. Wright and Halliwell, *Reliquiae Antiquae*, I, 289.

This portion of the MS. appears to be of the XV cent.; see Brown and Robbins, *Index*, no. 2633.

Choice is hard between marriage and hanging; but, since woman is the worse, "Drive forthe the carte!" Imbedded in a collection of Latin, English, and macaronic verses, mnemonic and proverbial. For the proverb "Wedding and hanging is destiny" see **91**.

234. Of lyghtnes most unsade.

By Henry Sponare.

(1) Ashmole 48 (31 four-line stanzas); ed. Wright, *Songs and Ballads*, p. 79.

On the basis of broadside contents Rollins, *MLN*, XXXIV (1919), 349, dates the MS. 1557-65.

A friend of mine and I often talk about woman's inconstancy, and he has asked me to find some means of dissuading them from it. So I went to "Godes holy booke" and found many mirrors there to set before the eyes of widows, maids, and wives, so that they might see how far they depart from the virtue of Biblical women. Pride, talkativeness, desire—these are the vices of women nowadays. Try and learn from the examples of Rebecca, Sara, Esther, Judith, Anna, and the rest. These were sober, humble, and chaste. God grant that modern women may be like them!

235. Of my lady wel me reioise I may.

By Thomas Hoccleve.

Humorous Praise of His Lady; or *La Commendacion de Ma Dame*.

(1) Huntington Library HM 744 (formerly Ashburnham Additional 133) (24 lines); ed. Sir Israel Gollancz, *Hoccleve's Works. II. The Minor Poems*, p. 37; Hammond, *English Verse*, p. 68; for other editions see Brown and Robbins, *Index*, no. 2640.

Furnivall, *Hoccleve's Works. I. The Minor Poems*, pp. viii, xxvii, gives his author's dates as 1368?-1450?. It appears to have been inserted into the Hoccleve "Series" of linked poems and therefore may be after 1420 (see **28**).

The third part of a "triple roundel" on Lady Money. Having sent her his complaint and been rebuked by this regal lady, who has great lords in her train, he writes a humorous catalogue of her charms, or feature-by-feature description. Like Chaucer's *Purse* (**325**) this is a satirical panegyric, a parody of the courtly love poem, and it reminds us of other parodies where the subject was actually a woman (see **226**).

236. Off noble men—both kyngys and pryncys royall.

Anonymous translation of Giovanni Boccaccio's *De claris mulieribus*. The editor believes the dialect is that of Suffolk and the author a disciple of Lydgate.

(1) British Museum Additional 10304 (256 rime-royal stanzas); ed. Gustav Schleich, *Die mittelenglische Umdichtung von Boccaccios De claris mulieribus,* Leipzig (Palaestra 144), 1924; for another (incomplete) edition by Zupitza see Brown and Robbins, *Index,* no. 2642.

(2) A Phillips MS. sold by Sotheby's in 1898 is mentioned by Schleich, p. 2.

Schleich dates the poem between 1433 and about 1440, which fits with the date of the MS. (according to Furnivall *ca.* 1440), the language, and an allusion to Lydgate's *Fall of Princes* (composed between 1431 and about 1438-39).

Though many books have been made in commendation of noble men, only one, Boccaccio's, is of noble women. So the author-translator writes of twenty-one noble ladies: Eve, Semiramis, Ops, Juno, Ceres, Minerva, Venus, Io, Europa, Libia, Camilla, Erythrya (Eriphyle), Amalthea, Circe, Medea, Mantho, Sappho, Carmenta, Thamyrys I and II, and Arthemisia. Schleich offers elaborate critical apparatus, including a parallel text of crucial parts of the original and a discussion of sources. For other derivatives of Boccaccio see Christine's *Cyte of Ladyes* (**46**) and Clapham's *Of the Nobilitie and Excellencie of VVomankynde* (**237**). In some measure the *De claris* also inspired Chaucer's *Legend* (**12**) and perhaps **80** and **247**. Boccaccio treats 104 or 105 ladies (Schleich, pp. 95-98); **236** has 21 and the *Legend* 10. The two later poems have 9 each, and Ovid's *Heroides* (**280**) has 18. Of them all only **80** and the *Legend* share a nearly identical list. Despite Boccaccio's great number Chaucer introduces four new names, **80** one, and **247** four or five; whereas Ovid's *Heroides* has eight not in any of the others. The *Legend* is called "IX good Women" in MS. Bodley 638 (*Summary Catalogue,* II, 200); and Chaucer's *Retractacion* lists the projected (?) number of legends variously as 15, 19, 20, and 25. Despite this interesting approximation in numbers, the translator of *De claris* does not seem to have been attempting a duplication of Chaucer, for he has only one heroine, Medea, in common with the *Legend*. He begins valiantly to put all of *De claris* into English, and renders the first ten stories in order. Then he skips about through Boccaccio's first 55 to select his other eleven tales. He passes over the last 50 stories completely, and ends with the apology that it is expedient for a man who has walked

ten or twenty miles to pause and rest a while. If the hearers like his
work he will "procede To the residue of ladyes notable." He may have
been Lydgate's disciple, but he certainly lacked his master's patience.

237. Of the Nobilitie and Excellencie of VVomankynde [prose].

Translated by David Clapham.
(1) T. Berthelet (1542). I have examined this from the reproduction of the Bodleian copy in the Edwards Brothers film
project (Film 1733, Case XII, Carton 71).

Agrippa's book was completed in 1529, and this translation
appeared in 1542. Since Clapham had translated Agrippa's *Commendation of Matrimony* around 1540, when Berthelet printed it,
and since that book sold well enough to merit a reprint in 1545,
we may perhaps conjecture that the second translation was made to
order between the years 1540 and 1542. Clapham received his LL.B.
at Cambridge in 1533.

This is the first of the translations of the *De Nobilitate et Praecellentia Foeminei Sexus* of Henry Cornelius Agrippa von Nettesheim, the
scientist, philosopher, and student of magic who was consulted with
regard to his contemplated marriage by Panurge (under the name of
Her Trippa, see Rabelais, Book III, chapter 25). Agrippa begins "And
thus betwene man and woman by substance of the soule, one hath no
higher preemynence of nobylytie aboue the other. . . . But all other
thynges, the which be in man, besydes the dyuyne substance of
the sowle, in those thynges the excellente and noble womanheed in a
maner infynytely dothe excell the rude grosse kynd of men," which we
shall prove not by sophistical logic, but by the best authorities. Her
name is better (Eve means "life," Adam "earth"). She was made in
Paradise and man without. She is more beautiful, and of a finer substance than he. She is more shamefast than man. She nourishes mankind and has a mother's pity. There follow countless examples from
Scripture and the classics. There is no deed done by man so noble that
woman has not at some time excelled it. And so he proceeds for countless pages, ending before his work attains too great a volume, and
inviting additions from others to this noble subject. For other translations see **214**.

238. Of the yong man and the euill disposed woman [prose].

Translated by Nicholas Leigh from the colloquy of Desiderius
Erasmus called *Adolescens et Scortum*.
(1) *A modest meane to Mariage,* Henry Denham (1568). I
have examined the Huntington Library copy by means of
microfilm.

Adolescens et Scortum appeared for the first time in Froben's
edition of August, 1523. For further remarks on the date see **189**.

Sophronius, a young man who has amended his life, converts his old friend Lucretia, a prostitute, to a life of chastity. A very special development of the theme of renunciation of love, which Preserved Smith (*A Key to the Colloquies of Erasmus,* Cambridge [Harvard Theological Studies, XIII], 1927, p. 22) believes to have been borrowed from Hrotswitha's drama *Paphnutius* (the Thais legend).

239. Of their nature they greatly them delite.

Ascribed by Stow to Geoffrey Chaucer, but rejected from the canon by Tyrwhitt and later editors.

  (1) Trinity College Cambridge R. 3. 19 (4 rime-royal stanzas).
  (2) Stow's *Chaucer* (1561), probably from (1). In many later
       editions including Chalmers, I, 560. For other editions see
       Hammond, *Chaucer,* p. 441.
  MS. late XV or early XVI cent.

Women delight to go on pilgrimages "To kisse no shrines but lusty quike images" (this first stanza lifted bodily from stanza 16 of **75**). When maids are married they lose their humility; "Beware alway, the blind eats many a fly" (see **166**). I have been so long in study that I am faint, so I say no more, but "pray God keepe the fly out of my dish." Thus I end, knowing that if maids and wives knew who I am I'd suffer. This was written in the lusty season of May.

Off women now þis I say for me (219).

240. On hye feest dayes, whan wyues go gay.

The Proude wyues Pater noster, that wolde gogaye, and vndyd her husbonde and went her waye.

The *STC* lists as no. 25938 three copies of an edition printed by John Kynge, dated 1560. These are at British Museum, Bodleian, and Huntington Library. I have been unable to collate these three extant copies, and am therefore unsure whether the discrepancies between the *STC* and earlier bibliographical descriptions are due to a faulty identification of two editions in the *STC* (which lists only the dated edition) or not. In the absence of a proper collation we may note the following facts and conjectures:

  (1) [Edward Vernon Utterson], *Select Pieces of Early Popular
       Poetry,* London, 1817, II, 143, based his edition on "Douce's
       copy," which was printed by John Kynge and apparently
       dated 1560. Hazlitt, *Remains,* IV, 149, seems to have collated
       this copy with (2), using Utterson as a base and incorporat-
       ing numerous corrections, including the title page of (2).
       Hazlitt (IV, 147) indicates that the dated copy had a wood-
       cut of a man with purses at his girdle; the undated copy
       instead had a woodcut of two women conversing (in Haz-
       litt, 72 eight-line stanzas).
  (2) Collier, *Bibliographical and Critical Account,* III, 246, and

Hazlitt, IV, 148, both saw a copy among the Selden tracts in the Bodleian, which is undated and has the woodcut of two women conversing on the title page. Collier gives a number of variants between (1) and (2) which in his opinion show the superiority of (2). If this is the Bodleian copy listed by the *STC*, we have two editions or issues by John Kynge erroneously identified. Harold Stein in *Library*, Series 2, XV (1934-35), p. 44, is of the opinion that this Selden copy was printed by William Copland between the years 1560 and 1568, but according to Hazlitt both (1) and (2) have "John Kynge" in the colophon.

(3) Stein describes the British Museum copy in the article cited. This is apparently the first of the copies listed by *STC*. It is dated 1560 and was printed by John Kynge.

(4) The Huntington Library copy mentioned by *STC* may be of either the dated or the undated edition.

(5) The issue is further complicated by *CHEL*, III, 553, which lists the entry to John Charlewood of January 15, 1581-82, as though it were an attested edition (for the entry see *Stationers' Register*, ed. Arber, II, 405). There were two entries in 1560, one on June 10 to Kynge (Arber, I, 128), the other to John Sampson (or Awdeley) on August 14 (Arber, I, 150).

1560 or before. Stein believes the poem was written much earlier.

Satire on woman's love for finery. At the saying of the Paternoster in church the proud wife's stream of consciousness is led by each phrase of the prayer into a meditation on fashions and methods of getting money out of her husband. At the end of the prayer she falls into conversation with her gossip, who tells her how to rule one's husband. She goes home and tries out the advice, but her husband refuses her the money she desires, and she finally steals it from him. The poem ends with a devout farced Paternoster. For French satires using this formula see *CHEL*, III, 553.

241. Ons dyd I aspyre to loves desyre.

To the tune of The downeryght squyre.

(1) Ashmole 48 (3 sixteen-line stanzas and one of twelve lines); ed. Wright, *Songs and Ballads*, p. 191.

On the basis of broadside contents Rollins, *MLN*, XXXIV (1919), 349, dates the MS. about 1557-65.

Once (the more fool I) I sought love and wooed my lady. She was full of laughter because she had brought me to the lure. Wanton, she gave what she desired, because she gained at my expense. We were to be married, but she has left me for any man who comes along. The more fool I. Rebellious lover; satire on woman's inconstancy, lust, and greed.

242. Ane of the warst þat evir was in erd.

(1) Advocates' Library 1. 1. 6 (1 rime-royal stanza); ed. Ritchie, *Bannatyne Manuscript,* IV, 23; see also Hunterian Club *Bannatyne,* I, cv.

1568 or before.

Satire against wicked Jezebel (among a group called by Bannatyne "Schort Epegrammis Aganis Women"). It might be from a longer piece, like *The Fall of Princes* or *The Remedy of Love* (see **255** and **142**), but I have been unable to find it in either of these prolific sources of isolated extracts. Jezebel was one of John Knox's favorite names for Mary Tudor; see Robert Louis Stevenson, *Familiar Studies of Men and Books,* New York, 1923, pp. 292-93, 331.

243. Ouer all gatis that I haff gon.

In Praise of Ivy.
Burden: "Nowell, nowell, ell, ell!
            I pray yow, lysten qwat I yow [tell.]"

(1) St. John's College Cambridge S. 54 (two-line burden and 9 four-line stanzas); ed. Greene, *Early English Carols,* p. 95 (no. 139); for another edition and parallels see p. 381.

MS. second half XV cent.

The poet, beginning with a *chanson d'aventure* setting, says he has traveled far but never seen so fair a branch as Ivy (symbolic of women), which is always green. Its letters spell *I*hesus, *V*irgin (worthy wife, mother, and maid), and *E*manuell. Ivy will always win in contest because of her meekness. Essentially a defense of women by witness of Mary; compare **291**, and for the Holly-Ivy controversy see **86**.

244. Pansing of lufe quhat lyf it leidis.

(1) Advocates' Library 1. 1. 6 (5 four-line stanzas); ed. Ritchie, *Bannatyne Manuscript,* IV, 96; see also Hunterian Club *Bannatyne,* I, cix.

1568 or before.

Both men and women should say good-by to the vanity of love.

245. Passing along through Redriffe.

Perhaps revised by Richard Johnson?
A New Song of a Curst Wife and her Husband; or possibly *a Man that his wyfe ys Master.*

(1) From Richard Johnson's *The Crown Garland of Golden Roses* (1612), ed. W. Chappell, London (Percy Society, VI), 1842, p. 78 (6 eight-line stanzas). For reprints of Johnson see *STC,* nos. 14673-14674.

Rollins suggests that this ballad may be identified with *Analytical Index,* no. 1655, "a man that his wyfe ys master," entered to John Cherlewood in 1562-63, or with **32**. It may be too late for our stated limits.

Chanson de mal marié. The poet overhears a husband describing his tormented married life. His wife scratches his face. He works all day and at night must report on all the money he has spent, for she goes through his pockets. If he fails to bring home five groats every evening she chides him unmercifully. So he has no control over borrowing and lending, and if he lives as long as Nestor it will be the same. Except when he is working, he dare not stray from her sight. With the variable refrain "My wife will needs be maister."

246. Pernitious peple parciall In despyte.

By [Robert?] Sempill.

Heir followis the defence of crissell sandelandis ffor vsing hirself contrair the ten commandis Being in ward for playing of the loun W' Every ane list geif hir half a croun.

(1) Advocates' Library 1. 1. 6 (14 eight-line stanzas); ed. Ritchie, *Bannatyne Manuscript,* II, 329; see also Hunterian Club *Bannatyne,* I, lxxxvii.

1568 or before. See **96**.

Half-humorous defense of a poor harlot who has been jailed for the exercise of her trade. Who among you may cast the first stone? Remember poor Susanna. Full of obscure local allusion to Sempill's friends and enemies. On date and subject matter see **96**.

Pray we to Our Lady dere (257).

Proface maistris Jyllian with your company (35).

247. Profulgent in preciousnesse, O Sinope queen.

Ascribed by Stow to Geoffrey Chaucer, but rejected by editors since Tyrwhitt.

The .ix. Ladies worthie.

(1) Trinity College Cambridge R. 3. 19 (9 rime-royal stanzas).

(2) Stow's *Chaucer* (1561) and later Chaucer editions, including Chalmers, I, 561. See Hammond, *Chaucer,* p. 441.

MS. late XV or early XVI cent.

Implied defense on the basis of nine women of martial valor. Skeat, *Chaucer,* VII, xiii, remarks on the unusual selection: Sinope, Hippolyta, Deifyle, Teuca, Penthesilea, Tomyris, Lampeto, Semiramis, and Melanippe. Four of these do not appear in any of the other catalogues mentioned under **236**. In view of the departure from the seminal lists of Boccaccio's *De claris mulieribus,* Skeat suggests the use of Orosius or Higden, who mention most of these Amazons. Actually, as the title implies, these are the Nine Feminine Worthies or "Les neuf Preuses,"

celebrated with their masculine compeers by Eustache Deschamps in his
Balade XCIII (*Oeuvres Complétes,* ed. Marquis de Queux de Saint-
Hilaire and Gaston Raynaud, Paris [SATF], 1873-1903, I, 200, 362).
Since Deschamps' Tantha is the English Teuca, and Marsopye (Mar-
pesia) the English Lampeto, the two lists are identical. But if the
Alceste of the *Prologue* be excluded, Chaucer's *Legend* also has nine
heroines, and the title of **247** therefore seems to recall the title "IX
good Women" affixed to the *Legend* by the scribe of MS. Bodley 638
(see **236**). *The .ix. Ladies worthie* should not, however, be confused
with another poem about nine ladies, *þe Cronycle made by Chaucier*
(**80**), which is merely an epitome of the *Legend*. **247** may well have
been intended as accompaniment to a pageant or a tapestry (see examples
in the note to Deschamps and in Huizinga, *Waning of the Middle Ages,*
p. 61).

Quha (see **Who**).

Quhat (see **What**).

Quhen (see **When**).

Quhome (see **Whom**).

Quhone (see **When**).

248. Refrain of youth thy vain desire.

    By "A. I." Could this be John Allde, the printer?
    *A godly ballad declaring by the Scriptures the plagues that haue
insued whordome.*

        (1) John Allde (November 25, 1566); ed. Lilly's *Collection,*
           p. 101 (25 four-line stanzas). *STC* (no. 14046) lists one
           copy, at the British Museum.

    The ballad is printed on the back of a waste sheet of a Prog-
nostication for 1567. It was entered to Allde in 1566-67 (Rollins,
Analytical Index, no. 512).

    Avoid the lusts of youth, which sting like the serpent. Remember
the punishments which came to the generation of Noah, to Pharaoh,
Abimelech, the Sodomites, the Sichemites, Potiphar's Wife, Bathsheba,
Zimri, Samson, Solomon, Herod, and many others. Pray to God that
he may save us from such sins and such punishments. And God save
our noble Queen!

249. Remembryng on the grete vnstabilnesse.

    By John Lydgate, on Madden's authority (MacCracken, I, xi).
    A Ballade on an Ale-Seller (*Hic nota de illis que vendunt ser-
visiam in Cantuar*).

        (1) Rawlinson C. 48 (11 rime-royal stanzas, last two fragmen-
           tary); ed. MacCracken, *Minor Poems of Lydgate,* II, 429.
    The MS. is of the XV cent. Lydgate died in 1448-49.

Satire on a beautiful ale-wife, whose wantonness and kisses and false oaths are to obtain money, and who deserves herself to be deceived. Let us praise only true women. Brown and Robbins, *Index*, nos. 2809 and 3823, appear to accept **334**, which immediately follows in the MS., as a mocking palinode.

250. Returne the, hairt, hamewart agane.

By Alexander Scott.

(1) Advocates' Library 1. 1. 6 (4 eight-line stanzas); ed. Ritchie, *Bannatyne Manuscript*, IV, 8; Cranstoun, *Poems of Alexander Scott*, p. 66; Donald, *Poems of Alexander Scott*, p. 42. For further editions see Cranstoun, p. 159, and Hunterian Club *Bannatyne*, I, ciii.

Cranstoun dates Scott's work 1545-68.

Rebellious lover; satire on a woman's inconstancy. Return, my heart, for the devil a crumb does she care for you. There are plenty of other women. The poem appealed to Allan Ramsay, who printed it in *The Evergreen* with two additional stanzas which intensify the sting of the satire (see Donald, p. 90; and Cranstoun, p. 159).

Right & noe wronge (36).

251. Rycht airlie on Ask Weddinsday.

By William Dunbar.
The Twa Cummeris.

(1) Advocates' Library 1. 1. 6 (6 five-line stanzas); ed. Ritchie, *Bannatyne Manuscript*, III, 14; Small, *Poems of William Dunbar*, II, 160, with variants of (2), (3), (4); MacKenzie, *Poems of William Dunbar*, p. 84; see for further editions Small, III, 249, and Hunterian Club *Bannatyne*, I, lxxxix.

(2) Magdalene College Cambridge, Pepys 2553; ed. W. A. Craigie, *Maitland Folio Manuscript*, I, 64, with variants from (3).

(3) Cambridge University Library Ll. 5. 10 (the "Reidpeth MS.").

(4) "A MS. volume of the Register of Sasines, Town Clerk's Office, Aberdeen." In his notes Small (III, 249) cites MSS. "M., B., K., and Ab." In the bibliographical introduction (I, cxciv, cxcvii) Mackay cites MSS. "B., M., R., and Mak." "K" is apparently a misprint for R; so the disagreement seems to be between "Ab." and "Mak." The Mackay introduction lists no "Ab."; but this appears to be identical with Aberdeen (Mackay's "A"); and this surmise is confirmed by MacKenzie, p. 215, who cites as authorities (1), (2), and (4). Mackay's "Mak." should mean Makculloch; but the poem is not found in George Stevenson, ed.,

Pieces from the Makculloch and the Gray MSS., Edinburgh (STS, LXV), 1918.

According to the *DNB* Dunbar's dates are 1465?-1530? Mackay in his introduction to Small (I, clix) notes the similarity to *Tua Mariit Wemen and the Wedo,* which is certainly before 1508. He would put the two among Dunbar's earliest productions, before the marriage of James IV and Margaret Tudor in 1503. The Aberdeen MS. is dated 1503-1504 by MacKenzie, p. 215.

Very early on the first day of Lent two gossips sat drinking wine and complaining that "This lang Lentern makis me lene." One of them, very fat, pretended to be faint; her friend said she inherited that trait from her mother, who would drink nothing but Malmsey. Refrain, said the fat one, from fasting now and let your husband suffer. Good counsel, said the other, for as a lover he's somewhat lacking. So sip by sip they drank two quarts and began to cheer up a bit. For similar satires on woman's love of the bottle see **107**. None of them have the daft wit of Dunbar, who picks the day after carnival for the gossips' heavy thirst.

Richt as þe biche in Jolyng in hir raige (282).

252. Right best beloved & most in assurance.

(1) Rawlinson C. 813 (9 rime-royal stanzas); ed. Padelford and Benham, *Anglia,* XXXI (1908), 395.

W. Bolle, in *Anglia,* XXXIV (1911), 274, observes that, although the MS. is of the time of Henry VIII, most of its contents are late XV cent. Brown and Robbins, *Index,* no. 2821, imply by inclusion a date before 1500.

Answer by a woman to a man's charges of faithlessness. She accuses him in turn, and suggests that his skepticism may come from his encounter with "some vnjuste" woman. The literal-minded verses, the meter of which walks on all fours, make it not at all impossible that the poem was written as it purports to be, by some earnest but untalented lady.

253. ryght frutefull Epystle . . . in laude and prayse of matrymony, A [prose].

Translated by Richard Tavernour from Desiderius Erasmus' *Encomium Matrimonii.*

(1) Robert Redman (n.d.). I have examined the book by means of microfilm (Edwards Brothers Film 1089, Case VII, Carton 39), from the copy in the British Museum (*STC,* no. 10492).

According to Preserved Smith (*A Key to the Colloquies of Erasmus,* Cambridge [Harvard Theological Studies, XIII], 1927), p. 12, the *Encomium Matrimonii* was written in 1518. The *STC*

dates Redman's edition [1530?]. It is dedicated to Thomas Cromwell, who died in 1540. The *DNB* gives Tavernour's dates as
(1505?-1575).

Counsel to a young man to marry and preserve his noble line, with
countless examples to reveal the nobility of matrimony, the great felicity
of a good wife, and the absurdity of celibacy (a little of which will go
a long way). A brilliant humanistic essay showing the temper of the
times. For, although many sober treatises on marriage existed in the
Middle Ages, and although the Church's central position would have
shared in very large measure our views of common sense and partnership
in marriage, none of these would have been likely to belittle clerical
celibacy as Erasmus does. Since the days of Hildebrand and his clerical
reforms celibacy was a matter not to be spoken of lightly. We find in
Erasmus not only the breath of new intellectual life, but also his individual blend of sober counsel spiced by wit, courtliness, and conventional
satire on women; compare, for instance, his references (sig. B7) to
Socrates and Xanthippe and (D5) to his friend Jovius' wooing a fourth
wife. Smith (pp. 12-24) points out that the *Encomium Matrimonii*
began a period of concern on Erasmus' part with the subjects of women
and marriage, and that this work blossomed especially in the August,
1523, edition of the *Colloquies,* which has at least five new pertinent
pieces. He also wrote a *De Matrimonio Christiano,* published in 1526.
These general treatises on marriage reflect the times and occasionally
refer to the woman problem, but the many medieval and renaissance
tracts on the subject cannot be included in this Index. See my Introduction, p. 72n.

254. Say me, viit in þe brom.

Tell Me, Wight in the Broom.

(1) Trinity College Cambridge B. 14. 39 (3 couplets); ed.
Brown, *English Lyrics of the XIIIth Century,* p. 32; M. R.
James, *The Western Manuscripts in the Library of Trinity
College, Cambridge,* Cambridge, 1900-1904, I, 441.

(2) British Museum Additional 11579; ed. Brown, p. 32.

MS. (1) was compiled at various times up to about 1253.

The wife asks the witching broom how to have her husband's love,
and the answer is "Hold þine tunke stille." For the Latin exemplum in
which (2) occurs see Brown, p. 180.

255. Seeing the manifolde inconuenience.

Ascribed by Thynne to Chaucer; rejected by modern editors
from Tyrwhitt on. See under date.

The Remedy of Love.

(1) Thynne's *Chaucer* (1532) (81 rime-royal stanzas) and later
Chaucer editions, on which see Hammond, *Chaucer,* p. 450.
Ed. Chalmers, I, 538; and in Skeat's *Facsimile,* p. 758.

Skeat, *Canon,* p. 113, believes that the language points to a probable date of about 1530: "How can we pretend that Thynne confined himself to printing genuine poems by Chaucer, when we find him thus inserting a poem which he must have known to have been written in his own lifetime? No MS. copy is known, or is likely to be found." Brown and Robbins, *Index,* no. 3084, appear to accept a date before 1500 for the *Prologue* (19 stanzas), but say nothing about the rest of the poem.

Observing the dangers of prosperity and the malady of love which encumbers youth, I am moved to pray to my lord Youth. "I am your subject, but pray you to accept sober counsel. Fie on age, with its pretended seriousness; well I know old men who live in adultery. If a young man rebukes Age he stands on his dignity. Yet Age has one advantage, experience. I too, young as I am, have experience; it is well known that God said a little child shall lead them. And so I end my prologue, calling on furious Alecto, her sisters, and jealous Juno to inspire me." So then follows the counsel to youth, drawn "for the most part out of the Proverbs of Solomon," that is, from Proverbs and Ecclesiastes. Fly the "miswoman," who is the root of all the trouble. She is honey and gall. Beware the strange woman. I tell you the tale of a woman who was loved by three men. She had them all to dinner, and when they were seated she winked at one lover, offered the cup to another, and trod on the other's foot under the table. I ask you a *questione d'amore:* "Which of these three stood now in grace?" One of the three was I, and this disgusted me against love forever. (His lady was scarcely as enterprising as Dunbar's Wedow, who could keep five men dangling at a feast. See **336**, lines 489-496.) So I leave the gentle meters of the Muses, and call on Hermes, the Furies, Pluto and his Harpies to guide me. If all the earth were parchment one could not write the falsehood of woman, who is the devil's brand and a stinking rose. Wine and women cause wise men to fall into heresy. Avoid therefore all women, except your wife. Solomon in his fifth chapter (actually Prov. 7:6-27) tells of how a lascivious wife lured a young man when her husband was from home, and put the youth on the "waies of hell leading to death." I weep and wail the misfortune of her husband. There follows some etymological play with the word "cokold." It is of course jealousy on the part of husbands which leads to the ruses of women and their disobedience. Wed therefore only if you can trust women. I do not gainsay matrimony, for better it is to marry than to burn. But married or not, love no wife or mistress too keenly. And if you have a wife keep her from being idle, mingle praise and blame with tact, and keep your eyes open for any rival, but breathe no word to your wife if you find one, for that but fans the flame. Essentially, then, this poem is what it purports to be, a remedy against too violent love of any type—for harlot, mistress, or wife. Its worldly wisdom is based primarily on Scripture. But one would be surprised if the author's knowledge of the "olde daunce" did not stem in part from

Ovid, the *Roman de la Rose,* Chaucer, and perhaps the matrimonial treatises of the early XVI or late XV century. There is, as Skeat says, no MS. version of the poem (which breaks off in Thynne rather abruptly). But extracts (perhaps taken from Thynne or another early print) appear in the Bannatyne MS. (see **118** and **306**, both ascribed in the MS. to Chaucer). The Bannatyne MS. also has a *Remeidis of Luve* (**263**), but this is a mere Rebellious Lover poem. For a quatrain on Love in Idleness labeled "Ouidius de remedio amoris" (middle or late XVI cent.) see Padelford, *Anglia,* XXXVI (1912), 115 (from MS. Arch Selden B. 26). Miss Spurgeon (*Five Hundred Years of Chaucer Criticism*) does not give specific references to the Chaucer allusions of such members of the Chaucerian apocrypha. One notices at least three possibilities: (1) the invocation of the Furies instead of the Muses (stanzas 19, 31—compare *Troilus and Criseyde,* i. 1-11; iv. 22-28); (2) the use of a key-phrase from the Marriage Group, "weeping and wailing" as the companions of wedding (stanza 59—*Clerk's Tale,* IV, 1212, *Merchant's Prologue,* IV, 1213, and *passim*); and (3) the use of the meaningful word "puruayaunce," a favorite of the Wife of Bath (stanza 79).

256. Shall I wed an agèd man.

The complaint of a widdow against an old man (To the tune of Trentham's Toy).

(1) Earl of Macclesfield, Shirburn Castle, Oxfordshire: MS. Shirburn North Library 119. D. 44 (9 eight-line stanzas and a concluding quatrain); ed. Andrew Clark, *The Shirburn Ballads, 1585-1616,* Oxford, 1907, p. 269.

The MS. is late, but the ballad is almost certainly to be identified with a broadside entered to William Pekering in 1564 (Rollins, *Analytical Index,* no. 2410).

Like the Wife of Bath this widow will marry a bachelor rather than an old man. Semi-sympathetic with the woman who speaks, but nevertheless a satire on woman's desire and on the marriage of youth by age.

257. Sche saw theis women all bedene.

In Praise of Women.

Burden: "Pray we to Oure Lady dere
For here holy grace."

(1) St. John's College Cambridge S. 54 (two-line burden and 6 four-line stanzas); ed. Greene, *Early English Carols,* p. 263 (no. 394); for another edition see p. 429.

MS. of the second half of the XV cent.

Our Lady saved women from care—maids, wives, and widows. Women are good and clean and courteous, and make good company. All our bliss came from a woman (the Virgin). When a man is in sorrow a woman can cure him with a kiss. Men are false and fickle and women are mad to trust them; dear Lady, pray thy Son to protect women from wicked men. Defense, therefore, using the three favorite themes: the Virgin Mary, the virtue of women, and the wickedness of men. Greene (p. 429) errs in speaking of this as a reaction to "the earlier medieval attitude of disapproval of women." Defense in just these terms was as much of a convention as satire.

258. She þat hathe a wantan eye.

(1) Rawlinson C. 813 (16 four-line stanzas); ed. Padelford and Benham, *Anglia,* XXXI (1908), 352.

W. Bolle, *Anglia,* XXXIV (1911), 274, observes that, although the MS. is of the time of Henry VIII, most of the pieces are of the late XV cent. It certainly precedes in date *A Dialogue bytwene the commune secretary and Jalowsye* (see **342**), which was printed about 1560 and made extensive use of it (see Bolle, p. 291).

Satire on woman's inconstancy, hypocrisy, greed, love of gossip, lack of secrecy, pride, wandering wit, idleness, and general lack of trustworthiness. Good women (that is, all women who read this poem) will think the poet does not mean them.

259. Sythe, Blackwood, you haue mynde to wed a wife.

Attributed by Merrill to Nicholas Grimald, but Rollins accepts the ascription of the title to "N. Vincent," who has not been otherwise identified.

N. Vincent. to G. Blackwood, agaynst wedding.

(1) *Tottel's Miscellany* (in the first edition of June 5, 1557, only); ed. Rollins, I, 95; for another modern edition see II, 226 (10 couplets).

Before June 5, 1557, and after 1548, when its Latin source, Theodore Beza's *Poemata* (the epigram *Ponticus Cornelio de uxore non ducenda*) was published (see Rollins, II, 226, for the text).

Counsel against marriage. One's wife will either be ugly and hateful, or fair and wanton; chaste and prolific (with all the troubles children bring) or barren and shrewish. There is no blessedness in marriage. For counsels on marriage involving similar dread alternatives see **163, 343**, and Dr. Walter Haddon's *Vxor Non est Ducenda* (cited Rollins, II, 227). Each of these three has a palinode (see **260**).

260. Sythe, Vincent, I haue minde to wed a wife.

Attributed by Merrill to Nicholas Grimald, but Rollins accepts the ascription to "G. Blackwood," not otherwise identified.

G. Blackwood to. N. Vincent, with weddyng.

(1) *Tottel's Miscellany* (in the first edition only); Rollins, I, 95; see also II, 226 (9 couplets).

Between 1548 and 1557 (see **259**).

Denies the dread alternatives of marriage in **259**. Each alternative may be dealt with. This answer is from Beza's palinode, *Cornelius Pontico de uxore ducenda.* Similar answers to attacks on marriage are comprised in Dr. Walter Haddon's *Vxor Est Ducenda* (Rollins, II, 227), **162**, and the last portion of **343**.

261. "Sire Clerk of Oxenford," oure Hooste said.

> By Geoffrey Chaucer.
> *The Clerk's Prologue and Tale* (for the *Envoy,* see **81**).
> (1)-(59) These authorities are the same as those cited for *The Wife of Bath's Prologue and Tale* (**58**). *The Clerk's Prologue and Tale* is imperfectly represented only in:
> (11) Cambridge University Library Mm. 2. 5.
> (12) Delamere-Penrose.
> (20) Harley 1239.
> *The Clerk's Prologue and Tale* appears (in every case imperfectly) also in the following MSS. which do not contain *The Wife of Bath's Prologue and Tale:*
> (60) Harley 5908.
> (61) Marquess of Bath, Longleat 257.
> (62) Royal Library, Naples, xiii. B. 29.
> (63) Phillipps 8299 (now Huntington Library, MS. HM 140).
> (64) Rawlinson C. 86.

(The foregoing list has been compiled from McCormick and Heseltine on the principles cited under **58**. Exclusive of the *Envoy* this prologue and tale, which begins the E1 fragment of the *Canterbury Tales,* consists of 1176 lines. The *Envoy* embodies lines 1177-1212. For certain spurious or canceled links which follow the *Envoy* see Robinson, *Chaucer,* p. 1009. For editions and commentary see Robinson, pp. 121, 814; Hammond, *Chaucer,* p. 303; Griffith, *Chaucer,* p. 97; Martin, *Chaucer,* p. 56; and the current bibliographies.)

Earlier editors placed it in the seventies (Skeat said about 1373), and considered that the *Envoy* and other modifications to fit it into the *Tales* were made much later. Several recent students (especially Tatlock and Sisam) have argued that *The Clerk's Tale* itself may well have been composed in the Canterbury period (about 1385-95). See Robinson, p. 815.

The Clerk tells the tale of Patient Griselda, model of all wives, and ends soberly with the statement that the tale is told "nat for that wyves sholde / Folwen Grisilde as in humylitee, / For it were inportable, though they wolde," but so that every person whatever his estate might be constant as Griselda in adversity. Since Griselda was so obedient to a mortal man, we should likewise receive in submission all that God sends us. But then, in a jesting afterthought, he points out that Griseldas are rare nowadays. For the love of the Wife of Bath and "al hire secte" he will now sing a song (the *Envoy*) counseling wives how to rule their husbands. In the opinion of most recent scholars, this tale forms the second section of the "Marriage Group"; and represents the ascetic Clerk's answer to the lusty Wife of Bath. Perhaps it is this incipient debate more than anything else which has led us too often to label satire on women as clerical or "monkish." We must not forget that Chaucer himself was not a monk, and that his most vitriolic spokesman for the satirical point of view was an experienced layman, the Merchant. For the next step in the debate (the Merchant's) see **339**.

262. Schir! thocht your Grace hes put gret ordour.

By Sir David Lyndsay.

Ane Supplicatioun directit frome Schir Dauid Lyndesay, knicht, to the Kingis grace, in Contemptioun of Syde Taillis.

(1) *The Warkis of the famous and worthie knicht, Schir Dauid Lyndesay. Newly correctit and augmentit.* Edinburgh, J. Scot, at the expensis of H. Charteris, 1568 (the *STC*, nos. 15658-70, lists this first edition of the works and twelve others before 1640); ed. Douglas Hamer, *The Works of Sir David Lindsay of the Mount, 1490-1555*, Edinburgh (STS, Third Series, I, II, VI, VIII), 1930-34, I, 117; David Laing, *The Poetical Works of Sir David Lyndsay*, Edinburgh, 1879, I, 128; Fairholt, *Satirical Songs and Poems on Costume*, p. 69; for further editions see Hamer, III, 143, and Laing, I, 286-289 (88 couplets).

(2) Laing mentions two separate or broadside editions which I have been unable to identify in the *STC*. He gives variants to one of them (I, 289).

Since the poem refers directly to Queen Madeleine, wife of James V, Hamer dates 1537-42, preferably 1539-41.

Satire on woman's fashions, especially the trains or "long tails" which sweep the streets and gather to themselves all the dirt in the city. It is all right for a queen or an empress [like Madeleine, who may have brought the fashion from France] to wear trains for dignity, but every lady in the land will ape her. Nay, even "mureland Meg, that milkit the yowis," has to wear trains. The dust rises in clouds when they walk down the street. Lovers fall out of love again when they see the filthy state of these trains. Another fault is wearing muzzles or mufflers. A woman's beauty need not be hidden (unless she is on some clandestine errand). Good women will not object to this rural rime; those who do are harlots whose face is red. "Tails" are satirized also in **309** and **369**.

263. So prayiss me as ʒe think causs quhy.

Remeidis of Luve.

(1) Advocates' Library 1. 1. 6 (8 four-line stanzas); ed. Ritchie,

> *Bannatyne Manuscript,* IV, 1; see also Hunterian Club
> *Bannatyne,* I, ciii.

1568 or before.

Rebellious lover; I'll treat you just as you treat me. Compare **299**.

264. Sum be mery, and sum be sade.

Of the Different Sorts of Women; or *Song on Woman.*
Burden to MS. (1): "Women, women, love of women
                        Maketh bare pursis with sum men."
Burden to MS. (2): "Women, women, women, women,
                        A song I syng even off women."
   (1) Balliol College Oxford 354 (two-line burden and 6 seven-
       line stanzas); ed. Greene, *Early English Carols,* p. 267 (no.
       401A), with variants of (2); ed. Dyboski, *Songs, Carols*
       (EETSES, CI), p. 113; Flügel, *Anglia,* XXVI (1903), 276;
       Denys K. Roberts, *Straw in the Hair,* London, 1938, p. 183.
   (2) Bodleian Eng. poet. e. 1; ed. Wright, *Songs and Carols*
       (Percy Society), p. 89; J. E. Masters, *Rymes of the
       Minstrels,* p. 30. Combined text of (1), (2), and **265** in
       Chambers and Sidgwick, *Early English Lyrics,* p. 214.
MS. (2), the earliest authority, is of the second half of the XV
cent.

> Some are merry, some sad, some busy, some bad, yet all are not so,
>   For sum be lewed,
>   And sum be shrewed;
>   Go, shrew, whersoeuer ye go.

This is the typical pattern of stanza and argument. The satirical charges
are against woman's folly, easily aroused anger, drunkenness, ugliness,
and talkativeness. In each case the charge is answered, but the residue
seems to be in the direction of satire, in view of the refrain and burden.
Yet one basic element in the conventional defense, the insistence on the
dangers of generalization, plays an important part in the poem. See **265**
for another version. Chambers, p. 368, notices a XVII cent. catch with
the same formula.

265. Some be nyse as a nonne hene.

Of the Different Sorts of Women; or *Song on Woman.*
Burden: "Women, women, loue of women
                Make bare purs with some men."
   (1) Lambeth Palace 306 (two-line burden and 7 seven-line
       stanzas); ed. Greene, *Early English Carols,* p. 268 (no.
       401B); Wright and Halliwell, *Reliquiae Antiquae,* I, 248;
       F. J. Furnivall, ed., *The Wright's Chaste Wife,* London
       (EETS, XII), 1888, p. 25. See also **264***;* and Brown and
       Robbins, *Index,* no. 3171.

The MS. is of the XV cent.

Another version of **264** which differs sufficiently to permit Greene to say (p. 431) that the two "probably represent the activities of at least two different authors, writing to the same air and according to an easy and suggestive formula." The relationship is a bit closer than Greene implies, since the burden, refrain, and two stanzas are practically identical. In addition to the charges cited under **264** we may notice the additional claims that woman is fastidious (as a nun's hen), wanton, flattering, and untruthful. He who made this song

> Came of the north and of the sothern blode,
> And somewhat kyne to Robyn Hode.

266. Som do entende.

Song on Deferring Marriage.

(1) Harley 2252 (5 four-line stanzas); ed. Wright and Halliwell, *Reliquiae Antiquae*, I, 258; Flügel, *Neuenglisches Lesebuch*, I, 140 (there wrongly printed as part of **225**).

MS. of the time of Henry VIII.

Counsel to young men to marry while they are young, and not to wait until they grow old in order to marry a wealthy wife. When they grow old the wealthy women won't have them.

267. Sum man luvis for leill luve and delyte.

(1) Advocates' Library 1. 1. 6 (1 rime-royal stanza); ed. Ritchie, *Bannatyne Manuscript*, IV, 40; see also Hunterian Club *Bannatyne*, I, cvi (no. 289).

1568 or before.

Earthly love against heavenly.

268. Sum wyfes of the borroustoun.

Sir Richard Maitland.

Satire on the Toun Ladyes.

(1) Magdalene College Cambridge, Pepys 2553 (lines 1-50 missing); ed. W. A. Craigie, *Maitland Folio Manuscript*, I, 299, with variants from (2); for further editions see II, 111.

(2) Magdalene College Cambridge, Pepys 1408 (22 five-line stanzas); ed. W. A. Craigie, *Maitland Quarto Manuscript*, p. 1; Fairholt, *Satirical Songs and Poems on Costume*, p. 91.

The *Maitland Folio*, which is the earliest authority, was composed 1570-85.

Satire on woman's vanity in clothes and cosmetics, with special reference to the bourgeois wives who ape the nobility and waste their husband's money.

269. Sum wemen wepyn of peure feminite.

Stanza 111 of Benedict Burgh's *Cato Major.*

(1) British Museum Additional 29729 (1 rime-royal stanza);
I have transcribed it for publication. Brown, *Register*, II, 89,
lists thirty MSS. and two editions of the whole poem. For
this stanza see Max Förster, *Archiv*, CXV (1905), 322.

Burgh died in 1483. Förster, *Archiv*, CI (1898), 46-47, dates
the *Cato Major* 1433-40. The MS. is in the hand of John Stow
(1525?-1605), but the Burgh extract appears on the flyleaf, probably
in another hand.

This "flower" from Burgh qualifies as a miniature satire on woman's
crocodile tears.

270. Somtyme Y louid, so do Y yut.

The note at the end of the poem, "desor mais," may mean
"henceforth I shall not love"; it may be a scribe's pen name (note
the numerous scribal signatures in the MS. cited by Greene, p. 340);
or it may be a kind of motto (see Huizinga, *Waning of the Middle
Ages*, p. 211). It is probably not the name of an author.

The Delivered Lover.

Burden: "Vp, son and mery wether,
                Somer draweth nere."

(1) Cambridge University Library Ff. 1. 6 (two-line burden
and 8 four-line stanzas); ed. Greene, *Early English Carols*,
p. 316 (no. 469); Wright and Halliwell, *Reliquiae Antiquae*,
I, 202; M. R. Adamson, *A Treasury of Middle English
Verse*, London, 1930, p. 149.

MS. second half XV cent.

Rebellious lover poem. I have escaped from the thralldom, and
can laugh at these lovers and sleep at night. May all who suffer someday
join with me in this song. The speaker may be referring to a constant
human love or marriage in his ambiguous first line, and hence intend
an insult to the courtly system with its "danger." But it is more likely
that the present love is *caritas* or heavenly love; in which event we may
recall that the carol type was largely developed by the Franciscan attempt
to secularize religious poetry (Greene, pp. cxi-cxxxii). The poem has
other obscurities. Greene (p. 452) would identify the speaker as "a
woman who has escaped from an affair with an unworthy lover and is
properly thankful." Presumably his conclusion is based upon mention
of some culprit, "that wyckid creature; / He and no mo" who "Ouer-
threw al my mater," since there is nothing else to suggest that a woman
is speaking. But it seems more likely that the wicked creature is the
perennial detractor or rival, Malebouche or Wikked Tunge, and that
the speaker is the usual complaining lover. Only courtly males were in
the habit of being "in danger" (stanza 1), of offering their "seruice"
(stanza 2), or of suffering from the lover's malady (stanzas 3, 5, 6).
This is not a parody courtly lyric, but it is similar in sentiment to that

genre, and does appear to echo a serious lover's complaint in the same MS. (Greene, no. 442).

Sum tyme wyfis sa grave hes bene (268).

271. Sore this dere strykyn ys.

The poem is signed "W. Cornysh" in MS. (1). As in **202**, Cornysshe may be only the composer of the accompanying music.

Burden or refrain begins "Blow ye horne hunter."

(1) British Museum Additional 31922 (six-line burden or refrain and 7 four-line stanzas); ed. Flügel, *Anglia,* XII (1889-90), 238.

(2) Royal Appendix 58 (burden or refrain only); ed. Flügel, p. 262, who cites another edition by Chappell.

The Royal MS., which is the earliest authority, was composed in the first quarter of the XVI cent., and Cornysshe is thought to have died in 1524.

Under the guise of hunting language (see **7**) the poet describes his encounter with an amorous wench.

271a. Spektakle of luf Or delectatioun of luf of wemen, þe lytill buk entitillit and callit the [prose].

Signed "per M G. Myll."

(1) Lord Talbot de Malahide, Dublin, MS. Asloan; ed. W. A. Craigie, *The Asloan Manuscript,* Edinburgh (STS, XIV, XVI), 1923-24, I, 271; see also I, viii.

The MS. was composed about 1515, in the reign of James V of Scotland. The translation is dated July 10, 1492.

As the author "was musing vpone þe restles besynes of þis translatory world" he found a little book in Latin which he decided should "be had in to our wulgar and matarnall toung." It consisted of examples told to a lusty squire by his father, a "gud ald knycht," in order to warn him against the delights of the flesh and the love of women. Aristotle, Ovid, "Hermes," St. Gregory, St. Bernard, Diogenes, Solenius, Socrates, Secundus, Seneca, Plato, and others among the saints and philosophers have all inveighed against lechery. Many examples are cited: against the love of women in general, against the love of young women, of married women, of widows and aged women, and of nuns. These stories are from the Bible, the classics, and medieval chronicle and romance. Many of them are unusual in Scots or English, among them the tale of Buridan and the Queen of Navarre. In his conclusion the old knight urges his son to marry a chaste woman of good family, and to rule her well. The translation was made in the city of "Sandris" (St. Andrews?) and Myll begs that women will not misjudge him, since any fault is due to his original. This original has not been identified. For an English *Spectacle of Louers* see **66**.

272. Stel is gud, I sey no odur.

Women Compared to Steel.

Burden: "War yt, war yt, war yt wele:
Wemen be as trew as stele."

(1) St. John's College Cambridge S. 54 (two-line burden and
5 four-line stanzas); ed. Greene, *Early English Carols,*
p. 266 (no. 400); see for another edition p. 431.

MS. of the second half of the XV cent.

The refrain and burden pretend to flatter women with the statement "Wemen be as trew as stele." But women are charged with being
as shrewish as Cain's brothers (the friars?), with falsehood, sharp
tongues, fickleness, ugliness, and flattery. Ironic praise, if we are to
give the poet any credit for calculating his effect correctly. Since the
Virgin Mary was called as true as steel (see Brown, *Religious Lyrics of
the XIVth Century,* p. 180) we may conjecture that our carol writer is
answering some defense of women in which the Virgin was cited as
usual. For other occurrences of this comparison see Greene, p. 431.

273. Somer is comen wiþ loue to toune.

The Thrush and the Nightingale; headed in the MS. *Ci comence
le cuntent parentre le Mauuis & la russinole.*

(1) Digby 86 (32 six-line stanzas); ed. with variants of (2)
F. Holthausen, *Anglia,* XLIII (1919), 53; ed. Hazlitt,
Remains, I, 50; Brown, *English Lyrics of the XIIIth Cen-
tury,* p. 101; for further editions and notes see Wells,
Manual, pp. 831, 1126, 1510, 1625, 1719.

(2) Advocates' Library 19. 2. 1 (Auchinleck MS.) (stanzas 1-4,
7-8, and first two lines of 9; in all 75 lines only); for
editions see Brown, p. 207.

MS. Digby, according to Wells (p. 422), is dated 1272-83, and
was associated with Redmarley, Worcestershire (*SWMl*), Brown
(pp. xxix-xxxiii) observes. Brown (*Register*) calls it "*Ca.* 1275."

When summer and love had come to our land I heard "a strif"
between the thrush and the nightingale on women's worth. The nightingale defended them and the thrush called them fickle fiends. Nightingale: women are courteous and bring men happiness. Thrush: they are
fair but false, and Alexander was harmed by them. Nightingale: there
is not one wicked lady among a thousand; they are meek and shamefast.
Thrush: they are lustful, I have found, Adam knew their wickedness.
Nightingale: they are the greatest joy that man can have when he holds
them in his arms. Thrush: Gawain sought far and wide and never
found a true one. Nightingale: you lie and shall be punished; I have
heard of them nothing but good. Thrush: think of Constantine's Queen,
who loved a deformed beggar! Nightingale: you shall be put in prison
for your false charges. Thrush: Think of Samson, whose wife sold him.

Nightingale: woman is beautiful, fair of speech, and consolation to man. Thrush: among a hundred there are not five chaste ones who do not work for man's destruction. Nightingale: the world was saved by Christ's Mother. Thrush: I was mad to strive with thee; for the Virgin destroys all my argument. For the first bird-debate on the subject of women see **112**. This is the second, and purports to be from a French *estrif;* the first suggests as its original a Latin *altercacio.* For other such debates see **129, 139, 286, 313,** and **323.** In view of the growing list of parallels between MS. Digby 86 and the most famous lyric MS. in Middle English, Harley 2253 (see Brown, p. xxxvii), we may note the following ties between this poem and pieces in Harley: (1) *Annot and Johon* (Brown, p. 136) appears to allude to a contentious thrush, perhaps to the thrush of this poem. (2) The first line recalls "Lenten ys come wiþ loue to toune," a courtly lyric which also contrasts the "nyhtegales" and the threatening "þrestelcoc" and complains that with all creatures wooing, including the worm under the clod, "wymmen waxeþ wounder proude." MS. Auchinleck actually confuses the two poems by altering "Somer" to "Lenten." (3) *Le Blasme des Femmes,* which appears in both MSS., shares with our poem an unusual allusion to Constantine's Wife. After a rather extensive search for this story (the results of which I intend to publish elsewhere) I have found only these two allusions (one Middle English and one Anglo-Norman) in England, although the story is widespread on the Continent. The exact meaning of these parallels is not entirely clear; interpretation awaits a painstaking comparison of these two great lyric anthologies of the XIII century in all their details. Work on the two has suffered so far by being limited either to the French pieces (Stengel) or to the English (Brown). All the contents, French, Latin, and English, deserve to be studied as a unit in order to reveal important relationships between early Middle English and the Continent, among them the *estrif* background of *The Thrush and the Nightingale.* Another interesting point is the possibility that our poem stems from that important class of educated men, the lawyers, who were neither unlettered nor members of the clergy. The legal form of *The Owl and the Nightingale* is well attested (see Atkins' edition, Cambridge, 1922, p. liii; and R. M. Wilson, *Early Middle English Literature,* London, 1939, p. 160). In *The Thrush* we have nothing like the elaborate legal setting of the earlier poem, but we may have echoes of the law-court in several places: (1) "I take witnesse" (line 46); (2) the threat of exile (84, 127, 179); (3) the nightingale's insistence on his legal domain (97).

274. Somer passed / and Wynter Well begone.

A translation of *Les Quinze Joyes de Mariage,* attributed to Antoine de la Sale, and probably composed in the early XV cent., perhaps as late as 1450 (on these disputed points see F. P. Wilson, ed., *The Batchelars Banquet,* Oxford, 1929, pp. xv-xvi). Hazlitt, *Remains,* IV, 73, assigns this early XVI cent. translation to "Henry Fielding," on what grounds I do not know. Wilson (p. xxxv) suggests that it was by Robert Copland, who did many translations from the French for de Worde.

The .xv. Joyes of maryage.

(1) Wynkyn de Worde [*ca.* 1507?]. I am indebted to Dr. E. L. Pafort, of the Pierpont Morgan Library, for a detailed description of the Morgan copy and for many other facts about the book. The *STC* (no. 15258) lists two copies, one at the Bodleian and another in the Harmsworth collection, and treats them as one edition. In Dr. Pafort's opinion "The Bodleian fragments (Douce fragm. e. 10 of only sigg. C4-5) belong to a different setting of type, slightly earlier, possibly [of] the year 1507."

(2) Wynkyn de Worde (1509). According to Dr. Pafort, two copies belong here, the Harmsworth copy, now HH 130/6 in the Folger Shakespeare Library, and the Macro-Heber-Britwell copy, not listed in the *STC,* and now no. 21589 in the Pierpont Morgan Library. Since the Folger copy is imperfect (lacking 6 leaves), the only perfect copy of any extant edition is in the Morgan collection. None of these has ever been reprinted, but there is a brief extract from the Morgan copy in Wilson, p. xxxvi.

The translation may have been made for the press, and perhaps, like the first edition, it may be dated about 1507. See under author for the date of the original.

The translation begins with a "Prologue of the translatoure," followed by a "Prohemye of the auctour," the former in eleven and the latter in thirty seven-line stanzas. The text proper, which begins "The fyrst Joy of maryage is this," is in couplets (I am unaware of the exact number). The original, in French prose, has been often translated into English, and has retained its popularity until the present day (as is evidenced by Richard Aldington's translation of 1926). For the history of its reputation in England see Wilson, pp. xxxv-xli. Too long to summarize here, it contains an ironic treatment of women's vices, and omits none of the usual charges. The formula on which it is based is that of the Five Joys of Mary—in itself a malicious bit of paradox, since the Blessed Virgin was conventionally cited in defense of her sex. Perhaps the most celebrated chapter is the third, in which the author describes the consolations bestowed on a woman in childbed by her gossips, and the harsh words endured by the husband from their lips. The author of *Les Quinze Joyes* refers in his prologue to Valerius and to Matheolus; he probably made direct use of the latter as well as of Jean de Meun and Deschamps. It will thus be seen that he was in the main current of the satirical tradition. The standard edition is that of Ferdinand Heuckenkamp, Halle, 1901.

Sythe (see **Since**).

Take hede and lerne, thou lytell childe, and se (75).

275. Take iij claterars.

    (1) The "Brome MS.," owned by the Hon. Mrs. R. Douglas Hamilton, Diss, Norfolk (may be in prose, but could be arranged into the semblance of 10 lines of verse on the model of the Bodleian version); ed. Lucy T. Smith, *A Commonplace Book of the Fifteenth Century*, London, 1886, p. 12.

    (2) Bodleian Eng. poet. e. 1 (10 lines); ed. Wright, *Songs and Carols* (Percy Society), p. 4; Padelford, in *CHEL*. II, 437; J. E. Masters, *Rymes of the Minstrels*, p. 20.

Both authorities are of the second half of the XV cent.

The first version has five triads: three "claterars"—a pie, a jay, and a woman; three shrews—a wasp, a weasel, and a woman; and the like. In each case the second line is hidden by a simple cipher, and the fifth triad has been swollen to four. The second version looks like someone's attempt to convert the first from a simple riddle to a carol, by prefacing a burden (?):

    Herfor, and therfor, and therfor I came,
    And for to preysse this praty woman.

These two lines, if repeated, would create a pattern of ironic denial of general satire on women much like that in **272** or **136**. The second version drops one of the original triads.

276. Tanglid I was in loves snare.

By Sir Thomas Wyatt (signed "T. V." in the MS.).

    (1) British Museum Additional 17492 (6 six-line stanzas); ed. Foxwell, *Poems of Sir Thomas Wiat*, I, 329; E. M. W. Tillyard, *The Poetry of Sir Thomas Wyatt*, London, 1929, p. 84.

Foxwell (II, 166) would place this among Wyatt's "Court group," which she dates 1532-35. Wyatt died in 1542.

Rebellious lover, with a rebuke of his erstwhile mistress' hypocrisy, and a refrain which is an outburst of joy at his escape from her net:

    But ha! ha! ha! full well is me,
    For I am now at libertye.

Foxwell (II, 166) says this poem is an imitation of Serafino's *First Barzaletto* (from the 1516 edition).

277. Tell you I chyll.

By John Skelton.
Here After Foloweth the Booke Called Elynour Rummynge. The Tunnyng of Elynour Rummyng Per Skelton Laureat.

    (1) *Certayne bokes, compyled by mayster Skelton*, R. Lant for H. Tab [1545?]. *STC*, no. 22598.

    (2) [Another edition], J. Kynge and T. Marche [1560?]. *STC*,

no. 22599. Ed. with "collations" from (1), (3), (4), and (7) by Dyce and Child, *Poetical Works of Skelton*, I, 109 (623 lines); from this edition by Henderson, *Complete Poems of John Skelton*, p. 99, and [Richard Hughes], *Poems by John Skelton*, London, 1924, p. 39; see also Dyce and Child, III, 88.

(3) [Another edition], J. Day [1565?]. *STC*, no. 22600.

(4) *Pithy, pleasaunt and profitable workes of Maister Skelton*, T. Marshe (1568). *STC*, no. 22608.

(5) *Elynor Rumming*, J. Busbie and G. Loftis (1609). *STC*, no. 22612.

(6) *The Tunning of Elynour of Rumming*, n.p. (1624). *STC*, no. 22613.

(7) *Elynour Rummin, the famous ale-wife of England*, S. Rand (1624). *STC*, no. 22614.

(The foregoing list is a compilation of information in Dyce and Child and in the *STC*; I cannot vouch for its completeness or accuracy. This poem may exist in others of the numerous collections cited in the *STC*. Skelton bibliography is still an uncharted wilderness.)

Referred to in *The Garland of Laurel* (*ca.* 1522-23), which gives us a certain upward limit (see William Nelson, *John Skelton, Laureate*, New York, 1939, p. 248). Friedrich Brie, "Skelton-Studien," *ESt*, XXXVII (1906-1907), 48, dates the poem about the same time as *Philip Sparrow*, *ca.* 1506-1512. There is no certain autobiographical content.

The most celebrated of the ale-wife poems. Skelton at his best, which implies everything that is peculiar to him, everything that is traditional in type, everything that is representative of his transitional age with its love for the grotesque. In the prologue he describes his heroine in all her incredible ugliness of dress and feature. Throughout his portrait is threaded with an elusive sympathy which recalls Chaucer's Wife of Bath and Dunbar's Kind Kittok, and which, like them, seems to suggest that the author was in part sketching from life rather than merely continuing satirical convention (Brie denies, however, that there was a real Elynour). The contrasts between flattering phrases like "comely gyll," "somwhat sage," and catalogues of ugliness like "lothely lere. . . . Scuruy and lowsy," and the merging of the two in oxymoron ("She is vgly fayre") are in part a reflection of this sympathy and in part an inheritance from the sarcasm of the parody panegyric (see **226**). *Primus passus* introduces us to Elynour's function as a brewer of "noppy ale," and to the horde of slatternly wenches and housewives who frequent her ale-stake. *Secundus passus* describes their lack of cash, Elynour's rebukes, and her marvellous and dreadful recipe for ale. *Tertius passus* describes the household goods which the gossips barter for drink. This theme is continued in the next four *passus,* intermingled with other startling portraits and lively horseplay. The poem is followed by Latin prose and verse bits which seem to indicate that the poet's intent was to satirize woman's garrulity, slovenliness, and drunkenness (Brie, however, believes that the Latin was composed separately). The closest parallel to the poem is "I shall you tell a full good sport" (**107**) under which I have collected further ale-wife poems. Brie (pp. 48-49) and Dyce and Child (III, 95) note the similarity to Lorenzo de Medici's *Simposio* or *I Beoni,* but feel that Skelton had probably never seen Lorenzo's work, composed before his death in 1492 but not printed until 1568. Nelson (p. 51) points out a parallel between *Elynour Rummyng* and the pulpit attacks of St. Thomas More on gluttony. But there is an artistic tolerance in the poem which is not evident in More. For excellent discussions of Skelton's satire on women, and on *Elynour Rummyng* in particular, see Arthur Koelbing, *Zur Charakteristik John Skelton's,* Stuttgart, 1904, pp. 47-56, and Worcester, *Art of Satire,* pp. 61-66. A lost play, "Mother Rumming. C[omedy]," named in Edward Archer's list appended to *The Old Law* (1656), which is reprinted in W. W. Greg, *A List of Masques,* London, 1902, p. xc, may have been a late adaptation of Skelton's poem. But it is more likely that Archer saw some edition of the poem and wrongly assumed it to be a play.

278. Thankit be god and his appostillis twelf.

Aganis mariage of evill wyvis.

(1) Advocates' Library 1. 1. 6 (6 eight-line stanzas); ed. Ritchie, *Bannatyne Manuscript,* IV, 36; see also Hunterian Club *Bannatyne,* I, cvi.

1568 or before.

Bachelor's rejoicing. A rich wife is proud and contentious, a poor wife extravagant. I loved in my youth and was tormented; but I was saved from wedding. There is no difference "Betuix the gallowis and the spowsing claith." (Compare the English proverb "Wedding and hanging is destiny"; see **25, 91, 292,** and Rollins, *Analytical Index,* no. 2216.)

279. The auncient acquaintance, madam, betwen vs twayn.

By John Skelton.

(1) *Dyuers balettys and dyties solacyous,* [Richard Pynson], (n.d.); ed. Dyce and Child, *Poetical Works of Skelton,* I, 28; Philip Henderson, *Complete Poems of John Skelton,* p. 29 (6 rime-royal stanzas).

Skelton's dates are (1460?-1529). Duff, *Century,* pp. 126-27, places Pynson's works between the years 1486 and 1528 (he died in 1530). Brie, *ESt,* XXXVII (1906-1907), 40, would date poems of this kind 1490-98.

A variety of Rebellious Lover poem, although the love seems to be long past. Satire on woman's lust under the guise of horsemanship.

280. The angry Greekes for Helens rape preparde.

Translated by George Turbervile.

The Heroycall Epistles of the Learned Poet Publius Ovidius Naso.

(1) Henry Denham (1567); ed. Frederick Boas, London, 1928.
(2)-(8) *STC,* nos. 18941-47, lists seven further editions before 1640: [1569], [1570?], [1580?], 1600, 1636, and two in 1639.

If we accept 1544 as Turbervile's birth year (see John Erskine Hankins, *The Life and Works of George Turbervile,* University of Kansas Humanistic Studies, no. 25, 1940, p. 6), and allow him at least sixteen years to attain the training and perseverance to undertake such a translation, we may place the composition of the book between the years 1560 and 1567. During these years he was presumably at the Inns of Court (Hankins, pp. 7-8). Two isolated epistles were entered to Denham in 1566-67 (Hankins, p. 29).

In addition to the twenty-one epistles ascribed to Ovid and the three masculine answers ascribed to Aulus Sabinus, Turbervile provides us with prose prefaces and dedications, and, at the end, a set of verses headed *The Translator to the Captious Sort of Sycophantes.* Twelve of the epistles are in poulter's measure, six in "fourteeners," and six in blank verse. For discussions of the translation see Hankin, pp. 29-30, 38-44; and Henry B. Lathrop, *Translations from the Classics into English from Caxton to Chapman,* University of Wisconsin Studies in Language and Literature, no. 35, 1933, pp. 132-34. Essentially the *Heroides* is a defense of Cupid's martyrs (as is shown by its medieval imitators, Chaucer and Boccaccio); the masculine answers make the whole group a kind of debate on woman's worth. A special study of Ovid's influence on the medieval and early renaissance pattern of defense could well be made, especially in view of his kindred importance as a source for the satirical tradition in the *Ars Amatoria* and the *Remedia Amoris.* The *Ars Amatoria* was translated into English for the first time by Thomas Heywood in 1598; the *Remedia* by F. L. in 1600(?) (see Lathrop, p. 317). There was also a *Flores* or selection from the *Ars Amatoria* printed by Wynkyn de Worde in 1513; according to Lathrop (p. 21) this school text carefully avoids the "dishonest" (which probably means most of the satirical) portions of the original. Ovid's influence on the *Roman de la Rose* (and thus indirectly on the Wife of Bath) is well known; for other early English *Remedies of Love* see **263, 255,** and **174.** On early medieval translations and imitations of Ovid see William A. Neilson, *The Origins and Sources of the Court of Love,* Boston ([Harvard] *Studies and Notes,* VI), 1899, pp. 170-81.

281. The bachelor most joyfully.

(1) British Museum Additional 5665 (10 lines); ed. Chambers and Sidgwick, *Early English Lyrics,* p. 211; for further editions see p. 367.

The MS. was composed in the first quarter of the XVI cent.

Bachelor's rejoicing. A single man may make love where he will; a married man dare not arouse the jealousy of his wife Joan.

282. The beistlie lust, the furious appatite.

Probably not by William Dunbar, although included without question by Small in his edition. None of the four MSS. really ascribes the poem to Dunbar, but in (2) and (3) these six stanzas are followed by another poem signed "Quod dumbar," which Small takes as a last stanza. All the modern authorities (Mackenzie, Craigie, Schipper) except Small reject it from the canon (see Mac-Kenzie, p. 226), since our six stanzas are plainly marked "Explicit" at the end. A similar error appears to have caused the "quod chaw-seir" at the end of the fragment in (4). MacGregor, the copyist of (4), may have been misled by the fact that the following poem in (1) is **54**, ascribed (also erroneously) by Bannatyne to Geoffrey Chaucer.

Ballade Against Evil Women (the heading in Bannatyne, *Ballatis Aganis evill wemen,* applies to several poems which follow).

(1) Advocates' Library 1. 1. 6 (5 rime-royal stanzas); ed. Ritchie, *Bannatyne Manuscript,* IV, 32; see also Hunterian Club *Bannatyne,* I, cvi.

(2) Magdalene College Cambridge, Pepys 2553 (6 rime-royal stanzas); ed. W. A. Craigie, *Maitland Folio Manuscript,* I, 391. For the last stanza of Small's edition see I, 391, and MacKenzie, *Poems of William Dunbar,* p. 154 (printed separately as *A Prayer* or *Ane Orisoun). Ane Orisoun* is one eight-line stanza.

(3) Cambridge University Library Ll. 5. 10 (6 rime-royal stanzas); ed. with *Ane Orisoun* and variants from (1) by Small, *Poems of William Dunbar,* II, 266; for another edition see III, 355.

(4) "The Dean of Lismore's MS." (2 rime-royal stanzas corresponding to stanzas 2 and 3 of the Maitland copy, with the first line of stanza 3 missing); ed. Craigie, II, 124. Apparently this is the famous collection made in 1512-26 by Sir James MacGregor, dean of Lismore in Argyllshire, and his brother Duncan, and called *The Dean of Lismore's Book* in accordance with the practice of Celticists. Its major contents are Irish and Scottish Gaelic. According to Rudolf Thurneyson (*Die irische Helden- und Königsage,* Halle, 1921, p. 52) it is now MS. Advocates' Library XXXVII.

1568 or before (the date of Bannatyne, the earliest authority). Mackay's attempt in his introduction to Small (I, clxix) to assign it to the years 1508-1513 and to consider **219** as its palinode is of no value, since there is clearly no authority for attributing the poem to Dunbar at all.

One of the most violent satires against women's lasciviousness in this handlist. Women are held back by the disapproval of neither God nor man; all their trust is in their god Cupid. Like the "fowlest tyk" women seek the most unworthy lovers on whom to bestow their virginity. No matter how many seemly servants a lady may have she will "tak a crippill or a creatour / Deformit as ane owle be dame natour" (compare the story of Constantine's Wife mentioned under **273**). The clerks teach us the malice, wiles, and "colorit eloquence" of women. Women could beguile a man who combined in him the wit and strength of Solomon, Aristotle, Samson, and Hector. Follow them if you would learn inconstancy; if not "frome subtill huris dissivir." The bitterness of the poem has naturally disturbed modern commentators, among them Pinkerton, who delivered himself of the rather remarkable statement "A poor satire on women (who can write a good one?)." If, like I. A. Richards, we believe that a poem should retain meaning even though the reader's opinions have changed from those of the poet's time, we may accord this poem some praise for its rhetorical force. It employs the device of alliterating adjectives found also in **229**, and like that poem recalls earlier Latin poems of a highly ascetic intention. Our concession to its artistic merit need imply no approval of its theme; and, we have seen, the argument that Dunbar did not write it need not be based on our personal distaste or our qualms about a great Scottish poet's honor. From an artistic point of view it is not unworthy of Dunbar.

283. The chief gynnyng of grace and of vertue.

By John Lydgate.
An Epistle to Sibille, or *Letter to Lady Sibille.*
(1) Ashmole 59 (20 rime-royal stanzas); ed. MacCracken, *Minor Poems of Lydgate,* I, 14.

MS. composed between 1447 and 1456. Lydgate lived from about 1370 to 1448-49.

A praise of good women, based primarily on Prov. 31:10-31. In the concluding stanzas Lydgate asks wives, maids, and widows to follow the example of the virtuous woman who is above rubies and to eschew idleness, and in the envoy he begs ruth on the dullness of his style from "my ladye which cleped is Cybille." MacCracken (I, xx) suggests that Lydgate wrote the poem for Lady Sibille Boys of Holm Hale. Since I have found no verbal parallels, it may be mere coincidence that Christine's *Livre du Duc des Vrais Amans (Oeuvres Poétiques,* ed. Maurice Roy, Paris [SATF], 1886-96, III, 160-173) has an exchange of letters with Sebille de Monthault, dame de la Tour, on the subject of virtuous womanhood. For other poems influenced by the same Biblical passage see **59, 94, 388** and **389**. In 1568-69 John Allde was licensed to print "a boke intituled to *ye prayse of good women ye xiij chapter of ye Proverbis."* Presumably this is an error for "ye xxxj chapeter." See Arber, I, 378; and Collier, *Extracts,* I, 181. Compare also Prov. 12:4.

284. The diuill Is not to daly stryf.

> (1) Advocates' Library 1. 1. 6 (3 couplets); ed. Ritchie, *Bannatyne Manuscript,* IV, 23; see also Hunterian Club *Bannatyne,* I, cv.
>
> 1568 or before.

In daily living a woman is worse than the devil himself. Compare Elynour Rummyng (**277**), who is sib to the devil, and the celebrated Belphegor, a demon who married a shrewish woman who finally was expelled from hell because she tormented the Satanic crew beyond endurance.

The fyrst Joy of maryage is this (274).

285. The flickeryng fame that flieth from eare to eare.

> *Of the choise of a wife.*
> (1) *Tottel's Miscellany* (in all editions); ed. Rollins, I, 195.
>
> 1557 or before.

Choose your wife not because of fame and beauty, but because of virtue.

286. The god of love, a! benedicite!

Ascribed to Chaucer by Thynne and later editors including the usually skeptical Tyrwhitt. But since Bradshaw and Skeat the Clanvowe mentioned at the end of the Cambridge MS. has been accepted as author, and the debate has been confined to his identity. The candidates are Sir Thomas and two Sir John Clanvowes. One Sir John died on October 17, 1391, perhaps too early to have written this poem. Brusendorff favors Sir Thomas (see below under date). On the still unsettled problem see Wells, *Manual,* pp. 831, 1126, 1404, 1510, 1625, 1719; Hammond, *Chaucer,* p. 421; Skeat, *Canon,* p. 107; and for the best recent summary C. E. Ward, *MLN,* XLIV (1929), 217-26.

> *The Cuckoo and the Nightingale;* or *The Book of Cupid, God of Love.*
> (1) Cambridge University Library Ff. 1. 6 (58 five-line stanzas).
> (2) Bodleian Tanner 346 (adds a *balade* with *envoy,* according to Brown and Robbins, *Index,* no. 3361); ed. *Flowre and the Leaf and the Boke of Cupide,* Kelmscott Press, 1896.
> (3) Arch. Selden B. 24 (lines 1-246 only).
> (4) Bodley 638.
> (5) Bodleian Fairfax 16; ed. E. Vollmer, *Berliner Beiträge zur*

germanischen und romanischen Philologie, XVI, 1898 (adds
a *balade,* according to Brown and Robbins).

(6) Harley 7333.

(7) Thynne's *Chaucer* (1532); ed. with variants Skeat, *Chaucer,* VII, 347. For further editions see Wells and Hammond.

The date, still a matter of dispute, seems to lie somewhere
between 1390 and 1410. Brusendorff (*Chaucer Tradition,* pp. 441-44)
and Ward, on the basis of an allusion to Woodstock Manor, believe
it was written for the courtship of Sir Thomas Clanvowe, who
married Perinne Whettenye in 1392 and received a grant from
Queen Anne at Woodstock. This date would fit well with the
borrowings from Chaucer. Skeat had noted a supposed imitation
by Clanvowe of Hoccleve's title for the *Letter of Cupid, God of
Love* (**49**), and therefore dated *The Cuckoo* "about 1403, or at any
rate soon after 1402, which is the known date of The Letter of
Cupid." Desirous of setting the date back to 1392, Brusendorff and
Ward argue that Hoccleve may just as well have imitated the
alternative title of Clanvowe. They appear to have forgotten that
Hoccleve's title was dependent on his source, Christine's *L'Epistre
au Dieu d'Amours,* and that there may consequently be some merit
in Skeat's suggestion.

The suffering poet, who in springtime feels the access of Cupid's
power, dreams of a forest full of singing birds. The poet chides the
lewd Cuckoo's song, and a Nightingale also takes up the cudgels against
the Cuckoo, who retaliates with an attack upon the followers of love.
The Nightingale finally puts his enemy to rout, and thanks the poet
with the promise of a Parliament of Birds on St. Valentine's Day
"Before the chambre-window of the quene At Wodestok." The poem
differs from other bird-debates (see **273**) by virtue of its elaborate love-
vision structure, inherited from the *Roman de la Rose,* perhaps through
such intermediaries as Deschamps, Machaut, and Chaucer. There are
echoes of Chaucer's *Parliament* and *Knight's Tale,* as well as the cult
of the daisy in the *Legend.* Thus it is among the earliest of a long line
of Chaucerian imitations.

287. The hart lovyt þe wood, the hare lovyt þe hyll.

(1) The "Brome MS.," owned by the Hon. Mrs. R. Douglas
Hamilton, Diss, Norfolk (4 lines monorimed); ed. Lucy
T. Smith, *A Commonplace Book of the Fifteenth Century,*
London, 1886, p. 11.

The MS. is of the second half of the XV cent.

The hart loves the wood, the hare the hill, the knight his sword,
the churl his "byll," the fool his folly, the wise man his skill, and "The
properte of a shrod qwen ys to have hyr wyll." The epigrammatic turn
is fairly unusual for the XV cent. See **13**.

288. The life that erst thou ledst my friend.

By "I. P." Rollins suggests identification with John Pitt or Pitts, or with another unidentified I. P. who wrote a broadside on "A meruaylous straunge deformed Swyne," published by Richard Jones in 1571.

Dame Beauties replie to the Louer late at libertie: and now complaineth himselfe to be her captiue, Intituled: Where is the life that late I led.

(1) *A Handful of Pleasant Delights,* Richard Jones (1584); ed. Rollins, *Handful,* p. 15 (8 twelve-line stanzas).

Rollins dates the poem about 1566, since it appears to answer a ballad, now lost, entered to Richard Jones about March, 1566 (see *Handful,* pp. 88-89, and *Analytical Index,* no. 2019).

Defense of women. Dame Beauty answers the lover who complains of the yoke of love by saying that these supposed torments are all his own fault anyway. A mild version of the defense on the basis of men's wickedness (and folly).

289. The man ys blest.

The Discontented Husband.

(1) Cotton Vespasian A. 25 (6 six-line stanzas); ed. Böddeker, *JbREL,* XIV (1875), 214 (for further editions see Böddeker).

Böddeker dates the MS. 1578, but many of the poems in it have been identified with earlier broadsides. Rollins, *Analytical Index,* nos. 3006-3007, suggests that this may be an answer to *Wemen be best when they be at Rest,* entered in 1557-58 to John Wally and Mrs. Toy, and in 1559 to John Sampson. For Collier's version of the original ballad see **382.**

The man is blest who lives in [domestic] rest; the man is cursed who first gave his wife her will. Now all women rule. Let us pray to God that he redress the balance. Satire on woman's shrewishness and desire for the mastery.

290. The mare is so mynyone.

Tanner ascribed this ballad to William Keth, according to Ritson-Hazlitt. Keth was an exile at Frankfort during Queen Mary's reign.

Burden or refrain:

"Ty the mare, Tom boy, ty the mare, Tom boy,
    Lest she stray
    From the awaye,
  Now ty the mare, Tom boy."

(1) Harley 7568 (four-line burden and 8 eight-line stanzas);

ed. Joseph Ritson, *Ancient Songs and Ballads,* 3rd ed., rev. W. C. Hazlitt, London, 1877, p. 175.

The editors note that Ames had placed this poem under the year 1547, "though for what reason does not appear." It is not entered in Rollins' *Analytical Index* (which means that it is not listed as a ballad in the *Stationers' Register*). There was a William Kethe who died about 1608 (see *DNB*) and who accompanied Ambrose Dudley, Earl of Warwick, to Havre in 1563 as minister to the (Protestant) English army. This poem may have been writen for that occasion (Kethe is known as a metrical translator of the Psalms printed in the English psalter of 1561); it could well have been used as a stirring marching song. But this is a mere guess on my part; anti-Catholic ballads could have been written in any of the last seventy years of the XVI cent. Since this poem and a related one in *Tom Tyler and his Wife* (**193**) are both undated, their relationship solves no problems.

Tom's mare is hard to rule. This simple point is developed with many variations. An allusion to "Avynion" makes it fairly certain that the mare is the unruly Catholic Church, and that it is therefore to be identified with Ames' "A ballet, declaring the fall of the whore of Babylone, intituled, Tye thy mare Tom-boye &c." But the author was probably not unaware that Tom's skittish horse was usually identified with his wife (see **327**, which has a very similar burden). The poem therefore begs to be interpreted on the surface as a satire on woman's shrewishness, and only beneath as a piece of Reformation satire. Whether the play *Tom Tyler* preceded this poem or not we do not know; but certainly Tom's difficulties with his wife must have existed in song, ballad, or proverb before "The mare is so mynyone."

291. The most worthye she is in toune.

In Praise of Ivy.
Burden: "Ivy, chefe off treis it is;
          Veni, coronaberis."
(1) Bodleian Eng. poet. e. 1 (two-line burden and 4 four-line stanzas); ed. Greene, *Early English Carols,* p. 95 (no. 138); Chambers and Sidgwick, p. 236 (with important notes on Holly and Ivy on p. 374); Wright, *Songs and Carols* (Percy Society), p. 85; for another edition see Brown and Robbins, *Index,* no. 3438.
MS. second half of the XV cent.

Defense of Ivy, perhaps in answer to the Praise of Holly discussed under **85** (for the tradition see **86**). Hence a defense of women which debates their worth with a praise (or rather boast) of men. The phrase "Veni coronaberis" links the poem with the Virgin Mary, that perennial defender of her sex; it comes ultimately from the *Song of Songs.* The

Virgin is elsewhere linked to Holly (see Greene, p. ciii). In **206** the
speaker mentions "the roughe Hollye / that turnethe itt ofte into Godes
bodye."

292. The prouerb olde whoso denieth.

Attributed to Edward Gosynhill by the *STC*, Corser (see below), and Collier (*Extracts*, I, 3; *Bibliographical and Critical Account*, II, 74) on the assumption that Gosynhill in his answer to
this poem, *Mulierum Pean* (**347**), is referring to himself as author
of both poems. There Gosynhill describes a dream in which a group
of women came to see him, and asked him to

> Consyder our grefe, and howe we be blamed
> And all by a boke, that lately is past
> Which by reporte, by the was fyrst framed
> The scole of women, none auctour named
> In prynte it is passed, lewdely compyled
> All women wherby be sore reuyled.
>
> Consyder therin, thyne owne good name
> Consyder also our infamye
> Sende forth some other, contrary the same
> For thyne and ours, bothe honestye
> The *Pean* thou write, and lyeth the bye.

Taken by itself this might have been accepted without question as
a frank admission of the authorship of the *Scholehouse*. Nor would
there be anything to deter us from such an inference in the dis-
similar positions of the two poems, one a lively satire and the other
a defense. The convention of satire and palinode is too old and too
continuous (Stesichorus, Ovid, Jean Le Fèvre, Boccaccio, Chaucer,
Lydgate, Dunbar, Pyrrye) to disturb us as a possibility in the case
of Gosynhill. But the question is complicated by a bibliographical
mystery. The *Scholehouse* itself says:

> A foole of late contriued a book,
> And all in praise of the femynie;
> Who so taketh labour it to ouer look,
> Shall prooue all is but flattery;
> *Pehan* he calleth it: it may wel be,
> The pecock is proudest of his faire taile,
> And so are all women of their apparail.

Hazlitt, *Remains*, IV, 105, objects to the inference that Gosynhill
wrote the *Scholehouse* on the following grounds.

   1. Gosynhill does not plainly state that he is the author of the
      Scholehouse, but merely says it was charged to him "by
      reporte."

2. Gosynhill signed *Mulierum Pean* with three acrostics and one
   distinct mention of his name (Hazlitt seems to imply that
   such a publicity seeker would name himself explicitly in the
   Scholehouse as well, if he had written it).

Miss White and Stein accept Hazlitt's arguments, and reject
Gosynhill's authorship of the *Scholehouse* with something like finality. The *CBEL* (I, 716) states flatly "Incorrectly attrib. to Edward
Gosynhill." These are strong arguments, and we must certainly
admit that the case for Gosynhill is far from proved. But there are
some factors which the exponents of anonymity have not considered.

   1. It is true that "by reporte" is ambiguous. But there is nothing
      in the poem to make us believe that the "reporte" is a false
      calumny. If Gosynhill was subject to an erroneous attribution
      he would no doubt have spent several stanzas telling us so,
      and reviling slanderous tongues.
   2. Gosynhill's failure to sign the *Scholehouse* may be due to
      several causes.
      a) Since the *Scholehouse* was a bitter attack on women, an
      untried author might well have been diffident in attach-
      ing his name to it. The attempt, conventional or serious,
      to beg off from the supposed dread results of writing a
      satire on women is well represented in many of the poems
      of this Index. Praise of women, on the other hand, re-
      vealed one as a courtly gentleman deserving of the favor
      of womankind.
      b) When he named himself in *Mulierum Pean* he was pre-
      sumably by that time the successful author of the *Schole-
      house* (which was to go into four editions during the
      century and to be constantly referred to by defenders of
      women as the satire *par exemple*). There was now an
      excellent reason for abandoning his feigned or real dif-
      fidence in acknowledging the satire; his name by this
      time meant something to the public, which, for all we
      know, may have been clamoring for it (remember *Wav-
      erley*). Moreover, his reputation among women would
      now be vindicated by *Mulierum Pean*.
   3. While this point may be coincidental, we should at least
      remark that the metrical structure of both poems is the same—
      rime-royal stanzas with a "broken-backed" four-accent line.
      It is perfectly possible, therefore, that Gosynhill was in effect
      signing his name to both poems in *Mulierum Pean*. But one
      further problem remains, the crisscross of references in the
      two poems. Hazlitt says, "It is difficult to explain how an
      allusion to the Paean could find its way into a tract printed

previously to the *Paean,* unless we suppose that Gosynhill
was dead when the later editions of the *Scholehouse of
Women* came from the press, and that somebody, not very
friendly to the original writer, introduced variations into the
text. We have never been able to meet with the first and
second editions, printed by Wyer and Petit." Miss White,
who had examined the Huntington Library copy of Petit's
edition (presumably of 1541; see below), invalidates Hazlitt's conjecture by the information that this first or second
edition preserves the allusion to *Mulierum Pean.* We must
therefore seek another explanation of the puzzle. I believe
that one is implicit in the lines quoted from *Mulierum Pean*
above. Gosynhill says that (according to report) he had
"framed" "a boke, that lately is past . . . the scole of women."
We may infer that this book has been published, and is identical with Petit's *Scholehouse* (and perhaps with the lost
Wyer). But the ladies counsel him to "Sende forth some other
. . . . The *Pean* thou wrote, and lyeth the bye." Now in the
Scholehouse he says merely "A foole of late contriued a
book . . . *Pehan* he calleth it." We may be allowed the conjecture that the *"Pehan"* had been written but not yet published. The difficulty, in short, will be resolved if we assume
that Gosynhill had written the two poems, and inserted *in
each manuscript* a reference to his other work. Petit (and
Wyer?) then published the *Scholehouse* anonymously. When
that satire proved successful, Middleton published *Mulierum
Pean* (probably in 1542) with Gosynhill's name attached and
the admission of the authorship of the first book retained
from the manuscript version. The words "lyeth the bye"
certainly suggest that the ladies who visited Gosynhill were
referring to a book which was already written and which
presumably lay by him in manuscript. A more careful collation of the editions may reveal new evidence, but in the light
of the facts which are available to me, I believe that this is
the most acceptable theory. It may be noted that the explanation of cross references in manuscript would not be entirely
invalidated if the *Scholehouse* were shown on other grounds
to be written by another; since such a hypothetical author
might well have exchanged manuscripts with Gosynhill (men
did not become deadly enemies because they took opposite
sides in the controversy about women). But the facts are most
simply explained on the theory that Gosynhill wrote both
tracts. (Hazlitt, *Remains,* IV, 143, adds a further conjecture

which cannot be followed up at this time: "*Thronis* . . . and
one or two other expressions, such as *tratise* . . . and *prent*,
. . . might favour a suspicion that the author of *The Schole
House* was a North Briton." One may remark that such cursory vocabulary tests are not usually very satisfactory even in
Middle English.)

The Petit edition (as described by Miss White) bears the title
*Here begynneth a lytle boke named the Schole house of women:
wherin euery man may rede a goodly prayse of the condicyons of
women.* According to Warton the Wyer edition omits the first "of
women" and has "prayer" instead of "praise."

(1) Thomas Petit. This edition is dated on the title page
    "M.D. XLi" and in the colophon "M.D. LXi"; which leads
    the *STC* (no. 12106) to date it without query as 1561. But
    Dibdin, Corser, Hazlitt, White, and Stein agree that the
    date of the colophon is erroneous, and that 1541 is the
    correct date. If an error had crept into the title page, the
    printer could have easily have seen and remedied it; but if,
    as seems more likely, an error was made in the colophon,
    resetting would be a more expensive process which might
    well have been foregone. Such typographer's logic is con-
    firmed by two other facts. First, Gosynhill's *Mulierum
    Pean* appeared as an answer to *The Scholehouse* probably
    in 1542 and certainly before 1547, when Middleton, its pub-
    lisher, died (for further remarks see **347**). Again, Thomas
    Petit's last printed book is dated 1548 (*STC*, no. 3363),
    and the last book printed for him is dated 1554 (*STC*, no.
    1010). The unique Huntington copy (*STC*, no. 12106) is
    described by Beatrice White, *Huntington Library Bulletin*,
    II (1931), 169-70.

(2) "Robert Wyer also printed an edition of *The Scole Howse*
    in 12mo, no date," according to Thomas Corser, *Collectanea
    Anglo-Poetica*, VII (1877), 32, who cites Dibdin and Ellis
    as authorities. See also *CHEL*, III, 552, and Hazlitt, *Re-
    mains*, IV, 97-98. The ultimate authority appears to have
    been Joseph Ames; see Ames-Herbert, *Typographical Anti-
    quities*, London, 1785-90, I, 375 (repeated without comment
    in Ames-Herbert-Dibdin). Warton appears also to have
    seen it; he dates it "1542, as it seems." H. R. Plomer, *Robert
    Wyer*, London, 1897, p. 51, is forced to fall back on Ames-
    Herbert. It is not mentioned in the *STC*, and thus it has
    had no independent witness since the XVIII cent. We have
    no way of knowing whether Wyer's edition preceded or fol-

lowed Petit's, but Corser is certainly wrong in saying that
Wyer did not print after 1542. William R. Parker informs
me that Wyer's very intermittent career lasted from 1530 to
[1556], if we are to accept the evidence of the *STC* (nos.
15128 and 21561). But 1542 is an attractive date on other
grounds than Corser's: Wyer did print the Vaughan-Burdet
Dyalogue defensyue (**323**) in that year, and the *Dyalogue*
is at least conjecturally an answer to the *Scholehouse.*

(3) John Kynge, 1560. The *STC* (no. 12105) lists a copy in the
British Museum and another in the Clawson collection; the
latter is now in the possession of Mr. Pforzheimer, according to Stein, *Library,* Series 2, XV (1934-35), 42. Described
by Stein, Hazlitt, and Corser. The *Scholehouse* was entered
to Kynge in 1557-58, which led Hazlitt to suggest that there
was an earlier edition by Kynge. No other evidence of such
an edition is available, and since Edward More's *Defence*
(**125**), an answer to the *Scholehouse,* was written and
entered to Kynge in the same years (1557-58), we may conjecture that Kynge picked up the *Scholehouse* for publication along with More's *Defence* and held it for three years
or so, when he published both of them together. No edition
of More before 1560 is known in spite of the date of preface
and *Register* entry; and it would be rather a coincidence
to assume lost editions of both More and the *Scholehouse.*
What caused Kynge's delay is unknown; we may recall,
however, that in these years Knox had raised the woman
question to a serious problem of state. The *First Blast* (**64**)
was published abroad in 1558, and John Aylmer's answer
(**84**) appeared in 1559, after Elizabeth had come to the
throne. If these events were a deterrent to the printer, their
efficacy vanished in 1560, when Kynge established a record
for himself with three and possibly five books on the
woman question (see Introduction, pp. 72-74).

(4) John Allde (1572) (147 seven-line stanzas). The *STC* (no.
12107) records only a copy at the Bodleian, which is edited
by [Edward Vernon Utterson], *Select Pieces of Early Popular Poetry,* London, 1817, II, 55. Utterson is reprinted with
variants of (3) by Hazlitt, *Remains,* IV, 105.

(The *STC* further lists, as no. 12104, *The vertuous scholehous*
[**337**], but this prose dialogue has no connection with our piece
except its title.)

If Petit's edition is the first, we may conjecture that the *Scholehouse* was written in 1541 or shortly before. This date squares with

the definite allusion in *Mulierum Pean* (1542?), the conjectural allusion in the Vaughan-Burdet *Dyalogue defensyue* (1542), and with certain events of the late 1530's which may have been alluded to in the *Scholehouse* (see end of next section).

The *Scholehouse* was the storm center of a controversy about women which lasted for over thirty years. Definite allusions appear in *Mulierum Pean* (**347**), Bansley's *Pride and Abuse of Women* (**39**) and More's *Defence* (**125**); conjectural allusions in *The vertuous scholehous* (**337**) and Vaughan-Burdet (**323**). Its unusual reputation or notoriety was probably, like that of the *Lamentations of Matheolus,* the result of its encyclopedic nature, which makes it hard to summarize. The writer has little plan other than to salt his rambling series of charges against the sex with proverb, jest, and example. Women are crabbed, untrustworthy, contentious, susceptible to flattery, evasive, untruthful, malicious, wanton, greedy, sensual, hypocritical in tears, guileful, vain, and unchaste. There is a lively description of a talk between a young wife and her old "gossip" which reminds us of *Les Quinze Joyes de Mariage* (**274**). Women love pilgrimages in order to find new lovers (see **75, 239**). They pretend to be ill in order to obtain fine wine and delicate foods. They chide their husbands into excessive ambition by asking him whether he is a man or a mouse. Wedding is like the gout—there is no cure for either. To call a man a cuckold is worse than calling him heretic. A woman once argued with the author that women were superior to men because they were made of man's rib, while man was of earth only. He answered that a rib is crooked, stiff, sturdy, and evil to rule. Put two bones in a bag and they will clatter like a woman. In reality God made woman out of a dog's rib, since the dog ate Adam's rib, which He had intended for the purpose. This is why women bark and bawl like a cur (on this tale, widespread in Europe from Russia to Flanders, see Oskar Dähnhardt, *Natursagen,* Leipzig and Berlin, 1907-1912, I, 114-23). The Man Who Married a Dumb Wife, which follows (see **352**), is probably from *A C. mery talys* (printed about 1525 by John Rastell), which supplied several other jests in the poem. There is a stanza of lying-song (see **69**): when the sea lacks water, the mill turns without wind, Etna is without fire, and a crow is white, then women will cease talking. Next comes a host of examples from classics and Bible. For instances of pride the author adduces "the book Bocas" (probably the original *De Casibus Virorum et Foeminarum Illustrium* rather than Lydgate's *Fall of Princes*); for proverbial triads he calls on Solomon. He ends his poem with a stanza incorporating the "destroying burden" *Cuius contrarium verum est,* the basis of a carol copied only a few years earlier by Richard Hill in his commonplace book (see **136**). In his envoy he offers his poem as a mirror to the ignorant. Like a preacher and a minstrel he speaks in the abstract: "No creature liuing spoken by name." Only the galled jade will wince. In a final list of authorities he calls on Solomon, David, *Genesis,* Jerome, Juvenal, "olde Tobye,"

Cato, Ovid and Martial. He assures the learned reader that he does not mean to "prohybe the Sacrament" of marriage, but writes merely "that the masculine might heerby / Haue some what to iest with the feminy." Clearly he does not wish to be confused with the older ascetic tradition, for though the Statute of Six Articles had been passed in 1539 with the proviso that attacks on celibacy and vows were heretical, England and the Continent were full of the reforming spirit which was finally to establish the "heresy" in the Church of England (see **361**). The author also shows himself a good subject of Henry VIII by his allusions to Wilsdon, Barking, and other "hallowes" as "stones" and "stocks," evidence that the dissolution of the monasteries (1536-39) had been recent enough to cause him to turn the old charge against woman's wantonness on pilgrimages (compare the Wife of Bath and **75**) into a timely attack on the shrines themselves. While it is not wise to push too far the search for historical causes of a literary work which stems from a tradition as old as satire on women, we cannot help recalling that these years made the tradition very meaningful to those in high place. For it was in this time that the legitimacy of Elizabeth was continually being questioned; and the very year preceding our conjectured date for the *Scholehouse* Henry had married and divorced a fourth wife and married a fifth. The author may have intended no allusion, but when he is so careful to emphasize that he jests and intends no specific reference to "creature liuing," we cannot help surmising that he was aware that his readers might spontaneously manufacture their own "key" for certain of the evil women he is describing. Henry's married life may also explain the printing of other satirical tracts by Copland about five years earlier (see **67**). These suggestions must be taken with caution, but they will at least help us to understand the milieu into which was born the most notorious English satire on woman of the sixteenth century.

The Proverb reporteth, no man can deny (91).

293. Tho smallere pese tho mo to the pott.

> (1) Sloane 1210 (2 lines, with a Latin distich); ed. Wright and
>   Halliwell, *Reliquiae Antiquae*, II, 40.

MS. of the XV cent.

Proverbial couplet: the fairer a woman the more "gyglott" or harlot. This couplet is quoted by **292** (lines 558-59).

294. The smoky sighes the bitter teares.

The louer accusing hys loue for her vnfaithfulness, purposeth to liue in libertie.

> (1) *Tottel's Miscellany* (in all editions) (8 six-line stanzas); ed.
>   Rollins, I, 167.

1557 or before.

Rebellious lover, with several unusual classical allusions. His lady is like "the rauening owle."

295. The Sonne in lawe, his Stepdame being dead.

By George Turbervile.

Of the cruell hatred of Stepmothers.

(1) Turbervile's *Epitaphes, Epigrams, Songs and Sonets* (1567) (1 five-line stanza); ed. Collier [1867], p. 189; also in Chalmers, II, 633.

1567 or before.

Stepmothers are malicious even in death. See **74**. From the Greek Anthology, ix, 67; according to Lathrop, *MLN*, XLIII (1928), 225, via the Latin of Janus Cornarius (also in the Latin of Sir Thomas More).

296. The sonne of Sirache / of women doeth saye.

By Robert Crowley.

Of Nyce Wyues.

(1) *One and thyrtye Epigrammes,* printed by Robert Crowley (1550) (18 four-line stanzas); ed. J. M. Cowper, *The Select Works of Robert Crowley, Printer, Archdeacon of Hertford (1559–1567),* London (EETSES, XV), 1872, p. 43.

1550 or before.

Jesus, son of Sirach (author of *Ecclesiasticus*), states that a woman's whoredom is revealed in her wanton eyes. What must we therefore think of the woman of London, with her garish apparel: cap like a sow's maw (compare Elynour Rummyng's "clothes vpon her hed / That wey a sowe of led" in **277**), tussocks of purchased and unnatural hair, bare bosom, middle as small as a wand (because made of wire bought from the "paste wyfes hande"), bum like a barrel with hoops at the skirt, shoes of stuff which may touch no dirt, and precious rings on her fingers. Modest women will not be disturbed by my writing; as for these "nice whippets," "I haue sayde they be whorelike / and so I saye styll." There is a pleasant stubbornness in this religious satirist and printer, soon to turn archdeacon. His satire is distinctly not for fun, but there was wit in him just as there was in Juvenal. Another poem, *The Woman's lesson,* is too didactic to be included here. But it is interesting to recall the title of the volume in which it appeared: *The Voyce of the last trumpet, blowen by the seuenth Angel* (1549). See Cowper, p. 99. In 1558 appeared John Knox's *First Blast of the Trumpet against the monstruous regiment of Women* (**64**). Ninian Winzet's *The last blast of the trompet of Godis worde agains the vsurpit auctoritie of Iohne Knox,* a Catholic tract published in Edinburgh (1562) which continues the heavenly orchestration, has nothing to do with women. See *Certain Tractates . . . by Ninian Winzet,* ed. James King Hewison, Edinburgh (STS, XV, XXII), 1887-90, I, 35.

297. The vse of Court richt weill I knaw.

(1) Advocates' Library 1. 1. 6 (5 six-line stanzas); ed. Ritchie, *Bannatyne Manuscript,* IV, 31; see also Hunterian Club *Bannatyne,* I, cv.

(2) Magdalene College Cambridge, Pepys 2553 (a garbled version of 16 lines); ed. W. A. Craigie, *Maitland Folio Manuscript*, I, 193; for other editions see II, 99-100.

1568 or before.

Silly lairds send their wives to court to solicit for their suits at law. The women wanton and spend the family silver and lose the suit; then they bring home a horn for their husband and a child who is not his. For the same theme see **301**.

298. The vertue of Vlisses wife.

Ascribed to William Gray by Dormer along with **6**, to which it is the sequel, and which is ascribed in the MS. to Thomas Norton. **298** does not appear in the MS., and apparently there is no basis for Dormer's ascription. See Rollins, II, 309.

An answere [to *Against women either good or badde*].

(1) *Tottel's Miscellany* (in all editions) (2 five-line and 1 seven-line stanzas); ed. Rollins, I, 202.

1557 or before.

Penelope's fame lives on, and Helens are virtuous today. Ulysses' rage and not his wife spilt gentle blood. Not Helen but Paris was to blame for the Trojan War. Since neither good nor bad do ill, I shall serve women with all my will.

þer beoþe foure thinges þat makeþ man a fool (387).

þer beon foure thinges causing gret folye (387).

Thair dwelt a larde in Fyffe (352).

298a. þer ys no merth yn noþir.

(1) Bodleian Douce 257 (2 four-line stanzas, beginning imperfectly); second stanza ed. Wright and Halliwell, *Reliquiae Antiquae*, II, 113. See Brown and Robbins, *Index*, Acephalous Poems No. *63.

MS. of XV cent.

Satire on marriage. There is no rest for a man who has a young wife or a harvest goose—"Moche gagil with bothe."

299. Thair is nocht ane winche þat I se.

(1) Advocates' Library 1. 1. 6 (4 eight-line stanzas); ed. Ritchie, *Bannatyne Manuscript*, IV, 16; see also Hunterian Club *Bannatyne*, I, civ.

1568 or before.

Rebellious lover. No woman shall beguile me; I'll counter every one of their tricks with one of my own. Compare **263**.

Ther is, right at the west syde of Ytaille (261).

There was never ffile: half so well filed (338).

Ther wer iij wylly, 3te wyly ther wer (275).

300. **Thir billis ar brevit to birdis in speciall.**

By "Mersar," according to the MS. (in lighter ink than the poem).

(1) Advocates' Library 1. 1. 6 (6 rime-royal stanzas); ed. Ritchie, *Bannatyne Manuscript*, IV, 73; see also Hunterian Club *Bannatyne*, I, cviii.

1568 or before. Possibly before 1508, when a certain Mersar was mentioned in Dunbar's *Lament for the Makaris* (see **19**).

Warning to women against wicked men. No man will marry a woman who has lost her chastity.

301. **Thir ladyis fair, That makis repair.**

By William Dunbar.
The Benifite of them who have ladies wha can be gude Solici-ters at Court; or *Of the Ladyis Solistaris at Court.*

(1) Advocates' Library 1. 1. 6 (6 eight-line stanzas with internal rime); ed. Ritchie, *Bannatyne Manuscript*, IV, 30; Small, *Poems of William Dunbar*, II, 168, with variants from other two authorities; see also Hunterian Club *Bannatyne*, I, civ, and Small, III, 259, for further editions.

(2) Magdalene College Cambridge, Pepys 2553; ed. W. A. Craigie, *Maitland Folio Manuscript*, I, 390; see II, 123, for variants from (3).

(3) Cambridge University Library Ll. 5. 10 (the "Reidpeth MS.").

Mackay in his introduction to Small, I, clxi, argues that this poem refers to the fixed Court at Edinburgh, which superseded the ambulatory Sessions of James I in 1503. He therefore places it among poems "probably written between 1503 and 1513." I am at a loss to see how he decides the court was either fixed or ambulatory, except (p. cxxiv) by the rather far-fetched inference "A novelty or an innovation is always a favorite subject for satire." Dunbar's dates were 1465?-1530?

By giving up their honesty ladies can do more in three days at the law court than their lairds can do in ten. See **297** (where the ladies are wanton enough, but with little recompense for their lairds), **231**, and **167**. In the last two the court is at the King's Palace rather than at the Law Session, but in all four poems women are charged with an excessive lust for those in high place. Dunbar's *Aganis the Solistaris in Court* (Small, II, 206) is a general satire against sycophancy.

302. Thir lenterne dayis ar luvely lang.

> By "Stewart" according to the MS.
> (1) Advocates' Library 1. 1. 6 (6 eight-line stanzas); ed. Ritchie,
> *Bannatyne Manuscript*, IV, 6; see also Hunterian Club
> *Bannatyne*, I, ciii.
> 1568 or before.

Rebellious lover. Though I mourn for my lady, I shall not waste
this beautiful spring on sorrowing. Never did a miller make so fair a
cake that its mate could not be supplied. "As gud luve cumis as gais."

303. Thise olde gentil Britouns in hir dayes.

> By Geoffrey Chaucer.
> *The Franklin's Prologue and Tale.*
> (1)-(54). It appears in all but five of the authorities cited for
> *The Wife of Bath's Prologue and Tale* (**58**). These five
> are British Museum Additional 25718, McCormick, Raw-
> linson 141, Rawlinson 149 (from which it may have been
> lost, since appropriate leaves are missing), and the Sion
> fragment. It is imperfect in the following MSS. (as num-
> bered for *WBProl and T*):
> (4) Bodley 686.
> (16) Egerton 2863.
> (18) Cambridge University Library Gg. 4. 27.
> (20) Harley 1239.
> (22) Harley 7334.
> (59) Trinity College Cambridge R. 3. 15.
> It appears in no MS. where it was not originally accom-
> panied by *WBProl and T*.

(The foregoing list has been compiled from McCormick and
Heseltine on the principles cited under **58**. For editions and commentary see Robinson, *Chaucer*, p. 827; Hammond, *Chaucer*, p.
314; Griffith, *Chaucer*, p. 103; Martin, *Chaucer*, p. 57; and the current bibliographies. *The Franklin's Prologue and Tale* form lines
709-1624 of the F² fragment, 916 lines in all. For a spurious end-link
see Robinson, *Chaucer*, p. 1010.)

Robinson (p. 826) observes that the use of Jerome against
Jovinian and echoes of the *G-Prologue* of the *Legend of Good
Women*, as well as the connection with the Marriage Group, all
indicate a late date (1390-95?). But there are also echoes of the
Teseide and the *Knight's Tale*, which suggest an earlier date (1380-
86?). The superb fitness of the tale as a climax to the Marriage
Group might argue that Chaucer chose it specifically with that
Group in mind, and therefore composed it during the later period,
recalling the materials of the *Knight's Tale* which he was adapting

for the *Canterbury Tales*. But the exact circumstances of the composition of the Marriage Group itself are a guess; and even Chaucer's
intention in the four "acts" of the Human Comedy which deal with
women and marriage is a matter of conjecture—brilliant conjecture
which students would find hard to abandon no matter what incon-
venient facts might be advanced against it.

In the ordinary sense in which we have interpreted the terms satire
and defense of women this "Breton lay" can scarcely be said to fit. But,
if we accept the theory of the Marriage Group, it is Chaucer's own contribution to the controversy, and its very lack of categorical fitness reveals
the stature of the man. After the discourse of the shrewish but sympathetic Wife of Bath, of the kindly but ascetic Clerk, and of that tormented *Jaloux,* the Merchant, we are introduced to a marriage which
violates the codes of courtly love and of misogynistic satire. It violates
them in order to transcend them; the generous Franklin (and we abandon our sense of the dramatic to identify him with his artistic creator)
tells us that the perfect marriage is one in which the husband abandons
his canonical rights over his wife by bringing to marriage the principles
of the courtly code. The idea of partnership in wedded life is not absent
from medieval religious writing; it is even implicit in St. Paul. But
perhaps we may say that Chaucer was the first layman to make it pala-
table as a theory to laymen. In this sense, then, he is a true forerunner
of humanists like Erasmus, Vives, and Sir Thomas Elyot.

304. These women all, / Both great and small.

Ascribed to "Heath" by Quiller-Couch, since (1) is followed
by "finis q mr. Heath." There are accompanying musical notes, and
it is uncertain whether Heath is the author, scribe, or composer.

In Dispraise of Women, or *Women.*

(1) Harley 7578 (5 six-line stanzas); ed. Ritson, *Ancient Songs,*
rev. Hazlitt (1877), p. 178; Sir Arthur Quiller-Couch, *The
Oxford Book of Sixteenth Century Verse,* Oxford, 1932, p.
39.

(2) Folger Library, MS. 1186. 2 (42 lines). Described by Seymour de Ricci, *Census of Medieval and Renaissance Manuscripts in the United States and Canada,* New York, 1935-
40, I, 385. I have not seen this version, but it appears to be
the same poem with at least two extra stanzas.

Quiller-Couch dates the poem "temp. Hen. VIII." The Harley
MS. is a collection of fragments bound together from the XV, XVI,
and XVII centuries. The Folger copy is said by de Ricci to be on
paper "*ca.* 1550."

Satire on woman's inconstancy, greed, and wantonness. They all
take after their mothers. Bound together by the playfully disclaiming
refrain "But I will nott say so."

Thir (see **These**).

305. Thys indrys day befel a stryfe.

The Old Man Worsted.

Burden: "Hey, howe!
　　　　Sely men, God helpe yowe."

(1) Bodleian Eng. poet. e. 1 (two-line burden and 4 four-line stanzas, reconstructed by Greene from what appears to be the burden and 2 seven-line stanzas); ed. Greene, *Early English Carols,* p. 274 (no. 409); Wright, *Songs and Carols* (Percy Society), p. 51; J. E. Masters, *Rymes of the Minstrels,* p. 27.

The MS. is of the second half of the XV cent.

A fight for the breeches between an old man and his wife, who pulls his beard and chases him outdoors. He complains that his house is filled with a continual smoke (an allusion to the three things which destroy a home—smoke, a leaky roof, and a chiding wife; see Greene, p. 434). The complaint reminds us of the *chanson de mal marié* (see Sandison, *"Chanson d'Aventure" in Middle English,* p. 52).

306. This work quha sa sall sie or reid.

Assigned to "Chauseir" twice in the MS., an ascription carried over from *The Remedy of Love* (**255**), of which these are stanzas 20-29 and 38.

(1) Advocates' Library 1. 1. 6 (11 rime-royal stanzas); ed. Ritchie, *Bannatyne Manuscript,* IV, 24; see also Hunterian Club *Bannatyne,* I, cv.

The Remedy of Love was dated by Skeat about 1530.

This extract comprises the counsels of Solomon to "flle þe mys-woman" and the story of the lady who had three lovers to dinner and managed to make love to all of them.

307. This worlde is ful of variaunce.

By John Lydgate, according to two of the MSS. Stow wrongly ascribed it to Chaucer. See Skeat, *Canon,* p. 119; MacCracken, *Minor Poems of Lydgate,* I, xv; Hammond, *Chaucer,* p. 421.

Doublenesse; or *Beware of Doublenesse.* Headed in the MSS. by several titles: "a balade made by Lydgate of wymen for desporte and game per Antyfrasim," "Balade made by Lydgate," "Lidegate of doubilnesse," "Balade of wymmens constaunce," and (in Stow) "A balade whiche Chaucer made in the praise or rather dispraise of women for ther doubleness."

(1) Bodleian Fairfax 16 (13 eight-line stanzas); ed. with variants from (2), (3), (4) by MacCracken, II, 438; with vari-

ants from (2), (3), (4), (5) by Skeat, *Chaucer,* VII, 291; for further editions see Hammond, pp. 421-22.

(2) Ashmole 59 (two stanzas missing).

(3) Harley 7578.

(4) British Museum Additional 16165 (one stanza missing).

(5) Stow's *Chaucer* (1561) and later Chaucer editions.

(The editors and commentators have failed to record the separate existence of the last stanza or "envoy" in two other MSS. See **230**).

Lydgate lived between the years 1370(?) and 1448-49.

Ironic praise of women "per antiphrasim." Faith and trust and constancy, the fresh flowers of summer, the crooked moon, the sun and the summer's day, the sea with his ebb and flow, Fortune's wheel, the wind, a snake and an eel, all these things are fickle—and only woman is devoid of doubleness. Women always drive their craft safely home. Those who accuse them are false. They are constant—they always win in the cast of the dice. Think of the faith of Delilah, Rosamund, and Cleopatra. Each single thing needs a balance-weight, and therefore doubleness is praiseworthy. Pure women, arm yourselves with doubleness that you may deal with wicked men. The same ironical praise of "doubleness" in women appears in Lydgate's translation of *Les Échecs Amoureux* (Ernest Sieper, ed., *Lydgate's Reson and Sensuallyte,* London [EETSES, LXXXIV, LXXXIX], 1901-1903, I, 162). A companion poem of **307**, "þis worlde is ful of stabulnesse," with the destroying refrain, "So as þe crabbe goþe forward," is a satire on all classes of men (including women); it is translated from the French (see MacCracken, II, 464). For another destroying refrain, supposedly by Lydgate, see **334**.

Tho (see **The**).

Thocht, Thoᵗ (see **Though**).

308. Thou art the hapiest man alyve.

Tetrastichs.

(1) "From a collection of wooden fortune cards, of the time of Queen Elizabeth, in the possession of Charles Babbage, Esq.," according to the editors, Wright and Halliwell, *Reliquiae Antiquae,* I, 249 (12 four-line stanzas). I have been unable further to localize these cards.

Time of Queen Elizabeth. They may be later than 1568.

Mingled satire on men and women, but all of it applying in some fashion to marriage and its evils. Each stanza would apply to a single victim, who in some fashion received the card as a "fortune." It is difficult to tell whether the whole Babbage collection was satirical, or whether Halliwell selected only the satirical cards. For the genre see **201**.

309. þou þat werred þe crowne of thornes.

(1) Ashmole 59 (5 couplets); I have transcribed it for publication. See **65**.

The MS. was composed between 1447 and 1456.

A prayer to Christ to destroy the pride of women's horns and long
tails and hoods like "Carrake sayles." Men also have their share of
vanity in dress. On "horns" see **232**; on "tails" see **262**.

310. Tho' all þe wod vnder the hevin þat growis.

(1) Advocates' Library 1. 1. 6 (1 eight-line stanza); ed. Ritchie,
Bannatyne Manuscript, IV, 23; see also Hunterian Club
Bannatyne, I, cv.

1568 or before.

If all the wood were pens, and all the sea ink, and all the earth
white paper, and all the men authors, they could not write the wickedness contained in one woman. For this formula see **118**, which follows
310 in the MS.

311. [Though Helen were so passing faire.

"[A ballad] of the greate myschances yat hapened vnto men
throwe the Cruelnes of wycked Women" (Rollins, *Analytical Index,*
no. 1042); called by Collier *The Wickednesse of Cruell Women.*

(1) Collier says it "has been preserved" and prints a poem of
8 eight-line stanzas in his *Extracts,* I, 132. He remarks,
"The historical accuracy of some of these details seems
doubtful, and the wording of the MS. (in the possession
of the Editor) is clearly incorrect in several places."

The ballad title was entered to William How in 1565-66. Collier is believed to have created this and other spurious poems to fit
the entry in the *Stationers' Register.* See Rollins, ed., *Handful,* p.
100, and his note in *JEGP,* XVIII (1919), 53. Collier's MS. has
recently turned up at the Folger Library. See Introduction, p. 80.

Men have been destroyed by Helen, Semiramis, Clytemnestra,
Jocasta, Pasiphae, Agrippina, Ciborea (mother of Judas). Men, beware
women. Ciborea, the only unusual woman in the poem, is well attested
in the Middle Ages. See Wayland D. Hand, *A Dictionary of Words
and Idioms Associated with Judas Iscariot,* University of California Pub-
lications in Modern Philology, XXIV, Berkeley, 1942, p. 290.]

312. Tho' I in grit Distress.

By Alexander Scott.

(1) Advocates' Library 1. 1. 6 (5 eight-line stanzas); ed. Cranstoun, *Poems of Alexander Scott,* p. 60; Donald, *Poems of
Alexander Scott,* p. 38; Ritchie, *Bannatyne Manuscript,* III,

351; for other editions see Cranstoun, p. 157.

Cranstoun dates Scott's work 1545-68.

Rebellious lover, with charges of unfaithfulness and "niceness" (wantonness).

313. Thoughe laureate poetes in olde antyquyte.

By Thomas Feylde.

A contrauersye bytwene a louer and a Jaye.

(1) Wynkyn de Worde (n.d.) (4 rime-royal, 78 eight-line, and 3 rime-royal stanzas). The *STC* (no. 10839) lists only one copy, at Huntington Library, which I have examined by means of microfilm. This is apparently different from the copy used by Thomas Dibdin in his edition for the Roxburghe Club (London, 1818), which was then in the possession of the Duke of Devonshire. There are numerous minor differences and a variant title page; the colophons, however, are identical. Collier, *Bibliographical and Critical Account,* II, 17, described a copy owned by Heber which also differed from that used by Dibdin; whether this is identical with Huntington I do not know. Edward Arber, *The Dunbar Anthology,* London, 1901, p. 192, has a modernized version (of Dibdin?).

(2) Wynkyn de Worde (n.d.). See (1).

Arber dates the book *ca.* 1508?; Spurgeon, *Five Hundred Years of Chaucer Criticism,* I, 70, says 1509 with no explanation. The *STC* dates it [1522?]. Our decision depends on an allusion made to Stephen Hawes (1475?-1530):

> Yonge Steuen Hawse whose soule god pardon
> Treated of loue so clerkely and well
> To rede his werkes is myn affeccyon
> Whiche he compyled of Labell pucell.

If this means that Hawes was dead Feylde's poem must be placed between 1530 and 1535 (when the printer died). Perhaps there is no necessity for assuming that Hawes' soul had left his body before these lines were written. Feylde, who lists Hawes along with Chaucer, Gower, and Lydgate, may have been misled by the conscious archaizing of *The Pastime of Pleasure* ("La Belle Pucelle") into concluding that Hawes was one of the laureate dead. Hawes would have been about 55 in 1530; and in those or any times this scarcely would seem to be an age meriting the adjective "young." The poem was certainly written after *The Pastime,* which was printed in 1509.

Though it is hardly a distinguished poem, Feylde's *Contrauersye* is

of considerable interest for several reasons: its relationship to the Chau-
cerians, its remarkable erudition, and its carrying on of the tradition
of bird-debate (see **273**). J. M. Berdan (*Early Tudor Poetry,* New York,
1920, pp. 128, 150) has some interesting remarks to make with regard
to its heritage in theme and meter from the Latin *conflictus.* The inter-
locutors, named Amator and Graculus, suggest a Latin source. But none
has been found, and we may recall that *The Owl and the Nightingale*
and *The Thrush and the Nightingale* have Latin or French titles and
no proved sources in these languages. Feylde does, however, display
considerable learning. In his prologue he refers to the treatments of
love by Ovid, Calaunce (Catullus?), Tibullus, Gallus, Sappho, and the
four English poets already mentioned. Neither Catullus nor Tibullus,
the latter of whom wrote "with style moche paynfull," was well known
before the XV century; they were printed together in the *editio princeps*
of 1472 (Venice) (see F. W. Hall, *A Companion to Classical Texts,*
Oxford, 1913, pp. 218, 280). We would seem, therefore, to be in the
presence of an author who combines his knowledge of medieval tradition with the New Learning. The editors observe many parallels to
Hawes and to Chaucer. The author begins with the conventional dream-
vision of a lovely "arbere" with trees and birds and flowers. He sees a
lover shouting to the high heavens of the pains of love, calling upon
St. George, Phoebus, and Hawes' Pucelle, as well as Nature, Cupid,
Fortune, and Death. The lover faints but soon recovers, and a Jay
addresses him: exile despair! Lover: her beauty torments me and I
have no grace. Jay:

> Loue is delycyous
> Loue is prymrose
> Loue is more precyous
> Than golde and topasyon
> Loue is a pretty cage
> For fowles of tender aege
> Loue is but dotage,
> When we haue all done!

(Compare **170**.) Love brings you but an hour in "cocke lorels bote"
(printed by de Worde with no date; assigned by the *STC* and the *CBEL*
to [1510?]). Natural affection, I will not deny, leads one to women,
but it is transitory. Take example of Grand Amour (from *The Pastime
of Pleasure*), Griselda, Jason, Hypsipyle, Thisbe and Pyramus, Helen
and Paris, Scylla and Minos, who were true lovers! What is become of
Phyllis and Demophoon, Alcmena and Amphitryon, Polyxena and
Achilles, Deianira and Hercules? Where are Semele and Jocasta, Cleopatra and Ixiona, Semiramis and Sylvia, Medea and Lucretia? Faithful
Penelope, deceitful Circe, woeful Niobe, good Esther—the pageants of
all are past. Therefore be content with Reason and let love alone. Lover:
I cannot escape from the toils of blind Cupid and his daughter Will
(Desire). I suffer like Tristram, Lamwell, Lamarock, Gawain, Lancelot,
Gareth, Craddock, Bevis, Eglamore, Terry, Triamore, Phaedra and The-

seus, Pasiphae and Taurus (so!), and twenty-six or so other sad ladies.
There are few today like Troilus and Griselda. "Trust is now treche
and loue is but lechery!" (From some version of the *Abuses of the
Age,* a popular bit of medieval *laus temporis acti.*) Although the Lover
already seems to have given up, the Jay continues with an attack on
woman's frailty, inconstancy, fair words and false mind, honey hiding
gall. As Guido says, they are never sure. Remember Cresyde in Chaucer. Women brought to grief Samson, Solomon, David, Aristotle,
Hercules, and Arthur. Priam, Paris, and many others were slain at
Troy for Helen's sake. Read of them in Guido (della Colonne) and
in Secundus ("Mulier est hominis confusio"—see Robinson, *Chaucer,* p.
860). Trust no woman, therefore. With that the Jay flew away, the
woeful Lover "Fast after yede," and the author woke up and wrote
this treatise. Go, little book; some may call you envious—those who
read and find them guilty, let them amend. I wrote this "by pastymes
plesaunce." But there was such a lover, called "F. T.," with a lady whose
name begins with "A.B." (Feylde's initials reversed; the lady, who is,
I presume, not cruel Barbara Allen, has never been identified.) So far
as I am aware, this remarkable compilation was not reprinted after de
Worde's time. But there is an entry in the *Stationers' Register* for
1557-58 to John Wally and Mrs. Toy, of "a ballett of the lover and of
the byrde" (Arber, I, 75), which may be identical either with Feylde's
poem or with **129**, the only two poems I know in which a lover discusses
woman's worth with a bird. Collier, *Extracts,* I, 7, believes the entry to
be for "a broadside formed out of the 4to tract" (out of Feylde, that is);
but Rollins, *Analytical Index,* no. 1581, makes no identification.

314. Though men account it shame.

    By George Turbervile.
    The Lover, seeing himself abusde, renounceth Love.
    (1) Turbervile's *Epitaphes, Epigrams, Songs and Sonets* (1567)
        (23 four-line stanzas); ed. Collier [1867], p. 165; see also
        Chalmers, II, 627.
    1567 or before.

Rebellious lover. Whatever men may say about changing one's
mind, there is virtue in repentance. I thought my "subtile lasse" was
like Penelope or Lucretia, but I was like a mouse in a trap and a man
swimming with a weight on his feet. Now I find solid earth beneath
me and good anchorage, and I will no longer serve a fickle wench or
be a silly sot of Cupid's crew.

315. Though they that wanted grace.

    By George Turbervile.
    Of the torments of Hell, and the paines of Love.
    (1) Turbervile's *Epitaphes, Epigrams, Songs and Sonets* (1567)
        (27 four-line stanzas); ed. Collier [1867], p. 241; see also
        Chalmers, II, 647.

1567 or before.

No matter how fierce the pains of Hell or the punishments of Tantalus, Tityus, Sisyphus, the Belides, Prometheus, and Orestes, no matter how sulphur burns and Cerberus bites, the worst pain of all is suffered by a lover. The abstract application and whimsical, exaggerated tone justify the inclusion of the piece here. Its original, a sonnet in *Tottel's Miscellany* (Rollins, I, 131), is spoken by a lover who is not yet cured, and who is therefore hardly to be classed as a satirist. Both poems, however, appear to stem from the satirical tradition in which love and marriage are described as hell or purgatory. See Robinson's notes, *Chaucer*, p. 804, to the *Wife of Bath's Prologue*, III, 489. The theme is as old as Matheolus, who in his XIII cent. *Lamentations* uses it in a daring conversation with God, who justifies His ways to men by offering heaven to those who have suffered their purgation on earth (see Dow, *Varying Attitude toward Women*, pp. 110-11). One is reminded of Socrates' acceptance of Xanthippe as a good discipline for his patience and philosophic calm. A ballad "shewying how maryage ys bothe parydice and also purgatory" was entered in 1565-66 to Richard Hudson (Rollins, *Analytical Index*, no. 2423).

316. Though wisdom wold I should refrain.

The complaint of a woman Louer, To the tune of, Raging loue.
(1) *A Handful of Pleasant Delights*, Richard Jones (1584) (7 eight-line stanzas); ed. Rollins, *Handful*, p. 50.
Rollins, p. 110, places it before 1566 on the evidence of the tune.

A scion of the medieval forsaken maiden's lament, on which see Sandison, *"Chanson d'Aventure" in Middle English*, pp. 47-50. Most such poems are too particularized for defense and too sympathetic for satire; but this late piece is made general by its warning to "comly Dams" against wicked men, and it enters the controversy by virtue of the masculine answer, **108**, which follows it in *A Handful*.

Ty the mare, Tom boy, ty the mare, Tom boy (290).

Tie, tie, tie the mare, tie (327).

317. To Adam and Eve Crist gave the soveraignte.

By John Lydgate. Stanzas 1-4, on Adam and Eve, are from *The Fall of Princes*, Book i, 519-60, 631-37; stanzas 10-15 from Book i, 6336, 6414-19, 6441-68. According to MacCracken, *Minor Poems of Lydgate*, I, xvi, the others were probably added by Lydgate.
Examples against Women.
(1) Digby 181 (15 rime-royal stanzas); ed. MacCracken, II, 442.
According to Bergen (I, ix), *The Fall of Princes* was begun in 1431. Since these extracts are all from the First Book, they may have been made shortly after that date. But they could have been put together at any time before Lydgate's death in 1448-49.

Adam and Eve had Paradise "Which vertu hadde agayn all mal-
adie," but through Eve they lost that blissful life. Solomon lost his
kingdom to Jereboam by his lust for strange women. Rachel mocked
her own father, Judith killed Holofernes, and Job's Wife "hym rebuked
& on a donghyll left him lye." "Dalida the double" deceived her
mighty husband, Samson, shore him of his strength, and turned him
over to the Philistines. No pestilence is worse than a false and variable
woman. These old examples should teach men to beware. Some women
are steadfast, but many are not. Lydgate's adaptation of his own work
indicates that he would not have disapproved of the many extracts which
were later made from *The Fall of Princes* (see **142**). Presumably he
lifted a few stanzas on Adam and Eve, wrote several new ones on the
perils of womankind, added a number from his stock on Samson, and
appended a concluding stanza which was new. Portions of Adam and
Samson are joined with Dido in another MS. (see **350**).

318. To false report and flying fame.

Against a gentlewoman by whom he was refused.
(1) *Tottel's Miscellany* (in all editions) (5 six-line stanzas); ed.
Rollins, I, 199.
1557 or before.

Rebellious lover: there are plenty of women as good as the "gyllot"
I once thought was a paragon. She tried to make me her thrall, but I
am free. Answered by **373**.

319. To loue, alas, who would not feare.

The lady forsaken of her louer, prayeth his returne, or the end
of her own life.
(1) *Tottel's Miscellany* (in all editions) (8 or 9 six-line stanzas); ed. Rollins, I, 172; see also II, 290.
1557 or before.

Like **316**, this is a forsaken maiden's lament. Its references to
Dido and Aeneas show a blending of classical lore with the popular or
pseudo-popular lament. Qualifies as a defense on the basis of its final
stanza, beginning "By me all women may beware." Dido reminds us
of the *Heroides* and its imitations. A separate *Letter of Dido to Aeneas*
was printed by Pynson in his 1526 edition of Chaucer (see Hammond,
Chaucer, p. 436).

320. To love vnluvitt it is ane pane.

By Alexander Scott.
The MS. ends the poem with "Quod Scott quhen his wyfe left
him," which has been used as a title by Donald.
(1) Advocates' Library 1. 1. 6 (5 five-line stanzas); ed. Ritchie,
Bannatyne Manuscript, IV, 17; Cranstoun, *Poems of Alexander Scott*, p. 73; Donald, *Poems of Alexander Scott*, p. 45;
for further editions see Cranstoun, p. 164.

Cranstoun dates Scott's work 1545-68.

A wanton man has taken my beloved from me, which has broken my heart. But why do I mourn her and slay myself with melancholy like a fool? "As gude lufe cumis as gaiss." A simple Rebellious Lover poem, with a light touch at the end. The seriousness with which the MS. colophon has been taken (see Cranstoun, p. x) is a beautiful example of what scholars may do with the autobiographical fallacy. The description of his lady by such terms as "my souerane," "þat sweit may," and the emphasis throughout the poem on love, not marriage, would be scarcely applicable to a wife in medieval or early renaissance times. If Scott had wanted to satirize his wife he had a full stock of other conventions to draw on. It is of course possible that "wife" is a mere bit of devotional intensity (compare *Knight's Tale*, 2775, 3062, and Robinson's note to the former line in his *Chaucer*, p. 784), and that it really means "sweetheart" or "betrothed." It is also possible that this poem was addressed to his wife before he married her. But the most likely explanation is that Bannatyne wrote the colophon with little or no authority.

To my trew loue and able (335).

321. To saie you are not fayre, I shall belye you.

> (1) British Museum Additional 10336 (1 four-line stanza); ed. Halliwell, *Selection from the Minor Poems of Dan John Lydgate*, p. 271.
> MS. appears to be of the XV cent.

Parody of a courtly panegyric, with an ironic reversal: "Speake faire or foule, I am sure to goe without you." Cited by Halliwell as a parallel to **194**.

322. To onpreyse wemen yt were a shame.

> *In Praise of Women.*
> Burden: "I am as lyght as any roe
>   To preyse wemen wher that I goo."
> (1) Harley 4294 (two-line burden and 3 four-line stanzas); ed. Greene, *Early English Carols*, p. 264 (no. 396); Wright and Halliwell, *Reliquiae Antiquae*, I, 275; Chambers and Sidgwick, *Early English Lyrics*, p. 197; M. R. Adamson, *A Treasury of Middle English Verse*, London, 1930, p. 118.
> The carols in the MS. are in an early XVI cent. hand.

The "unpraise" of women is a shame; remember your mother and the Blessed Virgin. Women are worthy things: they wash and wring and sing "Lullay" to you, and yet they have but care and woe. They serve a man both day and night and are ill repaid. The poem has usually been taken as a straightforward defense in view of its mention of the Virgin and its account of woman's work. But perhaps one may be

pardoned some suspicion about the poet's thorough sincerity. The first
line of the burden suggests the wild and unreasonable thoughts of youth.
For parallels see Gower, *Confessio Amantis*, iv, 2786, ed. Macaulay, II,
376; Brown, *English Lyrics of the XIIIth Century*, pp. 22, 140, 145;
Brown, *Religious Lyrics of the XIVth Century*, pp. 4, 138. In none of
these is such wildness of mind advanced as a desirable condition, and
there is consequently some doubt about the soundness of the praise in
our burden. See **42** for evidence that the Virgin might appear in a
satire on women. Finally, there is an odd ambiguity in the line "They
do the washe and do the wrynge." It is true that the gospel of work
was an intrinsic part of the defenses of Christine de Pisan (see Alice
Kemp-Welch, *Of Six Mediaeval Women*, London, 1913, p. 122). But
the grammar is unclear, perhaps intentionally so (see **22**). Eileen Power
("The Position of Women," *Legacy of the Middle Ages*, ed. Crump and
Jacob, p. 410) accepts as sober praise by reading "dothe" instead of "do
the." But all editors show a space, which must be in the MS. If so,
the may be the article, it may mean "for thee," or it may be accusative
and mean simply "thee." In lines 190-94 of Lydgate's *Mumming at
Hertford* (**190**) it is certainly the husbands who get washed and wrung
when their wives declare:

> Whoo can hem wasshe, who can hem wring alsoo?
> Wryng hem, yee, wryng, so als God vs speed,
> Til þat some tyme we make hir nases bleed,
> And sowe hir clooþes whane þey beoþe to-rent,
> And clowte hir bakkes til somme of vs beo shent.

And when Chaucer's Clerk concluded his counsel to archwives with
"And lat hym care, and wepe, and wrynge, and waille" he touched the
spark of the Merchant's married discontent, and the great debate over
marriage began to rise to the status of a holocaust.

323. To you maystres Arthur, my seruyce premysed.

Assigned by the *STC* and earlier bibliographers to Robert
Vaughan, who certainly wrote the Prologue and Envoy. But Miss
White has shown that Vaughan's introductory verses really say that
Vaughan received the text proper from "a frende of myne," and
that this interpretation is further confirmed by an acrostic, twice
repeated, in the initial letters of the four stanzas of "Robert Vaghane
to the reader," of the name Robert Burdet. She therefore suggests
with reason that Burdet is the "frende" and real author. On the
whole this theory deserves acceptance as an explanation of a somewhat unusual set of facts. But there is one flaw. The envoy contains another acrostic of the name "Margaret Vernon." The two
may therefore be parallel in intention, and both may refer to friends
or patrons of Vaughan. And we should be more certain of Burdet's
authorship if the acrostic had been part of his own verses, rather
than those of Vaughan. In the prologue Vaughan dedicates the

work to "the ryght worshypfull and his singuler good maystres Arthur Hardberde." Was Margaret Vernon her maiden name?

A Dyalogue defensyue for women / agaynst malycyous detractoures. At the end "Thus endeth the Fawcon and the Pye."

(1) Robert Wyer for Richard Bankes (1542) (8 eight-line, 4 six-line, 280 four-line, 1 six-line, 2 four-line, 3 eight-line, 1 seven-line, and 3 eight-line stanzas). The *STC* (no. 24601) lists copies at Huntington Library and in the Clawson collection (now dispersed). I have examined the Huntington copy by means of microfilm. For bibliographical descriptions see Beatrice White, *Huntington Library Bulletin,* II (1931), 165-72; Thomas Corser, *Collectanea Anglo-Poetica,* Part VII (1877), 30; X (1880), 319-23; Wright, *Middle-Class Culture,* p. 468.

If, as has been suggested by Corser, Wright, and White, this poem is an answer to *The Scholehouse of Women* (**292**), it must have been written in 1541 or 1542 (unless there was an earlier edition of *The Scholehouse*). The author says:

> I red an oracyon
> Most pleasauntly set forth, with flowers rethorycall
> Descrybynge the monstruous vyce of detraction
> The dowghter of eunye [*sic*], the furye infernall . . . .
> Bryngynge Innocentes, in to paynes depe
> And from theyr good names, it doth them cast downe
> By readynge this Aucthour.

So he determines to answer the envious book. This vague language might, of course, refer to any satire on women. The only factors which justify the identification with *The Scholehouse* are the knowledge that that book was particularly apt to evoke controversy, and the coincidence of dates and of printer (Robert Wyer is supposed to have printed *The Scholehouse* at about this time). We must be on our guard against arguing in a circle with regard to the dates of the *Scholehouse* and its answers. Gosynhill's *Mulierum Pean* has a certain reference to the satire and is undated; the *Dyalogue defensyue* is securely dated but contains only a conjectural allusion. Therefore we are in the midst of conjecture when we lump them all together in 1541 and 1542. And, as it will be seen in the next section, some doubt can be cast on the common assumption that the *Scholehouse* is the "oracyon" referred to by Burdet (or Vaughan).

Vaughan offers his service to Mistress Hardberde, who had received "Afore this tyme . . . My wrytynges vnworthye." Those who strive against women do so "throughe auaryce." On a journey a friend gave me this dialogue defensive to publish under my own name. I took the volume and saw that it was to favor "one in your case," but I did

not ask who. Thank him who made it, not me. To the reader Vaughan
says to ponder and be not prejudiced by arguments on the basis of "a
auncyent occasyon" (apparently he means the usual examples of evil
women). Do not accuse "thy nowrysshe and mother," but listen to the
Falcon and to his authorities as presented in the margin. Then "The
Auchthour speaketh." In December amid bitter weather I read an envious book which accused women. I was sorrowful and went out to a
pleasant arbor surrounded by three moats and three hawthorn hedges.
In it were ash, aspen, box, beech, cork, and a host of other trees (the
catalogue is fairly unusual), among them "Holy with his pryckes" (an
allusion to the Holly-Ivy strife?). There I saw a Falcon and a Pie
debating about women. The Falcon asserts that women are perfect,
bodily and spiritually. To defend the first he argues on the basis of
their creation by God and their beauty, the sign of perfection. To defend
the second he names many learned women (for knowledge is the "effect"
of spiritual worth): Carmenta, who invented writing, the Muses,
Minerva, Paula, and Eustochium. But this is mere worldly knowledge,
says the Pie (whose arguments, though lively, are all plainly made to be
confuted by the Falcon). The Falcon cites the supernatural knowledge
of prophets like Cassandra. The Pie trots out Eve and Helen of Troy;
the Falcon counters with Penelope, Susanna, St. Catherine, and the
Virgin Mary, and says that supposedly wicked women really owe their
reputation to the men, like Adam and Paris, who were really responsible.
Women are patient, as Aristotle says. Men, not women, killed Christ.
Against the Pie's charge that women trick themselves out in gay apparel,
and lay forth "Theyr brestes . . . as a Boucher doth his flesshe To be
sold in the shambles," the Falcon counters with the wicked men who
attack chaste women like Dina, Thamar, Lucretia, St. Ursula, and all
the virgin martyrs. The Falcon cites the authority of the Church. The
Pie says this has about as much authority as an eel's tail. The Falcon
traps him into admitting that Livy, for instance, is an authority because
he is received by the people—so, therefore, the Church. Then follows
some dispute about what the Fathers really said about fine raiment and
women. The Falcon objects to the dangers of generalization—it is as if
we should call all men murderers because Cain slew Abel. Man is not,
as the Pie had said, better than woman; experience and scripture agree
in saying man committed the first murder, the first bigamy (Lamech),
the first drunkenness (Noah), the first unfilial act (Ham), the first
tyranny (Nimrod), the first sin against nature (Sodom), and so forth.
Consider the evil politics of the present day. The Falcon then sums up
his case, that women are perfect in arts natural and spiritual, that they
excell men in daily life, that they have labored diligently to save our
souls from vice, and that examples favor them. The Pie charges that
he too is generalizing from a few good women. The Falcon admits that
there are bad women, but argues only that women in general incline
more toward virtue than men. The Pie warns the Falcon that his
reward will be doubleness on women's part. The Falcon wishes no
reward but to find the truth, and asserts that women are innocent and

therefore cannot be double. The Pie admits he's not getting anywhere in the argument. The Falcon asks him why he began inveighing against women in the first place; he answers that he had been moved by malice at the excellence of woman's nature. Why then, says the Falcon, pick on women rather than men? Because, the Pie admits, men are powerful and might harm me, while women are weak. With this the Falcon chases the Pie away. The author, who has told all just as he heard it, wishes to displease none but merely to oppose detraction. God help us all to expell envy from our hearts! And may the Savior bring all this company, man and woman, to Heaven's glory. Then Vaughan speaks to the Falcon, telling him his defense may prove unnecessary, since women when Reason reigns shall themselves answer the Pie. The Pie he tells to "Walke in the wanyond, and wayte for some water / To lyckar thy lyppes, that of lying are drye." (Possibly alludes to some such legend as that of the thirsty Raven; see Oskar Dähnhardt, *Natursagen,* Leipzig and Berlin, 1907-1912, pp. 249, 286.) In stanzas with Margaret Vernon's name in acrostics Vaughan asks women to forgive their malicious enemies. He bids his "treatyse" go forth to his wise lady, who will "sowe the togyther, with fyne sylke of Spayne / And make the an hyllynge, of fyne veluet blewe." The book is meant to "pleade in her ryght / As in the quarell," for her defense against slanderers. May she keep it in "her Expresse cofer." Here the poem comes to an end. There are many mysteries about it, among them its supposedly multiple authorship and its allusions to some particular woman (Mistress Hardberde?) who has suffered from slander. There also seems to be specific reference in the statement that the book which the *Dyalogue defensyue* is answering was written from avarice and the desire to please powerful men. Since we have lost the key, we can only recall that in the last years of Henry VIII's reign there was political profit in the accusation of women in high place. Cromwell, for instance, had lost his head for his championship of the marriage with Anne of Clèves. Another problem is that of the conjectured allusion to *The Scholehouse of women.* For although arguments of date, printer, and authority cited in the prior sections cannot be dismissed with finality, there is actually nothing in the poem which specifically identifies the satire being answered, and the only internal evidence which attaches it to the *Scholehouse* controversy seems to be certain similarities to another defense, *Mulierum Pean* (see **347**). Another satire, Feylde's *Contrauersye bytwene a louer and a Jaye* (**313**), shows more similarity in certain details to Vaughan-Burdet, and therefore may be a better candidate for the envious satire to which they allude. There are numerous parallels:

1. Feylde and Vaughan-Burdet share metrical variety and elaborate prologues.
2. To my knowledge these two are the only bird-debates in the XVI cent., and in each the satirical position is taken by very similar birds. The chattering Jay and garrulous Pie are closer to one another than the other satirists of tradition: owl, thrush, "merle," and nightingale (see **273**). (For another connection of the Pie

with the argument about women see **275** and Wulff, *Die Frauen-feindlichen Dichtungen,* p. 117.)

3. The dénouement of a pursuit by the victorious Lover and Falcon, present in both poems, is absent in earlier bird-debates.

4. Unlike earlier debates, each is addressed to a lady, and each therefore contains a device of semi-anonymity involving her: Feylde's last stanza with its "lover, called F. T." (presumably himself with initials reversed), and the *Dyalogue's* various acrostics.

5. When the author of the *Dyalogue* speaks of the "flowers rethorycall" of the envious book he is answering, he may be alluding directly to Feylde's Prologue with its reference to Chaucer as "Flower of rhetoric eloquence." Common as the expression was, the similarity is significant because it better characterizes Feylde's aureate style than the rough and popular vigor of the *Scholehouse.* If there is one thing the Scholehouse lacks, it is rhetoric in the renaissance sense of inner form and outward polish. The interpretation of these parallels awaits a closer study of the three texts and an attempt to identify the personages of the *Contrauersye* and the *Dyalogue.* Meanwhile we should observe that the evidence of printers offers one tenuous link between Feylde and Vaughan-Burdet. John Butler, a legatee of Wynkyn de Worde, who published the *Contrauersye,* was associated in some (yet unclarified) fashion with Robert Wyer, the publisher of the *Dyalogue* (see Duff, *Century,* pp. 19-20, 174, 175, 190). Other sources which suggest themselves for the *Dyalogue* are Chaucer's *Parliament of Fowls,* in which falcons also champion woman, and Cornelius Agrippa's *De Nobilitate . . . Foeminei Sexus,* translated by David Clapham and published in 1542 (see **237**) like the *Dyalogue,* and sharing some philosophical comments on woman's worth with the *Dyalogue.*

324. To yow, mastres, whyche haue be-longe.

(1) Rawlinson C. 813 (7 eight-line stanzas); ed. Padelford and Benham, *Anglia,* XXXI (1908), 382.

W. Bolle, *Anglia,* XXXIV (1911), 274, has shown that most of the contents are late XV cent., although the MS. is of the time of Henry VIII.

Rebellious lover, with more than the usual violence. His lady is wanton, greedy, tyrannous, and presumes on her wealth and beauty. Her many suitors are alluded to by the refrain, "hwer many dogges be att on bone." The rebellion is quite final. Compare the military metaphors in **81** and **230** with the ironic "for your defense take your bokelere" of the last stanza.

325. To yow, my purse, and to noon other wight.

By Geoffrey Chaucer.
The Complaint of Chaucer to his Purse; or *A supplicacion to*

Kyng Rychard by chaucier; or *La Compleint de chaucer A sa Bourse Voide.*

   (1) Bodleian Fairfax 16 (the first six authorities here named contain 3 rime-royal stanzas and the five-line Envoy); ed. with variants from all but (10) by Robinson, *Chaucer,* p. 635. For further editions and bibliography see Hammond, *Chaucer,* p. 392; Robinson, pp. 980, 1039; Griffith, *Chaucer,* p. 130; Martin, *Chaucer,* p. 75; and the current bibliographies.

   (2) Cambridge University Library Ff. 1. 6.

   (3) Harley 7333.

   (4) Magdalene College Cambridge, Pepys 2006.

   (5) Caxton's edition (1478?). *STC,* no. 5091.

   (6) Thynne's edition (1532), and later Chaucer editions (see Hammond, p. 392).

   (7) Harley 2251 (this and the next three authorities lack the Envoy).

   (8) British Museum Additional 22139.

   (9) British Museum Additional 34360 (formerly Phillips 9053).

  (10) Pierpont Morgan Library, MS. 4; ed. with variants from all other authorities and a new *stemma* by Curt F. Bühler, *MLN,* LII (1937), 5.

  (11) Gonville and Caius College Cambridge 176/97 (first two stanzas only).

Envoy probably written between September 30, 1399, when Henry IV was received as king by Parliament, and October 3 of the same year, when Chaucer obtained by royal grant an additional stipend of forty marks. The lack of an envoy in several authorities has led to the surmise that the poem proper was written for Richard II. See Robinson, p. 980, and Bühler, pp. 8-9.

Chaucer complains to his Purse as though he were complaining to his lady. Certainly a parody of the courtly panegyric, and related to the catalogues of ugliness described under **226**. It was imitated by Hoccleve in **235**, which may explain why Speght's second and third editions ascribed *Purse* to Hoccleve (see Hammond, p. 392). Such parodic poems on Lady Money were appearing as late as 1634 (see Rollins, *Analytical Index,* no. 3035).

326. Tobroken been the statutz hye in hevene.

   By Geoffrey Chaucer.

   Lenuoy de Chaucer A Scogan; or *Litera directa de Scogan per G. C.*

   (1) Cambridge University Library Gg. 4. 27 (7 rime-royal stanzas).

(2) Bodleian Fairfax 16; ed. Robinson, *Chaucer,* p. 634, with variants from (1), (3), (4), (5). For further editions see Hammond, *Chaucer,* p. 393; Robinson, pp. 978, 1038; Griffith, *Chaucer,* p. 133; Martin, *Chaucer,* pp. 75-76; and the current bibliographies.

(3) Magdalene College Cambridge, Pepys 2006.

(4) Caxton's edition (1478?) (first three stanzas only).

(5) Thynne's edition (1532).

On the basis of allusions to a great deluge of rain the usually accepted date is 1393. Brusendorff has suggested 1391. See Robinson, pp. 978-79.

A playful warning to Scogan, who has caused the heavens to pour forth in revenge for his renunciation of love. Chaucer fears that Love will punish "alle hem that ben hoor and rounde of shap, / That ben so lykly folk in love to spede." Such arch remarks recall *Merciles Beaute* (**403**), presumably by Chaucer. If the Marriage Group was composed or in the process of composition when *Scogan* was written, we may perhaps find an echo of the Clerk's *Envoy* in "wepe and wayle" (line 4). For a discussion of the meaning of the poem see Walter H. French, *PMLA,* XLVIII (1933), 289.

327. Tom might be merrie, and well might fare.

Burden: "Tie, tie, tie the mare, tie,
　　　　Lest she stray from thee away;
　　　　Tie the mare Tomboy."

(1) *Tom Tyler and his wife* ("second Impression" 1661) (three-line burden or refrain and 4 four-line stanzas); for editions see **193**.

This lyric may be later than 1568, since the date of the first impression and of the play's composition is unknown. But possibly it may be identified with broadsides such as that mentioned as entered in 1562-63 by Thomas Colwell (Rollins, *Analytical Index,* no. 2664).

A dialogue in which Tom Tyler complains of his shrewish mare (wife), and in which Tom Taylor advises the use of the bit.

Tom Tiler, Tom Tiler, / More morter for Tom Tiler (33).

328. Tom Tiler was a trifeler.

Burden: "Hey derie, hoe derie, hey derie dan,
　　　　The Tylers wife of our Town,
　　　　Hath beaten her good man."

(1) *Tom Tyler and his Wife* ("second Impression" 1661) (three-line burden or refrain and 6 four-line stanzas); for editions see **193**.

The dates of the first impression and composition of the play are unknown (see **193**). Although some other lyrics from the play, included in this index, may be identifiable with earlier broadsides, this one is so close to the facts of the play that it could scarcely have preceded it. But the first line of the burden is similar to the title of a ballad mentioned by Robert Copland in his prologue to **377**, perhaps written in the 1520's. See H. R. Plomer, "Robert Copland," *Transactions of the Bibliographical Society,* III, (1895-96), 219.

The Gossips sing a song of how Tom Taylor subdued Tom Tyler's wife, and of how these shrewish wives will take revenge with words and blows.

Turne up hur halter and lat hur go (31 and 104).

329. Tutiuillus, þe deuyl of hell.

> *On Chattering in Church.*
>
> (1) Bodleian Douce 104 (6 three-line stanzas); ed. Brown, *Religious Lyrics of the XVth Century,* p. 277; for further editions see p. 348.

Halliwell, in his edition of the poem, *Reliquiae Antiquae,* I, 257, said that the MS. was "of the end of the fourteenth century," but Wells (*Manual,* p. 234) and Brown (*Register,* I, 111) date it 1427. The story is much older, but the name Tutivillus appears first, so far as I know, with Gower. The name was very popular in the XV and XVI centuries.

Tutivillus writes down the names of women who chatter in church. Better stay at home than serve the devil in this fashion. He'll draw them all to Hell with his "kene crokes." God bless us all! I cannot pause here to tell the story of this little devil, whose two major functions in medieval exempla are to write down on a scroll the words women utter during a church service, and to put in a sack the syllables which priests skip over in saying mass. Briefly, the exempla are at least as old as the early XII cent., when they appear in collections of Jacques of Vitry, Etienne de Bourbon, and Caesarius of Heisterbach. Since the story of the devil with the sack is associated in some collections with the *Vitaspatrum,* it may be much older. The devil with the scroll has been associated with Gregory the Great, St. Augustine of England, and also with St. Martin of Tours. *A Narracio Sancti Augustini,* which is an English account of the devil with the scroll (there called "Rofyn"), was printed by Wright and Halliwell, *Reliquiae Antiquae,* I, 59, and described as a separate piece by Wells, *Manual,* p. 173. It is really part of a longer poem by John Audelay; see his *Poems,* ed. Ella K. Whiting, London (EETS, CLXXXIV), 1931, p. 75. Stories of this sort have been recorded as folk tales in France, England, Germany, Sweden, Finland, and Estonia. See the note to line 1049f. in *Peter Idley's Instructions to His Son,* ed. Charlotte d'Evelyn, Boston and London, 1935, p. 226. Some

macaronic lines on Tutivillus' duties will be found in Wright and Halliwell, I, 291 (from MS. Lansdowne 762).

330. Twoo lynes shall teach you how.

>By George Turbervile.
>*Turberviles aunswere and distich to the same* (**331**).
>(1) Turbervile's *Epitaphes, Epigrams, Songs and Sonets* (1567)
>   (1 four-line stanza); ed. Collier [1867], p. 14; and Chalmers,
>   II, 587.

Probably written between 1563, when Googe's poem (**331**) was
published, and 1567.

Tells Googe that if he suffers from love he should renounce it and
let reason rule.

331. Two lynes shall tell the griefe.

>By Barnaby Googe.
>*Master Googe his sonet of the paines of Loue.*
>(1) Googe's *Eglogs, Epytaphes, and Sonettes* (1563); ed. Ed-
>   ward Arber, London (English Reprints), 1910, p. 97.
>(2) Turbervile's *Epitaphes, Epigrams, Songs and Sonets* (1567)
>   (1 four-line stanza); ed. Collier [1867], p. 14; and Chalmers,
>   II, 587.
>1563 or before.

In love one burns and freezes as in Hell. Answered by **330**. These
two are printed as quatrains *abcb*, but they are actually fourteeners, as
Turbervile's title indicates.

ij Wyfes and one howse (332).

332. Two wymen in one howse.

>(1) Lansdowne 762 (2 couplets); ed. Wright and Halliwell, *Re-
>   liquiae Antiquae*, I, 233.
>(2) Corpus Christi College Cambridge 379; ed. M. R. James,
>   *A Descriptive Catalogue of the Manuscripts in the Library
>   of Corpus Christi College,* Cambridge, 1909-1912, II, 227.

Lansdowne, the earliest authority, is of the time of Henry VII
and Henry VIII. See Brown and Robbins, *Index*, no. 3818.

Two women in a house, two cats and a mouse, two dogs and a bone
can never agree.

333. Vnder ane birkin bank me by.

>*God gif I wer wedo now.*
>(1) Magdalene College Cambridge, Pepys 2553 (5 eight-line
>   stanzas); ed. W. A. Craigie, *Maitland Folio Manuscript,* I,
>   244; for another edition see II, 105.

The Maitland Folio was composed 1570-85.

Chanson de mal marié. The author overhears "ane heynd cheild" who has been married scarcely twelve months describing his evil wife. If he were now "ane wedo" he could choose anyone he wished. She nags me and beats me, "God gif I were ane wedo now!"

334. Vndir your hood is but oo contenaunce.

By John Lydgate, according to Madden, who is cited as authority by MacCracken, *Minor Poems of Lydgate,* I, xii. Its authenticity is supposed to rest on its rimes and its presence in the same MS. as a number of other Lydgate poems; the same arguments are used for **249**.

Ballade per Antiphrasim.
(1) Rawlinson C. 48 (4 eight-line stanzas, two badly damaged); ed. MacCracken, II, 432.

Lydgate lived from about 1370(?) to 1448-49; the MS. is of the XV cent.

Ironic praise of his lady with a "destroying refrain." You are as steadfast and as beautiful "As I goo loos, and teied am with a lyne." For this rather obvious type of irony see **136** and a poem securely ascribed to Lydgate, **307**. The "per antiphrasim" which appears in the title of both **334** and **307**, is presumably from the hand of John Shirley, who was in the habit of labeling Chaucer's or Lydgate's ironies with the phrase lest any reader miss the point. For other examples see Skeat, *Chaucer,* VII, 292, 515 (from MSS. Bodleian Fairfax 16 and British Museum Additional 16165), and Hammond, *Anglia,* XXX (1907), 327 (from MS. Ashmole 59). It is also in the incipit of a XV cent. tract on bleeding in MS. Trinity College Cambridge R. 1. 86: "Minucia alia fit per metathesim, alia per antifrasim." See M. R. James, *The Western Manuscripts in the Library of Trinity College, Cambridge,* Cambridge, 1900-1904, II, 25. The proverbial refrain "Though I go loose, I tyed am with a lyne," is used in a serious moralizing poem by Lydgate (see MacCracken, II, 832).

335. Vnto you most froward þis lettre I write.

Salutation: "To my trew loue and able
            As the wedyr cok he is stable
            Thys letter to hym be deliueryd."
(1) Rawlinson Poetry 36 (three-line salutation, 5 rime-royal stanzas, and two-line postscript, according to Robbins); ed. Rose Cords, *Archiv,* CXXXV (1916), 296; R. H. Robbins, *MLR,* XXXVII (1942), 416.
MS. second half of XV cent.

What might be termed a comic valentine from a lady to her former lover. You are well-featured and fresh-countenanced as an owl. So flat are your forehead, mouth, and nose that you look like a cat. If all the painters in the land were gathered they could not paint your body, on which the clothes hang like a broken wing on an old goose. The climax of this catalogue of uglinesses is the statement that a woman who loved such a man on a dark night would deserve hanging the next morning. For the answer see **221**, and for similar parody panegyrics see **226**. On the form of letter-exchange being parodied see Chambers and Sidgwick, *Early English Lyrics,* pp. 15-19; and Edward Arber, *An English Garner,* London, 1877-97, VIII, 227.

Vp, son and mery wether, / Somer draweth nere (270).

336. Apon the Midsumer ewin, mirriest of nichtis.
>   By William Dunbar.
>   *The Tretis of The Tua Mariit Wemen and the Wedo.*
>   (1) Chapman and Myllar (n.d.) (lines 1-102 lost). Described by the *STC* (no. 7350) as [Scotland? 1508?]. These fragments, now in the Advocates' Library (Edinburgh), were ed. George Stevenson, *Pieces from the Makculloch and the Gray MSS. together with the Chepman and Myllar Prints,* Edinburgh (STS, LXV), 1918, p. 247; ed. MacKenzie, *Poems of William Dunbar,* p. 85, with missing portions supplied from (2). On p. xviii the editor suggests that this portion of the fragments may have been printed in France.
>   (2) Magdalene College Cambridge, Pepys 2553 (530 alliterative lines); ed. Small, *Poems of William Dunbar,* II, 30; W. A. Craigie, *Maitland Folio Manuscript,* I, 98; for further editions see Small, III, 69; and Craigie, II, 71.

Certainly written before *ca.* 1508, the date of the printing. Mackay places it among poems written before 1503, during the looser times supposed to have existed before the marriage of James IV and Margaret Tudor (introduction to Small, I, clviii). Dunbar's dates are 1465?-1530? One wonders why a wanton poem of Dunbar's need be early when Chaucer's Wife of Bath is among his latest works, or why alliterative verse need be considered an early product of Dunbar's pen. However early the alliterative tradition may have arisen in England, Dunbar's single use of the device is skillful and deserves to rank as one of his many brilliant essays in metrical variety. There is no reason why the poem should not be placed as late in his career as the bibliographical evidence will permit.

The author overhears two wives and a widow, drinking and gossiping in a garden. The Widow wants to know what mirth the others have had in marriage, and whether they could have chosen better husbands. One wife wishes marriages were made to last for but a year. The other describes her old and ugly husband in a piece of realistic vituperation which will stand comparison with the wedding night of

January in the *Merchant's Tale*. Like January and the old husbands of the Wife of Bath he is always jealous, but the speaker sells her favors to him at a high price in gowns and jewels (compare *Wife of Bath's Prologue*, III, 409-411). The three gossips laugh and pass the cup around, and the Widow asks the first wife how she has fared. She answers that her husband is a lecher and unable to pay his marriage debt (compare the Wife of Bath's fourth husband). She suffers more than the wife with the old husband because old men are "at Venus warkis" no worse than they seem, whereas "I wend I iosit a gem, and I haif ane geit gottin." The Widow then confesses that she has always been a shrew, no matter how much a saint she may look. Women should be polite without and cruel and inconstant within—tigers in guise of turtle-doves. The first of her two husbands was an old dotard, easy to deceive; and she made the most of her opportunities with "a lufsummar leid, my lust for to slokyn." Her second husband was a wealthy merchant of middle age, and she made him obey like a servant by boasting of her noble blood (on this common theme of the French *chanson de mal mariée* see Sandison, "Chanson d'Aventure," pp. 51-52). The Widow reviled him to his face and to others, got all his property into her control, passed over to him the proper duties of woman, squandered money on dress and cosmetics, cuckolded him and thought of another when he made love to her, raised her children like barons' sons, and made fools of his children by a former wife. And so he is dead, and she is free. She flirts in church, keeps a sponge in her cloak to weep for her husbands when she sees their friends, keeps a secret lover but gives alms and therefore retains her reputation as a "haly wif," and does hospitality to the barons, knights, and bachelors of the parish. None is sent away.

> Bot, with my fair calling, I comfort thaim all:
> For he that sittis me nixt, I nip on his finger;
> I serf him on the tothir syde on the samin fasson;
> And he that behind me sittis, I hard on him lene;
> And him befor, with my fut fast on his I stramp;
> And to the bernis far but sueit blenkis I cast.

(See **255**.) There is nobody alive who will not have her love if he wishes. "This is the legeand of my lif, thought Latyne it be nane." (One of Chaucer's favorite jests. *Legend* is used unorthodoxly in *Miller's Tale, Shipman's Tale, Wife of Bath's Tale,* the rejected link between the tales of the Clerk and the Merchant, and the *Legend of Good Women*.) The three women all laugh merrily, cool their mouths with comfortable drinks, and keep the party alive till dawn (which, like the garden itself and the beauty of the speakers, Dunbar describes in his most aureate fashion). The poet ends with the question "Quhilk wald ȝe vvaill to ȝour vvif, gif ȝe suld vved one?" As parentheses throughout this summary show, Dunbar was influenced equally by the popular *chanson de mal mariée* and by Chaucer's Marriage Group.

337. vertuous scholehous of vngracious women, (The). A godly dialogue or communication of two Systers. The one a good and vertuous wedowe, out of the land of Meissen. The other, a curst vngracious, froward and brawlinge woman, oute of the mountaynes. To the honour and prayse of all good women. And to the rebuke and instruccion of suche as be vnpacient [prose].

Probably translated by Walter Lynne, who signs the preface. He was a bookseller, printer (?), and translator who came before 1540 from the Low Countries. See Duff, *Century*, pp. 95-96. According to C. H. Herford, *Studies in the Literary Relations of England and Germany in the Sixteenth Century*, Cambridge, 1886, p. 67, Lynne is translating from Wolfgang Resch, *Ein schöner dialogus oder gesprech, von zweien schwestern*, published in 1533 and again in 1565. On Resch see Karl Goedeke, *Grundrisz zur Geschichte der Deutschen Dichtung*, 2nd ed., Dresden, 1884——, II, 272.

Bale's title for the tract is *Dialogus duarum sororum*.

(1) No printer or date. *STC* (no. 12104) believes Lynne was the printer, and that the book was published about 1550. But *STC* is in error in calling it the first edition of *The Scholehouse of Women* (**292**), with which it has nothing in common except a portion of the title.

Presumably the *STC* arrived at the 1550 date because Lynne's activity as publisher or printer ends that year (William R. Parker informs me that Lynne's doubtful printing career covers no more than the years 1547-50). In 1550 he had been in England for over ten years, and there are traces of him as late as 1567. By 1571 his wife seems to have been a widow. If we wish to attach *The vertuous scholehous* to the earlier title we may well assume a date closer to 1541, when *The Scholehouse* was apparently first published. But the success of *The Scholehouse* lasted for over thirty years. I have been unable to compare the translation with the two German editions, a venture which might help somewhat in dating Lynne's work. My knowledge of the English is based upon the unique copy in the British Museum, a microfilm of which I have examined (Edwards Brothers Film 1252, Case IX, Carton 50).

The wayward Serapia "complayneth vpon her husbande, and wilfull children." Her godly sister Justina "instructeth and conforteth her in pacience, to be obedient vnto her wedded husband, and to bringe vp her children in the feare of God, with fayre wordes, & decent nurtour and correction, grounding the same in the holy scripture of God, & confirming the same by many goodly examples." This summary, from the preface of "Gwalter Lyn to the reader," is sufficient to explain the nature of the piece, which is long and rather tedious, and enlivened only by occasional satirical touches when Serapia gets in her innings. The translation of Resch is supplemented in this volume with two other products of the German Reformation, "A fruteful Predication or Sermon of D. Mart. Luth. concernynge matrimony" and "A briefe Exhortacion vnto the maryed couple, howe they shall behaue themselues in wedlocke." Although I have not carefully compared *The vertuous scholehous* with Erasmus' *Coniugium* (**184**), there are sufficient similarities between the two to suggest that Wolfgang Resch, a "Formschneyder zu Nürnberg," may have taken Erasmus, who was living in Freiburg im Breisgau, for his model.

Wa (see **Woe**).

Wald (see **Would**).

War yt, war yt, war yt wele (272).

338. Was neuer file yet half so well yfiled.

By Sir Thomas Wyatt.
The abused louer seeth his foly, and entendeth to trust no more.
(1) Egerton 2711 (sonnet—14 lines); ed. with variants from
   (2)-(5) by Foxwell, *Poems of Sir Thomas Wiat,* I, 21.
(2) British Museum Additional 17492.
(3) British Museum Additional 28635.
(4) British Museum Additional 28635 (another copy).
(5) *Tottel's Miscellany* (in all editions); ed. with variants from
   (1) by Rollins, I, 33.

Wyatt's dates are 1503?-1542. Miss Foxwell places the sonnets *ca.* 1528-41.

I was made a filing instrument to beguile others, so was I beguiled. The reward for guile is little trust. As the title (in *Tottel's Miscellany*) shows, this is a rebellious lover poem, which accuses women's falsehood and guile. Miss Foxwell (II, 35) in speaking of the "curiously modern" treatment of moral problems, and of Wyatt's attack on the double standard, is perhaps a bit too serious. The plays on the word "file," a rather colloquial metaphor for coward or deceiver, tend to lighten the poem. And its theme is not original autobiography, but the perennial threat of a lover to treat his lady in the same false ways as she has treated him. To us this may seem a rather obvious point; it is given meaning by the courtly code, which demanded that a lover remain faithful forever, but left the lady's duties in a somewhat ambiguous state. One pleasant look appears at times to have been enough to make the lover cry inconstant when no other pleasant looks appeared; and he might carry the charge on to a final "renunciation," on the grounds of reciprocal action. Compare **263, 299, 362,** and **376.**

339. Wepyng and waylyng, care and oother sorwe.
> By Geoffrey Chaucer.
> *The Merchant's Prologue, Tale, and Epilogue.*
> (1)-(52) It appears in all but seven of the authorities cited for
> *Wife of Bath's Prologue and Tale* (**58**). The seven are
> Bodley 414, Harley 1239, McCormick, Phillips 8136, Raw-
> linson Poetry 141, Sion College Arch. L. 30, and British
> Museum Additional 25718. In 32 out of the 52 the *Mer-
> chant's Tale* contains some imperfection, usually the lack of
> *Prologue, Epilogue,* or both. The *Epilogue* exists alone in
> (53) Mr. George A. Plimpton's MS. (New York).
> (The foregoing list is compiled from McCormick and Heseltine
> in accordance with principles cited under **58**. For editions and com-
> mentary see Robinson, *Chaucer,* p. 817; Hammond, *Chaucer,* p.
> 309; Griffith, *Chaucer,* p. 100; Martin, *Chaucer,* p. 57; and the cur-
> rent bibliographies. The *Merchant's Tale* and its links form lines
> 1213-2440, the concluding portion, of fragment E² of the *Tales,* in
> all 1228 lines.)
> Perhaps composed within the years 1385-95. See Robinson, p.
> 817.
> Chaucer assigns his most bitter attacks on women to the exponents
> of experience, Wife of Bath, Host, and Merchant, and his defense to
> the bookish and idealistic Clerk and the sanguine Franklin. The Clerk
> is a praiser of women because he tells the tale of a perfect wife, a tale
> taken from Petrarch, prince of courtly poets. Chaucer and his Clerk
> are subtle enough to blend idealism with a good-natured bit of satire in
> conclusion. But the Merchant's satire is not good-natured; it does not
> deal with the jest of woman's shrewishness, but attacks woman's lust
> and the guile with which women brilliantly hoodwink their husbands.
> If, as has been suggested, Chaucer originally intended the story of
> January and May for the Monk, its present assignment is excellent evi-
> dence of how he penetrated the surface of the Human Comedy; for the
> change would mean that he transcended literary convention and made
> the satirist leave the cloister. He does not therefore fall into the Refor-
> mation error, or willful perversion, by which monks are charged both
> with utter misogyny and perpetual lust. He leaves dramatic misogyny
> of the most pitiable sort to a man of affairs, the Merchant. But he is
> dramatic, and the Merchant is therefore neither Chaucer's final word
> on the subject nor a revelation of Chaucer's own married life. Chaucer's
> *senex amans* is traditional enough in satire and in *fabliau* (see Robinson,
> p. 917), but the classic opposition between January and May appears
> to have been originated either by him or by his contemporary Gower.
> Whatever its origin, the seasonal contrast was common enough in Eng-
> land after Chaucer's time. See **9**, **255**, and Spurgeon, *Five Hundred
> Years of Chaucer Criticism,* I, 18.

340. Weping haueþ my wonges wet.

Böddeker (*Altenglische Dichtungen*, pp. 455-56) suggested that the "Richard" mentioned in the last lines of the poem may have been the author, and identified him with the "Richard" who is the author of *La Besturne*, which appears in the related MS. Digby 86. His opinion appears to be followed by Josiah C. Russell, *Dictionary of Writers of Thirteenth Century England*, London, 1936, p. 111. Brown (p. 229) is noncommittal. It is not impossible that our poem is in a sense an answer to the Richard of *La Besturne*, who had referred to a "rimeur de engleterre" as an opponent.

I Repent of Blaming Women.

(1) Harley 2253 (6 twelve-line stanzas); ed. Brown, *English Lyrics of the XIIIth Century*, p. 141; see p. 228 for other editions.

The MS., or at least the poems in it, are of the late XIII century. Brown (p. xl) has tended to move the date of the contents backward in his more recent studies.

A defending palinode. The author repents the evil he had earlier written of women. Brown, in my opinion justly, opposes Böddeker's contention that the poem is "Eine Ironie." As he says, "Poetic extravagance . . . is not necessarily proof of ironic intention. If a medieval poet were setting out to satirize women he would hardly have introduced the Virgin as the climax of his argument." This is essentially correct, although the Virgin could appear in a poem which has satirical implications (see **322**; *L'Advocacie Nostre Dame*, summarized by Dow, *Varying Attitude toward Women*, pp. 92-95; and the parallels collected under **42**). When our poet says that since Christ was born "wommon nes wicked non," he may be guilty of a slight exaggeration. But this may be a mere answer to some list of wicked women from the Old Testament which he or another had compiled, just as he answers the *fabliau* tradition when he says

> þah told beon tales vntoun in toune
> such tiding mei tide, y nul nout teme
> of brudes bryht wiþ browes broune.

He does not fall into the artistic error displayed by Weddirburn in **101**, which piles up so many evil examples to be answered that the defender's intention is somewhat obscured. Certain attempts of modern critics to make ironies out of straightforward defenses seem to be due to a failure to realize the strength and frequency of the tradition of defense. Compare **42**. The seriousness of tone in our poem is further confirmed by the phrase "wonges wet," which appears elsewhere in religious poetry of great sincerity. See "vnwunne haueþ myn wonges wet" (in the same MS. and in a closely similar dialect) and "If sinnes in vr hert be sene, / Wit tere of ei mai was þam clene, / And wit wanges wete" (Brown, *Religious Lyrics of the XIVth Century*, pp. 4, 42).

341. Wel come be ӡe when ӡe goo.

The poem is signed "Childe," who may be the author, but who is more likely to be the composer of the accompanying music.

(1) Bodleian Arch. Selden B. 26 (2 eight-line stanzas); ed. Sir John, J. F. R., and C. Stainer, *Early Bodleian Music,* London, 1901, I, plate xcvii (facsimile), and II, 179; Chambers and Sidgwick, *Early English Lyrics,* p. 216; Padelford, *Anglia,* XXXVI (1912), 114.

Stainer (p. xxiii) and E. M. Thompson date the MS. about 1450-55.

Parody of courtly love poem. Compare **168** and **226**.

342. What a worlde is thys, I true it be acurst.

Collier, Hindley, and the *CBEL* (I, 716) attribute to Edward Gosynhill on the grounds that he may have written *The Scholehouse of Women* (**292**) and that John Kynge printed both. But the similarity to **292** consists of no more than that both are satires, and Kynge was the most active printer of satires and defenses in the XVI century. Moreover, whatever Gosynhill's connection with the *Scholehouse,* itself a conjectural matter, that poem was published nearly twenty years before Kynge printed a group of poems about women, among them this one.

A dialogue bytwene the commune secretary and Jalowsye, Touchynge the unstableness' of Harlottes.

(1) John Kynge (n.d.); the *STC* (no. 6807) lists one copy, at the British Museum. The edition by William Beloe, *Anecdotes of Literature and Scarce Books,* London, 1807-1812, I, 389, appears closer to (1) than to (2). Beloe used a copy in the Garrick collection which had been "thrown aside, as of no value."

(2) John Kynge (n.d.); the *STC* lists one copy, in the now dispersed Clawson collection. The *Huntington Library Supplement* (p. 42) lists a copy which may or may not be the same. It is apparently this edition which is followed by J. P. Collier in his facsimile by F. Shobul, printed in 1844 (25 copies only), and reprinted by Charles Hindley, *The Old Book Collector's Miscellany,* London, 1871, I, 6 (24 four-line stanzas). See Collier, *Extracts,* I, 108, where it is compared with a broadside entered in 1565 to Edward Sutton, "The Joyes of Jeloosey." See also Robbins, *Analytical Index,* no. 2096, and Collier, *Bibliographical and Critical Account,* II, 164. Collier mentions two copies, one preserved by Heber, and the other owned by "another gentleman."

These may or may not be identical with those now at the British Museum and Huntington.

Kynge printed from 1555 to 1561; apparently he died in the latter year (see Duff, *Century*, p. 86). The *STC* dates [1560?], presumably because of Kynge's four other poems about women in that year (see **292**). *A dialogue* is a revision of **258**, which is certainly as early as the time of Henry VIII and may be earlier. See the next section.

Jealousy wishes to marry but fears the horn. The Common Secretary tells him to pacify his mind and "Discharge your stomake." Jealousy then attacks women with nearly exact quotation of **258** (*A dialogue*, stanzas 5, 7, 9, 11, 13, 15, 17, 19, 21 correspond in order to **258**, stanzas 1, 2, 3, 4, 5, 6, 7, and 13, 9, 12, 13). His single stanzas are alternated with those of the Secretary, who expands on his remarks a bit more humorously but with little more kindness to the sex. The major conclusion is that if one does marry he should not pamper a wife in idleness, but rule her with a strong hand. We know nothing certain about the authorship of this unusual bit of patchwork. Perhaps we may conjecture that Kynge, who around 1560 was crowding his presses with satires and defenses, accepted knowingly or unknowingly an old poem, transformed into a new dialogue with a contemporary allusion or so by one of the crew of broadside writers. I am uncertain what the "commune secretary" is. Though it may be an authentic office of some sort, I should rather hazard the guess that it means "usual repository of secrets," or typical *confidant* of the jealous lover of courtly tradition. A common secret is no secret, of course. In a sense the common secretary is the opposite of a private secretary.

343. What lyfe is best to lead in citty or in towne?

"I.G." signs the second portion of the poem, and may also be responsible for the first. See under date.

A Paradox.

(1) Authority not cited in Lilly's *Collection*, p. 192 (11 couplets).

Most of Lilly's poems are from broadsides and MSS. before 1568. Several names which fit the initials "I.G." and which would aid in dating are suggested by the *STC*, nos. 11498-99. If they apply to the author of *An Apologie For Women-Kinde* (1605), cited by Wright, *Middle-Class Culture*, p. 484, the poem is probably too late for this index.

The first portion of the poem speaks not about women but about the paradox of life: the court has wit and wealth, the country health and quietness of mind; marriage brings solace and joy, bachelorhood "rest without anoy"; children are comforters and no children no charge; youth is lusty and old age wise—"Then not to dye or be vnborne is best, by my aduise." The second part purports to have found these verses on a wall; they are by one now married, which is the best end after all. What is said of men is more true of maids and widows, to whom I wish a good husband. The sequel, in other words, takes the first part to be a satire on marriage, now canceled because the author enjoys wedded bliss. There is another paradox of this sort signed "I. G." in Lilly's *Collection*, p. 227. Lilly says (p. 312) it is "evidently by the same writer . . . but it is on a separate paper, and apparently another essay." This second paradox is more melancholy: the needy are woeful, the wealthy subject to lawsuits; marriage is full of "carking," but wive not and never thrive; bearing children and barrenness are both sorrows; youth is witless and age sickly—"Then best it is to dye betime, or neuer to be borne." The writer of the second part of **343** thus seems to have been thinking more of the melancholy second poem, which begins "What lyfe is best? The nedy is full of woe and awe," than of the optimistic one which Lilly prints with it. Two other examples of the type, **163** and **259**, concern themselves directly with marriage. The form would seem to derive equally from the classical paradox, the scholastic disputation, and the satirical alternatives with regard to women in Jerome, Deschamps, and Chaucer. For its use by Shakespeare, see Introduction, p. 28.

344. What may I thinke of you (my fawlcon free).

By George Turbervile.
To a fickle and unconstaunt Dame, a friendly warning.
(1) Turbervile's *Epitaphes, Epigrams, Songs and Sonets* (1567) (12 couplets); ed. Collier [1867], p. 198; see also Chalmers, II, 636.
1567 or before.
Satire on a woman's inconstancy under guise of falconry. See **7**.

345. Quhat meneth this Quhat is this windir vre.

Ascribed in the MS. to "chauser," probably because the *Complaint of the Black Knight* or *Complaint of a Lover's Life*, from which these lines are taken, is called by Thynne and by Chapman and Myllar *The Maying and Disport of Chaucer*. Accepting Shirley's authority, as against that of six other MSS. and several early prints, Skeat (*Chaucer*, VII, xliii-xlv; *Canon*, pp. 102-103) and MacCracken (*Minor Poems of Lydgate*, I, xiv; II, 382) assign the *Complaint* to Lydgate. Miss Hammond (*Chaucer*, pp. 413-15) does not commit herself. Skeat gives ample evidence to show that the poem is not Chaucer's, but none of these three students of the Lydgate and Chaucer canons is aware of the selection in the Bannatyne Manuscript.
(1) Advocate's Library 1. 1. 6 (21 rime-royal stanzas); ed. Ritchie, *Bannatyne Manuscript*, IV, 82; see also Hunterian Club *Bannatyne*, I, cviii.

Skeat, Schick, Krausser, and others assign the *Complaint* to *ca.* 1402, on the basis of comparison with other works of Lydgate.

The original poem is a fresh and attractive, though somewhat diffuse, courtly poem in the form of a love-vision. The author incorporates the lover's plea for mercy and prays that all lovers may find happiness. Bannatyne or his original has skillfully cut out the courtly machinery, and the result is a set of melancholy charges against the inconstancy of women (comprising lines 302-434, 456-69 of the *Complaint*). This is excellent testimony for the satirical element which exists in many a courtly poem, and which needs only emphasis to be brought within the *querelle* proper. The author of the original *Complaint* was a true Chaucerian who incorporated echoes from the *Monk's Tale*, the *Legend, Mars, Venus, Anelida and Arcite, Troilus,* and others, and who built his whole poem around a situation similar to that found in the *Book of the Duchess.*

346. What no perdy ye may be sure!

By Sir Thomas Wyatt.

(1) Egerton 2711 (a "rondeau" in 15 lines); ed. with variants from (2) by Foxwell, *Poems of Sir Thomas Wiat,* I, 11; Padelford, *Early Sixteenth Century Lyrics,* p. 8; without variants by E. M. W. Tillyard, *The Poetry of Sir Thomas Wyatt,* London, 1929, p. 82.

(2) British Museum Additional 17492.

Miss Foxwell (I, xvii) dates all the rondeaus about 1528-29. Tillyard (p. 158) says "from its place in the MS. the rondeau would be later than the others, dating between 1532 and 1536." Padelford (p. 115) records the "mere conjecture" that the poem was directed against Anne Boleyn, who was beheaded in 1536. Wyatt himself lived from 1503(?) to 1542.

The lack of certain source has led Miss Foxwell (II, 25) to give the poem considerable biographical weight. It is an honest rebellion from the love of a false and capricious woman. But it seems to me we should be unfair to Wyatt's sense of humor if we assumed that he did not feel the explosive comedy of the oath on which the poem's recurrent effect is based.

347. What tyme ye crabbe his course had past.

By Edward Gosynhill, who names himself in the last stanza, and in the three preceding stanzas gives three acrostics, GOSINHL, GOSINHN, GOSINHL.

The prayse of all women / called Mulierum Pean. Uery fruytfull and delectable vnto all the reders. ¶Loke & rede who that can. This boke is prayse to eche woman.

(1) William Middleton (n.d.) (title page couplet and 155 seven-

line stanzas). The *STC* (no. 12102) lists only the copy at Huntington and dates [1542?]. I have examined the Huntington copies of (1) and (2) by means of microfilm. For bibliographical descriptions see Collier, *Bibliographical and Critical Account*, II, 73; Beatrice White, *Huntington Library Bulletin*, II (1931), 170-72; Thomas Corser, *Collectanea Anglo-Poetica*, Part VII (1877), 29.

(2) John Kynge (n.d.). The *STC* (no. 12103) lists copies at Huntington and in the now dispersed Clawson collection, and dates [1560?].

The *STC* date of 1542(?) for the first edition fits well enough with the conjectural date for the first edition of *The Scholehouse of Women* (**292**), to which this is an answer. Further complexities of relationship between the two poems are discussed under **292**. Middleton's edition bears McKerrow's Title-Page Border no. 7, and McKerrow accepts the *STC* date 1542(?) and cites as immediately prior recorded use a book of [1528?] and as immediately succeeding use one of 1547. On sig. E4^v of Middleton's edition there also appears McKerrow's Device no. 93. McKerrow does not list *Mulierum Pean* here, but reproduces as an identical unworn state Middleton's edition of *The Great Abridgment* (1542). Thus there is nothing in border to rule out, and much in device to recommend, the date 1542 for Middleton's edition. Kynge's edition is dated [1560?] by *STC* and by McKerrow, presumably because Kynge brought out three other books on the woman question in that year, all employing the same device (no. 111 identical with Title-Page Border no. 37$^\beta$) as is found in Kynge's *Mulierum Pean*. Kynge also used the device in the same year for two books not associated with the *querelle;* see McKerrow, *Title-Page Borders*, p. 40. It is noteworthy that Device 111 may have been once owned by Thomas Petit, the original printer of *The Scholehouse*, which Kynge printed beyond question in 1560. Middleton was admitted a freeman in July 5, 1541, and died in June, 1547; Kynge printed from 1555 to 1561 (Duff, *Century*, pp. 104, 86). Thus there is nothing in literary relationship or typographical evidence to cause us to abandon the *STC*'s dates of [1542?] and [1560?] for the two editions, or to rule out a date of *ca.* 1542 for the composition of the poem.

One January Gosynhill dreams that a company of women appear to charge him with the authorship of "the scole of women." For his own and their good names he is commanded to "Sende forth. . . The *Pean* thou wrote, and lyeth the bye." Venus then orders him to record her defense of women. Men have been accusing them ever since the Fall. Brute beasts do not slander their kind as men do. And yet how could men live without them? A good woman counseled Saul [but a

handwritten note in the margin of the Huntington copy observes that
the good woman was the notorious Witch of Endor]. Women tend
men when they are sick. Ceres invented grain, Carmenta writing,
Minerva wool and oil, Sappho the harp, and the twelve Sibyls prophecy.
Women feed you when you are born and after, wear their shoulders
lame by carrying you as an infant, pace the floors with you while fathers
"may lye and snowre full fast," and change your clouts when you are
unclean. When you are twelve months old you repay them by biting
the breast that feeds you and scratching with sharp nails. Your father
beats you, your mother is tender toward you. The story about the
Man Who Married a Dumb Wife (see **352**) and made her a tongue
with an aspen leaf is a pure lie, for any clerk will tell you that God
made all things perfect at creation, and that woman therefore could
not have been made without a tongue. Eve transgressed no more than
men, and Mary atoned for her. Woman was created out of man, but
man from the vile earth. Man, the adjective, can do nothing without
the substantive woman (on such "grammar of Venus," stemming originally from Donatus, Alanus de Insulis, and Jean Gerson's *Donatus
Moralisatus,* see Lewis, *Allegory of Love,* p. 106; Huizinga, *Waning
of the Middle Ages,* p. 190; and Paul Lehmann, *Die Parodie im Mittelalter,* Munich, 1922, pp. 152-56). God has always favored "the femyni-
tye." There are countless good women in the Bible and many wicked
men. Venus names Sarah, Rebecca, the daughter of Raguel, Dina,
Tamar, Rahab, Mary Magdalen, Judith, Deborah, Jael, Rizpah, and
others from the New Testament. There were the 11,000 Virgins, but
who ever heard of 11,000 good men? Women have the skill to run a
household, oversee the baker, brewer, butler and cook, and keep the
domestic accounts. A child is praised for mother wit, not father wit.
In the Envoy Gosynhill names himself, and says that though men will
envy his little book, women will praise it:

> Glory be thy garment so worthy thou arte
> Of syluer thy claspes, and of fyne golde.

He wishes no thanks except to be taken as a strong staff for womankind. This poem is raised above its companion defenses by its long
tribute to mother love, the most realistic, tender, and extensive I have
encountered among our four hundred pieces. The Vaughan-Burdet
Dialogue defensyue is usually said to be another answer to *The Scholehouse;* I have shown that this suggestion is by no means proved (see
323). But there are several indications that one of the two defenses
may have seen the other:

1. The love-vision setting which appears in both.
2. The discussion in both envoys of the way in which the book is to
   be bound.
3. The use of acrostics in each.
4. The refusal of thanks for their work by both authors, Vaughan
   because the text proper is really by Burdet, Gosynhill because
   his defense comes from a full heart,

5. Other parallels, such as the lists of noble women, and the emphasis in each on God's perfect creation (but these and others I have not mentioned may be conventional borrowings from various sources).

There is also much in Pyrrye's *The prayse of VVomen* (**94**) to suggest that the slavish Pyrrye had seen *Mulierum Pean.*

What! why dedist thou wynk when thou a wyf toke? (179).

348. Whatt women be in dede.

Signed in the MS. "quod Robert Jernegan."

(1) Trinity College Cambridge O. 1. 13 (1 four-line stanza); ed. M. R. James, *The Western Manuscripts in the Library of Trinity College, Cambridge,* Cambridge, 1900-1904, III, 13.

The MS. is of the XV cent., but these lines are added in a later hand (early XVI cent.?).

Women are fickle to their friends and spiteful to their foes.

349. When all men hathe spoken, and all men hathe sayde.

By John Wallys.

(1) Ashmole 48 (10 eight-line stanzas); ed. Wright, *Songs and Ballads,* p. 142.

Rollins in *MLN,* XXXIII (1919), 349, dates the MS. *ca.* 1557-65 on the basis of broadside contents.

Satire on shrewish wives by ironic praise of patient husbands. When the Recording Angel has reckoned up accounts in the end none will come closer to heaven "Then thes men that ar pacient, and hathe shrowes to ther wyuys." This theme is developed with rather heavy-handed humor and allusions to Socrates, each stanza ending with the refrain just quoted.

350. [When John Bochas consyderyd had and sought.]

By John Lydgate (an extract from *The Fall of Princes*).

(1) Trinity College Cambridge R. 3. 19 (number of lines not ascertained). I have not seen the extract. It is described by Brown and Robbins, *Index,* p. 638, as covering ff. 171-202. See also M. R. James, *The Western Manuscripts in the Library of Trinity College, Cambridge,* Cambridge, 1900-1904, II, 73.

From Books I and II of *The Fall of Princes,* which was begun in 1431 and perhaps finished in 1438 or 1439.

Since I have not examined the selection I am not aware of the exact tone of the extract. But it is said by Brown to be the sections dealing with Adam, Samson, and Dido, all of which involved considerable satire and ironic praise. Brown and Robbins, *Index,* no. 3983, add that extracts are also included from Chaucer's *Monk's Tale.* For another use of Adam and Samson (perhaps from Lydgate's own hand) see **317**; for another use of Dido and other extracts from *The Fall of Princes* see **142**.

When men motyth of byrdys of gret gentres (365).

351. When nettuls in wynter bryng forth rosys red.
When to Trust Women.
Burden: "Whan thes thynges foloyng be done to owr intent,
Than put women in trust and confydent."
(1) British Museum Printed Book IB 55242 (flyleaves of a copy of Trevisa's translation of Bartholomaeus Anglicus, *De Proprietatibus Rerum*); (stanzas 1, 3, 5, 6, 7 as printed in Greene's text of Bodleian Eng. Poet. e. 1; all except 3 have suffered damage). To be printed. Three stanzas only ed. Robert M. Garrett, "A Satire against Women," *Anglia,* XXXII (1909), 358.
(2) Bodleian Eng. Poet. e. 1 (two-line burden and 7 rime-royal stanzas); ed. Greene, *Early English Carols,* p. 269 (no. 402) with variants of (1), (3); Wright, *Songs and Carols* (Percy Society), p. 66; J. E. Masters, *Rymes of the Minstrels,* p. 18; H. M. Fitzgibbon, *Early English Poetry,* London, 1887, p. 144; a modernized version in Denys K. Roberts, *Straw in the Hair,* London, 1938, p. 181.
(3) Balliol College Oxford 354 (stanzas 1, 3, 5, 6); ed. with variants of (2) by Dyboski, *Songs, Carols* (EETSES, CI), p. 114; Flügel, *Anglia,* XXVI (1903), 277.
(4) The same book in which (1) appears contains a transcript of stanzas 1 and 3 in an XVIII or XIX cent. hand.
I am preparing a study of the three early versions in which the order of composition is conjectured to be as I have arranged the poems above. Bodleian Eng. Poet. e. 1 is of the second half of the XV cent. The copy in the printed book is later than 1495, when the book was published; but it was probably based on an older exemplar. Contemporary allusions have been incorporated into the Balliol version (composed perhaps in 1538).
A lying song. When nettles bear roses, and bulls of the sea sing a good bass, and sprats bear spears and go to war, and pies are mad poets, and sea-mews sell butter at market, and camels fly in the air, and apes are judges in Westminster, not to speak of several other rather difficult conditions, then one may put his trust and confidence in women. For the type see **69**. Greene justly compares this madcap animal jumble to grotesque medieval sculpture and illumination. When the history of grotesque is written it will be seen to have risen to its greatest height in the transitional period of the XV and XVI centuries. We may men-

tion the names of Brueghel, Dunbar, Skelton, the *Merlin Coccaie,* and
Rabelais, and compare the surrealism of the 1920's, another epoch when
fixed patterns of mind were breaking down.

352. Quhan wthair wyfes war glaid [beginning imperfect].

A Ballet shewing how a Dumb Wyff was maid to speik.

(1) Magdalene College Cambridge, Pepys 2553 (begins imperfectly, and preserves 5 twelve-line stanzas and eight lines
of another); ed. with variants of (2) by W. A. Craigie,
Maitland Folio Manuscript, I, 69, II, 65 (includes a discussion of other editions).

(2) Cambridge University Library Ll. 5. 10 (derived from the
Maitland Folio; but the copyist had seen a leaf of that MS.
which is now lost, and he therefore supplies 6 additional
stanzas). The extra stanzas are edited by Craigie, II, 66;
and a reconstruction of the poem from the two authorities
is provided by W. Carew Hazlitt, *Early Popular Poetry of
Scotland and the Northern Border,* London, 1895, II, 29
(according to Craigie this reconstruction was first printed
by David Laing in his *Select Remains of the Ancient Popular Romance and Poetry of Scotland,* Edinburgh, 1885,
p. 348, and involves additional lines supplied by C. Kirk-
patrick Sharpe).

The Maitland Folio was composed 1570-85.

A poetical version of the story of the Man Who Married a Dumb
Wife. He obtains an aspen leaf from the Devil, which he places in
her mouth instead of the tongue which she has lost or never had.
But when she begins to fulfill her womanly destiny and fills the house
with shrewish clatter, her husband repents and asks the Devil to have
her dumb again. The answer of the Prince of Darkness (supplied from
the jest-book version) rings down through the ages: "Al be it yet I haue
power to make a woman to speke but and if a woman begyn ones to
speke, I nor all the deuyls in hell that haue the more power be nat able
to make a woman to be styll, nor to cause her to leaue her spekynge."
This quotation comes from Jest 60 of *A C. mery talys* (W. C. Hazlitt,
Shakespeare Jest-Books, London, 1864, I, 87), of which the *STC* records
two editions by John Rastell, in 1526 and in [1525?] (nos. 23663-64).
This is the earliest version of the jest I have been able to discover. But
Rabelais mentions "la morale comedie de celluy qui avoit espousé une
femme mute," played at Montpellier when Ponocrates (a character) was
there. The plot is related by Epistemon, and involves a physician and
a surgical operation instead of a devil and an aspen leaf (Book iii, ch. 34).
Rabelais himself was at Montpellier from 1530 to 1531 or 1532; presumably he himself witnessed the comedy there, for his list of actors
includes several of his old friends. The comedy or its sources are not
identified in the editions (including the Édition Critique) which I have

at my disposal. The jest was reprinted from *A C. mery talys* in the
1557 translation of Erasmus' *Mery Dialogue, Declaring the Propertyes
of Shrowde Shrewes and Honest Wyues* (**184**). It was apparently added
by the printer to the colloquy in order to fill out blank leaves. The
original jest is alluded to in **292** and violently attacked in **347**. A
Scotch popular ballad, *The Dumb Wife of Aberdour* (not in Child),
is mentioned by Hazlitt, II, 28, and T. F. Thiselton-Dyer, *Folk-Lore
of Women*, London, 1905, pp. 65-66.

353. Quhen phebus fair w^t bemis bricht.

(1) Advocates' Library 1. 1. 6 (6 rime-royal stanzas); ed.
Ritchie, *Bannatyne Manuscript*, III, 356; see also Hunterian
Club *Bannatyne*, I, ciii.
1568 or before.

Lying-song. When the sun rises in the west, the sea is dry, the
ground is paved with gold, Arthur's seat is brought to Salisbury, clerks
pursue no benefice, fish fly, men desire no more wealth, and so on,
"Than will my reuerend lady on me rew." Involves scattered satire on
woman's desire for the mastery and on woman's cruelty. Not as satirical
as most members of the genre, for which see **69**.

354. Quhen phebus in to þe west rysis at morrow.

Ballat of vmpossibiliteis.

(1) Advocates' *Library* 1. 1. 6 (5 rime-royal stanzas); ed.
Ritchie, *Bannatyne Manuscript*, IV, 44; see also Hunterian
Club *Bannatyne*, I, cvi.
1568 or before.

Lying-song. When the sun rises in the west, there is no guilt in
the world, there are no April showers, no lover is jealous, Loch Levin
overruns East Lomond, the wind stands still, the Firth of Forth runs
up the hill, grain grows without straw, women say no man amiss,
Fortune's wheel moves not, and the like, "Than sall my lady luve me
and no mo." Satire on inconstancy. For the type see **69**.

355. When Phebus reluysant most ardent was and shene.

An anonymous translation of Guillaume Alexis's *Le Debat de
l'Omme et de la Femme.*

*An Interlocucyon / with an argument / betwyxt man and
woman / & whiche of them could proue to be most excellent.*

(1) Wynkyn de Worde (n.d.) (51 four-line and 1 twelve-line
stanzas). The *STC* (no. 14109) lists only one copy, at the
British Museum. Edited along with the French original by
Arthur Piaget and Emil Picot, *Oeuvres Poétiques de Guillaume Alexis, Prieur de Bucy*, Paris (SATF), 1896-1908, I,
145.

The de Worde print is dated by the *STC* [1525?], and the

editors date it not before 1525, but possibly as late as 1535, the time
of de Worde's death. Guillaume Alexis was perhaps born about
1425 and died in 1486 (Piaget and Picot, III, vi, xiv). The first
recorded French edition of *Le Debat* is dated [*ca.* 1490]; it was
printed by Pierre Mareschal and Bernabe Chaussard.

The author overhears a "stryfe" between a woman and a man. He
mentions Eve, she mentions Mary. He says women were never angels,
she says many chaste women have become so. He cites evil examples:
Potiphar's Wife, Bathsheba, Solomon's wives, Virgil's mistress, Helen
of Troy, Delilah; she opposes him with Mary, Esther, Judith. He makes
the usual charges of falsehood, extravagance, lasciviousness, shrewishness; she cites the Sibyls, Peter's denial of Christ, Mary Magdalen (to
whom Christ first appeared after the Crucifixion), the 11,000 Virgins.
She has the last word, and cites wicked men: Cain, Nero, Judas, the
persecutors of the Christians. The author leaves it to the reader who
won the debate.

356. When so you vew in verse.

By George Turbervile.
Disprayse of Women, that allure and love not.
(1) Turbervile's *Epitaphes, Epigrams, Songs and Sonets* (1567)
    42 four-line stanzas); ed. Collier [1867], p. 104; see also
    Chalmers, II, 611.
1567 or before.

When you hear about Lucretia and Penelope and Alceste in verse
you come to the rash conclusion that all women are virtuous. But there
are plenty of weeds in any garden. Griseldas and Cleopatras do not
live today. Modern women are deceitful, cruel; they weep crocodile
tears and sing like mermaids to lure men to their doom (compare
Donne's *Go and Catch a Falling Star*). There are many Helens, but
no Dianas. They laugh when they have a man in the toils. They are
as full of wiles as Sinon. Let us, like Ulysses, close our ears to the
sirens, trust not to rotten boughs, remember Medea, Circe, Cressida.
Argus with his hundred eyes could not watch them. Try yourself and
you'll find my words are true.

Whan sparrowys bild churches & stepulles hie (351).

357. Quhen þat the mone hes dominatioun.

Ballat of vnpossibiliteis compaird to the trewth of women in
luve.
(1) Advocates' Library 1. 1. 6 (5 rime-royal stanzas); ed.
    Ritchie, *Bannatyne Manuscript*, IV, 42; see also Hunterian
    Club *Bannatyne*, I, cvi.
1568 or before.

Lying-song. When the moon shines at noon brighter than the sun,
Tweed runs into Tay, the oyster is in season in June, no envy remains

in the cloister, English is Greek, February is flowery, the hound pities the hare, all countries are at peace, the red rose is blue, men are immortal, the snail is as swift as the swallow, and Troy is rebuilt, "Scho quhome I luve sall steidfast be and trew." For the genre see **69**.

358. When the wyntar wynddys ar vanished away.

> By John Wallys.
> (1) Ashmole 48 (10 twelve-line stanzas); ed. Wright, *Songs and Ballads*, p. 145.
> Rollins in *MLN*, XXXIV (1919), 349, dates the MS. 1557-65 on the basis of broadside contents.
>
> Ironic praise of woman's honesty: "For all the falsshede that man can comprehende / Fyrst sprang owt of a womans truthe." This variable refrain is similar to the destroying burden (see **136**).

Whane thes thynges foloyng be done to owr intent (351).

359. When woman fyrst dame nature wrought.

> By William Case.
> (1) Ashmole 48 (7 eight-line stanzas); ed. Wright, *Songs and Ballads*, p. 203.
> Rollins in *MLN*, XXXIV (1919), 349, dates the MS. 1557-65 on the basis of broadside contents. See **360**.
>
> When Dame Nature first created women she made them all wise and good. They are thrifty, seek their husband's ease, sorrow at their lover's pain, wear clean clothes only for their husband's eye, are never cruel and always true. These praises are bound by the ambiguous refrain "Thot thys ys true affyrm dare I, / I pray yow aske them yf I lye"; and to make sure that we get the point Case ends with "I say no more, but wot you why? / Me thynks I make to grete lye."

360. When women first Dame Nature wrought.

> By Richard Edwardes (see Ault, p. 45).
> *Of women.*
> (1) Cotton Titus A. 24 (5 eight-line stanzas); ed. Norman Ault, *Elizabethan Lyrics*, London, 1925, p. 45.
> According to Ault the poem was written before 1566. It is not in Edwardes' *Paradise of Dainty Devices*, published in that year. Presumably **359** and **360** were both written shortly after 1564-65, when a ballad probably to be equated with **386** was licensed to William Pekering.
>
> Nature created woman all wise and good. None are false, no lamb is so meek, if vice overcame all the earth women would still be good; "I pray you, ask them if I do lie." The last stanza is a lying-song (compare **69**): the eagle shall burn high mountains with his piercing eye, huge rocks shall float in the sea, the crab shall run and the snail swim,

sheep shall be wild and tigers tame; "Ha, ha! methinks I make a lie."
The first stanza is identical with Case's poem, **359**, and there are other
echoes. **360** is the more pointed of the two poems, especially in its
introduction of lying-song technique. But it is difficult to decide which
is the earlier, and which poet created the first stanza. Since both are
answers to **386**, which has a similar refrain and precedes **359** in MS.
Ashmole 48, we may surmise that a first stanza was set as an exercise
and that Case and Edwardes vied with each other in a conclusion.
But this is a purely conjectural answer to a bibliographical mystery.

361. When wreneys weare wodknyves, Cranes for to kyll.

> *A godlye sayng.*
> (1) Public Records Office, "State Papers of Henry VIII," accord-
> ing to the editor, F. J. Furnivall, *Ballads from Manuscripts,*
> London, 1868-73, I, 313 (7 four-line stanzas).

Furnivall believes the ballad may allude to the "Bloody Statute"
of 1539.

Lying-song satirizing priests' wives. Derived unmistakably from
351, which satirizes the faithlessness of women in general. The problem of the celibacy of the clergy, which was by no means so settled in
the Middle Ages as is ordinarily thought, greatly agitated English writers
of the XVI century. Even after the Act of Supremacy the English
Church called it heresy to deny this doctrine. The Statute of Six Articles
or "Bloody Statute" of 1539 affirmed it. A great many treatises on the
subject were written, most of which contain a discussion of the crucial
subject of woman's worth, but which cannot strictly find a place in this
handlist. I have recorded the following titles from the *STC*:

> 1. (No. 21804) James Sawtry, *The defence of the mariage of priestes,* Auryk,
> J. Troost, 1541.
> 2. (No. 17798) Philip Melancthon, *A very godly defense, defending the mariage
> of priestes,* tr. L. Beuchame, Leipzig, U. Hoff [Ipswich, J. Oswen], 1541.
> 3. (No. 20176) Bishop John Poynet, *A defence for mariage of priestes, by
> Scripture and aunciente writers,* R. Wolff, 1549.
> 4. (No. 17517) Thomas Martin, *A traictise declarying that the pretensed marriage
> of priestes is no mariage,* in acd. R. Caly, 1554.
> 5. (No. 24687) Jean Veron, *A stronge defence of the maryage of pryestes,*
> T. Marshe, [1562?].
> 6. (No. 17518) *A defence of priestes mariages agaynst T. Martin,* J. Kinston for
> R. Jugge [1567?].
> 7. (No. 17519) [Another edition of the last with additions by Archbishop
> Parker], R. Jugge [1567?].

For further material on the celibacy of the clergy see Cranstoun,
Poems of Alexander Scott, pp. 103-104; and the extensive treatment by
Henry C. Lea, *An Historical Sketch of Sacerdotal Celibacy,* 3rd and en-
larged edition, New York, 1907. For medieval satires on priests' wives
see Paul Lehmann, *Die Parodie im Mittelalter,* Munich, 1922, pp. 159-65.

362. Quhen ȝe were plesit to pleiss me hertfully.

> By Alexander Montgomerie?
> (1) Advocates' Library 1. 1. 6 (4 lines); ed. Ritchie, *Bannatyne*

Manuscript, IV, 9; James Cranstoun, *Poems of Alexander Montgomerie,* Edinburgh (STS, IX-XI), 1885-87, p. 279; see also Hunterian Club *Bannatyne,* I, civ.

1568 or before.

When you pleased me, I pleased you. Since you are pleased to please another be not displeased if I please whom I wish. Rebellious lover, satirizing woman's inconstancy.

When ever I marry, I'le marry a Maid (119).

[Where is the life that late I led?] First line of a ballad now lost, answered by **288**.

363. Wher wyving some mislike.

By Lewys Evans.

A new balet, entituled how to Wyve well; or *A balet of wyvynge.*

(1) Owen Rogers (1561) (21 four-line stanzas); ed. J. P. Collier, *Old Ballads from Early Printed Copies of the Utmost Rarity,* London (Percy Society, I), 1840, p. 37, from the unique copy owned by the Society of Antiquaries (*STC,* no. 10592).

1561 or before. It was entered in the same year under the title "A balet of wyvynge" (Rollins, *Analytical Index,* no. 2980).

Though we must commend the married life, yet it is full of care. Satire on woman's shrewishness, disobedience, and joy when she becomes a widow. Evans, who calls himself "schoolmaster," appears from other entries under his name in the *STC* to have indulged in frequent polemics against the Catholic Church.

364. Wherfor shuld I hang vp my bow vpon the grenwod bough?

The Forester Still Valiant.

Burden begins "I am a joly foster."

(1) British Museum Additional 31922 (six-line burden and 4 two-line stanzas); ed. Greene, *Early English Carols,* p. 314, no. 466; for further editions see p. 451.

The MS. is of the first half of the XVI cent.

If this has amorous significance, instead of being a mere hunting song, it may be classed as a bachelor's rejoicing (compare the related poems **83** and **97**).

365. Who carpys of byrddys of grete jentrys.

A Ballad.

(1) Trinity College Cambridge O. 9. 38 (13 eight-line stanzas); ed. Wright and Halliwell, *Reliquiae Antiquae,* I, 27.

(2) Rawlinson C. 86 (8 eight-line stanzas); ed. Rose Cords, *Archiv,* CXXXV (1916), 298.

Both MSS. transcribed for publication.

This portion of the Trinity MS. is of the late XV cent.; the Rawlinson MS. is of the same period.

Satire on faithless paramours under the guise of falconry, with the rebellious refrain, "Then plukked y of here bellys and let her fly." The author specifically exempts good wives, and asserts that his satire is directed against "small damsellys and tendere of age." For the type see **7.**

366. Who couthe suche a womman counterffete.

> (1) British Museum Additional 36983 (1 eight-line stanza); unprinted.

The MS. was composed about 1442.

Satire on woman's lasciviousness: this woman loves the rich for their gifts, the poor for their "fair condycion," the bishop for his absolution, the priest and clerk for their sweet singing, knights and squires for their prowess, and yeomen and grooms for their masculinity. The scribe has wittingly or not incorporated as a separate poem one stanza (one lot, that is) from the fortune-poem *Ragman Roll* (see **201**). Brown wrongly describes the fragment as "In praise of the B. V." (*Register,* II, 387).

367. Quha dewlie wald decerne.

By "M. A. Arbuthnot" (Alexander Arbuthnot).

Ane contrapoysoun to the Ballat falslie intitulit the properteis of gud Wemen; or *The Praises of Wemen.*

> (1) Magdalene College Cambridge, Pepys 1408 (28 eight-line stanzas); ed. W. A. Craigie, *Maitland Quarto Manuscript,* p. 86.

This poem may be later than 1568, since the Maitland Quarto was composed in the year 1585 and later. Arbuthnot's dates, however, are 1538-83, which leaves a margin of possibility that the poem belongs in this handlist.

Defense of good women in answer to a satire (as the title implies). This satire has not been identified. Arbuthnot offers the usual examples, scriptural and classical. Evil women are specifically excepted.

368. Quha hes gud malt and makis ill drynk.

By "allanis subdert."

> (1) Advocates' Library I. I. 6 (2 eleven-line stanzas); ed. Ritchie, *Bannatyne Manuscript,* III, 38; see also Hunterian Club *Bannatyne,* I, xci.

1568 or before.

Satire on ale-wives. Who brews evil ale from good malt, woe betide her! May she lie unburied seven years without a bell to clink or a clerk to sing; then may she sink to Hell, the man-slayer! But she who brews good ale, may she live long and go to heaven!

369. Who haues hornes als ha ram. and ha nech als a swan.

(1) Gonville and Caius College Cambridge 408/414 (1 four-line stanza); ed. M. R. James, *A Descriptive Catalogue of the Manuscripts in the Library of Gonville and Caius College,* Cambridge, 1907-1908, II, 476.

The MS. is of the XIII cent.

Satire on fashions, preceding an exemplum *contra mulieres ornantes se.* They have horns like a ram, neck like a swan, middle like a brock, and tail like a peacock. On "horns" see **232**; on "tails," **262**.

370. Quha lykis to luve.

By Alexander Scott.

(1) Advocates' Library 1. 1. 6 (6 ten-line stanzas); ed. Ritchie, *Bannatyne Manuscript,* IV, 94; Cranstoun, *Poems of Alexander Scott,* p. 78; Donald, *Poems of Alexander Scott,* p. 46; see also Hunterian Club *Bannatyne,* I, cix; and Cranstoun, p. 168.

Donald (p. 92), observing mention of "þe pest and plaig þat ringis," suggests that the poem is alluding to the Edinburgh plague of 1529. The assumption that a Scottish poet of the XVI cent. could not mention pestilence without being in the midst of it seems unwarranted. But if a specific allusion is intended, it is more likely to be the plague of 1568 (the other great one of the century), since Scott is thought to have been born about 1525. The poem appears in the last portion of the Bannatyne Manuscript, which was completed "in tyme of pest" (1568). Since Bannatyne is the sole authority for Scott in most of his recorded thirty-six poems, we may assume that the relationship between poet and scribe was close enough to permit inclusion of very recent poems. Cranstoun dates Scott's work 1545-68.

The torments of a lover, who has no wit but is like a "brutall best," "a fule vnwyce." Flee love like the pestilence; it is "Ane fyre sulfurius" that brings men down. Let Reason rule above "lathly lust," which is the net of Satan. A serious renunciation of earthly love, and of the cruel woman who spurns him.

371. Who so in wedloke doth intend.

A ballet of mariage.

(1) Cotton Vespasian A. 25 (2 eight-line stanzas); ed. Böddeker, *JbREL,* XIV (1875), 363.

This poem may have been composed after 1568, since the MS. has been dated by Böddeker 1578. But many of the pieces in it have been identified with earlier broadsides.

Counsel on marriage. The married man must embrace God's ordinance and live in God's fear, for marriage was established in paradise as a comfort to each. Marriage helps to stay "that filthie rage" which burdens every age, and brings consolation to man in health, sickness, wealth, and woe. God made man and woman one in flesh and bone, and they should be one in heart. May be classified as a defense.

372. Quha will behald of luve the chance.

By William Dunbar.

Inconstancy of Luve.

(1) Advocates' Library 1. 1. 6 (3 eight-line stanzas); ed. Small, *Poems of William Dunbar,* II, 172; MacKenzie, *Poems of William Dunbar,* p. 100; Ritchie, *Bannatyne Manuscript,* IV, 81; see also Small, III, 262, and Hunterian Club *Bannatyne,* I, cviii.

According to Mackay (introduction to Small, I, clxiv) "written . . . after he had given up thoughts of love," and hence "probably . . . between 1503 and 1513." Dunbar's dates are 1465?-1530?

Love is deceitful, inconstant, intemperate, and I renounce it. It is as easy to keep loyalty in love "As quha wald bid ane deid man dance, / In sepulture."

373. Whom fansy forced first to loue.

The answere [to *Against a gentlewoman by whom he was refused*].

(1) *Tottel's Miscellany* (in the second and later editions) (10 six-line stanzas); ed. Rollins, I, 238.

1557 or before. Since the poem to which this is an answer (**318**) is in the first edition of *Tottel's Miscellany,* and this appears for the first time in the second, it may be that the answer was composed for the second edition. This would place its composition between June 5 and July 31 of 1557.

Defense of a chaste woman against the lover who slandered her because of his own folly.

374. Quhome sould I wyt of my mischance.

By Alexander Scott.

A Complaint aganis Cupeid.

(1) Advocates' Library 1. 1. 6 (7 six-line stanzas); ed. Ritchie, *Bannatyne Manuscript,* IV, 97; Cranstoun, *Poems of Alexander Scott,* p. 83; Donald, *Poems of Alexander Scott,* p. 48; see also Cranstoun, p. 169, and Hunterian Club *Bannatyne,* I, cix.

Cranstoun dates Scott's work between 1545 and 1568.

Renunciation of love. The sins of blind Cupid are bitterly described.

375. Whye doth þe vaine fantasie.

Signed in the MS. "Experte, criede Roberte." Ritson identified this Robert with Henry Roberts (fl. 1585-1616), a prolific writer of news-sheets. Böddeker is noncommittal.

A Ballet.

(1) Cotton Vespasian A. 25 (9 twelve-line stanzas); ed. Böddeker, *JbREL*, XV (1876), 99.

May be too late for our stated limit. Böddeker dates the MS. 1578, and if Henry Roberts is the author 1568 is probably too early. But many of the poems in the MS. have been identified with broadsides written before 1568.

When you are young you may enjoy yourself with love, but when you marry be careful to choose an equal match. A wealthy wife cuckolds her husband. She who marries a widower is imprisoned in an old man's home. He who marries a widow is always compared with the first husband. Let ladies marry great men and "Matche kytt with the countre clown." So, lady (Böddeker prefers "laddie"), follow my advice.

376. Quhy sowld I luve bot gif I war luvit.

By Alexander Montgomerie? See Cranstoun, p. 384.

(1) Advocates' Library 1. 1. 6 (1 eight-line stanza); ed. Ritchie, *Bannatyne Manuscript*, IV, 9; James Cranstoun, *The Poems of Alexander Montgomerie*, Edinburgh (STS, IX–XI), 1885-87, p. 280; see also Hunterian Club *Bannatyne*, I, civ.

1568 or before.

Rebellious lover. Why should I love where love is not returned?

377. [Why should I muse, such tryfles for to wryte.]

By Robert Copland.

The seuen sorowes that women haue when theyr husbandes be deade.

(1) William Copland (n.d.). The *STC* (no. 5734) lists one copy at the British Museum and one at the Bodleian; but Stein, *Library*, Series 2, XV (1934-35), 45, observes that the Bodleian copy is merely a rotograph of the other. The *STC* dates [1568?]. Stein places it in Copland's Lothbury period, which Duff, *Century*, p. 33, dates from 1562 to 1568-69. One may perhaps assume at least one earlier edition printed either by Robert Copland or by Wynkyn de Worde. But none is extant, and it is not impossible that William Copland was in the possession of Robert's MSS. as well as his printing shop, inherited about 1548.

Plomer would place the composition of the poem around 1525-

27. See his "Robert Copland," *Transactions of the Bibliographical Society,* III (1895-96), 218. The conjecture is based on the known fact that Robert was printing and translating other satires on women (see **17, 35, 67,** and perhaps **75** and **274**) about this time. Plomer dates Robert's active life between about 1496 and 1547. For allusions in the prologue which may further narrow the date see next section.

Since I have been unable to see the poem I must rely on summaries in Plomer, Stein, and Wright, *Middle-Class Culture,* p. 471. It is plainly a gentle satire describing the "sorrows" of a widow who will not give up her widowhood. The title recalls *The .xv. Joyes of maryage* (**274**) printed twice by Copland's employer, Wynkyn de Worde, in *ca.* 1507(?) and 1509, and just possibly translated by Copland himself. Bibliographers have been especially interested in the prologue of **377**, which is packed with specific allusion to the bookseller's and printer's trade problems. Copland talks with a customer, "Quidam," who demands a good book to read. Copland refers to the sad lot of printers, who are asked to have the latest news "Of the Pope, of the Emperour, or of kynges, / Of Martyn Luther, or of the Great Turke . . .[of] the takyng of the French kyng," of jests and ballads. He does have "a very proper boke Of moral wisedome. . . . Or els a boke of comen consolation." But Quidam prefers "a boke of the wydowe Edyth," and will pay no more than a penny (Copland had asked fourpence). He then asks for the "prety geest in ryme" known as the *Seven Sorrows.* Quidam writes it out for Copland in a few minutes, and asks that it be well printed:

> Amende the englysh somwhat, if ye can,
> And spel it true, for I shal tel the man,
> By my souls, ye prynters make suche englyshe,
> So yll spelled, so yll poynted, and so peuyshe,
> That scantly one can rede lynes tow.

The "wardens" of the trade are worthy of blame for allowing such rude craftsmanship. Copland defends his trade against these calumnies. In his envoy he sends his little book out to the good ship, called Berthelet. But "medle not with a Scot." These allusions serve to place the date fairly close to 1525:

1. Luther must have begun to have news value for the English after 1517, when he nailed the Ninety-Five Theses to the Wittenberg church door. According to the *STC* his first appearance in English translation was in 1534.
2. The French king, Francis I, was captured at the Battle of Pavia on the 25th of February, 1525.
3. The Emperor (Charles V) began his war with "the Great Turke" in 1526. The allusion may be to earlier activities of Sultan Suleiman.
4. *The XII Mery Jests of the Wyddow Edyth* was printed in 1525 by John Rastell, according to *CBEL,* I, 714. The *STC* (no. 22870) lists only a reprint by Richard Jones in 1573.

5. Thomas Berthelet's printing career was from 1520 to 1555; John Scot's from 1521 to 1537 (Duff, *Century,* pp. 11-12, 149). Perhaps Copland is referring to Scot's print [*ca.* 1520-25] of *The boke of mayd Emlyn* (**380**), a rollicking satire on women, which was certainly printed before 1528, when Scot left St. Pulker's Parish. In 1528 Scot appears to have made amends with a reprint of William Harrington's *The comendacyons of matrimony.* There is no certain praise of women from Berthelet before 1540, when he covered himself with glory by issuing Elyot's *Defence of Good Women* (**53**) and Vives' *Instructions of a Christian Woman.* But Vives' Latin appeared in 1523, and there was time for Hyrde to complete his translation and put it in Berthelet's hands even before 1525. In any event the *STC* conjectures that the first edition of Vives by Berthelet was published in [1529?]. The data just provided assume that Copland's allusions are to Berthelet and Scot as friend and enemy of women; but it is possible that the allusion is rather to Berthelet's skill as a printer and Scot's lack of it.

378. Will still to wiffe woulde leade me.

By "I.C."

Of Will and Wit.

(1) Jesus College Cambridge 22 (1 six-line stanza); ed. M. R. James, *A Descriptive Catalogue of the Manuscripts in the Library of Jesus College,* Cambridge, 1895, p. 24.

The hand, according to Brown and Robbins, *Index,* no. 4167, is of the XVI cent., but they imply by their inclusion that the poem is before 1500.

Will (desire) leads me to marriage, but wit (reason) bids me beware. Yet if your will is wiving, farewell all thriving else. The stanza-form and the wive-thrive formula remind us of a poem by Thomas Tusser (**70**). For an early example of the conventional contrast between will and wit see Brown, *English Lyrics of the XIIIth Century,* p. 65; for other parallels see Brown and Robbins, *Index,* no. 4016.

379. Wyll ye complayne without a cawse.

A Ballet.

(1) Cotton Vespasian A. 25 (12 four-line stanzas); ed. Böddeker, *JbREL,* XIV (1875), 215.

This poem may have been composed after 1568, since the MS. has been dated 1578 by Böddeker. But many of the pieces in the MS. have been identified with earlier broadsides.

You who blame women because you have set your hopes too high are like the fox and the grapes. Women keep the race alive; "no man but that a woman bere / In woo and payne full fortye weekes." Women shall always have my praise.

380. Wyll ye here of meruaylles.

> *The boke of mayd Emlyn that had .v. Husbandes and all kockoldes; she wold make theyr berdes whether they wold or no, and gyue them to were a praty hoodefull of belles.*

> (1) John Skot (n.d.) (414 lines). The *STC* (no. 7681) lists only the copy at Huntington. Three times edited, by George Isted for the Roxburghe Club, 1820; by E. F. Rimbault, *Ancient Poetical Tracts of the Sixteenth Century,* London (Percy Society, VI), 1842, p. 13; and by Hazlitt, *Remains,* IV, 83. Rimbault used a copy owned by T. Caldecott, which may be identical with Huntington; Hazlitt reprinted Rimbault.

The *STC* dates [1525], whereas Hazlitt says [*ca.* 1520]. Rimbault (p. viii) notes that a British Museum copy of Isted's reprint has 1515 in handwriting, but knows no authority for that date. Skot, whose printing life includes the years 1521 to 1537, was located until 1528 in the Parish of St. Sepulchre, which corresponds to the colophon: "Imprynted without Newegate, in Saynt Pulkers parysshe." According to Rimbault a woodcut on the title page of woman and man with bells is taken from Pynson's 1509 edition of Barclay's *Ship of Fools.* It is possible that Robert Copland alludes to this satire when he tells his book to "medle not with a Scot" in *The seuen sorowes* (377) [*ca.* 1525?-30?]. The widest possible limits are thus 1509-1528, and if Copland's allusion is accepted, the book may well have been published *ca.* 1525.

A very lively description of wanton "mayde" Emlyn, "Drawne out of Gospelles" (compare **79,** *The gospelles of dystaues,* printed by de Worde about 1507-1509). Like the Wife of Bath she has had five husbands, like her she anticipates her husbands' charges of lovemaking by countercharges, like her she has married at least one young and lusty husband, one old dotard, and one impotent through lechery. On this frame the author strings a series of charges against woman's lust, vanity, greed, and murderous disposal of a husband she is tired of. Unlike the Wife of Bath she comes to a bad end, to the stocks, the stews, beggary, and finally death. Her story is often compared to Walter Smith's *The XII Mery Jests of the Wyddow Edyth,* printed in 1525 by John Rastell. But Edith is a picaresque rogue taken from life, akin to the rascals of Harman, Awdeley, and *Lazarillo de Tormes,* whereas Emlyn is the typical archwife of medieval satire.

381. With bemes schene / thow bricht cytherea.

> By Gawin Douglas.
> *The prollog of the fourt buik of virgell Treting of the Incommoditie of luve and Remeid pairof.*
> (1) Advocates Library 1. 1. 6 (4 eight-line and 33 rime-royal

stanzas); ed. Ritchie, *Bannatyne Manuscript,* IV, 108; see also Hunterian Club *Bannatyne,* I, cix.

Douglas' *Eneados* was completed on July 22, 1513, and first printed in 1553. For this edition and three extant MSS. of the whole translation see John Small, *The Poetical Works of Gavin Douglas,* Edinburgh, 1874, 1, cxliv; IV, 231, 235.

Attack on carnal love, with examples of those harmed by it: Solomon, Samson, David, Aristotle, Virgil, Alexander, Hercules, Narcissus, Theseus, and the like. The terrible power of love is described, bawds and old lechers are reviled, and women are counseled to choose Reason as guide rather than Venus. Dido may be a warning to "lusty ladyis quhite."

With lullay, lullay, lyke a chylde (192).

382. [Women are best when they are at rest.

Women Best, When at Reste.

(1) Collier, *Extracts,* I, 23, remarks: "We never heard of any printed copy of it, but it is contained in a MS. collection of productions of the kind, made at least two centuries ago, in the possession of the Editor, from which we quote it, observing that it had probably undergone some changes between the date of the . . . entry and the period when the MS. was written." His 7 four-line stanzas are the only authority for an extant version.

"[A ballet] called . . . wemen be best whan thay be at Rest" was entered in December 4, 1559, to John Sampson, and in 1557-58 there was an almost identical title entered to John Wally and Mrs. Toy. Rollins (*Analytical Index,* nos. 3006-3007) believes the poem is related to **289**. Collier is believed to have created **382** and other spurious ballads to fit entries in the *Stationers' Register.* See Rollins, *Handful,* p. 100, and his note in *JEGP,* XVIII (1919), 53.

A good woman is one who is at rest, but that is seldom. They go out on rainy days and ruin their fine clothing, they talk of their husbands' vices with their friends, they chide the poor man all day and all night. Therefore leave them alone. If this poem is by Collier, it is one of the least inspired of his forgeries.]

383. Womanhood, wanton, ye want.

By John Skelton.

(1) From *Skelton Laureate agaynste a comely coystrowne,* (n.p., n.d.). The *STC* (no. 22611) assigns it to R. Pynson as printer and does not date it. Edited with variants from (2) by Dyce and Child, *Poetical Works of Skelton,* I, 25; ed.

Philip Henderson, *Complete Poems of John Skelton*, p. 35
(4 rime-royal stanzas and a couplet).

(2) *Pithy, pleasaunt and profitable workes of Maister Skelton*,
T. Marshe, 1568. *STC*, no. 22608.

Skelton's dates are 1460?-1529. Brie, "Skelton-Studien," *ESt*,
XXXVII (1906-1907), 84, would date this poem 1490-98.

Satirical address upon his mistress's hypocrisy and wantonness. A
postscript directs it "To mastres Anne, that farly swete, / That wonnes
at the Key in Temmys strete." See "Masteres anne, / I am your man"
(**187**). For the satirical significance of "key" see "Kytt hathe lost hur
key, hur key" in Greene, *Early English Carols*, p. 310.

384. Wymmen beth bothe goud and schene.

>*In Praise of Women.*
>Burden: "Wymmen beth bothe goude and truwe:
>   Wytnesse on Marie."
>
>(1) Harley 7358 (two-line burden and 5 four-line stanzas); ed.
>   Greene, *Early English Carols*, p. 263 (no. 395) with variants
>   from (2); ed. Wright, *Songs and Carols* (Warton Club),
>   p. 106; Wright, *Songs and Carols* (1836), sig. F2ᵛ; Cham-
>   bers and Sidgwick, *Early English Lyrics*, p. 198; Mary G.
>   Segar, *A Mediaeval Anthology*, London, 1915, p. 108.
>
>(2) Sloane 2593 (omits the burden and second stanza and be-
>   gins "Of hondes and body and face are clene"); Wright,
>   *Songs and Carols* (Warton Club), p. 11; Wright, *Songs
>   and Carols* (1836), sig. B2; W. Hales and F. J. Furni-
>   vall, *Bishop Percy's Folio Manuscript*, London, 1868, III,
>   545.

The earliest authority, MS. Sloane, was written in the first half
of the XV cent.

Defence on the basis of woman's cleanness (probably in the sense
of chastity, but we should remember how well small boys are reputed
to wash behind their ears), their *gentilesse,* their gift of grace, their
silence, and the comfort they bring us in sorrow and in care. Each virtue
is illustrated by the refrain "Wytnesse on Marie." For other examples
of this type of defense see **42, 219, 145**, and the poems listed under
Praise of Women in Index II.

Wymmen beth bothe goude and truwe (384).

385. Wymmen ben fayre for t . . . .

>Burden: "Of alle thynges that God. . . ."
>(1) Cambridge University Library Additional 5943 (formerly
>   belonged to Lord Howard de Walden) (two?-line burden
>   and 3 three-line stanzas, all badly damaged); ed. Greene,
>   *Early English Carols,* p. 322 (Appendix, no. vii).

(2) An imperfect version on last flyleaf of same MS. The MS. is of the first quarter of the XV cent. (from about 1417 to 1425).

Badly damaged, but apparently a defense of women on the basis of their beauty, their powers of consolation, and Christ's Mother.

Women ben good for lo[ve] (137).

386. Women to praise who taketh in hand.

In Praise and Dispraise of Women.

(1) Ashmole 48 (7 eight-line stanzas); ed. Wright, *Songs and Ballads,* p. 201.

(2) Richard Johnson, *The Crown Garland of Golden Roses* (1612), ed. W. Chappell, London (Percy Society, VI), 1842, p. 52 (1 additional stanza).

Rollins in *MLN,* XXXIV (1919), 349, dates the MS. 1557-65 on the basis of broadside contents. This piece is equated by Rollins (*Analytical Index,* no. 3008) with the ballad entry in the *Stationers' Register* in 1564-65 to William Pekering: "Women to please Who taketh in hande . . . anombre muste Dyspleasse." On the title see **210.**

Those who praise women shall displease many; those who dispraise them live at their ease. They are man's only comfort. They spin and labor hard to save a penny. These three stanzas are bound by the refrain: "Ask them if that I lye." Then follow stanzas of dispraise. If a husband chides she does not answer back, "Except she crowne him with a stoole." She will "take him" on the face with her ten commandments (or nails). She will not pay her marriage debt unless he gives her a new piece of finery. She discusses her brawls with her gossips, as they drink together. And so I appeal to all good wives, "To know if that I lye." This poem pretends, like Pyrrye's *The praise and Dispraise of Women* (see **210**), to show both the good and bad aspects of women. But Pyrrye's tract contains a formal satire and a formal defense, whereas this poem is ironic in its praise and straightforward (though playful) in its satire. Pyrrye's attempts to cover both sides of the woman question is a bit laborious, and this jesting bit is very likely an answer to it. In turn it appears to have given rise to two sequels, **359** and **360.**

Women, women, love of women (264 and 265).

Women, women, women, women (264).

387. Wurship, women, wyne, vnweldy age.

By John Lydgate, but ascribed by Stow to Chaucer.

Quatuor infatuant, honor, etas, femina, vinum; or *Sayings of Dan Johan;* or *Bon Consaile;* or *Four Things that Make a Man a*

Fool (headed in MS. Ashmole "þe Philosofar writeþe for a souereine notabilite þat foure thingis makeþe þe prudence of man to falle").

(1) Bodleian Fairfax 16 (the first nine authorities begin as stated and consist of 1 rime-royal stanza); ed. MacCracken, *Minor Poems of Lydgate,* II, 709, with variants of (2)–(5).

(2) Harley 7578.

(3) Harley 116; ed. Förster, *Archiv,* CIV (1900), 301 (Brown, *Register,* II, 399, who notes the first seven and last seven items here listed, observes that Förster's citation of MS. Harley 4733 is erroneous).

(4) Harley 2251; ed. Brusendorff, *Chaucer Tradition,* p. 465; see also Hammond, *Anglia,* XXVIII (1905), 21.

(5) Ashmole 59.

(6) Trinity College Cambridge R. 3. 19; ed. Skeat, *Canon,* p. 124.

(7) Advocates' Library 19. 3. 1.

(8) British Museum Additional 16165 (according to Mac-Cracken, I, xvii). Not listed by Brown and Robbins, *Index,* no. 4230.

(9) British Museum Additional 34360 (according to Mac-Cracken, I, xvii—perhaps a confusion with "Worldly worship is ioye transitory," which he prints in volume II as a sequel to this poem?). Not listed by Brown and Robbins.

(10) Pierpont Morgan Library, MS. 775.

(11) Copenhagen, Royal Library 29264.

(12) British Museum Additional 29729 (another version, beginning "þer beoþe foure thinges þat makeþ man a fool," also 1 rime-royal stanza). The same version in (13) and (14).

(13) Trinity College Cambridge R. 3. 20; ed. MacCracken, II, 708; see also Hammond, *Chaucer,* p. 454.

(14) Stow's *Chaucer* (1561); ed. Skeat, *Chaucer,* VII, 296.

(15) Cambridge University Library Gg. 4: 27(b). This version, also of 1 rime-royal stanza, begins "þer beon foure thinges causing gret folye," and appears in the next three authorities.

(16) British Museum Additional 29729.

(17) Trinity College Cambridge R. 3. 20; ed. MacCracken, II, 708.

(18) Stow's *Chaucer* (1561); ed. Skeat, *Chaucer,* VII, 296.

The earliest authority seems to be John Shirley's MS. Ashmole 59, composed 1447-56. Lydgate lived from 1370(?) to 1448-49.

Honor, women, wine, and age make men lose their reason, but all poets agree that "women moste maken men to madde." The two versions in authorities (10)-(16) lack the special sting against women, which may account for their relative lack of popularity. In his copy of (9)

Shirley glosses "Ye wilbe shent, Dane Iohan lydgate for your triew seyeng," and in the same authority the stanza is assimilated to **75**. Authority (6) assimilates it to **226**. **255** (stanza 37) has the following lines:

> Wine and women into apostasie,
> Cause wisemen to fal, what is that to say,
> Of wisedome cause them to forget the way.

Compare also one of the proverbs in **213**. The original Latin proverb was probably derived from Vulgate *III Esdras,* chapters iii-iv, in which Darius asks three young men what is the strongest thing on earth. The first answers "wine," the second "the king," and the third carries the day with "women." See R. H. Charles, *The Apocrypha and Pseudepigrapha of the Old Testament,* Oxford, 1913, I, 29-32. The popularity of this parable is shown by its expansion in *A Pretie new Enterlude bot pithie and pleasaunt of the Story of Kyng Daryus* (Thomas Colwell, 1565); ed. Alois Brandl, *Quellen des Weltlichen Dramas in England vor Shakespeare,* Strassburg (Quellen und Forschungen, LXXX), 1898, p. 359. Collier, *Extracts,* I, 115, notes the licensing of a "pleasaunte Recytall" on the same subject to William Griffith, 1565-66. To my knowledge the earliest treatment in English, which Lydgate may have seen, is that in Gower's *Confessio Amantis,* vii, 1783-1984 (ed. Macaulay, III, 281-86).

388. Wald my gud lady lufe me best.

> By Robert Henryson.
> *The Garmont of Gude Ladeis.*
> (1) Advocates' Library 1. 1. 6 (10 four-line stanzas); ed. G. Gregory Smith, *The Poems of Robert Henryson,* Edinburgh (STS, LV, LVIII, LXIV), 1906-1914, I, 102; Ritchie, *Bannatyne Manuscript,* III, 252; Fairholt, *Satirical Songs and Poems on Costume,* p. 59; W. M. Metcalfe, *The Poems of Robert Henryson,* Paisley, 1917, p. 209; H. M. Fitzgibbon, *Early English Poetry,* London, 1887, p. 49; for several other editions see Smith, I, lxiv; Hunterian Club *Bannatyne,* I, xcv.

Henryson's uncertain dates are from about 1430 to 1508. Smith (I, xxiii) says "There will be less chance of quarrel with the most meticulous in chronology if we content ourselves with *'floruit* 1470-1500.'" Brown and Robbins, *Index,* no. 4237, imply by their inclusion that it is before 1500. See next section.

If my good lady will love me and follow my will I will make her a goodly garment: her hood of honor and governance; her "sark" of chastity, shame, and dread; her kirtle of constancy; her gown of goodliness, renown, and pleasure; her belt of benignity; her mantle of humility; her hat of "fair having"; her tippet of truth; her neck ribbon of ruth; her sleeves of hope; her gloves of good behavior; her shoes of "sickerness"; her stockings of honesty. The basis of this poem is didactic; but Henryson's gentle hand makes it a defense of good women. It may have been modeled on Olivier de la Marche's *Le Parement des Dames* (Olivier died in 1501-1502—see Fairholt, p. 59, and Smith, I, lxiv; and for a discussion of both the French and the English, see Hentsch, *De la Littérature Didactique*, pp. 179, 185). Both poems derive ultimately from Proverbs 31:17-25, and I Timothy 2:9-10. For other treatments of the woman of Proverbs whose virtue is above rubies see Rollins, *Analytical Index*, no. 2217; and the parallels collected under **283**. Panurge (Rabelais, Book iii, ch. xxx) fears that this paragon among women is dead. A longer poem on the same theme as Henryson's, **389**, is usually thought to be derived from him. Another use of the garment metaphor is found in **182**.

389. Wald my gud ladye that I Luif.

(1) Advocates' Library 1. 1. 6 (17 four-line stanzas, peculiarly numbered in the MS., as though some stanzas had been lost); ed. Ritchie, *Bannatyne Manuscript*, III, 295 (with facsimile); see also Hunterian Club *Bannatyne*, I, xcviii. 1568 or before.

Another "garment of good ladies," probably based on **388**.

390. Wrapt in my carelesse cloke, as I walke to and fro.

By Henry Howard, Earl of Surrey.

A carelesse man, scorning and describing, the suttle vsage of women towarde their louers.

(1) *Tottel's Miscellany* (in all editions) (15 couplets); ed. Rollins, I, 25; see also II, 150.

Surrey's dates are from about 1517 to 1547.

Renunciation of love, with satire on woman's hypocrisy, coyness, desire for the mastery, and guile. So wily is this woman of tender years that the poet asks "What will she do, when hory heares are powdred in her hedde?"

391. Ye are to yong to bryng me in.

An old louer to a yong gentilwoman.

(1) *Tottel's Miscellany* (second and succeeding editions) (4 eight-line stanzas); ed. Rollins, I, 255. 1557 or before.

Old in wisdom and experience, this rebellious lover can avoid the lures and wiles of a young lady. Akin to the renunciations found in **26** and **154**. Could this be the poem or tract which led to the defense called *Iane Anger her protection for Women. To defend them against the Scandalous Reportes Of a late Surfeiting Louer, and all other like Venerians that complaine so to bee overcloyed with womens kindnesse* (1589), cited Wright, *Middle-Class Culture*, p. 476?

392. Ʒe blindit luvaris, luke.

By Alexander Scott, according to the last stanza of Bannatyne.
(1) Advocates' Library 1. 1. 6 (19 eight-line stanzas); ed.
Ritchie, *Bannatyne Manuscript*, IV, 102; Cranstoun, *Poems of Alexander Scott*, p. 85; Donald, *Poems of Alexander Scott*, p. 61; for other editions see Cranstoun, p. 170.
(2) Magdalene College Cambridge, Pepys 2553 (omits two stanzas and a half, including the ascription to Scott); ed. in a text parallel to (1) by Donald, p. 61; ed. W. A. Craigie, *Maitland Folio Manuscript*, I, 294.
Cranstoun dates Scott's work 1545-68.

Attack on sensual love, with reference to woman's cruelty, wantonness, greed, and guile. Cranstoun, p. 170, compares **394** and **381**. Donald also compares (p. 93) with **394**, and says it is "Ane ballat maid to þe derisioun and scorne of wantoun men," as the other is against women. This is a just characterization, but it is noteworthy that Scott did not make his companion piece a defense of women, and that he preserved many satirical touches against the sex which men trust too much.

393. Ye loving wormes come learne of me.

Doubtfully ascribed to John Lyly by Bond; this ascription rejected on grounds of date by Rollins, p. 102.

A Warning to Wooers, that they be not ouer hastie, nor deceiued with womens beautie. To, Salisburie Plaine.

(1) *A Handful of Pleasant Delights*, Richard Jones (1584); ed. Rollins, *Handful*, p. 43 (5 eight-line, 4 six-line, and 4 more eight-line stanzas); ed. R. W. Bond, *The Complete Works of John Lyly*, Oxford, 1902, III, 465.

Jones registered the ballad in July, 1565 (see *Handful*, p. 102; and Rollins, *Analytical Index*, no. 3047).

Warning against love, on the basis of proverbs and classical examples. Love your equal lest you marry a shrew. I do not malign every woman, but he who loves not venom must shun the toad.

> Lay not the fault on womans backe,
> Thousands were good,
> But few scapte drowning in Noes flood;
> Most are wel bent,
> I must say so, least I be shent.

The extensive series of allusions is annotated by Rollins, *Handful*, p. 102; it includes Brooke's *Romeus* and the Hercules-Aristotle legend.

394. Ʒe lusty ladyis! luke.

By Alexander Scott.
Ane Ballat maid to the Derisioun and Scorne of wantoun Wemen.

(1) Advocates' Library 1. 1. 6 (13 eight-line stanzas); ed. Ritchie, *Bannatyne Manuscript,* II, 339; Cranstoun, *Poems of Alexander Scott,* p. 19; Donald, *Poems of Alexander Scott,* p. 55; see also Hunterian Club *Bannatyne,* I, lxxxvii. Cranstoun dates Scott's work 1545-68.

Satire on woman's lasciviousness. **392** appears to be a kind of palinode involving men.

395. Ye old mule that think your self so fayre.

By Sir Thomas Wyatt.

(1) Egerton 2711 (a "rondeau" in 16 lines); ed. Foxwell, *Poems of Sir Thomas Wiat,* I, 10; Padelford, *Early Sixteenth Century Lyrics,* p. 9.

Miss Foxwell places it in "the second Court period, 1533-6" (II, 24); elsewhere she says "*circ.* 1532" (I, xvii). Wyatt lived from 1503(?) to 1542.

A violent attack on an old woman who tries to repair her lost beauty. It has been associated with Anne Boleyn, whom Sanders (1586) called "Mula Regina"; but Miss Foxwell does not credit the suggestion (II, 24; see also Padelford, pp. xlv, 116). There is no reason to go out of our way to read autobiography or historical allusion into the poem, which belongs to a widespread genre discussed under **226**.

396. Ye shul be payd after your whylfulnes.

MacCracken suggests William de la Pole, Duke of Suffolk, as author; but Robert Steele believes that it was composed in English by Charles of Orleans, in whose personal manuscript it is preserved.

(1) Bibliothèque Nationale fonds français 25458 (a roundel of 12 lines); ed. Robert Steele, *The English Poems of Charles of Orleans,* London (EETS, CCXV), 1941, p. 222; Hammond, *English Verse,* p. 222.

(2) Grenoble, Bibliothèque, MS. 873; ed. H. N. MacCracken, "An English Friend of Charles of Orleans," *PMLA,* XXVI, (1911), 176; for other editions see Brown and Robbins, *Index,* no. 4256.

Suffolk lived from 1396 to 1450; Orleans (1394-1465) was captive in England from 1415 to 1440.

Rebellious lover: you shall be paid in your own coin.

397. You Ladies falsly deemd.

The lamentation of a woman being wrongfully defamed. To the tune of Damon & Pythias.

(1) *A Handful of Pleasant Delights,* Richard Jones (1584) (printed as 37 lines; apparently 6 six-line stanzas, each followed by a two-line refrain); ed. Rollins, *Handful,* p. 56.

On the basis of the tune Rollins assigns the poem to the lost 1566 edition of *A Handful*.

Defense of women against "false disembling men." Cites Susanna and the Duchess of Savoy.

398. You that in play peruse my plaint, and reade in rime the smart.

Translation of Petrarch's "Voi ch'ascóltate in rime sparse il suono."
The louer asketh pardon of his passed follie in loue.
(1) *Tottel's Miscellany* (in the second and succeeding editions) (7 couplets); ed. Rollins, I, 219.
1557 or before.
Renunciation of love. For another version see **399**.

399. You that in rime dispersed here the sownd.

Translation of Petrarch's "Voi ch'ascoltate in rime sparse il suono."
(1) British Museum Additional 36529 (14 lines—a sonnet); ed. Rollins, *Tottel's Miscellany*, II, 320.
John Harington the Elder, who wrote the MS., died in 1557.
Renunciation of love. See **398**.

400. Yyng men, I red that ye bewar.

Beware of a Shrewish Wife.
Burden: "In soro and care he led hys lyfe
That haue a schrow ontyll his wyfe."
(1) Bodleian Eng. poet. e. 1 (two-line burden and 3 four-line stanzas); ed. Greene, *Early English Carols*, p. 271 (no. 404); Wright, *Songs and Carols* (Percy Society), p. 43; Chambers and Sidgwick, *Early English Lyrics*, p. 209; J. E. Masters, *Rymes of the Minstrels*, p. 23; for other editions see Brown and Robbins, *Index*, no. 4278.
The MS. is of the second half of the XV cent.
A trapped husband warns young men to avoid marriage. Greene (p. 433) believes the poem is influenced by **75**. See also **165**.

401. Yyng men, I warne you euerychon.

A Young and Hen-pecked Husband's Complaint.
Burden: "How hey! It is non les:
I dar not seyn quan che say, 'Pes!' "
(1) Sloane 2593 (two-line burden and 5 four-line stanzas); ed. Greene, *Early English Carols*, p. 271 (no. 405); Wright, *Songs and Carols* (1836), sig. C4; Wright, *Songs and Carols* (Warton Club), p. 70; Chambers and Sidgwick, *Early English Lyrics*, p. 207. For other editions see Brown and Robbins, *Index*, no. 4279.

The MS. is of the first half of the XV cent.

Chanson de mal marié; a young man warns others his age to beware of marrying an old and shrewish wife.

402. Yowre counturfetyng with doubyll delyng.

Signed "Willm. Newarke," who may be the composer of the accompanying music, the author, or both.

    (1) British Museum Additional 5465 ("the Fairfax MS."); ed. Bernard Fehr, *Archiv,* CVI (1901), 56 (1 eight-line stanza).

The MS. was composed in the early years of the XVI cent. Robert Fairfax, the original owner, obtained a Mus.D. from Cambridge in 1504 and another from Oxford in 1511; he died in 1529 (Fehr, p. 50).

Satire on woman's inconstancy and hypocrisy; rebellious lover.

403. Your yen two wol slee me sodenly.

Ascribed to Chaucer by Thomas Percy in the 1767 edition of the *Reliques,* II, 11; the ascription accepted by Koch, Skeat, and Robinson, on the basis of the Chaucerian contents of the MS., and style and meter. Rejected by Brusendorff, *Chaucer Tradition,* p. 440.

Merciles Beaute; or *Chaucer's Roundel;* or *An Original Ballad by Chaucer.*

    (1) Magdalene College Cambridge, Pepys 2006 (a "triple roundel," in three parts of 13 lines each); ed. Robinson, *Chaucer,* p. 638; for other editions and bibliography see Robinson, p. 982; Hammond, *Chaucer,* p. 436; Griffith, *Chaucer,* p. 127; Martin, *Chaucer,* p. 73; and the current bibliographies. Brown and Robbins, *Index,* no. 4282, mention further editions and a XVII cent. transcript by Ainsworth in British Museum Additional 38179.

The MS. is of the XV cent. If the poem is by Chaucer, it is before 1400. Koch would date it about the same time as the *Parliament of Fowls* (in the early eighties?). If it is based on a ballade by the Duc de Berry (Robinson, p. 982) it must be later than 1389.

Rebellious lover. In the first part of this triple roundel the lady's eyes will bring quick death to the lover. In the second part we have a dramatic shift, where the lover observes that "Daunger" has chased Pity from his lady's heart. In the third the drama rises to its climax: since the lover has escaped from Love so fat, he refuses to return to Love's prison lean. This frank avowal of the stages of unrequited love seems typical enough of Chaucer, who could rebel against the courtly code without losing his sense of humor. Several parallels have been suggested in XIV cent. French poetry (Robinson, p. 982).

Youre swete loue wyth blody naylys (221).

INDEX II

INDEX III

(Since there is considerable bibliographical interest in the arrangement of the Marriage Group of the *Canterbury Tales*, which comprises entries **58, 81, 261, 303,** and **339** of Index I, I have indicated in each case the exemplars of this Group as *MG*. Other itemizations have appeared unnecessary, except in the case of the extensive anthology in the Bannatyne Manuscript, where I have preserved the classifications established by the scribe.)

A. MANUSCRIPTS

BRITISH MUSEUM

Cotton Caligula A. 9 . . . . **112**
Cotton Cleopatra C. 6 . . . . **211**
Cotton Cleopatra D. 7 . . . . **175**
Cotton Titus A. 24 . . . . **6, 360**
Cotton Vespasian A. 25 . . . .**3, 45, 218, 289, 371, 375, 379**
Cotton Vespasian D. 9 . . . . **30**
Egerton 2711 . . . .**61, 160, 196, 202, 338, 346, 395**
Egerton 2726 . . . .*MG*: **58, 81, 261, 303, 339**
Egerton 2863 . . . .*MG*: **58, 81, 261, 303, 339**
Egerton 2864 . . . .*MG*: **58, 81, 261, 303, 339**
Harley 78 . . . .**55, 109**
Harley 116 . . . .**182, 387**
Harley 372 . . . .**9, 82**
Harley 1239 . . . .*MG* (*MchT* missing): **58, 81, 261, 303**
Harley 1701 . . . .**212**
Harley 1703 . . . . **99**
Harley 1758 . . . .*MG*: **58, 81, 261, 303, 339**
Harley 1764 . . . .**150**
Harley 2251 . . . .**57, 75, 166, 185, 220, 227, 232, 325, 387**
Harley 2252 . . . . **191, 225, 266**
Harley 2253 . . . . **140, 169, 340**

OXFORD COLLEGES

C. LIST OF ABBREVIATIONS AND REFERENCES

The following list contains only titles used frequently and therefore
abbreviated in Introduction and Index I. Abbreviations for periodicals are
not entered, since I have followed the standard usage of Wells' *Manual*.

ALLEN, PHILIP S. *Medieval Latin Lyrics,* Chicago, 1931.
ANDREAS CAPELLANUS—see PARRY.
ARBER, EDWARD. *A Transcript of the Registers of the Company of Sta-
tioners of London, 1554–1640,* London and Birmingham, 1875-94.

AUDELAY, JOHN. *The Poems of,* ed. E. K. Whiting, London (EETS, CLXXXIV), 1931.

Bannatyne Manuscript. W. Tod Ritchie, ed., *The Bannatyne Manuscript Writtin in Tyme of Pest 1568,* Edinburgh (STS, New Series, XXII, XXIII, XXVI; Third Series, V), 1928-33.
———. *The Bannatyne Manuscript,* Printed for the Hunterian Club, 1896.
BOEDDEKER, KARL, ed. *Altenglische Dichtungen des MS. Harl. 2253,* Berlin, 1878.
BROWN, CARLETON, ed. *English Lyrics of the XIIIth Century,* Oxford, 1932.
———. *A Register of Middle English Religious and Didactic Verse,* Oxford, 1916-20.
———, ed. *Religious Lyrics of the XIVth Century,* Oxford, 1924.
———, ed. *Religious Lyrics of the XVth Century,* Oxford, 1939.
——— AND ROSSELL HOPE ROBBINS. *The Index of Middle English Verse,* New York, 1943.
BRUSENDORFF, AAGE. *The Chaucer Tradition,* London, 1925.

CBEL. *The Cambridge Bibliography of English Literature,* ed. F. W. Bateson, New York and Cambridge, 1941.
CHEL. *The Cambridge History of English Literature,* ed. A. W. Ward and A. R. Waller, Cambridge and New York, 1907-1917.
CHALMERS, ALEXANDER, ed. *The Works of the English Poets from Chaucer to Cowper,* London, 1810.
CHAMBERS, E. K. *The Mediaeval Stage,* Oxford, 1903.
——— AND F. SIDGWICK, ed. *Early English Lyrics,* London, 1926.
CHAUCER, GEOFFREY. *The Complete Works of,* ed. Fred N. Robinson, Boston, Mass., 1933.
———. *The Complete Works of,* ed. Walter W. Skeat, Oxford, 1894-97.
CHILD, FRANCIS JAMES, ed. *The English and Scottish Popular Ballads,* Boston, Mass., 1883-98.
COCKAYNE, OSWALD, ed. *Hali Meidenhad,* rev. F. J. Furnivall, London (EETS, XVIII), 1922.
COLLIER, JOHN PAYNE. *A Bibliographical and Critical Account of the Rarest Books in the English Language,* New York, 1866.
———. *Extracts from the Registers of the Stationers' Company,* London (Shakespeare Society), 1848.
CORSER, THOMAS. *Collectanea Anglo-Poetica,* [Manchester]: Chetham Society, 1860-83.
CRAIGIE, W. A., ed. *The Asloan Manuscript,* Edinburgh (STS, New Series, XIV, XVI), 1923-24.

———, ed. *The Maitland Folio Manuscript,* Edinburgh (STS, New Series, VII, XX), 1919-27.

———, ed. *The Maitland Quarto Manuscript,* Edinburgh (STS, New Series, IX), 1920.

CRANSTOUN—*see* SCOTT.

CRUMP, C. G., AND E. F. JACOB, ed. *The Legacy of the Middle Ages,* Oxford, 1932.

DNB. Dictionary of National Biography, London and New York, 1885-1901.

DONALD—*see* SCOTT.

DOW, BLANCHE H. *The Varying Attitude toward Women in French Literature of the Fifteenth Century: The Opening Years,* New York, 1936.

DUFF, E. GORDON. *A Century of the English Book Trade,* London, 1905.

DUNBAR, WILLIAM. *The Poems of,* ed. John Small, Edinburgh (STS, II, IV, XVI, XXI, XXIX), 1883-93.

———. *The Poems of,* ed. W. M. MacKenzie, Edinburgh, 1932.

DYBOSKI, ROMAN, ed. *Songs, Carols, and Other Miscellaneous Poems, from the Balliol MS. 354, Richard Hill's Commonplace-Book,* London (EETSES, CI), 1908.

EDMONDS, J. M., ed. and tr. *Elegy and Iambus,* London, 1931.

EETS. Early English Text Society.

EETSES. Early English Text Society, Extra Series.

FAIRHOLT, F. W., ed. *Satirical Songs and Poems on Costume,* London (Percy Society, XXVII), 1849.

FLUEGEL, EWALD, ed. *Neuenglisches Lesebuch,* Halle, 1895.

FOXWELL, A. K., ed. *The Poems of Sir Thomas Wiat,* London, 1913.

FURNIVALL, F. J., ed. *Jyl of Breyntford's Testament,* Printed for Private Circulation, 1871.

———, ed. *Political, Religious, and Love Poems,* London (EETS, XV), 1866. Revised edition, 1903.

GREENE, RICHARD L., ed. *The Early English Carols,* Oxford, 1935.

GOWER, JOHN. *The Complete Works of,* ed. G. C. Macaulay, Oxford, 1899-1902.

GRIFFITH, DUDLEY D. *A Bibliography of Chaucer, 1908-1924,* Seattle, Wash., 1926.

HALLIWELL, *Selection—see* LYDGATE.

HAMMOND, ELEANOR P. *Chaucer, A Bibliographical Manual,* New York, 1908.

————, ed. *English Verse between Chaucer and Surrey*, Durham, N. C., 1927.

HAZLITT, WILLIAM C., ed. *Remains of the Early Popular Poetry of England*, London, 1864-66.

HENTSCH, ALICE A. *De la Littérature Didactique du Moyen Age S'Adressant Spécialement aux Femmes*, Cahors, 1903.

HOCCLEVE, THOMAS. F. J. Furnivall, ed., *Hoccleve's Works. I. The Minor Poems in the Phillipps MS. 8151 (Cheltenham) and the Durham MS. III. 9*, London (EETSES, LXI), 1892.

————. Israel Gollancz, ed. *Hoccleve's Works. II. The Minor Poems in the Ashburnham MS. Addit. 133*, London (EETSES, LXXIII), 1925.

HUIZINGA, J. *The Waning of the Middle Ages*, London, 1927.

HUNTERIAN CLUB—*see* Bannatyne Manuscript.

JAMES, MONTAGUE R. *A Descriptive Catalogue of the Manuscripts in the Library of Corpus Christi College Cambridge*, Cambridge, 1909-1912.

KEMP–WELCH, ALICE. *Of Six Mediaeval Women*, London, 1913.

KILGOUR, RAYMOND L. *The Decline of Chivalry as Shown in the French Literature of the Late Middle Ages*, Cambridge, Mass., 1937.

LANGLOIS, ERNEST, ed. *Le Roman de la Rose*, Paris (SATF), 1914-24.

LEFRANC, ABEL. *Grands Écrivains Français de la Renaissance*, Paris, 1914.

LEA, HENRY CHARLES. *History of Sacerdotal Celibacy in the Christian Church*, 3rd ed., New York, 1907.

LEWIS, C. S. *The Allegory of Love*, Oxford, 1936.

LILLY's *Collection*. [Joseph Lilly], *A Collection of Seventy-Nine Black-Letter Ballads and Broadsides*, London: Joseph Lilly, 1867.

LOWNDES, WILLIAM T. *The Bibliographer's Manual of English Literature*, London, 1857-64.

LYDGATE, JOHN. Henry Bergen, ed., *Lydgate's Fall of Princes*, London, (EETSES, CXXI–CXXIV), 1924-27.

————. J. O. Halliwell, ed., *A Selection from the Minor Poems of Dan John Lydgate*, London (Percy Society, II), 1840.

————. Henry N. MacCracken and Merriam Sherwood, ed., *The Minor Poems of John Lydgate*, London (EETSES, CVII; EETS, CXCII), 1911, 1934.

MARTIN, WILLARD E. *A Chaucer Bibliography, 1925–1933*, Durham, N. C., 1935.

M[ASTERS], J. E., ed. *Rymes of the Minstrels*, Shaftesbury, Dorset, 1927.

MACAULAY—see GOWER.

McCORMICK, SIR WILLIAM, AND JANET E. HESELTINE. *The Manuscripts of Chaucer's Canterbury Tales*, Oxford, 1933.

MacCRACKEN—see LYDGATE.

MacKENZIE—see DUNBAR.

McKERROW, R. B., ed. *A Dictionary of Printers and Booksellers in England, Scotland, and Ireland, and of Foreign Printers of English Books 1557-1640*, London, 1910.

————. *Printers' & Publishers' Devices in England & Scotland 1485-1640*, London, 1913.

———— AND F. S. FERGUSON. *Title-Page Borders Used in England & Scotland, 1485-1640*, London, 1932.

MONTAIGLON, ANATOLE DE, AND JAMES H. ROTHSCHILD, ed. *Recueil de Poésies Françoises des XV° et XVI° Siècles*, Paris, 1855-78.

OAKDEN, J. P. *Alliterative Poetry in Middle English, The Dialectical and Metrical Survey*, Manchester, 1930.

———— AND ELIZABETH R. INNES. *Alliterative Poetry in Middle English, A Survey of the Traditions*, Manchester, 1935.

PADELFORD, F. M., ed. *Early Sixteenth Century Lyrics*, Boston, Mass., 1907.

PARRY, JOHN JAY, tr. *The Art of Courtly Love by Andreas Capellanus*, New York, 1941.

PLOMER, H. R. "Robert Copland," *Transactions of the Bibliographical Society*, III (1895-96), 211-25.

POWER, EILEEN. "The Position of Women"—see CRUMP AND JACOB.

RICHARDSON, LULU McDOWELL. *The Forerunners of Feminism in French Literature of the Renaissance from Christine of Pisa to Marie de Gournay*, Baltimore and Paris, 1929.

RIGAUD, ROSE. *Les Idées Féministes de Christine de Pisan*, Neuchatel, 1911.

RITCHIE—see Bannatyne Manuscript.

RITSON, JOSEPH. *Ancient Songs and Ballads from the Reign of King Henry the Second to the Revolution*, 3rd ed., rev. W. C. Hazlitt, London, 1877.

ROBINSON—see CHAUCER.

ROLLINS, HYDER E. *An Analytical Index to the Ballad-Entries in the Registers of the Company of Stationers of London*, in *Studies in Philology*, XXI (1924), 1-324.

————, ed. *A Handful of Pleasant Delights (1584) By Clement Robinson and Divers Others*, Cambridge, Mass., 1924.

SANDISON, HELEN E. *The "Chanson d'Aventure" in Middle English,* Bryn Mawr, Pa., 1913.

SATF. Société des Anciens Textes Français.

SCOTT, ALEXANDER. *The Poems of,* ed. James Cranstoun, Edinburgh (STS, XXXVI), 1896.

———. *The Poems of,* ed. A. K. Donald, London (EETSES, LXXXV), 1902.

SKEAT, WALTER W. *Chaucer—see* under CHAUCER.

———. *The Chaucer Canon,* Oxford, 1900.

———, ed. *The Works of Geoffrey Chaucer and Others, Being a Reproduction in Facsimile of the First Collected Edition 1532* [William Thynne], London, [1905].

SKELTON, JOHN. *The Poetical Works of Skelton and Donne,* ed. Alexander Dyce, rev. Francis J. Child, Boston, 1879.

———. *The Complete Poems of John Skelton Laureate,* ed. Philip Henderson, London, 1931.

SMALL—*see* DUNBAR.

SPURGEON, C. F. E. *Five Hundred Years of Chaucer Criticism and Allusion, 1357–1900,* Cambridge, 1925.

STC. *A Short-Title Catalogue of Books Printed in England, Scotland, & Ireland and of English Books Printed Abroad 1475–1640,* ed. A. W. Pollard and G. R. Redgrave, London, 1926.

— *Huntington Library Supplement to the Record of Its Books in the Short Title Catalogue of English Books, 1475–1640,* by Cecil Kay Edmonds, *Huntington Library Bulletin,* IV (1933), 1-152.

STS. Scottish Text Society.

STSNS. Scottish Text Society, New Series.

Summary Catalogue of Western Manuscripts in the Bodleian Library at Oxford, by Falconer Madan *et al.,* Oxford, 1895——.

Tottel's Miscellany, ed. Hyder E. Rollins, Cambridge, Mass., 1928-29.

WADDELL, HELEN. *The Wandering Scholars,* 7th ed., London, 1934.

WATSON, FOSTER. *Vives and the Renascence Education of Women,* New York, 1912.

WELLS, JOHN EDWIN. *A Manual of the Writings in Middle English 1050–1400,* New Haven, Conn., 1916 (with eight *Supplements* to 1941).

WORCESTER, DAVID. *The Art of Satire,* Cambridge, Mass., 1940.

WRIGHT, LOUIS B. *Middle-Class Culture in Elizabethan England,* Chapel Hill, N. C., 1935.

WRIGHT, THOMAS, ed. *Songs and Ballads with Other Short Poems, Chiefly of the Reign of Philip and Mary,* London (Roxburghe Club), 1860.

——, ed. *Songs and Carols of the Fifteenth Century,* London (Percy Society, XXIII), 1848.

——, ed. *Songs and Carols from a Manuscript in the British Museum of the Fifteenth Century,* London (Warton Club), 1856.

——, ed. *Songs and Carols Printed from a Manuscript in the Sloane Collection in the British Museum,* London, 1836.

WULFF, AUGUST. *Die Frauenfeindlichen Dichtungen in den Romanischen Literaturen des Mittelalters bis zum Ende des XIII. Jahrhunderts,* Halle a. S., 1914.

GENERAL INDEX OF
PROPER NAMES

GENERAL INDEX OF PROPER NAMES

(The titles of poems and prose works which form major entries in Index I are listed in Index II. Here they are listed only when they appear elsewhere in the text of the Introduction or of Index I. A classification of the localities in which the authorities for major entries in Index I are to be found is provided in Index III, and these localities are not repeated here. The names or works of modern scholars, and subjects, except for proper names, are likewise not included here.)

351

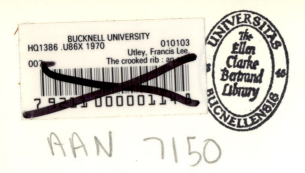